Total Life Coaching

Also by Patrick Williams (with Deborah C. Davis)

Therapist as Life Coach: Transforming Your Practice

A Norton Professional Book

TOTAL LIFE COACHING

50+ Life Lessons, Skills, and Techniques to Enhance Your Practice . . . and Your Life

Patrick Williams
Lloyd J. Thomas

W · W · NORTON

NEW YORK · LONDON

For information about permission to reproduce
selections from this book, write to
Permissions, W. W. Norton & Company, Inc.
500 Fifth Avenue, New York, NY 10110

Composition and book design by Viewtistic, Inc.
Manufacturing by Hamilton Printing
Production Manager: Leeann Graham

Library of Congress Cataloging-in-Publication Data
Williams, Patrick, 1950–
Total life coaching: 50+ life lessons, skills & techniques to enhance your practice—and your
life/Patrick Williams & Lloyd J. Thomas.
    p.   cm.
"A Norton professional book."
Includes bibliographical references and index.
ISBN 0-393-70434-3
1. Personal coaching. 2. Conduct of life. I. Thomas, Lloyd J. II. Title.

BF637.P36W55 2004
158'.3—dc22   2004046531

W. W. Norton & Company, Inc., 500 Fifth Avenue, New York, NY 10110
www.wwnorton.com
W. W. Norton & Company, Ltd., Castle House, 75/76 Wells Street, London W1T 3QT
4 5 6 7 8 9 0

Dedications

To Socrates . . . the first inquiring coach.
—Pat

To Darcy, my life partner and greatest love.
—Lloyd

Contents

SECTION 4
Living Life with Integrity

Acknowledgments

The profession of life coaching has revitalized our deep desire to make a difference and help people live as authentically as possible. No other profession allows you to work by phone, with no geographic boundaries, and with highly motivate and interesting clients who want to live their lives more purposefully.

More than anyone, we want to thank our coaching clients who, over the past decade, have enriched our lives. They are some of the most exciting, fun, joyful, and wonderful people we have ever met. We thank you all!

To Deborah Malmud and her excellent staff at Norton Professional Books, Michael McGandy, Andrea Costella, we thank you for for believing in this project, and for your dedication to ensure that the final product was professional, readable, and useful. Without your work, this book would have never been finished.

My (Pat's) individual thanks goes to my co-author, Lloyd. Thank you for your wisdom, your creativity, and mostly for your partnership on this project. The life lessons in this book were previously created by you. My role was to take what you had written before and add coaching language and coaching conversations to your concepts.

I (Lloyd) want to express my deep appreciation to my co-author, Pat. Thank you for your support, your friendship, and your belief in me and what I write. Thank you for introducing me to the profession of coaching, for being the great life coach you are, and for sharing your vast knowledge of coaching with me. It has been a joy for me to work with you on this book.

After months of work, we gave birth to this final product. We hope you find it enhacing to your life and valuable to your clients.

Total Life Coaching

Introduction

Life coaching is more than a collection of techniques and skills. It is more than something you do. Life coaching reflects who you are. It is your authentic being in action within a specific relationship. Who you are, your personhood, is the basis for effective life coaching. Coaching is rooted more in your being, than in your personal abilities. You coach because of who you are. Even though you may learn many specific coaching skills, they will need to be absorbed into your being.

If you are reading this, you may have already received training as a helping professional (e.g., counselor, therapist, coach, pastor, teacher, manager, or supervisor). Or, you may simply be interested in the profession of coaching or want to make changes in your life. This book is designed to enhance your professional practice, satisfy your curiosity, and empower you to change your life. Regardless of your background, we believe you will benefit from reading the philosophy and practical information contained in *Total Life Coaching*. Its focuses primarily, however, on the personal and professional coach.

As life coaches and writers, our intention is twofold: (1) To assist you in developing your personal, effective combination of coaching skills to be successful in creating desired outcomes in your own life; and (2) To enhance your coaching skills so that *you* become a catalyst for your clients' success. As we manifest these intentions in the book, readers will not only create their own desired outcomes in life, they will also coach others from the inside out, a coaching style that is much more effective than any other, because life coaching is more about *being* a coach than *doing* coaching.

Regardless of the personal coaching techniques or skills you may have learned, you may still not be the most effective coach you can become. We define authentic coaching as, "effective self-expression in the coach/client relationship so that you catalyze your clients' manifestation of their own desired outcomes." Coach training usually focuses on learning techniques to influence the behavior of clients. *Total Life Coaching* addresses such questions as: From whom do these coaching techniques emanate? What makes a good coach great? How can coaches incorporate techniques into their personalities to authentically contribute to their clients' well-being? What lessons from human history can coaches and clients learn to realize their potential as professionals and as people? How might these lessons be effectively and authentically coached? How catalytic of others' development is your self-expression? How effectively do your clients attain the results they really want?

Have you designed your life the way you want? If your deepest desires were fulfilled, how would your life change? Formal education neglects at least seven essential areas of learning:

- How best to learn
- How to maximize your wellness
- How to live your life *on purpose*
- How to design and create the life you desire
- How to be a catalyst for others' growth and development
- How to be a good spouse
- How to be an effective parent

After our formal education, we spend about 90–95 percent of our time functioning within these seven areas. *Total Life Coaching* focuses specifically on these areas. Life coaching is really filling the void in our formal education.

We usually take for granted the human skills of learning and creating, rarely studying them or consciously choosing to strengthen them. We may be taught a specific subject and expected to learn it. But teachers fail to teach individuals in the exact way they learn. We don't teach people how to discover who they really are. We don't teach them:

- Self-awareness
- Living within their own boundaries of integrity
- Spirituality and life purpose

- Social/relationship skills
- How to achieve their potential
- How to contribute their unique gifts to society
- How to creatively benefit from change
- How to use their personal strengths to overcome their weaknesses

In other words, *we are not taught how to design and implement a fulfilling life!*

Life is continuously providing us with information or messages. When we do not listen, the messages become lessons. When we do not learn, the lessons become problems. When we don't address the problems, they become crises. When crises are left unresolved, they create chaos in our lives. Great coaches seek to live on the levels of messages and lessons, not waiting for them to become problems, crises, and reactions to chaos. They also strive to have their clients live at that same level.

Total Life Coaching recommends that you keep life's processes on the message and lesson level. It makes living (and life coaching) so much more effective and enjoyable. In fact, coaching on the lesson and message levels is so important that we have written this book in a format that reflects life lessons and the messages contained within each lesson.

We want life coaches to: avoid coaching on the levels of problems, crises, and chaos; to reawaken an awareness of their own inner identity; discover a personal/professional vision and purpose; sharpen their coaching skills; and live in such an intentional manner that they are the catalyst for their clients' success and well-being. Doing so will not only enrich their own lives, but also bring their personalities directly into the coach/client relationship.

Most people are completely unaware of how they create what happens in their lives. This book will lead you down a direct path through the problems, crises, and chaos you may often encounter when you choose to take control of your life (and lifestyle). You will be empowered to make the necessary internal and external changes to become not only a highly successful coach, but the person you want to be. It is written in the Gospel of Thomas that "What you bring forth out of yourself from the inside will save you. What you do not bring forth out of yourself from the inside will destroy you." When you are an *authentic* life coach—one who brings to the coaching relationship what is genuinely within—you will be much more effective in assisting your clients to create their own desired outcomes.

When you consciously choose your responses to life, you purposefully create the life you desire. Most of us are not taught to consciously respond to life's events. Rather, we usually react automatically to what happens. When you only react to events in your life, you create a lifestyle predicated on external circumstances. When you plan for and choose your responses, you recapture your birthright to design and engineer your own lifestyle according to your preferences and desires. In other words, you take charge of the nature and quality of your life. By doing so, you create, or at least powerfully influence, your personal destiny.

In any endeavor, two essential factors build your foundation for success:

1. Consciously recognize that you already possess the power to respond in ways that create what you want; and
2. Through effective use of that power, generate the results you desire for your life and for the lives of your clients.

These two principles for success pervade your personal life, your life coaching, your career, and your creation of circumstances that benefit you and others.

As a life coach, you need to be intimately familiar with the personal qualities, characteristics, and abilities that the most successful people on earth have used to fulfill their own lives. You not only need to be aware of these successful life lessons, you need to know how to best coach your clients, so they develop them in themselves.

Total Life Coaching guides you step-by-step through the complex process of learning life's most essential lessons. It also provides the professional life coach, therapist, counselor, or consultant with exercises, concepts, and practical applications for catalyzing purposeful living in your coaching clientele. It teaches you the proven principles people use to become successful, however you define *success*.

We define *success* as the "attainment of any state with which you are content." Success brings peace of mind and is highly individualized. One person's success may not be considered a success by another person. Success and achievement are different. Achievement is the attainment of any goal. When you reach or desired goal, you may or may not be content—you may or may not be successful.

Structured "recipes" for coaching each of the 52 life lessons are presented in the nine sections of the book. Each section includes:

- The life lesson itself, presented in no specific order of importance
- The messages contained within the lesson
- Coaching objectives for your clients regarding each lesson
- What you need to know about the lesson to provide the framework (context) for coaching it

- Coaching methods, exercises, questions, and language for bringing each lesson to your clients
- Sample coaching conversations that exemplify the coach/client dialogue for the coaching of each life lesson

The Coaching Exercises included throughout this book will facilitate the client's integration of the specific life lesson into their own lives. It is often recommended that as an authentic life coach, you also complete these exercises so you have first-hand knowledge of the impact they may have on your clients.

One of the hallmarks of authentic life coaching is being able to ask powerful and evocative questions called "coaching questions." Many coaches know these as powerful questions, evocative questions, or purposeful inquiry. Powerful or evocative questions during coaching elicit responses in the moment, whereas purposeful inquiry is a process of leaving the client with a question to ponder and contemplate—a kind of Socratic inquiry. These are all questions to which the coach does not know the answer. Unlike statements disguised as questions, like "Why did you do that?," which imply a judgment, a powerful question is one that evokes new thoughts, emotions, visions, metaphors, and ideas. It is usually open-ended, beginning with the words *What, How, Where,* or *Who,* and rarely begins with the word *Why. Why* questions force the client to defend or justify themselves. Near the end of each life lesson, we present Coaching Questions and Inquiries, designed to assist clients in focusing on issues that will catalyze the coaching outcomes clients have set for themselves. Pure coaching lies in the inquiry.

We believe that all knowledge is useless, unless it is put into a language that others can understand. Learning new language associated with life coaching is critical to enhancing your coaching skills. Therefore, we include examples of words and phrases commonly used in the coaching profession that, when used, will strengthen your coaching abilities. They are phrases that you may want to speak to your clients in order to accelerate their progress of reaching their coaching goals. We call these phrases *coaching language.* Using coaching language is not to create new jargon, but to shift and expand clients' thinking.

In the margins throughout this book, are quotes from highly successful people who have addressed the information being presented. Hopefully, they will stimulate your thinking and validate your own conclusions.

At the end of each section are Questions and Statements for Your Reflection. We invite you to use these to stimulate your own thoughts about your coaching style, practice, clients, and your life.

You may read *Total Life Coaching* from cover to cover, or you may identify the area of successful living your client is working on and read only the most relevant lesson(s). You may want to use it as a textbook for coach training. You may want to share it with your clients. Regardless of how you read and use this book, you will no doubt enhance your practice, your coach/client relationships . . . and your life!

SECTION 1
Creating a Personal Identity

Knowledge of self is the source of our abilities.
—Lao Tzu

LIFE LESSON 1
What you believe about yourself defines who you are.

MESSAGES

1. In order to become an authentic life coach, be willing to change your childhood beliefs and the beliefs you've left unchallenged.
2. If you truly believe you are an authentic coach, then you are.
3. There are effective methods for shifting your beliefs.
4. Commit to discovering your authentic self-concept.
5. Effective life coaching modifies the client's self-concept.

The objectives for Lesson 1 are: 1) To understand that clients control the beliefs they hold about themselves; 2) To realize the number of possible beliefs is infinite; 3) To see the benefit of having a coach assist the client to shift his or her belief system by conscious choice; 4) To adopt beliefs necessary to define you as an authentic life coach; 5) To assist your clients to consciously choose and form a personal identity.

Framework Needed for Coaching Your Clients

Any *habitual pattern of thinking* is called a *belief*. Your basic beliefs about yourself, the people around you, and the world are the source of your perceived limits and problems as well as the source of your joy and fulfillment. Beliefs are the elements from which you create your experienced reality. They determine how you respond to that perceived reality.

Most of your core beliefs were formed when you were a child, unable to reason, dependent on others, and relatively helpless. For example, when children see everyone in their environment functioning more effectively than they are, they accurately conclude they are inadequate, incompetent, and dependent by

The purpose in life seems to be to acquaint man with himself.
—Ralph Waldo Emerson

comparison. You bring into adulthood your own core childhood beliefs. Belief modification is a continuous process unless you choose to "cling to" to earlier beliefs even when confronted with new information. The quality of your life, your lifestyle, and the reality you create—fortunately or unfortunately—are nothing more nor less than what you *believe* them to be. With clients we coach, this principle often presents itself as the inner critic or the gremlin that clients need to challenge so they can move to the level of success they want.

Who you believe you are, is who you are. You form your beliefs about yourself early in your life. As you grow into adulthood, you form new beliefs and update old ones. Your core beliefs form the context out of which all else evolves. If you believe yourself to be competent, you will behave in ways that reflect and strengthen competence. If you believe yourself to be a life coach, you will behave in ways reflecting your concept of a life coach. Conversely, if you believe yourself to be inadequate, your behavior will reflect inadequacy. If you believe you are a novice coach, you will probably never risk behaving like a professional coach. If your self-concept is negative, you will probably remain in a state of needing to improve.

This same wisdom applies to your clients. When your clients were children, they formed a child's view of themselves based on adult input. That childhood self-concept was formed with immature cognitive conclusions, early emotional experiences, and the feedback they perceptually received from their primary caretakers. As adults, however, your clients now have the capacity to modify—by conscious, rational choice—their beliefs and perceptions about their self-concept. They can also choose who they want to be.

Many professionals who have made the transition to the evolving field of life coaching—sometimes referred to as personal coaching—have backgrounds, experiences, and sometimes even coach training that *could* instill in them confidence in their new belief about themselves as a coach. However, when we learn something new, we often believe we have to be perfect or very experienced in order to feel confident. In order to gain valuable experience as a coach, we need to change our beliefs and behave as if we were already coaches.

We recommend you adopt a full practice mindset. This means that after you receive good, foundational training in coaching and are working with a mentor coach, you begin to act as if your practice is filled with exactly the clients you want. Identify the type of clients with whom you would ideally like to work. Design and implement the daily time schedule you would have if your practice was filled. Behave in ways that reflect a highly successful life coach. This attitude helps you detach from the notion of needing clients. It also allows you to authentically present yourself to potential clients or referral sources. Be passionate about your uniqueness as a person and your unique way of being a coach. Not everyone can be a coach. No one will ever coach exactly the way you do.

The reality outside your skin can never force you to change your mind or modify your beliefs. You do however have the capacity to change your mind. You can change your own belief systems by making new choices, taking new actions, and experimenting with new responses.

Responding to life is actually an evolutionary skill. We have a natural first response or reaction to events, especially stressful events. If you use your internal seven-second-delay switch, you can pause and reflect long enough to see that there are many choices about how to respond to any given situation even in an emergency. You possess that personal power. Limiting beliefs can be modified. You can update your beliefs. You can change your mind. You have that awesome freedom. As the adage goes, "Like a parachute, your mind works best when it is fully open."

When you exercise the freedom to change your thinking pattern, when you consciously alter your beliefs and your worldview (your perceptual paradigm), you also miraculously transform your perceived reality.

Exercises and Information

Below are examples of eight common childhood beliefs which, when your clients act upon them, can create great amounts of stress. Your clients perhaps at one point held these beliefs and, when taken as truth in the present, they can create problems, stress, self-defeat, and even illness. These beliefs were created when your clients were children—when they had minimal ability to reason or think rationally; therefore, we identify these beliefs as nonrational.

Presented along with each nonrational belief are *current clues*. These are present thoughts, feelings, or behaviors that might be operative if your client is currently holding that belief.

Dealing with Nonrational Beliefs

As an exercise, invite your clients to read each non-rational, stressful belief, and decide if the current clues are present in their lives. If they are present, that's okay—it simply demonstrates the presence of a non-rational belief that, with your coaching, they may want to modify. As adults, your clients can accomplish such modifications simply by choosing another belief. Having a personal coach to guide, support, and provide accountability can help clients immensely, rapidly propelling them toward the results they desire and toward the life they envision.

Nonrational, stressful belief 1. *Having love, recognition and approval from my family, friends, co-workers, and peers is important. If I don't please people, they may choose to reject, criticize, or abandon me.*

Current clues:

- Fears possible rejection or disapproval from others
- Ignores or feels ambivalent about an existing relationship
- Feels a lack of recognition
- Fears blame or criticism
- Jealousy
- Always does "the extras" or feels compelled to do so
- Is afraid to say "no"
- Always wants peace and harmony at any price
- Fears what people will think
- Always obeys without questioning
- Always meets perceived deadlines
- Always tries to be nice

> Search thine own heart. What paineth thee in others in thyself may be.
> —John Greenleaf Whittier

Example: If every time you say yes when you really wanted to say no—or if on those rare occasions when you do say no you feel guilty—you are responding irrationally from your non-rational belief system. When this happens you become stressed and you begin to tolerate this feeling. You are suffering from what Oprah Winfrey calls "the disease to please."

Healthy goal: Self-love, self-appreciation, and self-dependence.

Coach to create the desired belief: Help your client recognize that the likelihood of getting love, approval, and recognition from family, friends, and peers all the time is practically zero. People are, at best, irregular and inconsistent with their approval and caring. The most important person for your client to have love and approval from is herself.

Coaching language: Ask the client to read and recite the following coaching language out loud, three times daily, or until the current clues are replaced or simply disappear: I am good just the way I am. I appreciate my talents and abilities. I depend on myself for getting my needs met.

Nonrational, stressful belief 2. *I must be completely competent, consistent, and almost perfect in everything I do.*

Current clues:

- Fears being criticized or put down

- Afraid to make mistakes
- Afraid to fail
- Strives to maintain the image of looking good
- Needs and always tries to establish credibility
- Always unsatisfied with performance
- Experiences every relationship as a competition
- Desires mastery/power over everyone and everything undertaken
- Always dependable, even when it hurts or violates integrity
- Always drives for rapid completion of any task
- Consistent to the point of inflexibility
- Regularly procrastinates
- Cheats to accomplish desired outcome

Example: When you do something that does not meet your standards or expectations, you get upset with yourself and, in time, can become depressed.

Healthy goal: Self-acceptance, self-caring, self-approval.

Coach to create the desired belief: Advise your client that all human beings have inadequacies and weaknesses. When we have unrealistic expectations of ourselves and others, we set ourselves up for disappointment and failure in relationships, careers, and self-interests. All human beings make mistakes, and from these mistakes we learn lessons and grow.

Coaching language: I accept myself totally. I like who I am. I deserve to be cared for. My needs are important and I take full responsibility for getting them met.

Nonrational, stressful belief 3. *I need someone or something stronger than myself to rely on.*

Current clues:

- Feels helpless/powerless
- Fears not being in control
- Low level of self-confidence
- Afraid of personal responsibility and seeks to avoid it
- Feels shame and is afraid of being shamed or blamed
- Regularly breaks promises
- Exaggerates or blows things out of proportion
- Experiences a great deal of anxiety/worry
- Unwilling to take risks, even safe ones
- Feels attached to or dependent upon others

- Always complies with requests
- Always backs down or accedes to others' opinions

Example: You become stressed or agitated when you're asked to learn something new in a short period. You lose sleep worrying about how you'll do it.

Healthy goal: Increased self-confidence. Autonomy.

Coach to create the desired belief: Assure your clients that they can depend on themselves to address their own needs, or arrange for their desires to be addressed by others by making direct requests.

Coaching language: I can depend on myself. I can learn and develop, becoming stronger all the time. I am capable of learning new skills. I am confident that I am always growing. I enjoy new experiences. It is okay for me to learn at my own pace. I always give myself permission to ask directly for what I want.

4. Nonrational, stressful belief 4. *The past determines the present.*

Current clues:

- Superstitious or engages in superstitious behavior
- Believes it is useless to try anything new or different
- Unable to change
- Feels doomed, pre-destined, or believes that fate always prevails
- Rationalizes unwanted actions by defining themselves as a creature of habit

Example: Your client refuses to submit a manuscript to other publishers after having been turned down by some in the past. She believes she will never be published.

Healthy goal: Self-acceptance.

Coach to create the desired belief: Teach your clients that generally, the past only influences the present in their beliefs and expectations. At any given time, their beliefs and expectations may be examined, adjusted, and changed. This is called personal growth, which leads to different actions and healthy new experiences.

Discuss with your clients the concept of reframing. Ask them to redefine their past in a way that allows them to let it go and see it as experiential learning.

Coaching language: I can comfortably and easily release the old and welcome the new into my life. I trust that the present is perfect. I'm aware of the immediate moment. I can let go of past resentment.

Nonrational, stressful belief 5. *Anger is automatically bad and destructive. It needs to be closely controlled, avoided, or not shown.*
   Current clues:

- Lacks self-control
- Unaware of own emotions
- Adheres to the "don't-ever-rock-the-boat" position
- Strives to never hurt anyone, except perhaps oneself
- Hides feelings

   Example: You become quiet and withdrawn when you feel hurt. You become afraid or uncomfortable when people yell, even when they are not yelling at you.
   Healthy goal: Constructive emotional self-expression and self-support.
   Coach to create the desired belief: Let your clients know that anger is a normal, healthy, functional, human emotion. Anger is often cleansing; it needs to be expressed. Deal with anger as it happens, rather than allowing it to build up. Your clients can use anger to powerfully support themselves in pursuit of what they want or need. Anger only becomes unhealthy when allowed to build and fester—which can lead to rage or a destructive expression of anger. Anger expressed when it is immediately present (or shortly thereafter) creates room for the more desirable emotions of contentment, love, and happiness. Studies have shown that suppressed anger eventually manifests itself physically, emotionally or both. Unfortunately, many people endure a lifetime of suppressed anger and unfinished business.
   Coaching language: I understand that all my feelings are natural, normal, and okay to feel and experience. Sometimes anger may be channeled to support myself and what I need. I'm responsible for all of my emotions.

> The first step to knowledge is to know that we are ignorant.
> —Lord David Cecil

Nonrational, stressful belief 6. *I am not smart enough to become a doctor, lawyer, life coach, accountant, or anything else I believe is above me.*
   Current clues:

- Remains in academia for an inordinate amount of time
- Feels under pressure to perform
- Holds unrealistically high expectations of others
- Parents or caretakers are seen as "professionals"
- Siblings have excelled

> Whatever your mind can conceive and believe, it can achieve!
> —Andrew Carnegie

■ Strives to associate only with friends who have high goals or friends who are highly successful and look down on anyone who isn't

Example: Your clients believe people who become professionals are super smart and have done well in school their whole lives. Your clients believe they are average students and don't possess the tools necessary to become any better than they already perceive themselves to be.

Healthy goal: Increased self-confidence.

Coach to create the desired belief: Let your clients know that coaching regularly involves working with the client's mind-set. This means the coach facilitates change in how clients observe, rationalize, create stories, take responsibility for their choices and ultimately how they reinvent themselves.

Coaching language: I possess the talents, abilities, and tools to eventually become anybody or have anything I desire, if I put my mind to it. I am intelligent. When I apply myself, I can study and learn anything. If I choose to be a professional, I am confident that I will achieve that goal.

Nonrational, stressful belief 7. *I'm not attractive enough.*

Current clues:

■ Believe they are too fat, too thin, out of shape, too short, too tall, or too anything
■ Judge themselves to be inadequate in any way

Example: Your clients believe that to be attractive they need to resemble the thin and beautiful men and women in magazines. Your clients' inner voices say, "I will never be like that."

Healthy goal: Self-acceptance. Accurate self-image or self-concept.

Coach to create the desired belief: Let your clients know they are attractive just the way they are. A common coaching strategy in this situation is the use of affirmations or statements of intention relevant to the clients' desired results. The coach invites clients to practice making statements and phrases about how they want to improve themselves. Then working together, the coach helps the client create action plans.

Example: Your client regularly repeats, "I'm enjoying what I do every day at work" and the acts *as if* this affirmation was accurate.

Coaching language: If there is anything I desire to change about myself, I'll do that because I want to, not because I feel I *have* to. Trying to attain "perfect" looks is unrealistic and I know that unrealistic goals will only leave me disappointed. I recognize that the media portrays beauty unrealistically. I also realize that makeup, camera angles and airbrushing all contribute to a model's perceived perfection.

Nonrational, stressful belief 8. *I need to earn hundreds of thousands of dollars in order to be happy.*
   Current clues:

- Lives in an unnecessarily large house
- Drives a luxury car as a sign of having "made it"
- Always wears expensive clothing, even at home
- Dines at "exclusive" restaurants when one can't afford it
- Sacrifices in order to hire a housekeeper, maid, cook, chauffeur, or any other unnecessary help
- Feels one must have the best of everything

Example: You see Mr. and Mrs. Jones, who live in an upscale neighborhood and drive expensive cars, appearing very happy. Seeing that only reinforces that you need money and possessions in order to attain true happiness.
   Healthy goal: Contentment. Peace of mind and acceptance of the present situation while moving toward creating more wealth.
   Coach to create the desired belief: Offer your client the following information: Happiness is defined only by you. Happiness is an internal state of being. Happiness is almost never continuous. Your happiness depends on the attitudes you have toward yourself, others and the world.
   Coaching language: I realize that money and material possessions may make life easier, but they are not the key to happiness. I will maintain a positive attitude and be happy while I am on my journey to attain my goals. I will appreciate the material possessions that I accumulate, but will always know that they are not the reason for my happiness.

Assessing Your Self-Concept

Below is an assessment to help your clients understand their own self-concepts. Your clients can use it to evaluate their own beliefs about themselves.

Instructions: Score each of the statements using the scale below. Be objective and honest when you respond.

0 = Not at all true for me
1 = Somewhat true/true part of the time
2 = Fairly true/true half of the time
3 = Mainly true/true most of the time
4 = True all of the time

> Full wise is he that can himself know.
> —Geoffrey Chaucer

___ 1. I don't feel anyone else is better than me.
___ 2. I am free of shame, blame, and guilt.
___ 3. I am a happy, carefree person.
___ 4. I have no need to prove that I am as good as, or better than others.
___ 5. I do not have a strong need for people to pay attention to what I do.
___ 6. Losing does not make me feel inferior to others.
___ 7. I feel warm and friendly toward myself.
___ 8. I do not feel others are better than I am because they can do things better, have more money, or are more popular.
___ 9. I make friends easily.
___ 10. I speak up for my own ideas, likes, and dislikes.
___ 11. Other peoples' opinions or attitudes do not hurt me.
___ 12. I do not need praise to feel good about myself.
___ 13. I feel happy for others' good luck, especially if I know them well.
___ 14. I do not find fault with my family, friends, or others simply because it seems to be the thing to do.
___ 15. I don't feel that I must always please others.
___ 16. I'm open and honest and not afraid of letting people see my real self.
___ 17. I am friendly, thoughtful, and generous. I do not blame others for my problems or mistakes.
___ 18. I enjoy being alone.
___ 19. I can accept compliments and gifts without feeling uncomfortable or guilty.
___ 20. I can admit my mistakes and/or defeats without feeling pain or feeling diminished in any way.
___ 21. I feel no need to defend what I think, say, or do.
___ 22. I do not need others to agree with me or tell me that I am right.
___ 23. I do not brag about myself, what I've done, or what my family has and does.

__ 24. I can accept constructive criticism.

__ 25. I say what I mean and I mean what I say.

Total score: ___

To learn your own Self-Concept Index simply add all the scores.

> *Possible range is 0 to 100*
> 90 or above = You have a good self-concept.
> 75 to 90 = You could use some work.
> 50 to 75 = You should focus attention on updating your self-concept.
> Under 50 = Make building a positive self-concept your priority.

Sample Coaching Conversation

Coach: Let's check in. What progress did you make this week?

Client: I am so busy, I didn't do anything we talked about last week. Other things took precedence as usual.

Coach: You believe you are too busy to focus on your coaching goals?

Client: Yeah! I don't like it, but this is typical.

Coach: When you say this is "typical," it sounds to me that you hold a belief that this is the way it has been for you and always will be.

Client: Yeah, that's what I really want to change.

Coach: Great! What would change if you believed you had all the time you needed? How would you behave differently if you believed you were in control of your schedule?

Client: I'm not sure.

Coach: Then are you willing to design a fieldwork assignment to experiment with these new beliefs?

Client: Sure.

The coach and client address alternative beliefs and fieldwork assignments, and near the end of the coaching call, the coach might say:

Coach: On our next call, what if you brought a list of changes you think would occur if you had all the time you needed, and you were in control of your activity schedule.

Client: Yeah, I can do that!

Questions and Inquiries

Remember, as we stated in the introduction, the process of using powerful and evocative questions in the coaching conversation can be twofold: to get a response now (in the moment) or to leave the question for inquiry and contemplation between sessions. Many clients look forward to hearing their weekly inquiry, and it can maintain their connection with coaching between calls (or visits) while deepening their learning. Some examples of useful coaching queries follow:

1. Who do you believe you are, really?
2. What beliefs can you identify that are left over from your childhood?
3. What is the basis for your current beliefs? What accurate information do you have for maintaining these beliefs?
4. Can changing your beliefs about yourself and your situation change your life?
5. Do you believe you behave in a manner that is congruent with your self-concept? What beliefs do you need to modify to make your self-concept congruent with how you want to be in the future?

LIFE LESSON 2

Updating your belief system is how you learn and requires paradigm-shifting.

MESSAGES

1. Learning = modifying your perceptual paradigm.
2. In order to evolve, you must be willing to continually shift your perceptual world.
3. The authentic life coach assists clientele in making shifts in their perceptual paradigms.

The objectives for Lesson 2 are: 1) To understand the paradigm-shifting process. 2) To be able to identify significant elements in your clients' perceptual paradigms. 3) To be able to effectively coach paradigm-shifting in your clients.

Framework Needed for Coaching Your Clients

Throughout history, the phrase *nosce te ipsum*—"know thyself"—has been advocated as a foundational stone for authentic living. If you want to be most effective with clients, you first need to become more knowledgeable about yourself as a life coach. A critical element of your self knowledge is to become acquainted with how you learn best, or how you modify your perceptual world by incorporating new information.

The phrase *paradigm shift* was coined in 1962 by Thomas Kuhn in his classic book, *The Structure of Scientific Revolutions*. Kuhn demonstrated how almost every significant change in science begins with a break in scientists' conceptualization of "the way things are"—the old paradigms.

For example, the Egyptian astronomer, Ptolemy, believed the Earth was the center of the universe. Along came Copernicus, who believed the sun did not move through the sky, but that the Earth moved around the sun, and a scientific revolution took place. The old paradigm was overthrown, or at least shifted, to account for the new information. A new map was created and everything took on a different interpretation. Now, almost everyone believes the Earth goes around the sun, and not vice versa. This belief, however, is only a pattern of related ideas. The whole question is one of perspective. If you view the Earth from the sun, the Earth seems to rotate around you. If you view the sun from the Earth, the sun seems to rotate around you. From another paradigm, both the Earth and sun are suspended in space—their motions are caught up in the larger rotational motion of the galaxy, and the galaxy itself is rushing away at a tremendous speed from the apparent source of the Big Bang. Perception is all about point of view and, as we have seen, point of view is your current interpretation based upon your particular map (perceptual reality) of the universe.

Many people experience a fundamental paradigm shift when they face a life-threatening crisis. They suddenly see their priorities in a different order, their values change, their thinking about themselves shifts, and their feelings are modified. They may assume a new and different role. Everything changes. Why wait until tragedy or trauma forces you to update your perceptual world? Do it now—by conscious choice—and enjoy the results.

You can make conscious growth and rational change your path of least resistance. You affect change simply and easily when you modify your basic belief systems (maps) about yourself, your body, your life, and your death. The cognitive habits most in need of modification are your early-developed views of the world—your childhood and your immature cognitive conclusions.

> It is the nature of a man . . . to protest against change, particularly change for the better.
> —John Steinbeck

Exercises and Information

Below is an assessment tool to acquaint you and your clients with some common early conclusions (beliefs) and possible alternatives that can catalyze perceptual paradigm shifts.

How would some of your clients' basic core beliefs or conclusions shift if they incorporated in their view of the world the beliefs listed in the right hand column of the table below? If you adopted the *new beliefs* below, how would your life coaching change? How would your life change?

Early Conclusions	New Beliefs
I can't.	I can.
I am dependent.	I am autonomous.
I am helpless.	I am powerful.
I am unlovable.	I am lovable.
I am not good enough.	I am always okay.
Some feelings are good and some are bad.	All my feelings are natural and safe to experience.
I can't control my health and well-being.	I exert powerful influences on my health and well-being.
I can't learn.	I am always learning.
I can't change.	I am always changing and transforming myself.
I am a victim of events.	I am free to choose how I respond to any event.
I die and that's the end.	Death is a natural part of life. It completes the full cycle of life and death.
My body is physical matter.	My body is an energy field of endless transformations and infinite information.
I do not control what happens to me.	I am the result of all the concepts, ideas, and beliefs I hold.
I do not create my own reality.	I create my own reality.
There is an objective world independent of me, outside my skin.	The objective world is created by my internal responses.
Mind and body are two independent entities.	Mind and body are two aspects of the same informational energy field.
My mind is created (and trapped) only by my brain.	My mind is infinite and boundless.
Humans are separate from one another.	Humans are all a part of the same unified field. We are individual, but connected.
My perceptions are automatic and outside my control.	My perceptions are learned, and I can change them.
Meaning is contained in the event.	I create and ascribe any meaning to all events.
We are our bodies, our egos or even our personalities.	Who we really are is not our bodies, our egos, These are all aspects of the ongoing transformations of the informational energy field we create.
Suffering, pain, sickness, and death are parts of natural reality.	We are not the victims of suffering, pain, sickness, or death. Since I create my own reality, I can choose those changes and the meanings I ascribe to them.

Early Conclusions	New Beliefs
We have no influence on nature.	We influence nature and can become masters of natural law. Our intentions can become the triggers for all possible transformations in life.
We have no say in what happens to us.	We can create wellness, joy, or any experience we want. Our intentions, thoughts (beliefs), and perceptions become our reality.
I can't trust life.	I always trust my being alive.
I can't trust everyone.	Whether or not I trust is always my choice.

Obviously, this list of basic paradigm comparisons could go on and on. Invite your clients to generate their own lists. Add your own conclusions and beliefs to the list and see what transpires in your coaching practice, and in your own life.

Coaching Your Clients' Belief-System Shifts

Your contributions to the coach/client relationship need to facilitate the shifting of your clients' perceptual paradigms (belief-systems). Such shifts and consequent new beliefs need to support the creation of *their* desired results.

A paradigm shift commonly experienced by clients and coaches, occurs when the coaching relationship becomes understood as a co-creative partnership focused on the paradigm of "real possibility through chosen change," rather than a coach/client relationship focused on "fixing" the client. Our society believes in an old paradigm of pathology (the medical model) that implies that you have to be broken or wounded to seek help in creating a better life. As a profession, life coaching seems to be an evolutionary step beyond psychotherapy. Life coaching represents a shift toward creating your desired outcomes and consciously creating the future that the client desires.

In order to catalyze your clients' perceptual paradigm shifts, you—as the coach—need to be familiar with the process. We shift our perceptions all the time. Change is constant. Every moment our atoms change, our thoughts and beliefs change, our emotions are ever-flowing, and our relationships are in flux.

Coaching Tips

One of your responsibilities as a life coach is to assist the perceptual paradigm shifts your clients want or need to make. Below are some coaching tips for catalyzing the shifting process.

Become familiar with your own shifting process. Share with your clients the ideas of paradigms, perceptions, beliefs, and making shifts. Inform your clients about the shifting process. Let clients know what a perceptual-paradigm shift is. Describe the benefits of updating their beliefs, especially about themselves. Give clients examples with which they can experiment. Share your own shifting process.

> Progress is a nice word. But change is its motivator and change has its enemies.
> —Robert F. Kennedy

Describe the impact a specific belief may have on your clients. Speculate about the transformations that may occur with a new perceptual paradigm.

Below is a practical example of the possible benefits of a paradigm shift:

Example: Shifting from reacting to responding.

Before the shift: one of your clients tends to become upset and react emotionally to the behavior or language of others. She reacts to her own emotions by avoiding others, becoming bitter or cynical, losing energy, and withdrawing. Such reactions undermine her personal power and she releases that power onto others by placing blame. She is controlled by external events and becomes judgmental; her perspective narrows; her mind becomes closed; and she is unaware that she has the freedom and power to choose how to respond to any given event.

After the shift: Suggest to your client that she will become more self-controlled, self-directing, and autonomously choose her own actions and behavior. She will step away from the role of victim, become response-able, and empowered. She will take full responsibility for the consequences of her choices and actions, and begin to live consciously and congruently with her chosen purposes and goals.

Discuss what your clients need to do to make the shift. Ask your clients to:

- Develop keen and accurate self-awareness.
- Develop an accurate self-concept.
- Be truthful to themselves and tell others the truth (tempered with tact, of course).
- Make the connections between current choices and future results (consequences).
- Behave in ways that are in their best interests.
- Become self-protective and self-determined.

In order for them to:

- Be autonomous.
- Be self-responsible.
- Be honest.
- Maintain their integrity (wholeness).
- Be willing to be true to themselves.
- Identify core values and personal desires.
- Be self-caring.
- Set boundaries.
- Make conscious choices.
- Reprogram their subconscious minds.

Make your clients aware of the possible hazards of a shift. Let them know:

- Any new habit is difficult until with practice it becomes easy (learning curve).
- They may experience a decrease in their comfort levels and their sense of security.
- They may experience an increase in anxiety (fear).
- They will make mistakes (you always do when you begin practicing any new behavior).
- Other people may react negatively to their shift (out of unfamiliarity, if nothing else).

Relay to your clients the benefits that make the shift worth the effort. You can accomplish this by:

- Sharing your own beliefs about the consequences of the shift
- Not focusing on the rationale for shifting or the justification for maintaining the status quo
- Telling the truth about how you think the lives of your clients would change
- Supporting your clients through their experimenting and mistakes
- Mutually assessing your clients willingness and their commitment to the shift
- Making certain that the shift is linked to your clients' value system or their purpose

Ask directly for your clients to make the shift, using the words "Will you . . .?" Make your clients accountable for their shifts by:

- Asking your clients to demonstrate how they have shifted or modified their perceptual paradigm.
- Reinforcing the shift by acknowledging and appreciating it, and by validating its consequences, once you and a client know the shift has occurred.

Continue to challenge your clients to persist in strengthening their shift(s). As their life coach:

- If they make very small, incremental shifts, or make big deals about little shifts, challenge them to make greater ones.
- Don't push the client too quickly to make another new shift in their belief system. It usually takes about three weeks to make new, shift-associated behavior automatic or habitual. Attempting many shifts at once slows down the integration process.
- Ask the client to share the shift with others and their subsequent new beliefs, actions, attitudes, and perceptions.

Key Points About Shifting

Below are some critical points to keep in mind when you coach your clients to make shifts.

1. Shifts occur only when clients are open to them. Shifts occur more often as a result, rather than by intention. Therefore, avoid making a shift a "coaching goal." Belief-system shifts are evidence that learning has occurred. People don't usually learn if they feel emotionally or intellectually threatened by the change(s).

2. Shifts occur when clients already have become aware of their internal life and have accomplished at least some personal, internal changes. Shifts occur most effectively when:

- Clients' values are clear.
- Their fear is minimal.
- Their self-awareness is sharp.

- Their self-esteem and self-confidence is strong.
- They are truthful about themselves.
- They acknowledge their own response-ability.
- Their self-acceptance is constant.

Belief-shifting rarely occurs:

- In the presence of fear
- When dependence is present
- When clients are reactive, rather than responsive
- When clients are highly stressed
- When clients are very needy

3. Shifts are comprehensive. The resulting change is fundamental. When you shift your awareness, your belief system (perceptual paradigm), and your priorities (values), everything realigns. Accurate awareness usually comes from changes in thinking and behaving, and not through gathering new information or insights.

4. There are an infinite number of key shifts to make. When you shift your beliefs, you are moving up at least one level of development. You learn and grow. Your conscious awareness expands. You are nearer to your desired outcomes.

Ask your clients to make, one at a time, all shifts that are essential to creating their own desired outcomes. Plant as many seeds as possible by expanding your own awareness of the many shifts you can make. Make your clients aware of the many possible shifts, give them all at once, and let them choose the right ones for them.

> Get used to thinking that there is nothing Nature loves so well as to change existing forms and to make new ones like them.
> —Marcus Aurelius

Practical and Powerful Methods to Catalyze Perceptual Paradigm Shifts

For the first three years of life, children actively organize their sensory input into perceptions. They attribute meaning to those perceptions and create basic conclusions or cognitive maps by which they make behavioral adaptations in order to survive. Some of these conclusions remain useful and vital for the remainder of their lives; some become irrelevant and require updating. Some conclusions, once useful and necessary, become self-defeating and even self-destructive. When the latter occurs, a basic perceptual paradigm shift is required.

Over a period of several years, co-author of this book, Lloyd J. Thomas, asked many of his clients to tell him what actions contributed most to their making perceptual shifts. Below are some of the most common answers they shared:

- Sought out more information
- Became more observant of their inner life
- Became more selective about what was important to them
- Engaged in some form of meditation or breathing control
- Realized their own wholeness or integrity
- Reframed some historical events in their lives
- Learned how to use their natural creativity
- Used pain as a teaching/learning event
- Engaged in imagery (imagination/visualization)
- Prayed
- Revised the meaning given to earlier experiences
- Engaged in some kind of self-discipline
- Learned to let go of resentments through forgiveness
- Read inspirational literature
- Became more self-assertive
- Recorded and interpreted their dreams
- Experienced love (both being loved and loving)
- Balanced their activity/rest cycles
- Imitated a chosen role-model (hero)
- Acted as if their beliefs were different
- Listened to music
- Reprioritized their values
- Danced
- Learned a new language
- Practiced selectively focusing their attention
- Became more self-aware, self-caring, and self-centered
- Played more
- Laughed more
- Never repressed their crying (or other strong emotions)
- Experimented with new ideas and behaviors
- Became more curious and enhanced their curiosity
- Practiced one new habit for three weeks

- Increased their touch/physical contact
- Learned how to really listen
- Engaged in body work (tai chi, yoga, massage)
- Took more risks
- Confronted their own personal issues

Sample Coaching Conversation

Client: What I want to get most out of our coaching is help with my new business.

Coach: Tell me more. How can I help?

Client: Well, I have this idea about a business, but I'm not a businessman, so I don't know what to do.

Coach: What have you done so far?

Client: I've started a training program for cable TV installers. After being one for many years, I saw the need for a lot more information to be available for technicians to be profitable.

Coach: Will you be more specific?

Client: Well, I've done two weekend seminars and created a notebook of information with all the things I think will make their job more profitable.

Coach: Did you make money on these two seminars, or sell the notebook to participants?

Client: Oh yes! More than eighty people paid a registration fee and purchased the available notebook.

Coach: So you had this idea, organized the seminars, had paying customers, and sold your notebook. It sounds like you already are a businessman to me!

Client: I guess so!

Coach: As a businessman, what other skills do you want to strengthen or learn?

> Things do change. The only question is that since things are deteriorating so quickly, will society and man's habits change quickly enough?
> —Isaac Asimov

Questions and Inquiries

1. What perceptual paradigms are you willing to identify?
2. Which ones are you willing to challenge or change?
3. What techniques are you willing to use to modify your perceptual paradigms?

LIFE LESSON 3

Conscious awareness is the key to successful lifestyle creation.

MESSAGES

1. Your personal perceptual paradigm is a combination of your self-concept and your level of self-esteem.

2. You can choose who you want to be and how much you value who you are.

3. An authentic life coach *always* interacts with clients to unconditionally increase their level of self-esteem.

The objectives for Lesson 3 are: 1) To expand your client's awareness of who they really are; 2) To understand that everyone is growing and changing and no one is ever finished; 3) To increase your own level of self-esteem; 4) To understand that self-awareness is the critical method for developing an accurate self-concept; 5) To update and upgrade the self-concepts of your clients to be positive and useful.

Framework Needed for Coaching Your Clients

The primary psychological factor dividing humans from other animals is the conscious awareness of the *self* as a separate being. Self-awareness is being conscious of everything that goes on inside you: your sensations, feelings, thoughts, perceptions, memories, images, experiences, and so on. Self-awareness allows us to remember a past, anticipate a future, and be conscious of the present. Self-awareness is also what divides and separates individuals from other human beings. Along with this self-awareness is the capacity to evaluate and judge the self and others.

An unexamined life is not worth living.
—Socrates

Being conscious of your own mental processes, and then practicing control of those processes, can empower you beyond your wildest imaginings.

Ten percent of the quality of your life is based on what happens to you and 90 percent on how you *respond* to what happens to you. The significance of events is determined by the meaning *you* assign to them. The habitual way you see events and respond makes up your awareness. A healthily developed awareness includes the capacity to accurately and clearly perceive and give meaning to everything that affects your life. Self-awareness is the means whereby adults define themselves or, in other words, develop a self-concept. This awareness determines all behavior. Self-awareness can be accurate or inaccurate, positive or negative. *You* determine its style and content.

Who you think you are today is at best incomplete, and is probably inaccurate. We formed a sense of self when we were children. We identified with our parent(s) or caretakers so we believed we were like them. We also used the information from our senses (sight, sound, taste, touch, smell etc.) to form beliefs about ourselves.

The more you learn about yourself and how you function, the larger your self-awareness becomes. Just because you are not consciously aware of all the activities you do, doesn't mean you don't do them. You digest food. You perspire. You produce all kinds of biochemicals. You even create and destroy your body cells on a regular basis. You may not be aware of how you do it, but if *you* don't do these things, who does? And you certainly don't incorporate your abilities to stay alive as a part of your self-concept. But if you don't stay alive, who does? Maybe you need to expand your awareness of who you are to more accurately reflect the reality of your true self. Each one of us is, at a fundamental level, a field of energy and information. Who keeps that field in the form of a human body? If not you, who?

Perhaps the philosopher, Tielhard de Chardin (1976), was accurate in stating that we are not physical beings having a spiritual experience, rather we are spiritual beings having a physical experience.

Once your clients become more fully aware of who they really are, they can use that knowledge to generate almost any outcome. Their personal awareness of their own abilities and how they can best use those abilities makes them the most powerful and creative creatures on the face of the earth.

Self Esteem

You live with yourself closer and longer than with anyone else. The most critical relationship you can experience in life is the one you have with yourself.

Wouldn't it be great to have your closest friend always inside you, no matter where you go or whatever you do? Nourish that friendship and you will never consent to feeling inferior again.

As we discussed in Lesson 1, your self-concept is defined as "Who you believe you are." The value you place on that belief defines your level of self-esteem. Your self-esteem is rooted in how valuable you believe you are. If, as a child, you were told that you were beautiful, smart, caring, loving, affectionate, outgoing, etc., you probably have a positive, valuable self-concept and high self-esteem. Unfortunately, by the time children are ten years old they have received several thousand negative and thousands fewer positive messages from the influential people around them. Children perceive themselves as unable to function as adequately as they see others around them functioning. When they compare themselves to adults, they almost always feel inadequate. When they compare themselves to what the media portrays as "normal," they tend to develop an inaccurate self-concept and less than optimal self-esteem.

Many people believe what they do *is* who they are. They draw their identity from the role they play in their family, daily relationships, or career. Who you are, however, is always different from whatever you do or how you perform. You are the actor in this play called *life*. You are *not* the actions you take. We were once asked, "If you are not what you do, what choices do you have for defining yourself?" Our answer to that question was, "The number of choices you have for defining yourself is infinite."

> The ability to divorce one's mind from one's actions is a symptom of psychological aberration.
> —Walter Goodman

Building a positive self-concept and raising your level of self-esteem helps you enjoy life. You can survive with a negative self-concept, but it will be difficult for you to be happy. When your self-esteem is low, or is not regularly looked after and raised, your emotional life can become enormously painful. This negativity and pain leads to further beliefs and feelings of inadequacy, weakness, inability to cope, anger, depression, and feeling victimized by life.

Exercises and Information

Below are some coaching exercises and information for expanding your clients' self-awareness and self-esteem.

Expanding Self-Awareness

Here are a few quick methods you can suggest to your clients that will invite them to expand their self-awareness. Learning how to most effectively use these suggestions, however, often requires a lifetime.

Encourage you clients to:

Pay attention to their senses. Our senses include seeing, hearing, touching, smelling, tasting, kinesthesia, and intuition. In the normal human body, these senses are fully functioning by the age of twelve to fourteen. You can separate these senses from each other through a variety of exercises. For example, invite your clients to wear blindfolds for twenty-four hours and ask them to observe how much more they use their other senses. Next, ask them to wear a blindfold *and* earplugs for another twenty-four hours. Have them observe how much they use the other five senses. Then, have them spend time in a flotation chamber which minimizes their sense of sight, sound, touch, smell, taste, and kinesthesia. They will be acutely aware of their intuition and mental activity. Challenge your clients to begin to be aware of how—and in what proportions—they combine these senses to create what they experience.

Experiment by giving new meanings to language. The basis for humor and comedy is to look at experiences from a different (and often unexpected) point of view, thereby giving new meaning to common experiences.

Practice the skill of mindfulness. An ancient skill, mindfulness is being fully aware (conscious) of your experiences at any given moment. How you feel, how you move, how you think, and what you sense. To accomplish this, your clients need to slow everything down. Challenge them to take the time to be aware of colors, textures, and shapes, bodily movement, and what they are thinking and feeling right now. Being aware of all that is going on inside and outside of their bodies and minds can be a flood of overwhelming experiences, but doing so will make your clients more aware of themselves and their place in the environment.

Get to know and control mental activity. The qualities of a powerful, healthy mind are tranquility and peacefulness, gentleness (without fear or anger), silence (without words, images, or memories), restraint and control, purity and lack of clutter, and receptivity (openness). To become more fully aware of these qualities, the practice of meditation is probably the most helpful. Invite your clients to learn how to meditate.

Make the distinction between who they are versus what they do or how they perform. Many people grow up believing that their actions define them.

They believe they *are* the role or roles they play. Our professions or activities are all habitual behaviors in which we engage. They do not define us as people. We are defined by who we really are as human beings, not by what we do or how we behave.

Increase self-esteem. Self-esteem is genuine self-love. Advise your clients that if they believe themselves to be valuable, they need to treat themselves accordingly. Your clients cannot have sound self-value until they give up or let go of the defensive attitudes of fear, shame, guilt, and remorse, and completely stop negatively value-judging themselves. Your clients need to become more curious and investigative of themselves and their present-moment experience, without attributing any value to that experience. Your clients are the valuable observers or experiencers of their existence. They are not *what* they experience.

Changing the Cycle of Low Self-Esteem/Negative Self-Concept

Clients demonstrate a low level of self-esteem when they exhibit some or all of the following feelings or behaviors:

- Unnecessary self-protection
- Fear of rejection or abandonment
- Unwillingness to take risks
- Inability to address personal wants and needs
- Development of self-destructive thinking patterns that characterize them in a negative way
- Limited ability to form close, personal relationships or friendships
- Weakened ability to address and solve problems

Negativity tends to snowball. If your clients feel unhappy and dislike themselves, they will protect their fragile self-esteem by defending it in ways that temporarily may make them feel better, but ultimately will make them feel worse. In turn, this defensive behavior makes them think less of themselves—and the grim cycle is complete. As a life coach to your clients, it is your job to help them break this cycle.

The best method for you to help clients raise their level of self-esteem is to become unconditionally constructive in all you think, do, and say about your clients. Avoid thinking or saying anything that makes them "wrong."

> Life is not easy for any of us. But what of that? We must have perseverance and, above all, confidence in ourselves. We must believe that we are gifted for something, and that this thing, at whatever cost, must be attained.
> —Marie Curie

Refrain from making internal judgments about them. Figuratively surround your clients in a fog of acceptance. If they are engaging in negative behavior, share with them what you believe the consequences for them will be if it continues. Ask them what they think the outcome will be if they continue to behave negatively.

Below are some suggestions for escaping the vicious cycle of a negative self-concept and low self-esteem. Some of these tools may work better for your clients than others. If you want your clients to develop more accurate and highly-valued self-concepts, have them try several of the following:

Learn to notice and identify negative or self-criticizing thoughts. Become aware of how much they think negatively about themselves and diminish their personal importance.

Speak positively to themselves. Tell them to stop the insults and self-criticism. Have them practice positive and affirming self-talk.

Convert all their "should's" into "could's." If they feel they should do something that is not particularly important to them, or is based on what other people think they should do, ask them to forget it. Challenge them to do only those activities that will reinforce their positive self-concept and strengthen them.

Encourage them to exercise. Physical exercise is an excellent way for your clients to strengthen their self-concepts. In addition to improving their appearance and health, physical exercise nurtures positive thoughts and feelings, as biochemicals released by the brain during exercise create a natural and healthy high.

Learn to differentiate between the things that they can control and things they cannot. Send your clients the message that they have absolutely no power to change another person's chosen behavior. Ask them to recognize and use their personal power to change themselves and design and engineer their *own* lives in the way they choose—leave changes in others' lives to the others!

Learn from their mistakes without self-punishment. There are no mistakes, only lessons. Humans learn through experience. The only time we encounter problems is when we fail to learn the lessons life constantly sends our way the first time they occur.

> No one can make you feel inferior without your consent.
> —Eleanor Roosevelt

Learn from past errors and then let them go. Encourage your clients to practice self-forgiveness and learn self-acceptance.

Affirmations for Raising Self-Esteem

The following Affirmation Sets are helpful for reinforcing an increased level of self-esteem. Invite your clients to memorize one set per week. Have them repeat the set to themselves until it becomes part of their current, unconscious belief system. Let them know that they must exert every effort to internalize these sets if they want to build and nourish a higher level of self-esteem.

> Nothing is more unpleasant than a virtuous person with a mean mind.
> —Walter Bagehot

Set 1

1. I accept complete responsibility for my own well-being—for everything I think, say, and do.
2. I choose to direct my life in constructive channels.
3. I refrain from negatively criticizing myself and from accepting the negative judgments of others.
4. I make decisions and accept the consequences of my actions.
5. I discipline myself by controlling my thoughts, desires, images, perceptions, and expectations.

Set 2

1. I think for myself and act accordingly.
2. I allow myself the freedom to succeed or fail without feeling guilty, inadequate, or "less-than."
3. I don't blame others for my problems, defeats, or mistakes.
4. I get satisfaction from doing my work conscientiously and well.
5. I refuse to accept blame, shame, or guilt.

Set 3

1. I accept problems as challenges to my awareness and its development.
2. I purge myself of all blame, shame, and guilt.
3. My current goals and objectives motivate me, so I don't procrastinate.
4. I see things through to their logical conclusions.

5. I do not allow personal comparisons to affect my self-esteem. I avoid comparing myself to others.

Set 4

1. I make every effort to achieve and maintain a positive self-concept.
2. I am authentic—true to my own needs, values, and convictions.
3. I do not try to prove my worth through my accomplishments.
4. I will not base my identity (who I am) on my roles (what I do).
5. I accept myself totally and unconditionally.

Set 5

1. I stand up for my opinions and convictions.
2. I do not rely on others for financial or moral support.
3. I face reality honestly and resist nothing I cannot change.
4. Fear of failure or defeat does not hold me back.

Set 6

1. I do not require others to agree with or approve of what I think and do.
2. I do not let others talk me into things against my better judgment.
3. I am patient, kind, and gentle with myself.
4. I avoid over-indulgence and do nothing in excess.

Set 7

1. I walk erectly and greet everyone with a smile.
2. I learn lessons from my mistakes.
3. I never try to impress others with my worth or importance.
4. I love being me.

Coaching Language

- "You are an intelligent, conscious, spiritual being."
- "You have a lot more personal power than you may have imagined."
- "You have infinite organizing power."

- "The source of all awareness and knowledge is always available to you."
- "You are always expanding your conscious awareness."
- "(For you) I am a life coach, and coaching is my chosen profession."

Sample Coaching Conversation

Setting: A client seeks coaching to improve her law practice.

Client: Nothing we've come up with before seems to be changing anything about my practice.

Coach: Why did you want to become a lawyer in the first place? I mean, what drew you to the practice of law in the beginning?

Client: Well, my Dad always expected me to become an attorney. After all, it has been a family tradition, and I would be the first woman lawyer in the family.

Coach: In your heart of hearts, do you really want to be an attorney, successful or not?

Client: (long pause) Not really, but I can't change now.

Coach: (after more silence) Really? If you weren't an attorney, who would you be?

Client: I guess I always wanted to be a marine biologist, or work around the ocean and marine life.

Coach: So that part of you that wanted to be a marine biologist, how could that be nurtured or experienced today?

Client: I guess I could volunteer at the local marina, or take classes in marine biology.

Coach: What I would like for you to consider is separating your career from your self-concept. In other words, let's find outlets for your personal passion about marine biology and perhaps integrate it with the practice of law.

Questions and Inquiries

Here are some questions to ask your clients that may help them clarify their self-concept and self-esteem.

1. Who are you?
2. How do you think?

3. How do you create?
4. How do you control your actions?
5. How do you feel?
6. What makes you different from others?
7. How are you the same?
8. How do you realize your potential as a unique individual?
9. How can you design and develop a future that you really want for yourself?
10. Where do you start? (This question is answered by: You start by getting to know yourself.)
11. How would you function differently if you saw yourself as a spiritual being?
12. What are the implications for you to view yourself as a field of infinite organizing power?
13. Are you living up to your potential as a human being? Does anyone?
14. Given your new self-awareness, how will you be different a year from now?

LIFE LESSON 4
Your value system guides you toward success or failure.

The objectives for Lesson 4 are: 1) To understand and share with your clients the importance of a clear value system; 2) To identify your own personal values; 3) To assist your clients to understand their personal values; 4) To help clients learn where and how their current values may have originated; 5) To learn how to change value systems.

Framework Needed for Coaching Your Clients

A prankster once broke into a fashionable store and switched the price tags on all the merchandise. On articles of low value he placed high price tags, and on the truly precious articles he placed low price tags. A witness to the proceedings remarked, "How true to life! So many of us have the wrong price tags on our values; and we are not even aware of it."

To understand the role your values play in your life, it might be helpful to compare yourself to an automobile. Like the engine in a car, your body, emotions, wants, and needs are the driving force or energy provider to move you through life. Your mind/thinking is like the steering wheel, directing the movement of the vehicle (behavior) and guiding it in specific directions. Your value system acts like the rules of the road. The rules protect you and help you get to where you want to go, in a safe and efficient manner.

Being unaware of your emotions, wants, and needs and not addressing them is like turning off the car's ignition. You won't go anywhere. Failure to think about where you want to go and how you want to get there is like stepping on the accelerator and letting go of the steering wheel. You will certainly move, but you will have no control over the direction or the best way to arrive at your destination. Without awareness of the rules of the road—your values—you might just drive on the wrong side of the road or try to go in a straight line to your destination, when there are curves in the road. You will be endangered and without guidance as to the most effective way to reach your desired goals. When you follow your values you are assured that your behavior is protective and supportive of your self and your desired future.

For the first five years of life, we learned and incorporated most of our values from our parents. We imitated them and learned to like what they liked or accepted. We valued what they thought was important: if they were caring, we became caring; if they spoke English, we learned to speak English; if they were friendly, we learned to value friendliness; if they were angry and abusive, we came to believe those qualities were normal and important; if they were fearful, we learned to fear, and so on.

> The good things in
> life are not
> necessarily the
> rarest, nor the
> most costly.
> —Chinese proverb

In adolescence, we became free to choose our own values. We tended to question—if not rebel against—the values held by our parents and teachers. We sought and experimented with alternative values to see how well they fit. Since we were never adults before, we didn't know what values would work best, so we tried out many different ones. Sometimes the ones we chose worked well; sometimes they might have been self-defeating or downright destructive.

As a life coach, learning about the values your clients developed in their past may prove beneficial. What were the outcomes created by those who followed a certain value system? What values proved useful to you in your past?

Exercises and Information

Here are some questions to ask your clients that may help them clarify their personal values.

Inquiries

Ask your clients to answer the following questions and give them to you.

- Who do you most admire?
- What values did (do) they live by?
- Do you want the same outcomes for your life as they had in theirs?
- Who would you like to follow to become the most successful person you can be?
- What values guide (or guided) their behavior?
- Who do you want to be like when you are 25? 30? 50? 70? 90?
- When you die, how do you want to be remembered?
- What legacy do you want to leave to your children and grandchildren?
- What values have worked best in the past to promote your health, wealth, happiness, and prosperity?

> Today we are afraid of simple words like *goodness* and *mercy* and *kindness*. We don't believe in the good old words because we don't believe in the good old values anymore. And that's why the world is sick.
> —Lin Yutang

Sample Coaching Conversation

Setting: To have your clients change their childhood value systems, you need to ask them how they would behave differently if they were following a new value.

Coach: So, you value being physically fit and yet your habits to support that value have been inconsistent. Let's try acting as if you are physically fit and you love regular exercise. Try that now.

Client: I can imagine feeling fit and finding time in my day to exercise and take care of my body. I can see that in my future, but I also know I never seem to find the time to get started.

Coach: There is no time to find. You have to make time. This week, I want you to practice a physically-fit mindset. Act as if you are physically fit even if you don't do anything differently, and report back to me. If this is a value and not a *should*, you will start allowing it to manifest in your daily life.

When your clients are confronted with a difficult situation or choice, and they value courage (or any other value), ask questions such as:

"What would *courage* do in this situation?"
"What would *faith* do?"
"What would *love* do?"
"What would (*your client's value*) lead or direct you to do?"

Then, invite your clients to follow their values in all of their actions.

In the coach/client relationship, an authentic life coach always behaves in accordance with the values he or she has chosen, remaining alert to the impact that his or her value-based behavior has on the coaching relationship.

Questions and Inquiries

1. Are you comfortable with where you are headed in your life?
2. Do you regularly get where you want to go?
3. Do you efficiently achieve your desired goals?
4. Does your behavior work for you, for others—or is it destructive?
5. Do you fail to achieve what you want?
6. By following your values, do you get where you want to be in life? If not, change your value system.

If you or your clients do not like the direction in which your lives are going, or the outcomes you believe will occur, choose different values and behave accordingly. As adults, you are free to do that. Don't misuse or neglect that freedom.

> We live in a vastly complex society which has been able to provide us with a multitude of material things, and this is good, but people are beginning to suspect that we have paid a high spiritual price for our plenty.
> —Euell Gibbons

LIFE LESSON 5
You are responsible for your standards.

MESSAGES

1. Understand and believe in the value of high personal standards.
2. Be willing to continuously raise your standards.
3. Realize that there is a direct correlation between the standards you set for yourself and your personal satisfaction.
4. Realize you have the power to raise your standards at this very moment.

The objectives for Lesson 5 are: 1) To increase your awareness of the personal and professional standards you have now; 2) To have clients imagine and create new, higher personal standards for themselves; 3) To have clients take actions that support attainment of the highest standards they set for themselves; 4) To continue to raise the bar for yourself and your clientele throughout life; 5) To set higher standards for your coaching practice.

Framework Needed for Coaching Your Clients

Personal standards are those internal aims you have for yourself, your clients, and the world. Your behavior is a direct reflection of the standards by which you have consciously or unconsciously chosen to live. If one of your personal standards is to be a life coach, you will begin to think and behave like a life coach thinks and behaves. You can always choose different standards. You can always choose to behave in ways to meet those standards. You are the only one who has the power, and therefore the responsibility, to set and meet your own personal standards.

The results and outcomes your client may experience in her life or business are directly related to the standards she has set for herself and her business. For example, if she believes she will be satisfied and fulfilled with a business that generates an income of $50,000 a year, then that is the income standard toward which she will strive. If she behaves in ways that support the generation of $50,000 a year, she will also attract customers in numbers that will create that amount of income, and nothing more. She has limited her desired outcome to a specific amount.

The standards you consciously or unconsciously set for yourself, limit or expand your capacity to grow, learn, earn, experience and enjoy your lifestyle! If you desire growth, fulfillment of your potential, a full coaching practice and new experiences, reset your standards differently enough to include and support such development!

Exercises and Information

Here are a few main areas where your clients need to focus when evaluating their standards.

> The quality of a person's life is in direct proportion to their commitment to excellence regardless of their chosen field of endeavor.
> —Vince Lombardi

- *Self-Concept*
  Is it accurate and updated from childhood?
- *Level of Desire and Willingness*
  Are your clients willing to do whatever is necessary to manifest their desired outcomes, and to become the person they desire to be?
- *Interpersonal Relationship Network*
  Have your clients sought out (or attracted) relationships with people who are supportive of their envisioned outcomes, or who have already accomplished what your clients want to do? Have they found and connected to role models who already are who they want to become?
- *Personal Expectations*
  Do your clients fully expect to reach the standards they have set? The more solid their expectancies, the more likely they will behave in a manner that will fulfill those expectations.
- *Self-Conduct*
  Are your clients' thinking habits, emotional habits, and behavioral habits consistent with meeting their chosen standards? Does their habitual way of functioning support them in maintaining their own standards?

Sample Coaching Conversation

Setting: The client is consistently late for his or her coaching call.

Coach: One of the roles I have as your life coach is to model high personal and professional standards. Therefore, before we start today, I need to have a conversation about your frequent tardiness for your coaching sessions.

Client: I know, I know. I'm sorry.

Coach: Are you late for other appointments in your life?

Client: Oh yes, it happens all the time.

Coach: One of my personal standards is to be respectful of others and to be on time for any appointments with them. I also hold myself to a standard of being ten minutes early for meetings. That allows me to settle in, take a breath, and be fully present. Is being on time a standard you would like to have as well?

Client: Of course. I always intend to be on time.

Coach: Will you practice this standard beginning with our sessions? And maybe later extend it to other areas of your life?

Client: I'll give it a shot.

Coach: Great! What do you think of this? Next week, I want you to be ready ten minutes before our scheduled appointment. Use that time to focus on our coaching, our objectives, what you want from the session, and allow yourself to be fully present when you call.

Client: Okay. I like that.

Catalyzing High Personal and Professional Standards

Note: The following exercises and suggestions are offered as relevant to a coaching practice but are applicable to any client as well.

Are you making your coaching practice worth living? Here are some questions for stimulating your thinking about your personal and professional standards.

- Who am I . . . really?
- What roles do I play as a life coach?
- Who do I want to become in the future? Is that the person I really want to be?
- What are my standards for being a coach?

- With respect to my standards for life coaching, what is my self-concept now?
- How do I see myself now?
- Who was I in the past? What kind of person was I during my personal history?
- As a life coach, what are my personal aspirations?
- What are my dreams for my coaching practice?
- Who am I not . . . really?

Exercises to Do Now

Have your clients complete the following exercise to help them raise their personal standards.

1. Make a list of ten people you admire and would like to emulate in some way. To what standards do they hold themselves?
2. Define your personal standards as a person.
3. Raise your standards by candidly answering the following:

I am someone who aspires to be: _____

_____

_____

In order to be who I want to be, do what I want to do, and have what I want to have, I am willing to: _____

_____

_____

_____

In order to grow, I must surround myself with people who are: _____

_____

_____

_____

I understand that realistic expectations lead to actions and results. I can reasonably expect the following from myself: _____

_____

_____

_____

What is essential to my success? _____

_____

_____

_____

My actions are a direct result of my beliefs, attitudes, and energy. In order to achieve greatness in my endeavors, my conduct will habitually be: _____

_____

_____

_____

> The important thing in life is to have a great aim and to possess the aptitude and the perseverance to attain it.
> —Goethe

Raising Your Practice Standards

You are the CEO of your coaching practice. Your business is life coaching. Your product is the value you bring to your clients. Client satisfaction is dependent on the services you provide. You may want to raise your practice standards to the level of the successful CEO of any company or organization.

Below are seventeen skills essential for executive success in your life-coaching practice. Aspire to strengthen them, raise your standards accordingly, and not only will you fulfill your own professional goals, you may also fill your practice!

1. Develop visionary thinking. Develop a clear vision for your coaching practice; maintain a long-term view of your practice and anticipate obstacles and opportunities; be creative in generating ideas for your future; generate ideas that capture your imagination and the imagination of your clients; challenge the current thinking and assumptions of your clients; seek breakthrough ideas and new paradigms that bring value to the marketplace.

2. Develop mature judgment. Seek to clarify complex issues; understand the problems and symptoms of your clients before developing a strategy to address them; remain mentally receptive to your clients' values and viewpoints, especially when they are different from your own.

3. Develop financial management skills. Create a comprehensive financial plan for your practice; perform a realistic financial analysis that evaluates your use of time, practice options, and marketability; recognize profitability and income potential in niches within the profession; track and manage the financial performance of your practice (budget, income, cash flow, debt, balance, etc.); become a student of financial management.

4. Have a global perspective. Grasp the position of your practice within the worldwide profession of coaching; familiarize yourself and stay abreast of the trends and qualification criteria for the profession; participate in a professional coaching organization (e.g., the International Coaching Federation); maintain personal curiosity and a wide range of interests in related professions; recognize and pursue prospects for alliances and worldwide opportunities.

5. Develop your strategic thinking and actions. Clearly identify your professional goals as a life coach; learn of the success factors that other coaches use; create specific strategies that distinguish your practice from competitors; always convert broad strategies into clear objectives and practical actions; always keep the desires of your clients in focus and develop strategies accordingly; identify and take the risks necessary to implement your strategies; develop contingency strategies and prioritize them.

6. Engage in action. Become accountable to a mentor coach for the success of your practice; strive for continuous improvement of your coaching skills (e.g., read, attend professional conferences); establish benchmarks for the development of your practice and track your attainment of them; confront problems and difficulties head-on and resolve them as soon as possible; comprehensively evaluate your practice four times a year.

7. Practice the principle of attraction. Create a co-learning relationship with clients, rather than a "knowing/ignorant" or "coach/client" relationship; recognize and acknowledge the talents and abilities of your clients, as well as their needs and desires; encourage your clients growth and development; appraise the strengths and weaknesses reported by clients; provide accurate and constructive feedback at all times; provide needed resources, tips, and experiences for the realization of your clients' desired outcomes; inspire commitment in your clients to the coaching process for the attainment of their goals; promote the courage and persistence of your clients.

8. Create a relationship that empowers the client. Develop a climate in which your clients stretch themselves beyond what they thought they could achieve; generate excitement, energy, and personal investment; encourage commitment to attaining coaching goals; communicate your confidence in your clients' ability and desire to create their desired outcomes; celebrate and reward all small and large achievements; foster autonomy and independence; promote collaboration.

Ethics stays in the prefaces of the average business science book.
—Peter Drucker

9. Become highly influential and develop your ability to negotiate. Always seek win/win solutions to conflict; express respect for the challenges, points of view, and brilliance of your clients; maintain a positive attitude and realistically optimistic outlook; seek to first understand the coaching needs of your clients and thereafter express your own; become self-assertive, not aggressive; be firmly flexible in any position you adopt; learn to actively and effectively listen; become genuinely curious and interested in your clients; develop your unique leadership style, but remain adaptable and versatile within it.

10. Build extensive and transformative relationships. Create and expand your professional, personal, and social networks; join groups to exchange ideas and generate support; keep in touch with contacts made in the past; recognize and appreciate individual differences in all people and groups; adapt your personal style to be congruent with the learning styles of others; cultivate collaboration and cooperation; always be of value and service to others; be trustworthy and dependable, thereby inspiring trust; be open, truthful, direct, and candid in all your communications; maintain a high level of personal integrity; treat others fairly; be consistent.

11. Practice effective communication skills. Keep all channels of communication open; keep others well informed; speak clearly and concisely; promote candid discussion, especially on sensitive or tough issues; express your opinions, ideas, and desires without intimidating others; listen to and acknowledge the input of others; ask questions that clarify issues or expand the awareness of your clients; encourage others to express different and contrary ideas; make certain that your non-verbal messages are congruent with your verbal ones.

12. Hone your speaking skills. Think of speaking as a strategic issue; deliver public speeches in a clear and well-organized manner; develop a persuasive and convincing speaking style; increase your speaking vocabulary; use an abundance of examples, illustrations, and metaphors to communicate your key ideas; speak with poise and credibility; learn to handle questions well, especially in adversarial situations; learn how to lead effective meetings of diverse groups.

13. Drive for client success. Set and pursue coaching goals that are extensive and that stretch your clients; communicate your commitment to the attainment of your clients' goals; hold your clients accountable for generating desired results; communicate trust and understanding of your clients doing what is in their best interest; "walk your talk" to present your clients with a role model; encourage a strong work ethic; stress priorities, persistence, and patience.

14. Foster appropriate risk-taking. Champion new ideas and fresh initiatives; create a relationship that encourages appropriate risk-taking; acknowledge break-through initiatives and thinking out loud; identify new opportunities and make them a reality in your own practice as well as in the life your clients; reward innovation; perceive so-called mistakes and failures as essential stepping stones to successful creation of desired outcomes.

15. Develop your own self-confidence. Stand up to destructive criticism; develop a willingness to make the lonely decision; have and maintain your sense of humor; give and share credit for accomplishments that are visible to others; be realistic in evaluating your own strengths and weaknesses; build on your strengths and delegate your weaknesses; acknowledge your own limitations and inadequacies; maintain your own dreams and possibilities.

> To be a success in business, be daring, be first, be different.
> —Marchant

16. Learn how to adapt. Welcome change; increase your repertoire of responses to new demands, challenges, and situations; maintain inner calm, especially when surrounded by chaotic stress or pressure; become aware of and cope with the political realities of any interpersonal situation; identify and practice your own personal stress-coping mechanisms; learn to quickly choose your desired responses rather than merely react; avoid anger when your plans are thwarted; realize that nothing is permanent and there are no decisions that cannot be altered by further decision.

17. Continue to evolve. Identify and clearly communicate your own values, goals, aspirations, and unique personal characteristics; effectively manage your use of time; shift from knowing to an attitude of learning; continue self-development; maintain a dynamic balance between your coaching practice and your personal life; prioritize your actions according to your values; never stop learning and expanding your awareness.

Coaching Language

- "My personal standards include: _____." (Recite them out loud)
- I ask directly by using the words `I want/need _____. Will you _____?'"
- "I live according to the highest standards I have set for myself."

Questions and Inquiries

1. What standards do you hold yourself to right now?
2. What standards can you raise immediately, and what impact will this have on your life?
3. When will you begin to live according to these higher standards?

LIFE LESSON 6

You protect your "self" by setting and maintaining strong boundaries.

MESSAGES

1. It is vital to your happiness and development to have extensive boundaries.
2. Identify the boundaries you want to set and teach others what they are.
3. Recognize when others overstep your boundaries.
4. Plan ahead for actions you will take when your boundaries are violated.

The objectives for Lesson 6 are: 1) To have the client realize the importance of identifying and setting their personal boundaries; 2) To assist the client in practicing responses when others overstep the boundaries they have established; 3) To plan with your clients actions they can take to immediately set new boundaries.

Framework Needed for Coaching Your Clients

Boundaries are similar to a moat around a medieval castle. Moats were built to keep enemies from having access to the heart of the empire. The farther the moat was dug from the castle's walls, the harder it was for the enemy to invade—and so it is with you. The farther out you set your boundaries, the more difficult it becomes for hurtful people to reach your heart.

Boundaries are rules you establish for yourself, and by which you teach others to abide. Others do not recognize your boundaries unless they are visible, or you communicate clearly what they are. For example, children will push or test the boundaries of their parents by acting out or behaving in ways that invite the parents to stop or correct them. Children may plead to stay up "just five more minutes," but smart parents will not change the rule. When children fail to learn or

experience parental boundaries, they become very uncertain of themselves, insecure with others, and cannot develop trust of the world. When parents establish
known and firm boundaries for young children, they feel secure, and they grow
up learning to respect the boundaries of others.

Every boundary has degrees of distance from you and from your heart. The
more extensive your boundaries, the more difficulty abusive people have affecting
you, and the easier it is for you to keep people who are harmful to you at a comfortable distance.

When you establish healthy boundaries, you feel more secure. Your level of
anxiety lowers, and you strengthen the trust you have in yourself, in others, and
in the world.

A cautionary note: If you establish boundaries that are too rigid or too extensive, you shut out all contact with others—a very lonely, isolated (albeit safe) position to adopt.

Many adults struggle to take time to practice self-care. If you value taking
time for yourself for reading, meditating, writing—but rarely do it—you have a
boundary that can be strengthened.

Coaches often request that their clients look at their calendar and make time
for what *they* want first, and then build their work life and schedule around that.
Of course, such scheduling has to be reasonable and realistic, but scheduling time
for themselves first, increases the probability clients will take the time they want
or need.

In order to clearly identify *your* personal boundaries, you need to decide what
is acceptable to you, and define what you consider to be unacceptable behavior
exhibited by others who affect your life. You then need to educate them about
your boundaries. Finally, you need to determine, and then inform, others of the
actions you will take if/when your boundaries are violated. Like any new
behavior, boundary-setting is difficult at first. But with practice, you will unconsciously and automatically set your boundaries.

Boundaries are very important in any relationship. They are a key part of
coaching clients to establish their own boundaries for themselves. Boundaries are
our personal lines of demarcation for privacy, confidentiality, or just plain personal space. They are rooted in our personal value systems.

In contrast to personal standards that are usually private, boundaries need to
be made public in order to be effective. A boundary is a personal line that people
do not cross, they help to create either personal safety or personal/professional
clarity.

If you are willing to be flexible with a personal standard in response to a specific condition, then it is a boundary. Flexible boundaries are best when you con-

> It is a blessed thing
> that in every age
> some one has had
> the individuality
> enough and the
> courage enough to
> stand by his own
> convictions.
> —Robert G. Ingersoll

sciously choose when and how to modify them. For example, if you expect a very important call, you might make an exception to the boundary off not having business calls at night. This becomes a choice you have made to adjust a professional boundary. If not taking business calls at night is one of your professional standards, however, you might simply say, "My evenings with my family are for us, and I do not schedule or answer business calls after 5:00 p.m. under any circumstances."

Exercises and Information

Unless they are made public, personal boundaries are completely ineffective. Here are some suggestions for clients to inform others of their boundaries.

Effective methods for clients to educate others about their boundaries

Encourage your clients to:

> In matters of principle, stand like a rock; in matters of taste, swim with the current.
> —Thomas Jefferson

1. *Inform* others about the effect their behavior has on them. Example: "When you behave that way, I feel . . ." "When you said that, I thought . . ."
2. *Make direct requests* using the words, "Will you . . ." so that others respond to them in the manner your clients desire. Example: "Will you listen to what I am about to say and then respond from your heart?"
3. *Teach* others clearly about how you want them to behave under specific and relevant circumstances. Examples: "Don't ever touch me when you are angry," "I am trying to eliminate hostility from our relationship, so please keep your voice down when we are interacting."
4. *Warn* others of the consequences of their actions. Make "if then" statements. "If you . . . then I will . . ." Examples: "When you ignore me, I will always react with anger." "If you disobey the rules, I will not interact with you for an hour." Be certain your clients know to carry out any warnings they do make.
5. *Leave the scene.* Leave the room, the restaurant, the area. If others consistently violate your established boundaries, invite them to leave the relationship. Example: "I am going for a walk to calm down. I will be back, but I don't know when."

Tip 1. Invite your clients to set their own boundaries because you have experienced how much better your interpersonal relationships become when *you* have done so.

Teaching example: You notice that one of your clients overpromises, then becomes frustrated with a long "to-do" list. Ask this client to say "no" to more requests or demands. A tactful way of declining is to say, "I'd prefer not to . . ." or "Let me think about it and get back to you." Such phrases invite your client to set boundaries.

Tip 2. Teach clients to be tactful and caring when they educate others regarding their boundaries. Your clients should never attempt to teach others about their boundaries when angry or defensive. Keep in mind that when clients set their boundaries, they are caring for and protecting themselves. Setting boundaries is not a means to ventilate their emotions.

Teaching example: Tell your clients, "Assertiveness is expressing your views or needs without intentionally hurting another. You can be tactful *and* truthful! Practice having courageous conversations with the people in your life. Be intentionally clear about your boundaries and communicating them well to those around you. Having this intention keeps the energy behind the communication respectful and controlled."

Tip 3. Realize that setting boundaries may be a completely new skill for your clients Let them know that like all new skills, boundary-setting seems initially difficult. With practice, however—small boundaries first—clients will master the skill and boundary-setting will become unconscious and automatic. At that point, setting boundaries will seem easy to clients.

Teaching example: Say to your clients, "Let trusted friends know that you are practicing setting and strengthening your boundaries. Communicate with them as a rehearsal, saying what you need and the results you want. They can help you feel comfortable and confident about establishing your personal boundaries. This is the same as an actor practicing his or her lines until the dialogue is delivered with the character and confidence that many rehearsals and practice allow."

Tip 4. Make certain your clients extend their boundaries to their interpersonal relationships. That way, they will allow others a chance to learn and grow with them in respecting their boundaries. It is a good idea for you as a life coach, to share with your clients your own progress in learning how to set and respect personal boundaries.

Teaching example: Tell your clients to let other people know what your boundaries are and why they are important to you. Share your progress and ask for feedback.

Tip 5. Establishing extensive boundaries allows your clients to put energy into living the kind of lifestyle they desire. Unclear boundaries distract and drain clients' energy, as they are forced to defend themselves, justify their behavior, and manage conflict. When they complain how others may have hurt them or invaded their personal space, you can be certain that their personal boundaries are unclear to them or to others. As clients ease their way into the changes generated by their new boundaries, they will have much more energy available for pursuit of their goals and desires.

Teaching example: A female client often got into conversations at work that she called "bitch sessions," wherein people complained about many minor things. She always felt trapped and drained after these conversations. Her coach requested that she begin choosing the conversations in which she would participate, and not to participate in the bitch sessions. Her coach suggested she tell others that she was practicing a new boundary of not complaining and, instead, was looking for solutions.

Tip 6. Clients are often unaware of their own boundaries and the fact that they may be entirely missing or consistently violated. Coaching is often necessary to increase their awareness of boundary absence or violation. Clients will gradually begin to see or feel when others are invading their personal space, lifestyle, or using them for their own purposes. Such sensitization is crucial for clients to really understand the cost to them of not having boundaries. Once they understand that, they will become eager to practice their own boundary-setting.

At the very least, clients need to set boundaries in the following areas:

- *Time.* This dialogue below is an example of how you can use the coaching approach to help a client set new or improved boundaries about time.

    Client: I want more time for my family and me. I always seem to have work or thinking to do, calls to make, or projects to do . . . and then there are unscheduled interruptions that add more to my time demands.

    Coach: Let's talk about ways you can take control of some of your time. Time is like money, if you don't pay yourself first, there won't be any left. How could you pay yourself first with the time you have?

    Client: I don't have a clue . . . I don't have enough time now.

    Coach: You have the same amount of time as we all do. Do you use a calendar or organizer to track your appointments and projects?

Client: Yes, but so often I have to squeeze things in.

Coach: By setting a new boundary on time, I ask that you write in your calendar appointments with yourself and your family. You may schedule in the things you want more time for and then other things will be scheduled around that. You'll have to experiment with this for awhile, but we will continue working on new boundaries and new habits, OK?

Client: OK . . . I want that very much.

- *Heart (Emotions).* While coaching clients on how to set emotional boundaries, you might create ways for your clients to have safe places where they can let their emotional selves be expressed, and help them see that emotions are important to feel—even when they are not happy feelings. It's important for clients to know that if we suppress our feelings, they build up into stronger emotions and unhealthy reactions. Exercises to clarify your clients' emotional boundaries might include journal writing, assertiveness-skill training, communication, or even taking one of the assessment tools on the market for measuring Emotional Intelligence (commonly called EQ).

- *Spirit.* Your clients' boundaries are strengthened when they are set to allow space, time, and energy for clients to attend to their own spiritual growth. You might help your clients give more purposeful time to their spiritual selves through meditation, spiritual practices, or further exploration of their life purpose and meaning.

- *Body.* Busy people often neglect their physical well-being. By setting new boundaries for clients to focus on self-care, they will increase their physical health and well-being. Coach strategies with your clients for them to be purposeful and intentional about their bodies. Physical activity and self-care are important aspects of total life coaching conversations.

- *Relationships.* Although relationships are affected by all of the above, we make special mention of this as an area for strengthening boundaries because what your clients contribute to any relationship reflects who they are as well as the habits they have. Without relationships, we never develop as human beings. So, having the time and desire to focus on our selves—our bodies, our hearts, our spirits—also includes attention to the kinds of relationships we choose and what we contribute to them.

> The only freedom which deserves the name is that of pursuing our own good, in our own way, so long as we do not attempt to deprive others of theirs, or impede their efforts to obtain it.
> —John Stuart Mill

Exercises to Do Now

You may want to suggest the following exercises for your clients to try as experiments in boundary-setting.

1. Bringing to mind the behaviors of others, have your clients make a list of all such behaviors they consider unacceptable in their presence.
2. Develop a plan with your clients for their desired responses when someone violates their boundaries.
3. Make a list of all new boundaries your clients want to incorporate into their lives.
4. Have clients inform others about their new boundaries.
5. Have your clients make direct requests that others respect their new boundaries.
6. Come up with acceptable alternatives to offer others who are currently violating your clients' boundaries.
7. If someone persists in violating the boundaries of your clients, invite your clients to walk away and/or terminate the immediate interaction or the relationship.

Coaching Language

Language you and/or your clients can use to set and inform others of your boundaries.

- "I want to eliminate _____ from my life. When you _____, I will leave the room."
- "I will no longer tolerate (accept) _____. Will you please respect (honor) my request to _____?"
- "_____ is no longer acceptable to me. Will you stop _____?"

Questions and Inquiries

1. What are the boundaries that are important for you to establish *right now*?
2. Who is currently violating your boundaries?
3. What will be the most effective action you can take to establish a boundary with this person(s)?
4. When will you take this action?

LIFE LESSON 7
You are responsible for meeting your needs.

MESSAGES

1. Identify what your needs are and distinguish them from wishes or wants.
2. Recognize when you need something.
3. Ask directly for what you want and need.
4. Educate others about your ever-changing needs.

The objectives for Lesson 7 are: 1) To learn to catalyze clients' power and responsibility to address their needs; 2) To teach how to ask *directly* for anything; 3) To identify—and avoid playing—psychological (emotional) games; 4) To increase the probability of your clients satisfaction and fulfillment.

Framework Needed for Coaching Your Clients

Everyone has needs. Some needs are related to survival; some are related to safety; some are related to comfort; some are related to growth; some are related to stability; some are related to change; some are related to happiness; some are universal; some are individual. Regardless of what they are, we all have needs.

When we are children and not yet capable of meeting our own needs, caregivers are responsible for figuring out what our needs are and addressing them to the best of their ability. When we are adults, we become totally responsible for identifying our own needs and for addressing them ourselves or arranging for others to meet them. We can be very skilled in getting our needs met, thereby living a fulfilled life, or we can be unskilled and live a barely sustainable existence.

As children, we learn about our needs and how to address them by observing how our parents inform us of our needs, and by imitating how they address them. If our parents were unskilled or ignorant about our needs, then what we needed was inadequately fulfilled.

Babies cry when they need something. Crying is their only signal to the outside world that they are needy. In the normal course of development, crying is replaced by language. Children learn to put their needs into language so that others can address them. They also experiment with ways of meeting their own needs.

When crying or language do not work to meet their needs, children learn other behaviors or activities they believe work. Almost all habitual behavior a child learns is a result of their behavior being linked to need fulfillment. We become socialized to the extent that what we do is reinforced by having what we need effectively addressed. If our behavior does not result in need fulfillment, we quickly drop it and try something else.

When nothing works to get your needs met, those needs live only as wishes in your life. Conscious or unconscious wishes have no power to energize you. Unidentified (and therefore unaddressed) needs are experienced as vague wishes without the power to motivate you toward meeting them. For example, you may wish to win the lottery, but never buy a ticket. You may wish to be happy, but never know or practice what is needed for you to experience happiness.

Emotions are bodily energy changes resulting from some unaddressed need. We feel fear when our need for safety is threatened. We feel frustrated when our goal-directed behavior is blocked.

> Man must cease attributing his problems to his environment, and learn again to exercise his will—his personal responsibility . . .
> —Albert Schweitzer

The primary purpose of emotional energy is to provide us with the necessary power to get our needs addressed and/or fulfilled. Up to a certain point, emotional intensity increases in direct proportion to the size of the need. When our need for rest is sufficiently high, we call it *fatigue*. When emotional needs are not addressed and emotional fatigue occurs, we collapse into helplessness and despair. We then have no energy to address what we need. When our emotional or physical needs are adequately met, we feel satisfied and content. This state of contentment we define as *success* at getting our needs fulfilled.

When you are an adult, there are only three sources of meeting your needs: your environment, you, and other people. When you learn to manipulate and control environmental elements that affect your life, you can effectively address your needs. For example, if it has snowed heavily and you need to get to work, you can wait for the maintenance crew to clear the snow or you can shovel it yourself. Environmental manipulation to address your needs is often very difficult and requires large amounts of time and energy.

If you can't or don't want to address your needs through environmental manipulation, then you have only two other resources for need fulfillment: yourself and others. If, for whatever reason, you are unwilling or unable to address your needs by yourself, then other people must (especially if they care about your health and happiness). Since most people resist being manipulated or controlled, you will have to learn other means for getting people to address your needs. In his book, *Games People Play*, Eric Berne defines *games* as all the indirect methods for manipulating others to do what you want. An example of a psychological game might be pouting as a means to address your need for attention. Unfortunately, most of us continue to use the psychological games we learned before we had language, when we were small children.

If others can't or don't want to supply you with what you need, then, unless you manipulate your environment or take care of your needs yourself, your needs go unmet and usually become greater. Learning as many skills as you can to address your own needs is, therefore, critical. A critical aspect of getting your needs met is learning how to ask others directly for what you want or need from them. Using effective language to tell others what you need, and then making a direct request, is crucial to having others address your needs—and is the only way to avoid playing psychological games.

In English, there are only two words for asking directly for anything: "Will you . . . ?" Every other phrasing is either indirect or not asking. "Would you . . ." implies a condition—"would you *if*" a condition were present—and is therefore indirect. The command or order, "Give me" or "Just do it," is not asking.

When the direct request "Will you . . ." is preceded by a statement of what you need, it increases the likelihood that you will receive what you ask for. That sure beats the odds of not asking or playing indirect games.

For example:

- "I want to season my food. Will you please pass the salt and pepper?"
- "I'm cold and need to be warmer. Will you loan me your jacket?"
- "I'm lonely, will you spend time with me?"
- "I need your attention. Will you pay attention to me?"
- "I want to increase my social network. Will you be my friend?"
- "I need information. Will you tell me . . .?"
- "I want to eliminate fear (anger) from my life. Will you speak to me more quietly (more gently)?"

The most effective methods to address your needs are to first identify and address them yourself through environmental manipulation or self-caring behavior; and secondly, to make an "I" statement, which provides a context about what it is you want or need, and then to follow by asking directly for what you need, using the words, "Will you . . .?

Exercises and Information

Here are a few suggestions for your clients to take full responsibility for getting their needs met.

1. Ask your clients to identify some recurring needs they have (for example, their need for food, water, rest, activity, attention)
2. Have them practice putting their needs in descriptive language, using "I" statements. Begin each coaching session by practicing these statements.
3. Ask your clients to come to the coaching session knowing:
    - What they want from the session;
    - What kinds of responses they want from you as their coach;
    - What outcomes they anticipate from getting what they want from the session.
4. Have clients practice asking directly for those things that will address/fulfill their needs.

Steps Toward Getting Your Needs Met

Share with your clients the following:

1. Realize that fulfilling your needs is not selfish. It is your primary responsibility.
2. Identify at least four personal needs you want to fulfill: honesty, food, caring attention, to be understood, etc.
3. Ask your friends to tell you what they perceive your needs to be.
4. Using the coaching language in the sample Coaching Conversation that follows, directly ask four trusted friends (or relatives) to address one of the needs identified in 2 or 3 above.
5. Practice making "I" statements about your needs, and quickly follow up with a direct request for meeting your need.
6. Ask directly for whatever would address your wants/needs.
7. Set up a structure or agreement for regularly addressing your four needs.

8. Develop a personal boundary (see Life Lesson 5) that will aid you in fulfilling your needs.

9. Acknowledge and appreciate yourself and anyone else who addressed one or more of your needs.

Sample Coaching Conversation

Setting: A client who has been frustrated with his work/life balance.

Client: I really am feeling overwhelmed. I have so many little things that take up my time and energy, I feel completely stressed out.

Coach: What is *not* happening for you that might happen if these little things were not taking your time and energy?

Client: I am not having any fun. I am not able to relax and play golf or spend fun time with my wife. I need more fun time.

Coach: It sounds like fun is at least one need you have that is not being met. I believe a key need we all have is to have fun in our lives, and it is important to you. Is that right?

Client: That's right on. But I feel so absorbed in my business projects that I'm completely drained. I'm not even able to have fun when I do go out with my family or friends.

Coach: I want to request that you write down on a blank page in your scheduling book a list of activities that would address your need for fun. Then pick three activities this week and take full responsibility for making them happen, just like you take responsibility for your business projects. I'll bet that if you have the fun time or the "self" time you need, you will feel even more energized and focused on those "little things" that drain you now. Are you willing to do that?

Client: Sure . . . that sounds good: I really do need this.

Coach: And you deserve it too.

Questions and Inquiries

1. What needs of yours are currently unsatisfied?
2. How can you better fulfill those needs?
3. What do you want (need) when you engage in psychological games?
4. How can I best coach you to take full responsibility for getting your needs and desires addressed?

LIFE LESSON 8
Appreciate who you are and your lifestyle.

MESSAGES

1. An "attitude of gratitude" is the key to your happiness and success.
2. The least stressful emotion you can have is gratitude.
3. Expressing genuine appreciation is a powerful reinforcement.
4. Begin every new endeavor with an appreciation for your current condition/situation.

The objectives for Lesson 8 are: 1) To understand and inform your clients of the importance of appreciation; 2) To identify personal qualities you can appreciate; 3) To coach your clients about how to live in the present with a positive attitude; 4) To catalyze in your clients a genuine appreciation for their uniqueness and a feeling of unconditional gratefulness for what they have; 5) To help your clients build new skills on a solid foundation of appreciation.

Framework Needed for Coaching Your Clients

How many times have we heard or made these comments?

- "No matter what I do, it isn't good enough."
- "No matter how much I give, it never seems to satisfy."

Let's face it, there are people who, no matter how much they have, never appreciate it. You could pour your heart out to them, work until you drop, share until you're empty, and they still wouldn't acknowledge your effort with a simple "thank you." Many people spend most of their time seeking approval and appreciation from others—their coaches, their parents, their peers, their teachers, their bosses, their colleagues.

People who need appreciation are often paired with people who never express it, leaving both caught in a destructive cycle: the more person A needs to be appreciated, the more he or she strives for the "thank you's"; the more person A seeks appreciation, the more obligated person B feels to express gratitude; the more obliged person B feels, the more likely he or she is to rebel and withhold appreciation; this leads to further emptiness in person A, and his or her increased need for appreciation.

People caught in such a cycle devoid of gratitude usually experience life as an endless dependency filled with fear, helplessness, hostility, anger and—above all—unfulfilled needs. Usually both parties in this cycle have large, unmet needs for personal validation and support. Both desperately need to feel appreciated and valuable.

Feeling appreciated and valued is critical to happiness and is a key factor in being successful. If you don't feel appreciated, you'll find it nearly impossible to express appreciation to others.

As children, our need to feel valued is addressed primarily by our parents. As grown-ups responsible for addressing our own needs (see Lesson 7), we often fail to appreciate ourselves. We also may not be aware of how good our life really is, especially when we compare what we have to what others have, and believe we have less.

> The deepest principle of human nature is the craving to be appreciated.
> —William James

If we don't appreciate who we are and what we have, we tend to maintain a helpless–hostile–dependency cycle (HHD). When we don't appreciate who we are, we feel helpless. When we feel helpless, we become angry and hostile. When we feel hostile, we look to others to address our needs, and blame them if they don't. When they don't appreciate us or provide with what we need, we feel helpless and angry and dependent more intensely, and the cycle is reinforced.

Breaking the HHD cycle can begin with saying "thank you." Saying out loud, "I appreciate . . ." or "Thank you for . . ." is the beginning of altering the HHD cycle. This "thank you" can be directed toward yourself or others, or life itself.

Thank you communicates many messages:

- I recognize you.
- I like you.
- I appreciate you.
- I have seen you.
- I have heard you.
- I acknowledge your effort, work, or accomplishments.

▪ (And best of all) I value who you are and/or what you do.

Feeling valuable as a person, as well as for what you do, is probably the most important consequence of receiving thank you's. When we feel valuable, we feel able to be valued, cherished, and loved.

Feeling valuable means we are important as individuals. When we feel personally valued, we no longer need to pursue approval from others. We no longer need to feel frightened of our own inadequacies. We are valuable for who we are as people. What we do—our behavior—may or may not be appreciated, but that isn't as important if we feel valuable as individuals.

When we are appreciated for who we are, the need for validation is filled and the HHD cycle is replaced by the confident–caring–intimacy (CCI) cycle. No wonder Nobel-prize winner, Hans Selye, said the healthiest emotion you can experience is gratitude. Selye's research about stress and its effect on human health indicated that an attitude of vengeance is the most harmful emotion, and that one of gratitude is the most beneficial. If you want to stay healthy and have less stress in your life, develop a habitual "attitude of gratitude."

> Two kinds of gratitude: the sudden kind we feel for what we take; the larger kind we feel for what we give.
> —Edwin Robinson

Regularly and persistently, saying to yourself or to others, "Thank you for being you," and "Thank you for what you do," is crucial to changing from the HHD cycle to the CCI cycle. This principle cannot be over-emphasized.

Make the distinction between *who* you are as a person and *what* you do as that person. You can always appreciate who you are. You may not always appreciate how you behave. In order to be successful at anything you choose to do, you first need to appreciate who you are. Then, any behavioral mistakes you make become much less frightening and are a source of learning. Your ability to learn is clearly one of the most positive capacities you have as a human being.

Adopt a position of gratitude for who you are and where you are in life and you increase the likelihood you will become who you want to become and get to where you want to go. You will also live with a positive mental attitude—a time-honored orientation for successful living.

Exercises and Information

Here are some ways your clients might develop a consistent attitude of gratitude.

Developing Gratitude

Invite your clients to keep a Gratitude Journal. Instructions for this might be: "Take a few minutes every evening to make five entries in a Gratitude Journal.

Gratitude is not only the greatest of virtues, but the parent of all others.
—Marcus Tullius Cicero

Write down at least five things you appreciated about your day, your relationships, and yourself. Make it a different five each day. You will develop the habit of focusing on appreciating who you are, those around you, and life itself. After all, being alive is really a gift. You can choose to appreciate it or not. If you choose to appreciate your life, you will enjoy living so much more."

Another coaching tip is to have your clients carry a small, pocket-sized spiral notepad everywhere they go. Have them seek out any events, activities, people, qualities, or circumstances for which they are grateful and immediately write down what they appreciate. At the end of the day, they can transfer their appreciations from the notepad to their Gratitude Journal.

Coaching Language

Teach your clients to make the following sentences a regular part of their vocabulary:

"The thing I liked most about _____ is . . . ."
"Thank you for _____."
"I appreciate it when you _____."
"I appreciate your point of view, and _____."
"I am grateful for _____."

Sample Coaching Conversation

Coach: I get a real sense in our conversations that you're not really aware of your unique gifts and what others appreciate you for?

Client: I am not even sure what you mean? What are my unique gifts?

Coach: That's what I would like you to become more aware of. I believe that we all have unique qualities that we are not always aware of. And if we can learn to appreciate those ourselves, and see what others also appreciate about us, it can help us in our career and personal life. Are there people in your life that you really appreciate for some unique qualities—something that is special about them?

Client: Sure, my wife, many colleagues, and my children.

Coach: It is my guess that you don't know what people appreciate about you. So I am going to ask you to have a personal treasure hunt. It is an experiment, if you are willing to play?

Client: Yeah sure, tell me what it is.

Coach: I want you to ask five people who know you well and who you trust to share with you what they think are your unique gifts or qualities. Ask them to tell you what they find special about you. I know this is not a typical question, but it is a powerful exercise. The whole idea of this exercise is for you to develop a keen appreciation for you and all your unique talents and abilities. Are you willing to play?

Client: Yes, I guess so. I will tell them it is an assignment from my coach, ok?

Coach: OK with me. Do the treasure hunt this week and next session report back to me on your list of qualities, okay?

Questions and Inquiries

- Will you tell me five things you like about me?
- What kinds of things do you appreciate about me?
- What do I do on a regular basis that you like?
- What are some of my accomplishments that you like?
- What kinds of actions would you like me to engage in that I don't right now?
- Will you tell me when I do things that you appreciate?

LIFE LESSON 9
Accurately identify your personal talents.

MESSAGES
1. Strengthen your talents to deemphasize your weaknesses.
2. Identifying your talents increases your self-esteem.
3. Everyone has talents.
4. A life coach acknowledges and appreciates each client's talents.

The objectives for Lesson 9 are: 1) To help your clients understand that everyone is talented in a variety of ways; 2) To help your clients become aware of talents they may have never recognized.

Framework Needed For Coaching Your Clients

What is a talent? We define talent as a developed and refined ability. We all have innate abilities and are completely unaware of many of them, or simply take them for granted. These inborn abilities are the seeds for future talents.

When you were a child, these abilities were either nourished or stifled by your experiences of pleasure or pain, respectively. For example, if you were encouraged to stand up and dance for your family, and you regularly received positive feedback for dancing in the form of approval and reinforcement, you would be inclined to develop your dancing ability into a talent. However, if while you were dancing your family ridiculed or laughed at you, you might suppress your dancing ability and it would never develop into a talent. You always have a 50/50 chance of developing and refining your innate abilities, based on internal or external positive feedback.

Exercises and Information

In order to assist your clients to identify and develop their talents (hidden or not):

1. Have your clients send you a list of all the abilities they know they have.
2. Ask your clients, "How do you plan to strengthen these abilities?"
3. Have your clients list those abilities they would like to transform into talents.
4. Ask your clients to list twelve new experiences they will pursue in the next year (one each month).

Inborn Abilities Most Healthy People Possess

Almost everyone has the ability to:

Be energized and energetic
Be fearless
Be humorous
Be faithful
Be trusting
Be confident
Make choices
Be able to form beliefs
Anticipate a future
Dream
Develop a sense of fairness
Love
Bond with others
Be ambitious
Become self-sufficient
Grow, change, and evolve

Have a specific attention span
Focus that attention
Imitate
Learn
Develop language
Think
Attribute meaning to sensations
Organize sensory stimulation into perceptions
Exercise sensory control
Care
Nurture
Be open and receptive
Commit
Create
Adapt

> There is something that is much more scarce, something rarer than ability. It is the ability to recognize ability.
> —Robert Half

The development or refinement of an ability is directly related to available energy, time, pleasure/pain patterns, and supportive or encouraging resources.

The best way to discover your hidden talents is to seek out and engage in new experiences. Placing yourself in new situations, engaging in new behavior, trying out new abilities all invoke your abilities to cope. Often, coping abilities—with practice—become talents. Once a month, expose yourself to a new experience. At

> If people knew how hard I have to work to gain my mastery, it wouldn't seem wonderful at all.
> —Michelangelo

the end of a year, you may have discovered and strengthened and developed into talents at least twelve abilities you never knew you had.

Almost any natural ability can be developed into a talent with practice, practice, practice. To feel positive about practice, you need to keep two things firmly in mind:

1. All undeveloped skills seem difficult until they become automatic (unconscious); and
2. Begin practice as if you were already skilled at whatever it is you want to develop into a talent.

When you were in school, you were probably told to identify and improve your weaknesses. What you weren't told is that if you spend a lot of time and effort improving your weaknesses, the best you can hope for is to develop minor frailties. On the other hand, if you were told to identify and strengthen your talents, you would develop outstanding personal skills. Improve your weaknesses or build on your strengths, which would you rather do?

The greatest hindrance to developing your talents is fear—fear of failure, disapproval, risk-taking, dying, incompetence, and losing. Each of these fears invites you to avoid putting yourself into new situations and practicing new abilities. The greatest antidote to these fears is trust. Trust yourself to cope with whatever life brings. You have coped up to this point in your life—and if you fail to cope, it's rarely fatal.

Coaching Language

Teach your clients to use the following phrases:

"I know I can _____."
"One of my talents is the ability to _____."
"I consider my ability to _____ a gift."
"I am the trustee of all my talents and abilities."
"I am willing to try new things and place myself in new situations."

Sample Coaching Conversation

Coach: You really developed a terrific list of unique qualities that people appreciate in you. Any surprises?

Client: Yes. I had no idea how much people appreciated my lightness, my optimism, and my ability to be a team player. That felt really good.

Coach: Yes, and the other qualities on your list like visionary leader and motivator, also point to your strengths.

Client: But I'm also aware of some of my weaknesses that I want to improve upon. I have trouble focusing on details, I get distracted with lots of possibilities, and sometimes I get stressed and become negative and sullen.

Coach: We'll work on those in our coaching over time. But I want you to know that if we focus on your strengths, and you find ways to utilize those, some of what you called "weaknesses" may not need to change. You will learn to use your strengths and delegate your weaknesses. For example, many leaders are visionaries, rather than detail-oriented people. They seek out people who believe in their big-picture thinking and who can take care of the details. Do you know people like that?

Client: Yes. My wife is great with details and organizing, and so is my office assistant.

Coach: Hmmm. Maybe that is one reason you're attracted to them? Next time, let's talk about how you will integrate their strengths into your so-called weaknesses. Is that okay with you?

Client: Sure.

Questions and Inquiries

- What have you always wanted to do, but thought you didn't have the ability to do?
- What hidden talents would you like to discover you had?
- What activities bring you joy, whether or not you are good at them?
- What talents did you have as a child that have diminished as an adult?
- What are your greatest weaknesses that you might delegate to someone else?

Coaching Summary

In Section 1, Creating a Personal Identity, we have offered nine life lessons to integrate into your life coaching practice. These lessons invite you and your clients to develop a personal identity based upon increased self-awareness and creating a lifestyle that is consciously chosen.

The Lessons

If integrated into your coaching practice, each lesson will dramatically enhance your coaching skills, your practice, your life, and your clients' lives.

Life Lesson 1

What you believe about yourself defines who you are. Defining who you are is where it all begins. As a young child, your identity was given to you by others. As adults, you can modify your personal identity by changing your beliefs about yourself.

Life Lesson 2

Updating your belief system is how you learn and requires paradigm shifting. Your beliefs are what drive your behavior and actions and need regular modification to remain relevant. Occasionally you may want to review the strategies in this lesson with a personal coach who serves as a guide for enriching your perceptual reality.

Life Lesson 3

Conscious awareness is the key to successful lifestyle creation. This lesson provides a way for each of us to view ourselves as works-in-progress. If we become more conscious of our personal identities, we are more likely to reflect our inner being in creating the outcomes we desire.

When coaching this lesson, you need to have conversations about your clients' lifestyles, values, purposes, and their meaning.

Life Lesson 4

Your value system guides you toward success or failure. Awareness of what you genuinely value provides critical guidance for creating the life you desire. Your values provide a map for your behavior and actions. When coaching clients to identify their values, it is important to prevent your own value system from influencing theirs.

Life Lesson 5

You are responsible for your standards. When you put this lesson into practice, you begin to define responsibility as "the ability to respond." Taking personal responsibility may not result in change, but the choices we make in our lives can and do affect our relationships and society in general. The standards to which we personally commit define the directions in which we take our lives.

Coaching the establishment of professional and personal standards invites clients to avoid placing blame and shame, and instead focus on intentions and actions.

Life Lesson 6

You protect your self by setting and maintaining strong boundaries. Setting strong personal boundaries allows us to know how we are distinct from all others and unique in the world. We need boundaries to clarify who we are and to protect ourselves from unwanted influence. With such clarification and protection, we are better able to give ourselves to others and to the world.

Life Lesson 7

You are responsible for meeting your needs. Each of us has needs and wants. As adults, if we do not address our own needs or arrange for them to be met by others or by our environment, they never get met. When our needs consistently go unmet, we perish. When we are skillful at getting our needs met, we thrive.

Life Lesson 8

Appreciate who you are and your lifestyle. An attitude of appreciation lowers your stress level, clarifies your current perceptual reality, and allows you to accurately assess where to begin any new endeavor. Appreciating who you are builds self-awareness and self-confidence.

Life Lesson 9

Accurately identifying your personal talents. At best, improving your weaknesses makes them minor. Identifying and building on your abilities transforms them into talents, strengthens you to excel and enriches your life.

Statements and Questions for Reflection

1. Updating your self-concept enables you to be authentic in all your relationships.
   Questions: "What childhood habits of thinking, feeling, and behaving do you want to keep?" "Which do you want to replace?" "What personal elements make you the best life coach you can be?"
2. You are completely responsible for creating your own reality, how you respond to any event or situation, and for addressing all your needs and wants.
   Questions: "What can you do now to become more responsible for yourself?" "How can you become totally responsible for your coaching practice?"
3. The standards and boundaries you set guide and protect you so you can safely and effectively create the outcomes you desire.
   Questions: "How do you envision your desired future outcome(s)?" "What standards and boundaries will support you in creating these outcomes?" What boundaries and standards will enhance your coaching practice?"
4. Maintaining a positive mental attitude is made easy by appreciating all that you are, all that you have, and all aspects of your current reality.
   Questions: "Are you keeping a gratitude journal?" "What do you appreciate about your coaching?"
5. Generating multiple talents enriches your life.
   Questions: "What abilities are you going to transform, by practice, into talents?" "What talents do you have for life coaching?"

SECTION 2
Developing Spirituality and Life Purpose

We are not physical beings having a spiritual experience. Rather, we are spiritual beings having a physical experience.
—Teilhard de Chardin

LIFE LESSON 10
Realize and appreciate your spiritual nature.

MESSAGES

1. Create awareness of that "something" within human beings that is separate from us, yet is a silent witness to us.

2. Our spiritual nature differentiates us from all other species.

3. Each one of us has a unique spiritual heritage that contributes to our happiness and well-being.

4. Coaching the spiritual development of your clients requires an awareness of your own spiritual development.

The objectives for Lesson 10 are: 1) To learn to distinguish among spirituality, morality, ethics, and religion; 2) To acknowledge that our true nature is spiritual, not physical; 3) To realize that coaching the spiritual development of your clients is a high calling for a life coach; 4) To be able to coach your clients' spiritual development.

Framework Needed for Coaching Your Clients

As life coaches, we believe the topic of spirituality lies at the heart of coaching. We consider coaching the spiritual development of your clients to be one of the highest callings a coach can follow. Many coaches and clients however, do not know how to engage in conversations about spirituality without confusing the topic with religion. Spirituality is often "the elephant in the living room." Everyone knows it is present, but pretends not to see it. You can do yourself and your clients a great favor by being willing to engage in conversations about spiritual beliefs, values, and methods of practice.

It is much easier to describe what spiritual is not than to define *spirit* and *spirituality* in direct terms. For example, the spiritual aspects of our lives are often confused with morality. Morality concerns issues of right and wrong. Morality reflects social tradition and consensus, and has roots in socially-defined behavior. Morality varies from culture to culture, and is often used as a basis for judgments that separate one group from another. On the other hand, we believe that the fundamental spiritual principles that form the ground work for all religions are nonjudgemental and unifying, not separative.

Spirituality is also not an ethical system. Ethics is a particular set of values and a code for translating socially-defined morality into daily activity. Ethics usually addresses the right way for us to conduct ourselves in social settings and relationships. Spirituality is much more concerned with the nature of the personal relationship we have with an external force or power—whether we identify that as a god, life force, love, higher power, collective unconscious, life energy, etc.—and what that relationship contributes to our interpersonal relationships. Spirituality is not concerned with discovering a right way to act.

Another common confusion is to equate spirituality with "being psychic." We all have the ability to be psychic. Being psychic is akin to having direct knowledge of matters of human consciousness and awareness. It can be a means of experiencing the spiritual, but it is not itself spiritual. Rather, our capacity for psychic ability is simply another means we have of gaining information from our internal and external environments. Psychologist Naomi Remen writes that we can use our psychic ability ". . . to impress others, to accumulate personal power, to dominate or manipulate—in short to assert (our) separateness and (our) personal power. The spiritual, however, is not separative. A deep sense of the spiritual leads one to trust not one's own lonely power, but the great flow or pattern manifested in all life, including our own. We become not manipulator, but witness."

Finally, spirituality is different from religion. A religion is usually a dogma, a set of beliefs *about* the spiritual and a subsequent set of practices or disciplines that are derived from those beliefs. History has shown that religious belief can be a reason for exclusivity and discrimination—as though each religion claims to have the exclusive truth about spirit. But spirituality is inclusive; it is the deepest sense of unity, belonging, participation, and universality.

Religion usually provides a gateway to the spiritual life. Unfortunately, most people seeking spiritual growth perceive the gate to be the goal, and they don't pass through it.

Probably the most important aspect in defining spirituality is the acknowledgment of spirit as an essential component of human nature. There is something in all of us that seeks the spiritual. This yearning varies in strength from person to person, but is always there in everyone. Even the mental health pro-

> If matter mute and inanimate, though changed by the forces of Nature into a multitude of forms, can never die, will the spirit of man suffer annihilation when it has paid a brief visit, like a royal guest, to this tenement of clay? No. I am as sure that there is another life as I am that I live today.
> —William Jennings Bryan

fession is beginning to recognize the need for people to include their spiritual life in any treatment or therapy they might seek. Until recently, the term *spirit* conjured concepts such as ghosts, mental aberrations, religious beliefs, or cults. Now, however, science is beginning to acknowledge the importance of body energy, energy fields, and the psychological factors that modify such fields. Some of these factors have previously been exclusively the domain of "spiritual" people. Not so anymore.

In his book, *Creating Affluence*, Deepak Chopra the former President of the American College of Physicians and Surgeons, wrote, "Even our human body is a field of infinite organizing power. There are six trillion reactions occurring in the human body every second, and every one of them is correlated with every single other reaction; every single other biochemical event knows what other biochemical event is occurring in the body. A human body can think thoughts, play a piano, sing a song, digest food, eliminate toxins, kill germs, monitor the movement of stars, and make a new baby all at the same time, and correlate each of these activities with every other activity."

Chopra went on to say, "So, inherent in the field itself is infinite organizing power. To know that field intimately, to have experiential knowledge of that field as one's own nature, is to automatically embody the infinite organizing power of the field."

Such knowledge is an awareness of internal experience and is not based on conscious awareness of information gained from the outside. Thus, knowledge of the field is internal, not external, in nature.

Almost any spiritual tradition contains certain truths and methods for realizing them. In his book, *How to Know God*, Chopra describes four basic *paths* to learn about spirit. As a life coach, you need to be intimately familiar with them. These paths are:

- The path of love
- The path of spiritual discipline
- The path of action
- The path of science

Lawrence LeShan, clinical psychologist and author of the book, *The Medium, The Mystic, and The Physicist*, wrote extensively on anecdotal research about all four of the paths above. The most deeply spiritual and poetic quotations he used were often from the viewpoint of the physicist. Clearly, even the deep pursuit of science leads to understandings, knowledge, and intuitive beliefs about spirituality.

Exercises and Information

In order to coach clients in developing their own spirituality, some of the information and exercises below may be very useful.

Personal Benefits from a Spiritual Practice

Let your clients know that regardless of the religious or mystical paths they choose, the benefits they derive from pursuing a spiritual practice can include:

> Love, hope, fear, faith—these makes humanity . . .
> —Robert Browning

- Developing compassion for self and others. Such compassion is based not on seeking some ideal of perfection, but rather on the capacity to let go and to love, to open the heart to all that is.
- Strengthening the human virtues of kindness, patience, flexibility, self-awareness, self-acceptance, understanding, wisdom, and knowledge.
- And—best of all—the loss of fear. As our spiritual lives evolve, our fears diminish. Almost all common psychological problems are based on fear. Lose your fear and you become spiritually well. Become spiritually mature and you lose your fear.

Spiritual Principles and Practices

Introduce your clients to some of the following principles that influence their spiritual life. As a life coach, you also need to fully understand these principles.

1. You attract into your life the people and events for which you are psychologically and spiritually ready.
2. As we stated in the Introduction, life is always sending us messages. If we don't hear or are not aware of these messages, they become lessons. If we don't learn the lessons now, they become recurring problems. If we fail to resolve the problems, they become crises. If we ignore the crises, they become chaos.
3. We are all connected, yet unique and distinct. We are not separate. We are aspects of a single energy field and are never destroyed, merely transformed.
4. Awareness of your true human nature as having a spiritual element makes life more expansive, enriched, and easier.
5. Awareness of the truth always sets you free, but at first, it may also make you miserable.

6. You are physically built to be happy and to experience life as pleasurable.
7. The human species and human civilization is developing and evolving itself. *You* are a powerful influence on both.
8. We already possess all we need to be happy.
9. Serving others reflects your genuine spiritual nature. True service begins with extreme self-care.

Live by the above principles and you and your clients will genuinely experience what Joseph Campbell called "the rapture of being alive!"

> The most beautiful and most profound emotion one can experience is the sensation of the mystical...It is the source of all true science.
> —Albert Einstein

Common Spiritual Practices

Familiarize your clients with some of these common spiritual practices. Most have been used throughout history to help people become more aware of and develop their spirituality.

Meditation. Some common methods for meditating include focusing attention, concentrating; silencing internal dialogue, ceasing mental activity, repeating a word or phrase (mantra), totally relaxing the body and mind, and practicing imagery.

Body movement. Throughout the ages people have danced, twirled, drummed, and jumped in order to alter their state of awareness.

Music. Music stimulates the right side of the brain, it can also calm all other mental activity. It invites your states of consciousness to shift.

Singing and chanting. Vocalizing sounds, words, and repetitive phrases are effective ways to connect with the unconscious mind.

Focusing on natural beauty. Being in a natural versus a manmade environment can generate what Abraham Maslow calls "peak experiences," which are essentially spiritual. It also invites you to experience "oneness with the natural world."

Worship. Whatever form it takes, worshipping a higher being, spirits, life force, or a god alters your physical, mental, and emotional state. The act of worship itself is spiritual.

Contemplative prayer. Praying can take the form of praise, expression of gratitude, and petition (requesting). Contemplative prayer occurs when you focus on whatever you are experiencing at the moment and acknowledge what is. It is an opening of the mind to contemplate the experience of being alive.

Tips for Coaching Your Client's Spiritual Development

> Our humanity were a poor thing were it not for the divinity which stirs within us.
> —Francis Bacon

Tip 1. Don't pressure your clients to become more spiritual. Express your opinion that spiritual development is an essential aspect of a great life, but don't push your clients to focus on or pursue their own spiritual path.

Tip 2. Invite your clients to experiment with some spiritual principles or practices. Make certain that the suggested principles or practices are appealing to your clients. Invite them to try them out and see what happens.

Tip 3. Avoid focusing on or arguing about the truth or falsity of your clients' spiritual beliefs. Most so-called spiritual beliefs have more to do with religion or religious doctrine than they do with personal spiritual development.

Tip 4. Make certain your clients are aware that being on a spiritual path, or developing a full spiritual life, does not make them better than anyone else. If anything, increased spiritual awareness usually reflects the unity and equality of humanity.

Tip 5. Make certain you fully understand the reasons your clients want or need spiritual development. Clients seek spiritual development for a variety of reasons: to become enlightened; to enhance their ability to love; to more fully understand life; to heal themselves; to feel superior to others; to escape a difficult situation; to engage in a philosophical or intellectual exercise; to expiate guilt; or to seek "salvation." Be sure you know the motivations for the spiritual growth of your clients.

Tip 6. Become an example or model of what is spiritually possible. You may want to develop within yourself some of the qualities of a genuinely spiritual person described below.

Qualities and Characteristics of the Spiritual Person

Your clients may want to emulate a person who has a highly-developed spiritual life. This may help them to recognize the personal qualities that are usually displayed by someone who is truly spiritual. The founder of Coach University, the late Thomas Leonard, came up with a list of characteristics of the "truly spiritual" person. Share it with your clients in order to facilitate their identification with some of the developmental consequences of expanding their spiritual lives.

You can tell if someone is truly spiritual if:

- They are graceful in their communication.
- Their personal standards are extremely high.
- They don't let "toxic" people close to them.
- They experience bliss regularly, and not just during meditation or prayer.
- They attract other spiritual people.
- They are free of addictions.
- They have virtually no worries.
- They have the money they need.
- They live as they wish (often simply).
- They truly love others.
- Their cup is full and they can afford to give, serve, and contribute.
- They don't proselytize.
- You notice something extraordinary about them and you want some.
- There is a calmness and absence of concern about them.
- They are in touch with themselves.
- They are unconcerned with results and outcomes.
- They are graceful in all situations, not hooked by or reactive to circumstances.
- They are quick to learn and respond.
- They don't talk much about their spirituality; it's a given, not an identity or goal.
- They connect with others in healthy ways.

> Our secular lives need the vision, reverence, piety, values, reflection, service, and commitments offered by a spiritual sensibility.
> —Thomas Moore

Sample Coaching Conversation

Coach: I noticed on your life assessment, you rated your satisfaction with your spiritual development a 5 out of 10. What does that mean?

Client: I really did not know how to measure that. I am not very active in church anymore.

Coach: Spiritual development is not the same as religion, although for many people their religion or church is where they focus on their spiritual development. How would you describe the spiritual side of your life?

Client: What comes to mind are the times I feel so close to nature, when I see beauty in living things, and when I feel ecstatic about something I am experiencing.

Coach: Do you believe you have a spiritual nature? Some part of you beyond and before your physical and mental qualities? I do not want to intrude on your values or religious beliefs. I am just asking for your thoughts.

Client: Sure I do believe that, but I cannot prove it. I guess that is why the major religions talk of faith?

Coach: That is true. We cannot always prove what we know intuitively. In my coaching experience, the spiritual side of a person usually relates to life purpose, meaning, or a feeling of connectedness. Does that fit for you?

Client: Yes. But I don't think about that much.

Coach: That is an area that becomes important in life coaching. I have an idea. I'd like to request that you take fifteen minutes every morning next week to sit quietly in a peaceful place. Call it meditation or contemplation, but just sit and allow your mind to be quiet and your breathing to relax. After fifteen minutes, I would like you to then write freely about your thoughts and experiences. Will you do that, or would you like to amend that request in some way?

Client: Sure, that sounds like a good use of time. Are you saying that is a way to be more spiritual?

Coach: For me, it is. Time spent like that as a regular practice allows our internal chatter to become quiet for us to listen to our inner voice and to the wisdom from the world around us, especially nature and everyday wonders. I think you will enjoy it, and I think this is a crucial foundation for more effective and purposeful living. Thanks for being willing to experiment.

Questions and Inquiries

1. Who do you know that you would consider truly spiritual?
2. With what spiritual principles do you want to experiment?
3. What spiritual practices do you want to learn or develop?

4. How can you bring your spirituality into your daily living?
5. How can we bring spirituality into our coach/client relationship?
6. How can you bring to and maintain your spiritual life in all of your relationships?

LIFE LESSON 11
Your spiritual life is more important than your mental, emotional, or physical life.

The objectives for Lesson 11 are: 1) To learn some useful methods for identifying your clients' spiritual signposts; 2) To recognize some perceptual shifts your clients may want to make; 3) To assist your clients to discover and understand their own spiritual paths.

Framework Needed for Coaching Your Clients

Your clients may or may not recognize the spiritual path they are currently following. They may not recognize the spiritual signposts that mark their progress. On our spiritual journeys, there are always markers identifying and guiding our progress. Such markers may include:

- A growing, deep appreciation of external quiet and internal silence
- An increase of inner joy
- A profound sense of acceptance and contentment
- A dynamic internal serenity
- Increased delight in every aspect of being alive

■ Greater sense of awe and wonder
■ A profound sense of gratitude for being alive

One of the major signposts toward spiritual health is our willingness to do away with useless protection, remove unnecessary hardness, and allow our spiritual selves to emerge. To do so requires being open to people, life events, and to ourselves. It means learning to discriminate between people and events that present a real danger, and those that do not. It means learning to cherish yourself, your self-awareness, your feelings, thoughts, values, and perceptions of your nature as a human being. It also means being gentle and respectful with the qualities of others.

Most great spiritual teachers possess a certain quality of relaxed concentration in which they neither respond out of anger or fear, nor seem to cling to life out of desire. Truly spiritual people are free. They allow their vital energy to move them gracefully and effortlessly through traditions, habits, techniques, philosophies, theories, and emotions. They have reached the highest state of awareness or enlightenment, when they realize, as Mika Sayama wrote in *Samadhi*, that "consciousness or awareness is the base and form of all things"

There are myriad paths that converge into this state of spiritual awareness. Some experiences along the way may include meditation; communication; removal of boundaries that create separateness and dualistic thinking (explained later); acceptance of self and others as spiritual beings; joyful and energetic expression of laughter, sadness, and sexuality; constructive and supportive use of anger and fear; the discovery of the meaning and use of pain and suffering; promotion of human contact, nurturing, and love; and—finally—the acceptance of death as an integral part of life.

Exercises and Information

Some classic disciplines for enhancing one's spiritual awareness and development are presented below.

> The man who has no inner life is the slave of his surroundings.
> —Henri Frederic Amiel

Meditation

The value of prayer and meditation is important to spiritual growth. The state of awareness sought through meditation is one in which all internal dialogue, imagery, and thought cease (Kelsey, 1976). The mind becomes blank or void. Electroencephalography has demonstrated that the electrical pattern of the brain's activity changes to a pattern of sleep or deep relaxation, yet the meditator is fully awake and aware. Some hypnotic trances are also conscious states similar to those electronically-monitored meditative states.

Invite your clients who desire spiritual growth to engage in regular meditation, prayer, relaxation of mind and body, thought cessation, and internal quieting.

Communication

Life is not a problem to be solved but a reality to be experienced.
—Soren Kierkegaard

Let your clients know that perfect communication occurs when the meaning they give to their perceptions (ideas) is reproduced within you and you experience those reproduced meanings as your own. In your coaching conversations, you may want to practice and perfect your communication habits (refer to Section three). When your perceptual world and the perceptual world of your clients coincide sufficiently for you to agree on the meaning of any given personal experience, then you have communicated. Since such communication is totally abstract and unavailable on a physical, sensory level, perfect communication always occurs on a spiritual level.

For perfect communication to occur, the defensive barriers we build around our personal, experiential world must become permeable enough to allow what we "know" to be externalized. Such vulnerability also makes us receptive to communication from others. Mutual vulnerability to communicative exchange is necessary before any meaningful spiritual contact can be made.

Teach your clients that perfect (spiritual) communication involves sensitivity, openness, listening, skillful verbalizing, and vulnerable receptivity. If your clients want to enhance their spiritual awareness, coach them on the practice of these skills.

Removing Dualism

An invaluable signpost to guide your clients on their respective spiritual journeys is to eliminate all dualistic thinking from their awareness. Realizing that the universe is connected is no easy task. The threat of nuclear destruction, the pervasiveness of the Internet, and economic worldwide growth have raised our consciousness and provided clarity to the point where some of us are beginning to acknowledge the interconnectedness of world political systems and the people who comprise them. The next step in human awareness is to realize the essential unity of all life and experience.

Western thought usually takes the form of Aristotelian categorization. Westerners tend to analyze, break down into elements, and separate out the parts of any given whole or unity. Contemporary physicists are now demonstrating that all phenomena are fundamentally united (LeShan & Morgenau, 1982). Mystics and people of spirit have known this for centuries.

Note: Hoping your clients can *think* their way out of dualism without some belief in *oneness* or *unity* may be unrealistic. According to some enlightened ones, thought, itself, is separating and dualistic in nature, and direct experience of oneness is the only thing that can experientially carry a person beyond dualism.

Probably the best way to coach the elimination of dualistic thinking is to invite your clients to begin thinking the following: "Everything I think, say, and do has an impact on everything else in the world." Focus on the nature of that impact or influence. Play with the notion that your clients' thoughts are events that influence the experience of others, no matter what the physical distance between them. Plenty of spiritual people say that thought is pure energy and when it becomes understandable it affects everything. Contemporary physicists believe that when an atom vibrates, its effect is felt on the other side of the universe.

Acceptance

In order to accept that their present-moment experiences are perfect as is, your clients need to know that the human body is an open energy system. Use the following information to help your clients view themselves in this way:

> We take in food, water, air, and light. We combine these elements metabolically and create waste products and energy. Body energy, in turn, is expended in two ways: heat production and movement. If our energy stops creating heat or movement, we die. In order to stay alive, we accept those elements of life which we need. We transform them. Then we project them out of our bodies through both heat and movement. Energy exchange can not happen if we fail to accept ourselves and our needs. Self-acceptance is rooted in our biology and is therefore essential for our self-awareness to evolve. Energy, self-awareness, mental acknowledgement and acceptance of what is, and unconscious bodily movement all occur on a spiritual level.

Your clients need to know that acceptance of others is implied if they are accepting of the world and their own experiences. Failure to accept others prevents us from becoming fully human, as witnessed by what happens to a child left without human contact for any great length of time: the child fails to become much more than a biological creature.

Acceptance of our current situation allows us to make rational and realistic decisions and judgments. When we deny or hide from reality, we never have accurate information to use in our decision-making processes. Accepting our immediate condition is critical to living in the present moment and allows us to reduce our internal stress level.

Acceptance means practicing both giving and taking—not just passive reception—in all our relationships. We give to the earth, we take from the earth. We give to others, we take from others. We give to ourselves, we invest ourselves in living. This dance of giving and taking is what acceptance is all about. It is another signpost *en route* to our spiritual destination.

Energetic Expression of Emotions

Closely related to giving out energy is the expression of laughter, tears, and sexual energy. Infants cry as a signal they are not receiving something they need. Laughter, the first cousin to tears, is a signal of satisfaction and delight. Needy children do not laugh. Extremely or habitually needy children neither laugh nor cry.

If you have ever attempted to stifle a laugh or a sob, you're certainly aware of the amount of energy required to do so. Blocking our laughter and our tears hinders our effective use of energy and creates unnecessary tension in our bodies. Such tension prevents us from using our energy for other forms of self-expression. Constructively using our fear and anger allows us a powerful means by which to move toward any desired outcome. Holding our emotions inside merely increases body tension and stress.

Fully expressing sexuality is another way of releasing body tension and energy. Some spiritual leaders indicate abstinence as necessary for spiritual growth, while spiritual types of a more contemporary nature advocate full sexual expression as an expression of spiritual unity.

Sexual expression and release are obviously necessary for the continuation of the human species. It is a drive, a need, and a motivation. Acceptance of our human sexuality and its expression is as crucial to our evolution as any other basic human need, motivation, or biological phenomenon such as hunger or thirst. That we are sexual beings is not as important as *how* we express our sexuality. Like other powerful emotions such as fear and anger, what we do with our sexuality is critical to our physical and spiritual well-being.

Human Contact

Most people are now aware of the essential survival value of human contact. Infants crave tactile stimulation. The human nervous system fails to develop normally when stimulation of the skin by contact is absent, and our blood chemistry changes in direct proportion to the amount of contact we receive.

In order for nurturing and love to be effectively expressed, human contact must be made. Our relative comfort with hugs, massages, caresses, and skin-to-skin contact is certainly a sign of progress toward physical, psychological, and spiritual health.

Our spirit can be compared to a radio receiver. If the radio is not "tuned in" to the frequency pattern of the "sender," contact is not made, and no meaning is discovered nor given. Contact with others and with spirit is the foundation stone for any type of spiritual development.

Embracing Death

The last signpost of spiritual development is how we accept our own mortality, indeed, the mortality of all things. Death, like birth and growth, is natural to life. Death is not the opposite of life, but the opposite of birth. Both birth and death are universal life experiences. Everything and everyone that lives, dies. Every person who realizes life to its fullest welcomes death as a new life experience.

Fear of death prevents most spiritual development. As discussed earlier, fear leads to self-defensiveness. Self-defensiveness is what helps develop and maintain the ego. Spiritual evolution demands that once we have developed healthy egos, we must be willing to let them "die" if we are to reach the higher planes of spiritual maturity.

> Those who do not know how to I live must make a merit of dying.
> —George Bernard Shaw

The realization that our human spirit, our awareness, does not fully live until the body dies, has been a message delivered by most spiritual people throughout history.

If the signposts along *your* spiritual path seem too few and far between, or too many to reach in a single lifetime, know that your spiritual journey never ends. Your spiritual path is like the horizon. As we move toward a place on the horizon, the horizon retreats, ever inviting us to move onward. Perhaps all life is a never-ending journey toward a horizon seen only dimly in the distance. Perhaps we must trust in the process of moving toward it and, at the same moment, be fully aware of the process of our walking.

Common Elements of Spiritual Development

As a life coach, you need to identify for your clients the common elements or phases of spiritual development that characterize spiritual evolution. Ask clients whom you are coaching spiritually to identify what element(s) they think they are currently experiencing. Make them aware that as people evolve spiritually, they commonly experience certain aspects of development. Naturally, these elements are not usually experienced in a linear fashion. Spiritual development is never linear, but rather organic, like the growth of a tree one root running in one direction, a second root in another. In many spiritual traditions, the opening of the lotus flower is a common metaphor for spiritual evolution.

The following are some of the most commonly experienced developmental elements of spiritual evolution, beginning with:

> As I grow to understand life less and less, I learn to live it more and more.
> —Jules Renard

A gradual or sudden
Awakening
leading to
Exploration and Experimentation
and
Emptying Your Inner Life
so you require
Effective Nourishing of Your Spiritual Life
to
Satisfy Your Spiritual Hunger
so you are enabled to
Let Go of Mind and Ego
which leads to the
Dark Night of the Soul
resulting in a
Rebirth of Your *New* Self
that allows you to
Synthesize Your Spirit with Your Lifestyle
so you will realize that the
Endpoint is Not the End
and you continue your
Effortless Spiritual Evolution.

Tips for Coaching Spirituality

Coaching spirituality is highly dependent on your own realization of certain spiritual principles. Coaching spirituality rests primarily on the willingness of the coach to introduce conversations about spiritual principles into coaching sessions. How are these principles meaningful to your clients? Where does spirituality fit in their lives? What have they read that is profoundly spiritual to them? Do they have a place (church, synagogue, mosque, or study-group) where they engage in provocative discourse about these principles? If you are passionately engaged with these questions, then the conversations with your clients will be fruitful and stimulating.

Some common spiritual principles include:

- There is much more energy inside and outside our bodies than we can ever consciously experience with our five senses.
- We know, courtesy of Albert Einstein, that energy and physical matter are identical, proving that there is an essential unity in all things human and non-human.
- There is a flow and synergistic collection of energy that's bigger than any of us. A cathedral is much more than a pile of individually stacked stones.
- Our fundamental human nature is the same as the essence of all nature.
- The potential for greatness exists in all human beings, indeed, within all living and non-living things. Our potential for spiritual growth is infinite.

The spiritual benefits derived from coaching spiritual development include the following:

- When we expand our awareness of our own true nature, we increase our knowledge and awareness of everyone else.
- When we relate to others with synergistic energy, we create better outcomes than we could alone. The benefits of fearless cooperation are far better than relating competitively and fearfully.
- When we acknowledge our full interconnectedness, we move toward our own integrated wholeness.

> ... a spirituality that doesn't touch every single aspect of daily, personal, and commercial life is bogus.
> —Thomas Moore

- When we expand our sense of self, our ability to put into words and articulate our spirituality is greatly expanded.
- When we are in touch with our spiritual nature, we heal more rapidly from all injuries.

Twenty-Three Aspects of a Spiritual Life You Need to Be Able to Catalyze

Unless an authentic life coach has had experience in the personal development of some of the aspects listed below, he or she may not be able to effectively catalyze some of the following elements in the spiritual lives of clients. Just as an obstetrician does not have to give birth to a baby before he or she can assist someone else in that activity, a coach who has neither learned a great deal about nor directly experienced some of the aspects listed below *can* provide the necessary coaching as long as he or she is cognizant of the possibility that a client's spirituality might become trivialized because the words are too big or the concepts too unfamiliar to be useful.

Nonetheless, a client may seek coaching on:

inner peace	personal fulfillment	meditation and prayer
personal power	natural balance	unity and connectedness
happiness and joy	maximum health	integrity (integrated wholeness)
spiritual bliss	personal passion	individual spiritual journey
mindfulness	vitality and well-being	self-discovery
grace (flow)	creativity	truth
spiritual awakening	personal foundation	personal paradox
love	forgiveness	

Sample Coaching Conversation

Coach: Given our recent conversations about spirituality and purpose, and the fact that you wanted to spend some more time on that today, I want to clarify my role. Although as your coach, I am diligent to avoid giving you advice or answers, there are some things I love to teach. So, I would like to slip into the role of teacher for just a little while today. But, please note, what I am teaching is still just my thoughts, my beliefs. If they are helpful, then use them. If not, then ignore them or disagree with them, ok?

Client: OK.

Coach: I believe that our spiritual self is the most neglected self for most human beings. And yet, it is what makes us human. Obviously, spirituality has been the focus of philosophers, priests, religious leaders, mystics and so on for thousands of years, but modern man has confused spirituality with religious practice. How does that fit for you so far?

Client: I agree with those statements.

Coach: As we work together on developing your spiritual nature and how it relates to your everyday living, I would like for us to come up with some methods or spiritual practices that you can put into your life, ok?

Client: Yes, that sounds really good and something I have been intending to do.

Coach: What do you do now that feels like a spiritual practice?

Client: Every morning in the spring and summer, I tour our yard and look at the plants and flowers. I love seeing things grow. That feels very connecting for me.

Coach: Great. That is a spiritual practice and one that is taught by various spiritual teachers as a contemplative method. What else?

Client: I used to pray at meals, but I lost that habit.

Coach: Is that something that would be important to rekindle?

Client: I really would like to, just to be thankful for what we have and for being together. I do know that I pray to myself a lot during the day, especially as I wake up or go to bed. Just kind of a quiet inner dialogue.

Coach: That is also a good practice. Let's talk some more about other practices.

Coach and client can continue creating a list of possible spiritual practices to experience in everyday living, such as meditating, writing, reading, etc. As a coach, co-create a list of possible practices and then ask your client which ones they would like to include in their regimen.

Questions and Inquiries

1. What is your definition of spirituality?
2. How does spirituality increase the probability of your success (contentment) in life?

> The longer I live the more beautiful life becomes.
> —Frank Lloyd Wright

3. How do you resist the notion of your essence being spiritual in nature?
4. What is not spirituality?
5. What are you going to do to acquaint yourself with your own spiritual nature?

LIFE LESSON 12
You and your clients are already on spiritual paths.

MESSAGES

1. Your primary task in life is to follow your spiritual path.

2. The path to genuine happiness, success, and peace of mind is spiritual in nature.

3. Your daily living accurately reflects your level of spiritual growth.

4. All of your relationships are enhanced when you relate on a spiritual level.

The objectives for Lesson 12 are: 1) To assist your clients in identifying their personal spiritual paths; 2) To identify some spiritual shifts your clients may want to make.

Framework Needed for Coaching Your Clients

A *spiritual path* is a metaphor used to describe the development of the spiritual aspects of your life. The metaphor of a path reflects that you are clearly moving forward, while not always in a linear fashion, but in a focused way. The metaphor further implies that as you travel along this path, you are unable to reach any horizon as you progress toward new awareness, because the horizon is also ever-moving forward. As with any pathway, you encounter milestones and signposts along the route, and there is an endpoint. The endpoint to your spiritual journey is *enlightenment*. Once you reach enlightenment you continue to evolve, even though focused, conscious effort is no longer required for you to express or live out your spiritual evolution. Your spiritual growth simply happens. Much in the same way momentum carries a spaceship to its destination once the craft is free from Earth's gravity and traveling through the near-zero resistance of space, after you reach your spiritual endpoint—enlightenment—only occasional small course corrections are ever needed for your continued spiritual evolution.

Whether or not you are aware of it, you are already on your spiritual path. The question you must now ask yourself is, "Where am I on my path?" Many people are not aware they are sleepwalking—they don't even know they are already on a spiritual path.

Recognizing that you're already on a spiritual path commonly occurs when people experience a life crisis that forces them to seek assistance in order to cope. Sometimes spiritual awareness comes from someone who is obviously on a spiritual path of their own, and you are attracted to them or touched by them. You can also have a spiritual experience of your own and begin progressing through the phases listed below. Discovering your personal path is often facilitated by a life coach, spiritual guide, or someone who is already enlightened.

Exercises and Information

To accelerate on their spiritual paths, your clients need to be ready to shift, leap, grow, re-orient, and change. Like the caterpillar's metamorphosis from worm to moth, your clients need to be willing to transform themselves in order to fulfill their true nature as spiritual beings.

This process requires many paradigm shifts. Invite your clients to consider shifting:

> Death tugs at my ear and says: "Live, I am coming."
> —Oliver Wendell Holmes, Sr.

- From fear to love
- From defensiveness to trust
- From hiding to expressiveness
- From enclosure to openness
- From mind control to heart control
- From analysis to intuition
- From performance (doing) to being
- From reactivity to proactivity
- From responding to flowing
- From external control to internal control
- From darkness to light
- From knowledge to wisdom
- From narrowness to expansion
- From sleep (dream) to consciousness (awareness)

- From body/mind to spirit
- From judgment to acceptance

A critical outcome of making spiritual paradigm shifts is creating balance. Shifting from one extreme to another is rarely healthy. For example, if your client is living in a paradigm of fear, shifting to love is needed to rebalance his or her life. But clearly, you need to feel and use the fear response in appropriate situations. Only when fear dominates a person's life is the shift to love a rebalancing dynamic.

Clients Who Seek Spiritual Development

Below are descriptions of specific types of clients and methods for coaching their spiritual journeys.

The religious client. Your religious clients might live as priests, nuns, ministers, members of a religious order, or as lay persons striving to live according to the precepts of their religion. Religious people usually hold a specific set of beliefs and values, and they engage in practices prescribed by the teachings of a spiritual leader.

People who are religious can be labeled conservative, liberal, orthodox, fundamentalist, or strict, depending on *what* they believe and *how* they express those beliefs.

Religious clients usually live in an ethical manner. They have a caring and supportive community and usually seek to serve, love, and be of value to others. They are committed to living out the beliefs and doctrines of the religious community to which they belong.

Coaching tips. If your clients are strong believers in their religion, they usually seek a coach with similar religious beliefs. If you do not hold beliefs similar to theirs, you need to be very gentle and caring when speaking of spiritual principles. Your religious clients have probably based their entire lifestyles upon the religious beliefs they hold. Not challenging or criticizing your clients' religion is important, and, as their coach, never attempt to modify their beliefs. Simply support and catalyze your clients' individual desires. Champion accomplishments that support the attainment of their personal coaching goals. Remain open to the value of their beliefs and seek to understand what they do for the client. Remain receptive to new learning yourself.

The mystic or metaphysical client. *Webster's New World Dictionary* defines *metaphysics* as "the branch of philosophy that deals with first principles and seeks to explain the nature of being or reality (*ontology*) and of the origin and structure of the world (*cosmology*)" and is "closely associated with a theory of knowledge (*epistemology*)."

Mysticism is defined as "the doctrines or beliefs of mystics; specifically, the doctrine that it is possible to achieve communion with God through contemplation and love without the medium of human reason." Furthermore, it is "any doctrine that asserts the possibility of attaining knowledge of spiritual truths through intuition acquired by fixed meditation"—a "vague or obscure thinking or belief."

A mystic may regularly practice ancient spiritual disciplines (e.g., meditation, contemplative prayer, chanting, drumming, vision questing) that create personally beneficial altered states of consciousness. These practices expand the client's spiritual awareness.

Coaching tips. You need to distinguish between your mystical clients and those who are involved with metaphysics. Each type of client needs to be coached differently. If they seek spiritual guidance at all, mystics usually seek it from a spiritual guru. They might seek coaching for more tangible or practical outcomes in their lives. As their coach, clearly identify their coaching goals. Proceed with patience and gentleness. They will move forward at their own pace and in their own time. You may want to provide them with vocabulary to express their mystical experiences. Perhaps you can explore their experiences and expand your own awareness.

Coaching clients who are involved with metaphysics presents a great intellectual challenge for the coach. By its very nature, metaphysics is complex and esoteric. It is critical that your clients who are involved with metaphysics are extremely clear about their desired coaching objectives. Ask your clients, "How do you want to be different after three months of coaching?" and, "What would you like from me as your coach?" Make the distinction between metaphysical beliefs and beliefs regarding coaching.

Your coaching may keep them grounded in cultural reality. It may also increase their awareness of generally accepted concepts of life, knowledge, and spirit. These clients are usually very insightful and sensitive. They are often visionaries who can make unique advancements in their own lives, the lives of others, and in the world. You need to understand and respect this. Simply assist them in creating the life they envision.

The Generation X client. The Generation Xer has been described as the generation following the post-World War II baby boom, especially those born in the USA and Canada between the early 1960s and late 1970s. Despite a need for a model, they characteristically avoid imitating anyone else in their social network or modeling themselves after anyone else. Some of their values include simplicity, honesty, respect, material accumulation, and financial success. They are usually busy, computer literate, impatient, and highly concerned about their own future.

Coaching tips. Work together to discover what your Generation X clients envision for themselves in the near future. Without playing the role of mentor, invite them to recreate and shift their perceptual paradigms. As their coach, be direct, simple, honest, and respectful in how you relate to them. Ask them how they would like to be coached, what they would find most useful, and reflect back to them the influence they have on you as their coach. Allow them to become *your* model if it is in your best interest to do so.

Clients who adhere to eastern philosophies. Your clients who adhere to eastern philosophies are generally Muslims, Hindus, Buddhists, Sufis, Taoists, or Westerners who have become attracted to eastern philosophies. They may be very devoted to their belief system. They have a great knowledge and respect for cultural history, especially their own. Their lifestyles reflect the practices of their religion in what they wear, eat, and in their manner of relating to the opposite gender. They often honor and respect the teachings of their older relatives and ancestors. You may find it useful to think of these clients as enriching your life and increasing your awareness of cultural diversity and essential human unity.

Coaching tips. As their coach, you must remain open, receptive, accepting, and interested in their perceptual world. Never become defensive of your own. Gently introduce them to the concept of paradigm shifts and invite them to experiment in seeing things in another way. Coaching should focus on adapting and integrating coaching activities into their perceptual world.

Coaching Language

- "I am nourishing my spirit today by _____." (Say it out loud.)
- "I am open and receptive to whatever the world has in store for me!"

- "I accept whatever I experience in the present moment."
- "I use all the events of my life to my highest spiritual advantage, seeking the gifts and teachings of each one."

Sample Coaching Conversation

After engaging in some small talk and updating of progress.

Client: We have coached now for several weeks and I am making a lot of progress on my work goals. But back when I scored my life assessment, remember I put a question mark by spiritual development? I want you to coach me in that area today.

Coach: Great. That is a conversation I love to have, even though it can be difficult to do in one conversation. If we open this topic, I want you to know that it may become a background conversation in your everyday experience. And the good news is that if you are living purposefully, spiritual development must be part of the process.

Client: Yes, I understand that. I just don't know where to begin to improve my comprehension of my spiritual path.

Coach: Let's start with this question? What does spiritual development or spiritual path mean to you?

Client: I get it mixed up with my religious training and what I was taught in my early life. How does religion fit with spirituality?

Coach: My view—and that is all it is, my view or opinion—is that all the various religions are systems and structures created to give meaning. They are practices, as defined by that religion, that help in one's spiritual growth. So religion and spirituality can fit together very well and a religious practice that is congruent with one's beliefs will offer great resources for charting your spiritual path. But sometimes, in my opinion, spirituality is experienced as a very personal experience. If I believe I have a spirit, or that I am a spirit, what am I doing to nurture that part of me?

Client: Wow. This does get heavy doesn't it? I do believe in God, but sometimes my beliefs are influenced by various schools of thought, philosophies, and religions.

Coach: How about if we keep religion out of the conversation as much as possible? Neither one of us are theologians or trained clergy, but I do

> The spiritual dimension of life is evident everywhere, not just in holy places and exceptional deeds.
> —Frederic Brussat

believe we can explore your spiritual development as you see it in your everyday life. Then you can decide if there is a religion or philosophy that connects with you. Fair enough?

Client: OK. Where do we begin?

Coach: How would you know if you were developing spiritually? What does that mean to you?

Client: I guess I would have a sense of a connection to the universe, to a sense that I am living my life with love.

Coach: When in your life do you feel most connected to that? When do you feel most at peace and love?

Client: When I am inspired by nature. Or, when I listen to very moving music or witness art that has an impact on me, or read some passage that jumps out at me.

Coach: That's it! For you to be more aware of your spiritual development, I would like to suggest some regular spiritual exercise. Just like you exercise your body, the same is true for your spirit. Would you be willing to engage in a purposeful activity everyday that would nurture your spirit? It could be the reading, music, or nature that you mentioned, or something else.

Client: Yes. How long each day?

Coach: What do you think is appropriate?

Client: At least thirty minutes, just like physical exercise, seems doable. And sometimes it would be longer, of course.

Coach: Super. Do that everyday for two weeks and report to me by email what your experience is. This is not rocket science. This is a personal experience. So, if you can do that we can discuss it the next several weeks as part of our coaching, ok?

Client: OK.

Questions and Inquiries

1. Spiritual gifts are the elements of your personality that are especially useful in your own spiritual development (e.g., sensitivity to your own thought processes, awareness of your intuition, the ability to deeply meditate). What are your own spiritual gifts?
2. How well do you match the characteristics (as described on page 87) of the spiritual person?

3. What aspects of your spiritual life do you want to strengthen?
4. What defines your current spiritual path? How would you describe the path you are on?
5. What paradigm shifts (as described in Lesson 2) are you interested in or focused on?

LIFE LESSON 13

When you discover your life's purpose, living becomes meaningful.

MESSAGES

1. Without purpose, you become a "wandering generality."
2. As a life coach, one of your professional goals needs to be "to coach and live on purpose."
3. When you live on purpose, you become passionate about being alive.

The objectives for Lesson 13 are: 1) To learn how to discover at least one of your life's purposes; 2) To discover your primary purpose in life; 3) To become passionate about your lifestyle.

Framework Needed for Coaching Your Clients

There is nothing more wasteful than accomplishing with great difficulty that which doesn't have to be done at all. One of the best ways to avoid wasting your life is to discover your purposes before taking action.

Designing and creating a successful life requires you to first discover the purposes for behaving the way you do. If you act without purpose, the lifestyle you are likely to create will be a wandering generality based upon old habits or reactions to circumstance. Neither of these is likely to prove effective in supporting you to create the outcomes you really desire.

Most of us learned to cope with the world when we were less than five years old. If we were successful at managing everyday life and the problems it presented, then the methods we practiced for coping were repeated. If we repeatedly confronted the same challenges and successfully resolved or conquered them, we usually practiced our coping methods until they became unconscious.

Almost all children fantasize or dream about who they are going to be when they grow up. When those imaginings are repeated often enough, they become programmed into their subconscious minds where they begin to guide their behavior. When children practice being the people of their dreams, they behave in ways they imagine they would if they were already in that make-believe situation. Young children usually call it pretending. Rarely do they understand that they are shaping their own personalities and beginning to define their purpose in life.

By the time we are adults, many habits we practiced as children may become obsolete. To engage in our unconscious childhood habits of coping may be downright self-defeating, but we continue to do the same old things because they are familiar, require less effort, and don't comprise our comfort zone.

One definition of insanity is to continue to do the same things over and over while expecting different outcomes. Similarly, it's "insane" for us to continue to engage in coping habits created by a five-year-old! But adults often do precisely that—and then they wonder how they "got themselves into this mess." We often can't figure out why, no matter what we do, we end up in the "same old place." As Gerald Nadler wrote in his book, *Breakthrough Thinking*, "Otherwise intelligent people take the same self-limiting thinking approaches every time without realizing they are stuck in time-worn ruts on the road to mediocrity."

Indeed, every challenge or difficulty you may encounter invites you to cope with it "on purpose." If you want to effectively manage your life, begin by reprogramming your unconscious with new solutions that are purposeful. Creating an adult lifestyle *without* purposefulness will likely reproduce exactly what you experienced as a child, and the outcome may or may not be satisfying or desirable.

> The most practical of all methods of controlling the mind is the habit of keeping it busy with a definite purpose, backed by a definite plan.
> —Napoleon Hill

By focusing on purposes, you ensure that your solution-finding efforts are directed toward realistic goals and values that are workable in the real world. At the same time, you imagine outcomes that are as close as possible to your ideal solutions.

Realize that the greater your purposes, the more options become apparent to fulfill them. A truly effective lifestyle focuses on the largest purpose you can ideally and practically seek to attain. The largest one, of course, is your Personal Life Purpose. Naturally, there are certain desired outcomes that elude attainment. But you can always control the purposes you set for your efforts. Start by redefining your purpose for solving problems and fulfilling legitimate dreams to give meaning and direction to your life. A hierarchy of purposes keeps you on a playful and enjoyable track, leading to the creation of your desired lifestyle. It also focuses your coping skills and prevents wasted effort. This approach guarantees that you're not going to be working on something that won't meet your needs. Besides, finding the right purpose greatly increases your chances of discovering an innovative and relevant—perhaps even creative—way to live on purpose.

Exercises and Information

Here are some practical methods for coaching your clients to discover and follow their own personal purposes.

Asking "Why"

Whenever your clients announce large projects or goals, be certain to ask, "What purposes are you fulfilling when you finish this project (or attain this goal)?" Let your clients know that to successfully create the lives they desire, they need to identify why they are doing what they are doing. Clarify for your clients that you are not asking them to justify or defend the project or goal, rather, you are inviting them to identify the purposes for taking action in the first place.

Inviting Imagination

Have your clients use their imagination to identify as many purpose as they can for solving their immediate coaching "problem." Don't ask, "What's wrong here?" or "What's the matter?" Instead, ask, "What are you trying to accomplish here?" "What do you want by way of an outcome?" "What difference will there be if you attain your goal or fulfill your purpose?" The first questions to ask a prospective client are, "After you have attained your coaching goals, how will you or your life be different?" and "As your life coach, how will I recognize those differences?"

Living "On Purpose"

Share with your clients the following example:

In their book, *Breakthrough Thinking*, co-authors Gerald Nadler and Shozo Hibino discuss the relatively minor problem of finding a missing key to a bicycle chain lock. Suppose you have just purchased a new, expensive bicycle. You also purchased a chain lock to secure the bicycle while it's unattended. Sometimes you forget your key to the chain lock because you haven't made carrying the key with you an unconscious habit.

You might say that your task or problem is to find a missing key. How could it be any more complicated than that? Well, another, broader, purpose is found by asking, "What's the purpose of finding the key?" At this point, your response might be as simple as "To use the bicycle." Next, you might ask, "What's the purpose for the bicycle?," which engenders another response, and so on. By following such a progression—where you ask the purpose of each purpose—a series of continually larger purposes can be found.

Another way of finding multiple purposes is to write down all the purposes you can think of, large and small. For the bicycle-key problem, you might come up with a list like this.

My purpose is to

- Locate the missing bicycle key.
- Secure the bicycle.
- Get to school or work.
- Have the key available at all times.
- Use the bicycle.
- Get exercise.
- Keep track of the key.
- Have transportation.

Notice that some of these purposes are broader in scope than others. "To keep track of the key" is a smaller purpose than "To have transportation." These different purposes can be arranged as a progression from small to large, from immediate to long-range, from minor to major. This ranking of purposes is called a *purpose hierarchy*. The reason to think in terms of purpose hierarchies is to find the level at which your efforts will produce the most effective results. Using the above list, ranking the purposes from small to large produces the following purpose hierarchy:

1. Locate the missing bicycle key.
2. Keep track of the key.
3. Have the key available at all times.
4. Secure the bicycle.
5. Get exercise.
6. Get to school or work.
7. Have transportation.

The number of ways you can find to achieve each purpose within a purpose hierarchy often grows as you ascend to higher levels. If your purpose is to "Locate the missing bicycle key," you might only have a mental picture of searching through desk drawers. Moving down the hierarchy to a larger purpose level reveals a wider range of solutions. The purpose to "Have the key available at all times" suggests designating specific storage locations for the key. To "Secure the bicycle" suggests alternate ways of parking the bicycle that don't necessarily involve keys. Even larger purposes, such as to "Get exercise," suggest many other solutions besides riding the bicycle: swimming, jogging, playing tennis, and so on.

There is no single, correct purpose level for discovering solutions to any problem. But there is a level, usually larger than the first, which addresses what really needs to be accomplished for a specific situation. This purpose level suggests a larger number of solutions, some of which may never have been considered in relation to the problem. These solutions represent creative, effective, and purpose fulfilling breakthroughs. It is critical for your clients to generate the greater purposes for their lives. The greater their purposes, the more options for purpose fulfillment will emerge.

After philanthropist Andrew Carnegie died, a worn and crumpled piece of paper, yellowed with age, was discovered in the top drawer of his desk. On it was written, in Carnegie's own handwriting, his personal purpose: "I am going to spend the first forty years of my life creating a fortune, and the second forty years giving it all away." Indeed, he did both. He had written down his personal purpose for how he was going to spend his life. It was that purpose that kept him on track to live his life in the manner he desired.

Insight-Gaining Exercises

Below are a few exercises designed to help your clients discover and clarify their personal purposes, and to help them gain insight in to what is genuinely true for them and their lives.

Exercise 1. Select an important question (see examples in Exercise 5). Quiet your body and still your mind. Take ten deep breaths. Then ask the question of your own intuition. Wait. Ask it again. Contemplate the question in silence. Answers *will* emerge.

Exercise 2. Ask one question at a time about yourself. Record or write down your first thought (answer). Look for themes or patterns in your responses.

Exercise 3. Have a trusted friend or coach ask you the questions and then merge your answers with his or her perceptions. Interact with each other until both of you agree about your understanding of the responses.

Exercise 4. Assume you will certainly die in one hour. Write your obituary or eulogy containing what you want people to know or remember about you.

Exercise 5. Take time now to quietly contemplate each of the following questions. Then, write answers as they bubble up from your subconscious.

- What motivates me?
- What energizes me?
- What brings me the most joy, pleasure, or satisfaction?
- What greatly interests me?
- What is it I really, really, really want in my life?
- What have I always wanted, but never got?
- What kind of people do I enjoy being with?
- Why am I alive at this time, in this place?

Example of Personal Purpose Statements

Share with your clients the following actual examples of personal life-purpose statements.

- My purpose is to live, learn, love, and laugh.
- I will become financially independent and raise a happy family.
- My life is to be of valuable service to others.
- My life's purpose is to be a healer in the world.
- The purpose for my life is to be loved and be loving.
- I will live in balance and harmony with all creation.
- To find God.
- I want to be a catalyst for growth.
- My purpose is to have a great time and enjoy life.

Discovering Your Passion

When your clients are aware of their life purposes, they usually become passionate about actions that are in line with those purposes. But you can also reverse the order by helping your clients first discover what they are passionate about. Thereafter, your clients can formulate personal purposes reflecting their passions.

Unlocking the passions of your clients begins by looking inside. Use these questions to help your clients unlock their passions:

- If I had all the money I ever wanted, what would I do with my life?
- If my family would support anything I chose to do, what would I do?
- If I had no family members to consider when I make future plans, what would those plans be?
- If I had three months during which I didn't have to make a living (no family to care for, no job responsibilities, and no house maintenance), what would I do with my time?
- If I knew for certain I had only six months to live, what would I do during that time?
- If I found a magic lantern, rubbed it, and awakened a genie who could grant me five wishes, what would I ask for?

Identifying the Roles of Your Clients

Let your clients know we each play many different roles in life. While most of these roles we fell into without much conscious thought or deliberate choice, we can generate greater meaning in the roles we play if we discover the purpose for each one. As described in our example of the missing bicycle key, applying purpose to our chosen roles often results in the discovery of many alternative choices to accomplish the same goals or fulfill the same purposes.

> Live not one's life as though one had a thousand years, but live each day as the last.
> —Marcus Aurelius

Invite your clients to make a list of all the "who's" they are at the moment (e.g., human being, male/female, spouse, father, brother, educator, student). Then, have them add a comment regarding how these roles affect them and others around them.

Say to your clients, "Build a hierarchy of purposes around each role you have listed. Ask yourself, 'What is the purpose of this role?' or 'Why do I want to continue to in this role?' In your answers, focus on the purpose you have for acting in these roles, rather than simply listing reasons or justifications for what you do."

Sample Coaching Conversation

Client: I thought about my life purpose statements this past week and I must say, it was very helpful. I have never really thought in such a focused way about my purpose.

> The ideas that would suddenly come to my awareness proved to be the most worthy, and were, in the end, found to be infallible in leading me to discoveries of great importance.
> —Leonardo Da Vinci

Coach: What did you discover?

Client: I do believe that I have a unique purpose for being here on earth, and when I find the things that bring me the most joy and that I value, then I must be closer to living my purpose.

Coach: Go on, say some more. [*This conversation requires the coach to facilitate contemplative answers from the client. If you, as the coach, start doing most of the talking, then it will distract from the clients' experience. Remember, there is a time to teach about purpose and a time to coach about purpose.*]

Client: Well . . . I actually found this experience to relate to our previous discussion about my spiritual development. I guess they have to be connected in that it is really my spirit's purpose I am discovering.

Coach: I believe you are right about that. So what did you discover about your spirit's purpose for you?

Client: That I am called to be a leader, both in my job and in the example of my life. I really pride myself on being a leader at work, but also in leading others to find joy and excitement in everyday living. In my church, in my Rotary Club, with my neighbors, and at work, people often tell me that my chronic optimism is contagious. They love to be around me because I am so upbeat.

Coach: That's really great. Now, did you come up with a purpose statement?

Client: I got a start on it, but it needs some more clarity.

Coach: How about if you work on it some more this week, and send me your statements as you formulate them. I will offer my observations. Just remember, this is your individual purpose statement. Let the words come from your heart. If they resonate and make you smile, then it is probably accurate. Later, we will talk about how to use this purpose statement in your daily life to monitor what you choose to do with your time and energy. When you are living on purpose you will feel energized, resourceful, focused, and fulfilled. So your purpose statement becomes a compass point for your true north.

Questions and Inquiries

1. Have you listed all your purposes for the actions you take?
2. Have you expanded the number of purposes for addressing a particular problem?
3. Have you further explored the purposes of addressing this problem?

4. What purpose(s) are you trying to accomplish or fulfill?

5. What are your even bigger purposes?

6. Do you truly know what you are trying to accomplish?

7. What larger purpose might eliminate altogether the need to achieve this smaller purpose ?

Coaching Summary

In Section 2, Developing Spirituality and Life Purpose, we have offered you four life lessons for working with clients in the areas of coaching spiritual growth and developing a life purpose. We've provided you with a framework for discussing these important issues with your clients. When you coach clients who you believe are ready to expand the coaching conversations into areas of spirituality and life purpose, these lessons and strategies provide you with practical methods your clients can apply to their lives.

The Lessons

The four life lessons are summarized below as reference points and reminders of where to begin.

Life Lesson 10

Realize and appreciate your spiritual nature. We believe that the issues of spirituality and life purpose are very uncommon topics of conversation. As a coach, you can help your clients begin to explore their thoughts, desires, and questions about their personal spirituality and life purpose.

Life Lesson 11

Your spiritual life is more important than your mental, emotional, or physical life. Spirit is really your essential core. Everything else exists and emanates from your spirit—your non-physical "self." As coaches, we do not pretend to be gurus or realized spiritual guides. We do believe, however, it is very important to offer this lesson to your clients. We also believe that they are hungry for such coaching.

Life Lesson 12

You and your clients are already on spiritual paths. This lesson is like one of those simple truths that is sometimes overlooked. If we are already on individual spiritual paths, does it not make sense to become more conscious and purposeful about the journey? Wouldn't we want to be coached about that?

Life Lesson 13

When you discover your life's purpose, living becomes meaningful. This is another lesson that reminds us all to be aware and appreciative of the opportunities in our lives, and to become more fully conscious of our choices and experiences. Another way to think of this might be to ask your clients, "What does my life want for me?"

Statements and Questions for Reflection

Coaching from your own spiritual life and developing the spiritual life of your clients requires a high level of comfort in defining and distinguishing it from religion. Coach your clients by being curious about their spiritual beliefs, understandings, and practices. Use *their* language to move them toward conversations about their own spirituality.

Ask yourself the following questions:

1. What is my comfort level in immersing my coach/client relationships into the realm of spirituality?
2. Am I comfortable with ambiguity, paradoxical thinking, realizing what I don't know—each of which are elements in the spiritual conversation?
3. What do I know about the spiritual aspects of life?
4. Am I open-minded and genuinely curious about the spiritual life of my clients?
5. How well am I able to suspend judgment of someone's belief system, religion, or spiritual practice when they differ from mine?

SECTION 3
Enhancing Communication Skills

"The Medium is the Message" because it is the medium that shapes
and controls the search and form of human associations and action.
—Marshall McLuhan

LIFE LESSON 14

When you know and use the principles of communication, you increase the effectiveness of your ability to communicate.

MESSAGES

1. Any leader needs to be able to communicate well.

2. As a life coach, you need to be able to communicate effectively and powerfully.

3. Effective communication requires knowledge of some basic communication principles.

The objectives for Lesson 14 are: 1) To clearly understand the basic principles of communication; 2) To learn how to prepare for all types of communication; 3) To become a more authentic communicator.

Framework Needed for Coaching Your Clients

Communication is the primary way we make contact with each other. It is the transformation of an idea in your mind into its external manifestation. Communication is essential to fulfilling our wants and needs in life. It is the one critical ingredient found in all successful relationships.

Communication is also at the heart of the coaching conversation. It all begins with listening and creating a conversational environment that invites the client to be heard, to try out new ideas, to communicate clearly, and to enjoy the process.

Language is the greatest human skill we can develop. Poor communication, or lack of it, can topple governments, stifle creativity, shrivel human development, and isolate individuals from one another. Indeed, communications skills can make or break a life.

Language is the way we transform our ideas, images, memories, thoughts, and feelings—our mental activity—into sequences of sound that we send into the world. The better we understand the natural principles governing our mental activity, the more likely we are to transform that activity into clear, accurate, and powerful language. Once we master our mental activity, our communication skills become more powerfully effective.

The Process of Communication

The purpose of all communication is to encode and transmit information in such a manner that the receiver perceives the information meaningfully and in the way the sender intended. Full understanding is the receiver perceiving the exact message the sender intends. When this takes place, perfect communication has been accomplished. Sending skills are half of the communication process. Receiving skills are the essential other half.

Below is a brief outline of the communication process.

> I have never been able to understand why it is that just because I am unintelligible nobody understands me.
> —Milton Mayer

Source: The idea or thought to be communicated originates in the mind of the communicator/sender.

Encoding: By mental process, the idea is converted into some useful or meaningful symbol, such as words, pictures, and behavior.

Transmitting: Some type of physical activity—speaking, writing, acting, etc.—sends the encoded message from the communicator to the receiver.

Medium: This is the method or manner in which the encoded message is transmitted, such as paper, behavior, telephone line, mail, and air waves.

Receiving: The message is received through one or more of the senses via receptor cells, and then sent through the nervous system to the brain.

Decoding: Mental processing of the message converts what is received into a symbol the receiver understands or finds meaningful. Ideally, the decoding is exactly the same as what the sender encoded. Usually, it is only similar.

Perceiving: Organizing and attributing meaning to the information or message received results in perception.

Seven Principles of Mental Mastery*

The more you know about how you think, the more likely you are to communicate successfully.

1. Principle of control. Your clients feel much more positively about themselves when they feel they are in control of their lives. As an authentic life coach, you need to demonstrate control of *your* life. The most powerful way to gain control of your life is to control your thinking. Your thoughts are physical energy events. They affect your reality. Through communication, they have an impact on the world outside you. Control of your life begins by controlling the nature and quality of your thoughts. Change your thinking and you will—indeed, you must—change your life.

> Think innocently and justly, and, if you speak, speak accordingly.
> —Benjamin Franklin

2. Principle of cause and effect. This principle says that for all results (effects) in your life, there were previous, causal events—whether or not you are aware of them. There are no accidents. All phenomena have causes. Learning about the causes of events however, does not necessarily change the results. As a coach, you need to learn what causes are directly related to the outcomes your clients desire, and only then can you begin to catalyze those results. Ask yourself, "What will cause the outcomes genuinely desired by my clients?," and "How can I best coach them to discover those causes and create those outcomes?"

3. Principle of belief. Whatever you believe with feeling becomes your reality. (This principle was thoroughly presented in Section 1.) The key is to have emotional responses involved with your beliefs. Your clients need to passionately believe their beliefs with all their heart.

4. Principle of expectation. Whatever you confidently expect to occur becomes a self-fulfilling prophecy. The higher you hold the expectations of yourself and your clients, the more likely you are to co-create the outcomes your clients desire. Expect the best from your clients. They will more likely live up to those expectations.

5. Principle of attraction. You are a living magnet. You invariably attract people and situations that are in harmony with your dominant thoughts. Rather than sell or market your business or profession to prospective customers or clients, develop it to the point where it becomes irresistibly attractive. You are the living source of information about your business. Who you are as an authentic person is more attractive than any marketing strategy.

6. Principle of correspondence. Your outer world always reflects the nature and quality of your inner world. You can tell what is going on inside by looking at what is going on around you. If you don't like what is occurring in your life, change your thinking, feeling, and the way you communicate who you are.

7. **Principle of mental equivalency (law of mind).** Your thoughts objectify themselves. Thoughts are often fleeting images, ideas, or language. They are not beliefs until they become habitual thinking patterns. You modify your perceptual reality when you modify your thinking patterns and the quality of your habitual thoughts. Repeat your modified thinking patterns until they become beliefs. Imbue your beliefs with emotions, and then they define your reality. Perfect communication occurs when the ideas in your mind are reproduced point for point in the mind of the receiver.

Exercises and Information

While coaching clients, an authentic life coach must remain consciously aware of certain words and actions that either enhance or inhibit the communication process. We call these *communication smoothers* and *communication busters*, respectively.

> The rarest courage is the courage of thought.
> —Anatole France

When we argue or are in conflict with another person, helpful, problem-solving communication usually stops. We often use communication busters to defend ourselves or to launch an attack. When you coach your clients to become aware of these communication busters, they are more likely to stop using them.

Using communication smoothers in your coaching conversations facilitates and clarifies your communication skills. When you coach your clients to become aware of these smoothers, they are more likely to use them.

Share some of the following common communication busters and smoothers with your clients.

Communication Busters

Use of the following communication busters usually stops all effective communication.

Saying nothing. People stop communicating either because they don't know what to say, are too afraid to say anything, or because they believe silence is a punishment. In any case, saying nothing abruptly stops communication. Communication is effective only as a two-way conversation.

Expressing what you *don't* want. Communication is disrupted when someone goes on and on about what he or she doesn't want. Imagine going into a restaurant and telling the waiter all the things on the menu you don't want. Phrases like "I don't want to . . ." or worse, "I don't want you to . . ." always break up communication.

Asking questions ("grilling"). When questioned, people often become defensive. "What do you want to do?" or "Don't you want to . . .?" may seem like harmless enough questions, but "I" statements always make for more effective communication. All questions can be revised to become "I" statements. For example, "I want you to tell me what you . . ." or better yet, "When you say that (or behave that way), I feel (or think) . . ." Statements about your own thoughts and feelings are the most useful antidotes to communication busters.

Complaining. Unless you follow your complaint with a possible solution, complaining simply muddies the waters of otherwise clear communication. For example, saying, "Hey, there's no more toilet paper in here!" might just elicit the response, "Thank you for sharing that." Complaints, absent possible solutions, serve only to abrade the communication process.

Blaming. Blaming is a type of communication buster that is nasty for both parties, the blamer and the blamed. The blamer merely feels weaker and more helpless because shifting responsibility to another through blame undercuts the blamer's own power and ability to respond to what's really bothering him. The blamed is made to feel guilty or inadequate and often simply stops communicating.

Accusations, criticisms, and negative innuendos. These are all tools of a frightened, defensive, or angry person that serve only to wreck the communication process. When we feel accused, we want to defend ourselves. When we feel criticized, we become fearful, hostile, or ashamed. When we are accused or criticized by innuendo, we feel helpless. All of these responses block the channels of communication.

"Me too" listening. This is a common trap for many of us that stops communication early and implies we aren't really listening. When we attempt to show empathy by saying, "Me too . . . I had that happen to me once," or "I know just how you feel," we are actually changing the focus of the conversation from the other person to ourselves. We need to listen long and deep before sharing elements of our life. When we do engage in self-revelation, we need to be certain that such a revelation facilitates the coaching conversation rather than inhibits it. Sharing experiences that are similar can create a bond, but shared too early, they will more likely create a barrier.

Communication Smoothers

> Good communication is as stimulating as black coffee, and just as hard to sleep after.
> —Anne Morrow Lindbergh

Human beings have a highly refined ability to communicate. Yet when two people argue, make assumptions, or become overly emotional, they often communicate poorly.

To introduce the concept of communication smoothers, you might first ask your clients:

- "When you are emotionally involved in a topic of conversation, how well do you communicate?"
- "If you are particularly sensitive to a certain issue, how well can you speak directly about it?"
- "When you don't want to hurt someone else's feelings, what kind of hidden messages do you send?"

To enhance and facilitate their communication, share with your clients some of the following "communication-smoother" methods and phrases.

Take responsibility. Good communicators are aware of their own ability to choose how they want to respond to someone else. They do not *react* to others. Rather, they *act* from within to express who they really are. Self-disclosure is their primary purpose for communicating. They know that their own thoughts, feelings, and opinions are not controlled by someone else or by external circumstances; therefore, they never blame others for their responses. They make "I" statements. For example, "I think . . .," "I choose . . .," "I'd prefer . . .," "I need (want) . . .," or "I feel . . ."

Wait and incorporate what the other says. Rather than continuing with a reply or stream of thought triggered by the last sentence spoken, wait and incorporate what the other person has said into your response. Most of us tend to ignore what others say and either override their talking with our own, or plan what we are going to say next while the other person is still speaking. Don't interrupt. Wait and take in what others are saying before choosing how you want to respond. They may be agreeing with you!

Focus on what is accurate. When we only focus on our disagreements or the inaccuracies of what our communication partner is saying, we become confused or respond to something entirely off topic. If you have a question about what you hear, say, "I understood you to say ___. Is that accurate?"

Don't contradict. What your communication partner is saying is always valid for him or her. Others always have a different frame of reference than you. The primary purpose of communication is to mutually understand each other's point of view. You may state your disagreement, but avoid the phrase, "Yes, but . . ." When you contradict, you invite defensiveness or justification rather than clarification.

Voice pitch and volume. Screaming may help you relieve anger, but it rarely invites others to listen to what you have to say. By screaming, you generate more heat than light, and you elicit defensive reactions from others. Take a deep breath. Imagine you have a pause button, and then communicate thoughtfully and with no emotional charge. You might even try reading aloud in order to practice articulation, voice tone, and pitch, and to increase your working vocabulary.

Understand and then be understood. We often get quiet or leave the room when we feel frustrated or when we want to use a non-response as a silent statement or communication weapon. If both communicating parties agree to a "cooling off" period, then both may want to leave or become silent. Otherwise, both should stay with the process until each is satisfied and feels understood.

Make summarizing statements. Regularly take the time to summarize what you have heard, what you have said, and what you both have accomplished in the conversation. Be sure to include your own understanding of what the other has said.

Listen to yourself. Do you like what you are saying and how you are saying it? Are you responding in ways that accurately reflect your true thoughts and feelings? Listening to others is a critically important half of the communication process. By listening to yourself you might learn something about yourself as well as the topic you are discussing.

Non-Verbal Communication

Eighty percent of communication is conveyed without words. Your facial expressions, tone of voice, body position and movement, and listening skills comprise that 80 percent. People more readily believe or understand *how* you say something rather than *what* you say.

Coaching conversations can take place over the telephone, while others take place electronically by fax or email. These types of communication obviously minimize the use of non-verbal skills, but if your clients want to improve their overall communications skills, they will still need to incorporate non-verbal communication principles into their repertoire.

It's likely that most of your clients were never taught effective, non-verbal communication skills. If they are not communicating well, this probably has more to do with their non-verbal communication skills than their use of words. Here are some tips to share with them—tips that will make that 80 percent of their communicating process the most effective it can be.

Communicate before you "need" to. If you feel compelled to speak or have a pressing need to put your thoughts into words, your words will probably be very different from your non-verbal expressions! For example, if you are angry and afraid to express it directly, there will likely be greater volume and higher pitch to your voice than if you were not angry. Your need will speak louder than your words. We call this discrepancy incongruent communication and it is very confusing to your listeners.

Communicate from within your own experience. Many times our communication process is reactive to someone or something other than our own thinking or feeling. When you communicate in reaction to a situation, the situation can control your non-verbal expressions. You don't want someone else controlling your expression, so keep your expression true to what you are genuinely thinking and feeling, which makes your communication an authentic expression of who you are.

Don't try to communicate when you are drug-affected. When you are under the influence of caffeine, alcohol, drugs, or any other substance—even stress or adrenaline—your body will always communicate differently than your words. Clean up your body. Clean up your life. You will be a better communicator.

Express yourself in ways that help your listener(s) know you are hearing them. If others don't feel heard, they will repeat themselves, escalate the speed and intensity of their language, interrupt you, and talk over you. Let others know you have heard and understand them.

When in doubt, tell the truth. In fact, not only when you are in doubt, but *always* express the truth of your experience in all your communications. Take full responsibility for what you say and how you say it. Be simple, direct, and genuine in your communication style. When you try to hide something from others, they usually know it anyway. Always be willing to share your perspective and belief in a conversation, but be aware it is only the "truth" as you see it.

Sample Coaching Conversation

A busy dentist has weekly staff meetings, but he finds them unproductive and often ending in poor follow-through by his staff.

> **Client:** I had another staff meeting Monday and I almost dread having them. They just don't seem to help our office to be more efficient and coordinated in our patient services.
>
> **Coach:** Tell me how you schedule these meetings and how the agenda is set.
>
> **Client:** My senior office assistant sets the agenda with me, but we only meet for an hour and often there is not enough time to do much more than respond to problems and concerns that have come up.
>
> **Coach:** Yes, that is really typical for businesses when they don't plan meetings more productively. You are all busy. How are you communicating the importance and purpose of the meeting?
>
> **Client:** I have a notice on the bulletin board and it is a regular Monday morning meeting. They all know about it.

People don't always care how much you know, but they know how much you care by the way you listen.
—Louis Vermeil

Coach: Do they have input into the agenda? Do they believe you want to hear their ideas, or just their complaints?

Client: Ah, good question. I want to hear their ideas and have them be more responsible for solutions, but we only seem to have time for the problems and I end up making a decision that seems reactive and often does not get implemented completely.

Coach: The way you communicate is more effective if you are a leader instead of the boss. Employees will help you make your office run more smoothly if they are clear on the expectations and supported in creating implementation plans. What do you think you could do to change the effectiveness of these meetings and the follow-up of ideas?

Client: I think I need to put in writing how I would like the meetings to go and that we have them to function more as a team. Right now, it feels like all we do is put out fires.

Coach: So how could you communicate this to the staff?

Client: I need to have an individual conversation with each of them to ask their ideas on making the meetings better, and truly tell them of my desire to change the experience.

Coach: Excellent. What else?

Client: We could set the agenda during the week, maybe even have a meeting planner in the staff area for them to put ideas on. And we need a follow-up system for the ideas we generate.

Coach: Great. And you do not have to be the one to do all that. That is their responsibility. Communicate that you value them and their ideas and be clearer about your desires for the meeting time, and things will probably be much better. Could you try that this week?

Client: Yes. I will let you know how it goes.

Questions and Inquiries

1. How well do you communicate what you are thinking and feeling?
2. What communication skill will you work to develop over the next three weeks?
3. Under what conditions do you shut down communication?
4. What beliefs of yours are operating when you shut down?
5. At what times do you inhibit your own authentic self-expression?

6. What personal beliefs are operating when you inhibit yourself?
7. Do you need to increase your vocabulary?
8. What are you going to do to lose any and all fear of speaking in public?
9. How can you improve your non-verbal communication skills?
10. How can you authentically deliver a tough message to someone with compassion, warmth, and concern?

LIFE LESSON 15

The art of listening is a vital communication skill and is fundamental to all interpersonal relationships.

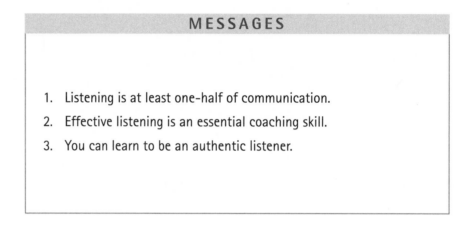

MESSAGES

1. Listening is at least one-half of communication.
2. Effective listening is an essential coaching skill.
3. You can learn to be an authentic listener.

The objectives for Lesson 15 are: 1) To recognize and hone the listening skills of your clients; 2) To understand some basic communication distinctions; 3) To learn what to listen for.

Framework Needed for Coaching Your Clients

If we do not listen, we cannot speak. If we do not listen, we do not think clearly. If we do not listen, we cannot communicate, we cannot love.

Listening is a skill; it can and must be learned. Listening can be taught, refined, and enhanced. Listening has been equated with so many other skills that it might be useful to list a few of the skills listening is *not*. Listening is not hearing, it is not thinking, it is not being passive, it is not comprehending, it is not remembering, and it is not judging or evaluating. Listening is not natural—and it is not easy!

Authentic Listening

Authentic listening means you reproduce within yourself an exact replica of what someone is communicating to you. Perfect listening combines several seldom-used human capacities, described below.

Openness. We must be open to at least the five usual senses of seeing, hearing, touching, smelling, and tasting. We can enhance our listening by being aware of other senses, such as movement, balance, muscular tension, and intuition.

Receptivity. You may be open in a passive manner to sensation, but receptivity is an active skill. Being receptive means you actively participate in accepting outside information.

Ability to pause. Refined listening means you have the ability to pause your own thinking and set your own thoughts aside while you are listening. If you rehearse your thoughts, words, ideas, or responses while someone else is sending you bits of information, then you'll miss those bits and will not have been listening very well.

> The greatest motivational act one person can do for another is listen.
> —Roy Moody

To listen, you must first clear the decks of all judgments and evaluations. Judgments only serve as blocks or filters to incoming messages. Judgments about the message or the sender—such as good, bad, right, wrong—all prevent or color the nature of the listening process and thereby distort your replication of the message you were sent.

Authentic listening. This means that you also hear and receive what is *not* said. One psychotherapist once called it, "Listening with the third ear." If I hear, "No, I never said I hated you!," and I am authentically listening, I will always check out the accuracy of what was meant by this remark from a vast sea of unspoken, possible meanings. Did the speaker mean, "I never said I hated you, but I do hate you," or "I never said I hated you because I don't hate you"? Listening means we ask about the speaker's intended meaning until it is clear to both parties.

You can enhance your ability to listen authentically by becoming aware of your own beliefs, conclusions, biases, filters, and frames of reference. If ten people witness an auto accident, there are always ten different reports of what happened. But if we know we were wearing rose-tinted glasses when we saw the accident, it helps us more accurately describe the color of the car. If we know we own and enjoy a Chevrolet sedan and dislike a GMC pickup truck, we may be more truthful in describing how we perceived the collision.

Listening to yourself. Listen to that still, small voice within. Listen to your own heart, your own feelings, your own imagination, and your own sense of who you really are. Listening to *you* enhances your own identity and your own sense of *self*.

Authentic listening is a learned art that broadens our awareness of others, the environment, and ourselves. Unfortunately, none of us currently listen perfectly, but we can certainly practice the art, and practice makes the skill automatic. With regular practice, we can all become authentic listening artists.

Exercises and Information

Here are some guidelines to help your clients learn to listen effectively and well.

Practice Authentic Listening

Authentic listening is a skill that takes practice. Without continued practice, our listening skills diminish and can become inactive.

1. Recognition. Recognize and share with your clients the benefits of good listening habits. Help them realize they can learn something of value from everyone and that usually, we only learn from others by listening to them.

2. Attentiveness. Have your clients focus their attention on the message sender's central theme. Ask them to keep their minds attuned to the major points and the "unsaid" meanings. Ask them to disregard distractions from the environment or even the digressions and irrelevancies common to most speaking.

3. Non-prejudicial. Tell your clients to avoid prejudice or "rehearsing" what they are going to say next. Advise them not to let a person's past behavior, appearance, manners, dress, or way of speaking influence their evaluation of what the speaker is trying to say. Invite them to evaluate the person's message on its own merits. Tell your clients, "Take your time, let what the speaker says have an impact on you, and then plan your response or let yourself be spontaneous."

He knew the precise psychological moment when to say nothing.
—Oscar Wilde

4. Calmness. Advise your clients to be calm and keep their attention focused. Until the other party to the communication has finished, your clients should not become overly excited for or against the ideas put forth. When something triggers in them a memory or a temptation to recall past people or events, your clients will want their attention to remain squarely on the present messages coming their way.

5. Non-directiveness. Encourage your clients to listen in a non-directive manner. Human beings are typically able to think four times faster than any other person can talk. We have ample time to sift, sort, analyze, and compare the ideas a sender is presenting. Advise your clients to avoid forming conclusions until the sender is finished. They may want to learn some method of noting essential ideas, but they should do this as unobtrusively as possible and in a way that doesn't interfere with remaining attentive.

6. Development. Support your clients work to develop their listening skills. One way to do this is by demonstrating good listening habits in your coaching conversations with them. Also, while your clients may be naturally more interested in themselves rather than in others, this is a communication weakness they must overcome. Furthermore, advise your clients to test their listening skills regularly by repeating to those with whom they are communicating what they understand to be the essence of the speaker's viewpoint.

Your Clients Need to Prepare for Listening!

Encourage your clients to:

- Concentrate—tune in to what is being said.
- Stay present. Eliminate *all* distractions.
- Accept that others are always "right" within their own perceptual world.
- Let go of the outcome. Openly listen without prejudice.
- Be genuinely curious. Everyone can teach something new.

Practical Tips to Give Your Clients

1. Face speakers directly. Maintain eye contact.
2. Listen attentively, with interest, and with patience.

3. Listen without interrupting the speaker overtly or covertly (in your mind).
4. Never rehearse what you are going to say before the speaker stops.
5. Pause to think about (rehearse) your reply *before* responding.
6. In your own words, reflect back to the speaker what you heard.
7. If you want clarification, ask open-ended questions that start with "what," "where," "when," "how," "who," or "why."
8. If you want commitment from the speaker, ask questions that require a "yes" or "no" reply.
9. Always be aware of your speaking/listening ratio.

Helpful Distinctions

In authentic coaching conversations, the coach often clarifies an issue by making distinctions. When coaching listening skills, helpful distinctions include hearing versus listening, listening *to* versus listening *for*, and listening *with* your inner responses, such as your intuition, emotions, and sensations.

Share with your clients these distinctions regarding authentic listening.

> A good listener is not only popular everywhere, but after a while he knows something.
> —Wilson Mizner

Hearing vs. listening. Hearing is the process of sound waves entering your ears, stimulating a tympanic membrane, rattling small bones, vibrating liquid, and finally generating an electrical impulse along the acoustic nerve leading to the temporal lobe of the brain. Hearing does not necessarily mean that anyone understands what was said. Listening, on the other hand, combines hearing with tuning in to what is said. Listening is attributing meaning to the patterns of electrical activity reaching the brain. This attribution of meaning, when done skillfully, results in full understanding of what is heard. This distinction between hearing and listening is crucial to understanding the communication process.

Listening to. For your clients to truly listen *to* someone else, they need to place themselves in the communication-sender's world. Like a television receiver, your clients must "tune in" to the channel, frequency, and energy of the sender. To listen effectively, they must know something about the sender, specifically:

- *Ideas and feelings.* For your clients to listen authentically, they must be aware of the context within which the sender is thinking, ranging from the language used to the sender's knowledge level. To determine how much the sender knows about the subject matter of the message, the receiver must ask directly for elaboration or clarification. In a group situation, there are many different knowledge levels.

To listen accurately to what senders are communicating, your clients need to listen to the emotions expressed about the message. Usually the content of a message is congruent with the feelings sent. Sometimes, however, the way senders say something belies what they mean, which can lead to humor or confusion—or both. If your clients do not grasp *both* the message and the feelings being conveyed about the message, they are not listening to what is being communicated. When clients recognize a discrepancy, they should simply say they don't understand and ask for further clarification.

- *Needs and problems.* When listening, your clients need to know that "senders" begin transmitting messages when they become uncomfortable with their thoughts and ideas remaining only in their minds. This discomfort is a result of some kind of personal need going unmet. When people send messages, they are usually asking for something from the receiver to address a need or a problem, even if it's simply a need for contact. If your clients want to perfect their listening skills, they need to listen for the possibly unspoken needs of every sender.

- *Sender's attitude toward the receiver.* If your clients want to enhance their receiving skills, they must be aware of the sender's attitude toward them. The attitude senders have toward their receivers affects their messages. If your clients are not aware of this attitude, they will probably not clearly comprehend the sender or the message. If your clients suspect senders do not respect them, they can:
  1. Become more knowledgeable about the subject matter.
  2. Be genuinely concerned about the personal needs of the sender.
  3. Show genuine concern about the perceptual world of the sender.

> There are few people who don't become more interesting when they stop talking.
> —Mary Lowey

What follows is a sample coaching conversation illustrating listening *to*.

Client: Wow, did things blow up at work this week! I had two employees come to me complaining about each other and I got stuck in the middle. I don't think I handled it very well.

Coach: (Thinking to himself) I'm hearing that he had two people complain and he thinks he didn't handle it well. (Aloud) So you feel caught in the middle, and you didn't handle it as well as you could have.

Client: Yeah! Exactly.

Coach: (Listening and responding to the facts) What did your clients complain about, and how did you respond?

Client: It was part of a team project and I don't remember the details. When arguments happen, I just shut off. I guess I didn't listen very well.

Coach: It sounds like you may want to change the way you listen. Is that right?

Client: Absolutely! Maybe if I listened better I would be able to handle this kind of situation differently.

Coach: If you listened differently, how might that change the way you handled the situation?

Client: I'm not sure, but I want to handle those situations differently.

Coach: Would you like to be coached today on listening differently?

Client: Sure.

Listening for. Listening *for*—distinct from listening *to*—involves anticipating and being sensitive and attentive to communications that are often so subtle (or never actually sent) that most people never become aware of them. When you listen for something, your attention remains vigilant. You never miss or discount the meaning of any message.

Your clients may want to listen *for* the following items:

- *Situations/problems.* What is happening? How long has this been happening?
- *Symptoms.* What is the client experiencing because of what is happening?
- *Sources.* Why is this happening?
- *Strengths.* Where does the sender feel naturally strong?
- *Tone.* What are the pitch, speed, clarity, and emotions in the sender's speech pattern?
- *Choice of language.* Does the sender speak using lingo specific to a particular subject?
- *Needs.* Is the speaker unconsciously asking for something?
- *Speaker's perspective.* Where is the speaker coming from? What is the speaker's point of view?

- *Bad habits/blocks.* What is the speaker doing intentionally that holds him back or blocks his success?
- *Successes.* What are the speaker's attainments? Progress? Wins?
- *Freedom.* Is the speaker doing really well? Does the speaker not feel as though he or she "should" be doing certain things?
- *Body language.* Most people can not express exactly what they are thinking or feeling. When face-to-face with a speaker, check for body language.
- *Emotions.* There are many important emotions:

  Happiness level: Will be loud and clear in an authentic conversation.

  Fear: May come from the speaker doing something for the first time, being alone, feeling ahead of themselves or pressure to perform, acting on perceived consequences, experiencing financial problems or inertia.

  Anger/upset: May be situational or come from weak boundaries, lack of reserves, withheld communication, or lack of integrity.

  Sadness: Feelings of loss, incompleteness with the past, regret, a missed opportunity.

  Tiredness: Lack of sleep, medical conditions, addictions.

  Resignation: Giving up, succumbing to circumstances, feeling hopeless, inability to self-generate.
- *Peace.* Self-acceptance, good self-esteem.
- *The overall picture.* Most important, listen for the overall picture—not just the pieces!

When your clients are unclear about their own understanding ask them directly for elaboration or clarification.

What follows is a sample coaching conversation illustrating listening *for*.

Client: Wow, did things blow up at work this week! I had two employees come to me complaining about each other and I got stuck in the middle. I don't think I handled it very well.

Coach: (Thinking to himself) I'm hearing that he is upset, stressed, stuck, and self-deprecating. (Aloud) So you feel frustrated and ineffective?

Client: Yeah, I sure do!

> **Coach:** (Listening for and reflecting on what is not being said) It sounds like you might benefit from learning how to respond differently in these situations. Is that right?
>
> **Client:** I guess so, because employees complain a lot to me and I don't know how to handle it.
>
> **Coach:** It sounds like you may want to change the way you listen to and handle complaints. Is that accurate?
>
> **Client:** Absolutely! Maybe if I listened better I would be able to handle this kind of situation differently.
>
> **Coach:** If you listened differently, how might that change the way you handled the situation?
>
> **Client:** I'm not sure, but I want to handle those situations differently.
>
> **Coach:** Would you like to be coached today on listening differently.
>
> **Client:** Sure.

Listening with. In authentic coaching conversations, the coach must always remain aware of his or her own inner responses and use this information to clarify what a client is saying, feeling, and wanting. The coach listens *with* a particular attitude, expectation, or feeling. A coach may have an immediate image, sensation, or intuitive sense about the client. For example, in the previous sample coaching conversation, the coach might have pictured an image of the client being pulled apart by his employees. This is something the coach should then share with the client. Accuracy of the inner response is not important. The coach's willingness to identify and share his or her inner experience is modeling authenticity. More often than not, this kind of sharing is highly relevant—and even if it's not relevant, the client will know the coach has been deeply listening and will respond accordingly.

What follows is a sample coaching conversation illustrating listening *with*.

> **Client:** Wow, did things blow up at work this week! I had two employees come to me complaining about each other and I got stuck in the middle. I don't think I handled it very well.
>
> **Coach:** (Thinking to himself) Interesting choice of words, "blow up." (Aloud) When you said that, I got this strong image of an explosion in your office.
>
> **Client:** Yeah, well it wasn't really an explosion. But I did feel the employees were putting me in an impossible position.
>
> **Coach:** (Listening with and sharing his inner response) I had the sense that you felt helpless and trapped. Is that the way it was?

Client: Yeah, now that you put it that way, I often feel caught. . . Like there's nothing I can do and there's no way out.

Coach: It sounds like you might benefit from learning how to respond differently in these situations. Is that right?

Client: I guess so, because employees complain a lot to me and I don't know how to handle it.

Coach: It sounds like you may want to change the way you listen to and handle complaints. Is that accurate?

Client: Absolutely! Maybe if I listened better I would be able to handle this kind of situation differently.

Coach: If you listened differently, how might that change the way you handled the situation?

Client: I'm not sure, but I want to handle those situations differently.

Coach: Would you like to be coached today on listening differently.

Client: Sure.

> The less men think,
> the more they talk.
> —Montesquieu

Barriers to Effective Communication

Below are some common language behaviors that effectively hinder the communication process.

Passivity. Communication requires energy, initiation, and responsiveness. If your clients remain passive, communication is slow at best.

Dominance. If your clients dominate the communication process, communicating becomes a one-way street and responses are hindered. Domination may occur through words, behavior, tone, threat, perceived authority, or manipulation.

Inappropriate self-disclosure. Your clients may talk too much *about* themselves rather than responding from *within* themselves. When your clients talk about themselves, the topic or focus of the communication changes.

Interrogation or grilling. People often protect themselves from meaningful contact by any one of the following patterns:

- Internal taboo against crying (or emotional expression)
- Talking exclusively about safe topics
- Avoiding uncomfortable issues
- Offering false reassurance

- Emotionally detaching from the topic or person
- Intellectualization (a common favorite)

Using crude language. Such language may be powerful, but it usually turns others off.

Using jargon. People often use words that belong exclusively to their area of expertise. For example, *legalese*, *medicalese*, or *psychologese*.

Moralizing or admonishing. Your clients should avoid imposing their own value judgments on another's communications. Avoid making other people wrong. Avoid telling others that their ideas or opinions are bad or wrong. Suggest to your clients that they simply say, "I disagree."

Patronizing. Condescending words, tone, or behavior—as though your clients were talking to a person of less value than themselves—always make the recipient feel defensive and block communication.

Inept confrontation. Arguing or being dogmatic in language or attitude.

Pressure tactics. Using threat—implied or explicit—to persuade someone about a topic.

Insensitivity to feelings. Being callous or unaware of your own feelings and the feelings of others.

Coaching Language

> We hear and comprehend only what we already half know.
> —Henry D. Thoreau

- "Let me see if I heard (understood) you correctly. You're saying _____."
- "I don't think I am clear about what you are saying. Will you say more about _____?"
- "I want to hear more. Will you elaborate on _____."
- "I'm sorry, I was distracted. Will you repeat what you just said?"

Sample Coaching Conversation

The following exemplifies one of the most common conversations a coach can have when the client needs or wants to improve the effectiveness of communication in an important relationship.

Coach: How did it go this week with your staff meetings? [*The client had agreed to discuss with each staff member the strengths, weaknesses, and opportunities that they see in their role and in the company.*]

Client: I completed each interview and practiced listening in the way we discussed. It was really powerful. But I need to continue the discussions. I don't think they all really believed that I wanted to hear the positive and the negative.

Coach: Ok, so what do you need to do to continue the dialogue and have your staff communicate what you want?

Client: Since this is a change in my leadership style, it will probably take some time.

Coach: And they must know that you really hear them, that you really care about and understand what they are saying.

Client: Yes. I do want that. How do I make that happen?

Coach: I think you probably know or already have some ideas. What could you do differently than you have in the past?

Client: In the past, I heard their complaints or criticisms and reacted personally, like *the boss*. For them to trust me, they really need to be heard and understood. I know I appreciate that when I speak to others.

Coach: Yes, that is the lesson here. You have improved your listening and now you can improve your responding. As the employee speaks, make sure you clarify what you think they are saying, and keep doing it until they feel completely understood. Now, what are some ways you could do that?

Client: I could say things like, "So, what you are saying is . . ., right?" or "It sounds like you feel . . . and that you would like to . . ., right?" I know I used to speak in order to defend or explain myself before the other person finished talking.

Coach: That's it. If you combine authentic listening with communicating for clarity and understanding, your staff will feel heard. It is my experience that even if you can't do what they want, they will understand you and be a team player.

Questions and Inquiries

1. Do you prepare yourself to focus on what individuals are trying to say to you?
2. When someone is sending you messages, do your own thoughts, feelings, or external events easily distract you?

3. Do you understand the importance of the art of listening?
4. Are you willing to practice your listening skills?
5. Do you understand the difference between listening *to* and listening *for*, and listening *with*?

LIFE LESSON 16

Successful communication hinges on how well others understand what you are saying.

MESSAGES

1. Effective coaching depends upon how well coaches are able to put their thinking and feeling into words.

2. Sending messages via language can take several forms: speaking, writing, or acting.

3. "Languaging" is translating your mental and emotional life into symbolic form and sending it out into the world.

The objectives for Lesson 16 are: 1) To learn how to express your thoughts and feelings during your communication; 2) To learn to send accurate and congruent messages simply; 3) To understand that coaching is primarily relating with words; 4) To understand that "languaging" is an art and a skill that can be mastered.

Framework Needed for Coaching Your Clients

Languaging is putting into action the thoughts and feelings you have. This action can be speaking, writing, illustrating, or behaving. Your language includes your tone of voice, your body language, and your vocabulary. If you want to become a great communicator, you need to master the skills of languaging.

Exercises and Information

Authentic listening is a language receiving skill. Below are communication skills that are involved in sending messages.

Communication-Sending Skills

Communication-sending skills to sharpen as you communicate with your clients include: conceptualizing, encoding, speaking, and touching.

Conceptualizing. Conceptualizing makes use of your clients' ability to think, fantasize, imagine, create, and to do all this with clarity.

Psychologists have demonstrated that thinking is, in reality, sub-vocal speech. If you want your clients to think more clearly, more accurately, or more completely, increase their usable vocabulary. One famous leader made it a daily practice to read out loud at least one page of the dictionary.

Words are the imprint of your ideas. They are the tangible, meaningful expression of thought. Often, you don't really have an idea, nor can it be fully conceived, until you put it into words. It is often as important to put your thoughts into words for your own understanding as it is for you to send your thoughts to someone else. Thinking aloud, talking to yourself, or recording your "ramblings" and listening to them, all improve your thinking ability.

Fantasizing is often regarded as useless. Not true! Albert Einstein almost failed the third grade because he spent so much time staring out the window daydreaming. What is important is the nature of your fantasy. Following your fantasies with questions such as "What if . . .?," "How might that . . .?," or "What would happen if . . .?" enhances the clarity of your conceptualizing.

Imagining is turning your fantasies into pictures. Images help clarify your thoughts, focus your fantasies, and program your central nervous system. Using images regularly saves time—and often solves problems.

Creativity is the ability to take two or more separate ideas, thoughts, fantasies, or images and synthesize them into a totally new idea, thought, fantasy, or image. Synthesis is the key to any newly-created event. Allowing your thinking, fantasies, and images to freely wander in your mental processing is the key to synthesizing. It's like the action of random molecules joining to form a compound that has none of the properties of the original molecules.

Using these abilities—which we all have to one degree or another—enhances the clarity of our conceptualizing and makes the source of our communication ability richer, more precise, and more powerful.

Encoding. The three methods of encoding personal concepts are through words, pictures, and behavior (actions). Make these distinctions clear and demonstrate them to your clients.

> You talk when you cease to be at peace with your thoughts; and when you can no longer dwell in the solitude of your heart you live in your lips, and sound is a diversion and a pastime. And in much of your talking, thinking is half murdered. For thought is a bird of space, that in a cage of words may indeed unfold its wings but cannot fly.
> —Kahlil Gibran

Words are used more often than any other encoding method. Consequently, the value of a large, usable vocabulary becomes obvious. Proper use and selection of words is more than just grammar or syntax. It's the ability to choose words that send your meaningful message as clearly as possible and convey that meaning to others.

> We shall never understand one another until we reduce the language to seven words.
> —Kahlil Gibran

Most people believe they understand and use words well. As an experiment, ask any group of people what the word *face* means. The word *face* has twenty-nine different meanings in the English language and probably no one asked could come up with the actual dictionary meaning. A word, after all, is merely a symbol. Its meaning, as well as its value as an encoding tool, is limited by what it means to the listener.

Here is some advice when using words: keep the sentences short and the words simple. Write or speak to express your thoughts and not to impress your listeners. To convey your meaning is far more important than to impress your listener(s) with your brilliance. Directness and simplicity are marks of a good communicator.

Visuals are a second method for encoding your communication. Examples of visual encoding include photographs, graphs, samples, charts, models, etc. that reach the brain through the sense of sight. Pictures can be used to depict something that is intricate, complicated, or a mass of data. Combined with words, they can make your meaning doubly powerful or clear. Pictures can speak to our aesthetic sense, something words cannot always do. Contemporary public speakers tend to express their ideas using slides, films, charts, or models. Despite the usefulness of pictures, they are rarely effective when used alone. They are visual aids to word communication.

Communicating *behaviors* are non-verbal expressions of our ideas. It was the earliest form of communication available to you as a child. What you do and how you act is a powerful means of communicating to others. When what you do communicates something different than what you say, others always "hear" what you do and understand/respond accordingly.

Smiles, sneers, laughs, or other facial expressions enrich our communication. Ritualistic behavior such as shaking hands or hugging has meaning as well. Refusing to act or behave also has powerful meaning. Giving someone the "silent treatment" or ignoring them sends a very powerful and usually threatening message. It is always important to make what you send congruent with how you send it. If the non-verbal, emotional message differs from the spoken word, your communication becomes confusing—but it's the non-verbal message to which people usually respond.

Speaking. A survey once concluded that the most frightening prospect for most people is to give a speech in public. What is so threatening about public speaking? Learn to be comfortable speaking in public and you increase the creative power of your words.

Ask your clients to increase their speaking vocabulary by choosing five words every week from the dictionary. Practice using these words daily in regular conversation. By the end of a week, these new words will be programmed into their subconscious so they will more likely use them in their daily lives.

Touching. Finally, there is the language of touch. Unfortunately, in our culture, most touching between adults has taken on sexual overtones. But touch is an exceptionally powerful communication tool. A slap, an arm around the shoulder, a hug, a punch—all communicate feelings so much clearer than words. The need to be touched, to stimulate the receptors of the skin, is powerful. If nothing else, touch keeps the peripheral nervous system in good working order. Physical affection (sexually expressed or not) is essential to our sense of well-being. Therefore, its value in communicating is exceptional.

Sample Coaching Conversation

Client: One of my coaching goals is to improve my ability to communicate more effectively in team meetings and especially in my public presentations to shareholders, at board meetings, and during corporate retreats.

Coach: Where do you think you need the most improvement?

Client: I do well with the structured presentations with my PowerPoint slide show and prepared graphs, but I sometimes get nervous and fumble with words when the Q and A session begins.

Coach: That is very normal. To improve your ability, we can work on some strategies together. Do you pause very long before answering questions? And do you believe you need to know the answer to all questions?

Client: Oh, that's a great question. I know I don't pause long at all. I jump right into an attempted answer and I find that sometimes I did not even hear the question properly. And yes, I believe my responsibility is to know all the answers. Isn't it?

Coach: No, it isn't.

Of course you should be knowledgeable of your area of expertise, but a good leader is also one who can say, "I don't know," and then lead a discussion to find out who has the ideas or sources to get to an answer. That involves *everyone* in the answer.

Pausing before answering can give you time to think—to respond rather than react. You know more than you give yourself credit for, but if you don't pause your language mine might be closed off and the words won't come. Pause, breathe, and then respond, and you'll find the words flow more easily. When your client can not find the the right word or phrase, have them play with it until it comes to them, or you, as their coach, cue them.

Questions and Inquiries

1. How do you know when you are clearly and accurately languaging your thoughts and feelings?
2. How can you improve your languaging skills?
3. How important is it to you to improve your communication skills? Why?

Herein lies the tragedy of the age: not that men are poor—all men know something of poverty; not that men are wicked—who is good? Not that men are ignorant—what is truth? Nay, but that men understand so little of men.
—William DuBois

LIFE LESSON 17

Feedback is a way of giving and receiving communication that assists and enhances your relationships.

MESSAGES

1. Without corrective feedback, living becomes perilously unreliable.
2. Accurate feedback is critical to "staying on track."
3. An authentic life coach is always providing constructive feedback to clients.

The objectives for Lesson 17 are: 1) To learn the skill of giving feedback as an effective communication tool; 2) To understand the distinctions between constructive, critical, and destructive feedback; 3) To enhance your ability to coach another person to consider changing his/her behavior through feedback; 4) To become aware of the elements of constructive feedback.

Framework Needed for Coaching Your Clients

Sending and receiving feedback is a specialized form of communication.

Giving and Receiving Constructive Feedback

Constructive feedback is a way of giving and receiving help. It is a corrective mechanism for individuals who want to learn how well their behavior matches their intentions. It's also a means for establishing one's own identity, for answering the question: "Who am I and how do others perceive me?"

Destructive feedback is any communication that makes the receiver wrong (as a person) or diminishes his or her character in any way. Examples of destructive feedback include criticizing, castigating, manipulating, blaming or accusing.

Giving feedback is a way of helping others to consider changing their behavior. Feedback is communication to another person or group that gives information about how that person or group affects others. Like a guided-missile system, receiving feedback helps you keep your behavior on target and thus, better achieve your goals.

Giving feedback is a normal element of coaching, but asking for feedback is also a particularly useful request for a coach. Feedback from clients keeps you informed about whether or not the influence you have on them is what you want it to be. Feedback helps clarify your own behavior and its affect on others, and it increases self-awareness.

Here are some criteria for giving useful, constructive feedback:

> Treat people as if they were what they ought to be and you help them to become what they are capable of being.
> —Goethe

Make feedback descriptive rather than evaluative. By describing your own reactions, you leave it up to the receiver to use your feedback or not. By avoiding evaluative language—"You should have . . ." or "You ought to . . ."—you reduce the need for the receiver of your feedback to react defensively. When a receiver becomes defensive, your feedback falls on deaf ears and becomes useless.

Make feedback specific rather than general. To be told that you are dominating is not as useful as to be told, "Just now, I felt forced to accept your arguments or I felt afraid you would attack me in some way." Specific feedback is always better than general feedback.

Make sure your feedback takes into account the needs of both the receiver and giver of the feedback. Feedback can be destructive to both the communication process and the relationship itself. It is most destructive when it serves only your own needs, is attacking or defensive in nature or fails to consider the needs of the person on the receiving end.

Constructive feedback is directed toward behavior, about which the receiver can do something. If the receiver cannot do anything with the feedback you are giving, keep it to yourself. When a person is reminded of some shortcoming over which he or she has no control, frustration is only increased.

Provide feedback that is solicited, rather than imposed or volunteered. Feedback is most useful when the receiver has asked the kind of question which those observing him or her can readily answer. Taking the risk of asking for feed-back from others is usually worth it—you get valuable information about yourself as well as the giver of the feedback. Abandon your fear of receiving negative feed-back. It can be most helpful in teaching you about yourself.

Provide feedback that is well-timed. In general, feedback is most usefully given at the earliest opportunity after the given behavior is observed. Providing feedback about an action you observed two weeks ago is an example of poor timing—but of course, this depends on the receiver's readiness to hear it.

Constructive feedback is always "checked" to ensure clear communication. One way of doing this is to have the receiver rephrase the feedback according to his or her understanding of what you've said. If what the receiver says corresponds to what you meant, then you can be more certain your feedback has been accurately received. When feedback is given in a group setting, both giver and receiver can check with others about the accuracy of the feedback by asking, "Is this feedback only one person's impression or an impression shared by others?"

> I want, by understanding myself, to understand others. I want to be all that I am capable of becoming . . . This all sounds very strenuous and serious. But now that I have wrestled with it, it's no longer so. I feel happy—deep down.
> —Katherine Mansfield

Exercises and Information

Authentic communication requires us to constantly reduce the gap between our intended communication and the communication perceived by our clients. For example, clients who receive informational feedback about their performance in all areas of their job description are said to have a 360-degree evaluation. Unfortunately, the usual result is that clients learn how to *act* differently based upon the feedback. They do not learn how to actually *be* different.

In the absence of new knowledge about who you are, you are left to keep doing what you do, all the while expecting different outcomes. As we've discussed before in Lesson 13 doing the same thing repeatedly while expecting a different outcome is not purposeful. Critical feedback can encourage you to change your observable behavior without altering any aspect of your personality. In essence, you develop a persona that you believe will satisfy (or silence) your critics, without ever changing on the inside. Your performance becomes incongruent with who you really are. All authenticity is lost.

In his book, *Leadership from the Inside Out*, Kevin Cashman describes what he calls "720° feedback." He says that such feedback begins with "inner 360°" informational input, which deepens and expands your self-understanding as well as your current and desired stages of personal development. This inner 360° stage,

Cashman says, "ensures that we begin to master a more authentic understanding of ourselves."

Only after the inner 360° assessment is made, do you engage in receiving the outer 360° informational feedback from external sources. When this comprehensive 720° feedback is received, coaches are provided a context in which to receive feedback from others as well as a context into which they can integrate this external feedback with their own self-awareness. With such comprehensive and integrated information, coaches are more empowered to serve their clients.

Sample Coaching Conversation

Coach: Let's talk today about your attempts to improve the feedback and communication you are sharing with your employees. What have you noticed?

Client: Well, giving positive feedback seems to be working. People have noticed my attempts and are taking them to heart. But sometimes when I try to compliment or acknowledge others I don't seem to always communicate it correctly.

Coach: The meaning of our communication is reflected in the response we get. In other words, what you mean to communicate may not be what is received. Do you ever say something and notice the reaction of the receiver is different than what you expected? Or a word you use is taken the wrong way?

Client: Absolutely. Often. What can I do about that?

Coach: Well, when that happens it's a perfect opportunity to request feedback. If you notice body language or a response different from what you expected, your meaning probably was not received as you intended. So check it out and clean it up. That is the mark of a great communicator. Make sure that what you intended your words to mean were actually received in that way.

Questions and Inquiries

1. What types of feedback to you characteristically give to others? Positive? Negative? Constructive? Opinions? Advice?
2. What types of feedback do you regularly request from others?
3. What is the nature of the impact you have on others? How do you know?

LIFE LESSON 18

Competition is primitive; cooperation is better; collaboration is best; and a synergistic relationship is superior.

MESSAGES

1. Life coaches should not compete with their clients.
2. A competitive coach/client relationship is destructive to the coaching process.
3. A co-active, collaborative, relationship empowers the client.
4. A synergistic relationship is the ideal relationship between client and life coach.

The objectives for Lesson 18 are: 1) To understand the distinctions between competition, cooperation, collaboration, and synergism; 2) To learn what synergy is; 3) To become comfortable with all three types of personal relationships: cooperative, collaborative, and synergistic; 4) To learn how to create the kind of coach/client relationship that works best for your clients.

Framework Needed for Coaching Your Clients

A recent television commercial tells us, "When companies compete, the consumer benefits." Indeed, competition between enterprises and businesses form the basis of the American economy. In fact, securing a competitive relationship generally determines how successful we are in business.

Competition is everywhere—but there is a personal cost Many times competition is destructive. It is always divisive and separating.

In a coaching relationship, competing with your clients is always destructive and is never beneficial to the clients. It sets up a win/lose relationship. When your clients lose, the coach/client relationship loses, and the coach loses as well. Authentic coaches always keep their clients' best interests in the forefront of their minds. Therefore, creating a competitive relationship with clients is "off limits" for life coaches. In fact, it is not coaching. If you engage in competitive relationships, you will probably not be hired as a coach.

> Two heads are better than one.
> —John Heywood

By the time we are in kindergarten, we begin to learn about the benefits of cooperation. But cooperation on a test is often confused with cheating. So, we usually don't understand what the benefits of cooperation really are.

As beneficial as competition is in some situations, you cannot be competitive unless you first learn to cooperate. In business, cooperation between employers and employees is crucial. In team sports, cooperation is essential to winning. In any setting, the fiercest competitors need to cooperate within an agreed-upon framework; otherwise, competition does not occur. The key for coaches is to create a cooperative relationship while avoiding a competitive one—but this is not an easy task.

After we learn to effectively compete and cooperate, we need to learn how to collaborate. Collaboration differs from cooperation in that it results in a brand new relationship. You can cooperate with someone and never change, but when you collaborate with someone you are always changed—you grow!

Collaboration means you and your clients function as a team, as a single unit. Collaborative teamwork is by far the most productive of all relationships. It defines the most effective and authentic coach/client relationship.

A cathedral is much more than a pile of rocks stacked on top of one another. When the result is greater than the sum of its component parts, we call this a *synergistic* outcome. When a life coach and a client form a synergistic relationship, the outcome is greater than the contribution made by each person involved. The most creative and beneficial outcomes of human endeavors have been those in which synergy has been involved.

If you want to leave a great coaching legacy with each of your clients, always strive for synergistic relationships with them. Not only is it important that you become the best coach you can be, it is even more critical that your relationships are the best they can be. Without quality relationships, your individuality shrivels and you never realize your potential as a human being. Develop superior relationships with others and you will grow into the person you were born to be.

Exercises and Information

The following are tips for developing collaborative and synergistic relationships. Competition exists and is useful at times, and cooperation is a helpful human strategy, but we believe that within *collaborative* and *synergistic* relationships, your clients will move to greater purposeful living and toward the efficient creation of their desired outcomes. We are not meant go through life alone. That is a notion brought to our culture in part by Alexis de Toqueville when he wrote of America's "rugged individualism" and praised us for the "pioneer spirit" that birthed our country. Yet this rugged individualism is also what separates us from one another. This idea, which idealizes doing everything alone, seems to have spread beyond the borders of America to most industrialized nations.

When coaching your clients (or using this lesson for your own personal evolution), we suggest you help your clients to:

1. Look for opportunities to involve others in their goals, creative ideas, and big visions. Great events in the world have always begun within conversations with others.

2. Be willing to let go of their favorite method for accomplishment in order to explore a new means of developing their ideas. As a coach, you might be the seed planter, but what eventually blooms within your clients may surprise even you.

3. Create special opportunities for creating synergy. Invite your clients to become spontaneous in their conversations. Ask them to spend time in a place that is sacred to them and have them invite others to join them. Ask your clients to form a master-mind group devoted to deep thinking, creative conversation, and soulful listening.

4. Realize that synergy is best developed when seemingly contradictory or outrageous ideas are blended and shaped into a final creation that mystifies all participants. A synergistic outcome emerges from multiple causes—synthesizing the energy, common dialogue, and various thoughts and visions of all participants, and then combining these elements in the crucible of creativity that allows everything to be synthesized—that is synergy.

Tips for Creating a Synergistic Coaching Conversation

Here are some suggestions for creating a synergistic relationship between you and your clients.

1. Prepare yourself for contact. View the coaching conversation as an opportunity to co-create with your clients a synergistic outcome. Get ready for the contact by reviewing your notes from previous conversations, recalling what outcomes your clients want from coaching, becoming aware of your own mental and emotional state, and remaining open to and focused on listening, under-standing, clarifying, and apprehending the entire conversation.

2. **Ask your clients:**
   "How are you today, at this moment?"

   - How are you feeling about yourself (good and bad)?
   - How are you looking at your relationships and your life?
   - How are you feeling about others?

   "What has happened since our last contact?"

   - What has occurred to you since our last session?
   - What breakthroughs and insights have you had?
   - Have you made any new choices or decisions?
   - Is there any relevant personal news you can share?

   "What are you working on?"

   - What progress have you made on your coaching goals, projects, and new habits?
   - What have you done that you are proud of?
   - What you are coming up against?
   - What ways can you move over, under, around, or through perceived obstacles?

   "As your life coach, how can I best assist you?"

   - Where are you stuck?
   - Where are you wondering about something?
   - What is your plan of action?
   - Do you need information, a strategy, brainstorming time, or advice?
   - How can I best coach you?

   "What's next?"

   - What is the next action, clarification, choice, or decision that will move you closer to your desired outcome?

- What do you want next for yourself?
- What new key habit do you want to strengthen?
- What do you want next for your relationships?

3. Always seek to fully comprehend your client before sharing your own thoughts, ideas, feelings, opinions, or knowledge.

- I am not certain I understood what you meant. Will you repeat that in different words?
- I believe I understood what you said. Are you ready for my thoughts on the subject?
- If you don't think I fully understood you, please let me know so we can be very clear with one another.

4. Speak with clarity and appreciation for your client's position and power.

- I am impressed with what you said so clearly.
- I appreciate the position you just stated.
- Wow! Well said!
- You have indeed communicated very powerfully and effectively.

5. Regarding your contributions to the coaching conversation, remember that your timing is critical.

- Is this an appropriate time to talk about _____?
- What did I just say that impacted you the most?
- Will you give me some feedback about what I just said?

The danger in communication is the illusion that it has been accomplished.
—George Bernard Shaw

Sample Coaching Conversation

Coach: [*After debriefing the clients' week*] So, what would you like from our coaching today? [*This is a great way to imply that the client is part of the equation. The coach did not ask, "What do you want from me today?"*]

Client: I need help with my sense of feeling overwhelmed. I am not accomplishing what I want. So I need you to tell me ways to combat that.

Coach: I am sure you would like me to tell you, but I find it more powerful if we come up with possible solutions together. My answers may not work for you. So let's work together on some ideas now, ok?

Client: Darn. You mean you are not just going to tell me the secrets? Somehow I know that (client chuckles).

Coach: First tell me what is overwhelming you and then we will do some possibility thinking together?

Client: Well, I have all these projects and obligations, such as . . .

This models the key to collaborative and synergistic coaching. Brilliant ideas often come out of the coaches mouth or the clients mouth. But they surfaced because of the nature of the coaching conversation.

Questions and Inquiries

1. In what areas do you tend to compete with your clients, customers, or friends? Knowledge? Income? Success?

2. What do you need to change in order to create cooperative (even synergistic) relationships?

3. How can you communicate so that *what* you say (and how you say it) is unconditionally supportive of others?

4. What can you say so that you never make others "wrong?"

5. What do you contribute to any relationship so that you increase the likelihood the two (or more) of you create mutually desired outcomes?

6. How often do you ask for the responses from others that will enhance the synergistic relationship?

LIFE LESSON 19

Authentic communication in situations involving conflict is a critical relationship skill necessary for growth and change.

MESSAGES

1. How you communicate when conflict arises is more important than the conflict itself.
2. Most coaching clients seek life coaching to resolve some type of conflict.
3. Abandon your fear of conflict.

The objectives for Lesson 19 are: 1) To understand the importance and value of conflict; 2) To identify the types of conflict and learn the methods of effective conflict management; 3) To learn the practical steps for resolving conflict; 4) To learn and practice the Conflict Communication Wheel method for addressing conflict; 5) To learn authentic communication skills in conflict situations.

Framework Needed for Coaching Your Clients

Nobody interacts very long without some conflict. Out of the crucible of conflict come creative solutions to problems. Conflict can also lead to the deterioration or even destruction of relationships. It all depends on *how* conflict is managed, *how* well you communicate, and *how* solutions are obtained.

There is a difference between conflict *solutions* and conflict *resolutions*. A *solution* to conflict is anything that brings the ongoing conflict to a halt. *Resolution*, by contrast, is when conflict not only stops, but all parties are satisfied with the outcome. Mutual satisfaction with the outcome is the primary goal of all effective conflict management skills.

Learning methods of conflict resolution and anticipating the usual outcome of these methods will greatly enhance your ability to effectively cope with conflicts and turn them into satisfying results.

> The next dreadful thing to a battle lost is a battle won.
> —Authur Wellesley

Conflict-Management Concepts

The five basic methods of conflict management are:

- Denial
- Suppression
- Domination
- Compromise
- Creative synthesis

Each of these methods can be used to solve conflicts. Each has their characteristic outcomes. How well you communicate using each method determines the nature of the outcomes. Each may be used appropriately or inappropriately.

Conflict management is a skill and, like any skill, it can be learned. But in order for this skill to develop and for you to be an effective communicator, conflict management must be learned, understood, practiced regularly and often, and maintained.

Method 1—Denial. Denial is a child's earliest method of problem solving—If they close their eyes, the problem disappears and is thereby solved. Conflict denial occurs when the manager solves the problem by denying its existence. This method results in no solution, except in the mind of the manager. The problem remains, but the conflict is over. It usually doesn't have a chance to begin!

Denial is appropriate to use when the issue is relatively unimportant; when the problem will resolve itself with the passage of time; when the conflict requires a different time or place to be resolved; when the conflict requires a "cooling-off" period; or when the parties involved need distance from their conflicting positions to gain more information or objectivity.

Denial is inappropriate to use when the problem or issue is an important one; when it is likely to pop up again; when it is not likely to disappear by itself, but become more significant; or when there is no other time or place as useful as the present to resolve it.

Denial outcome: A "no win/no lose" situation. Nobody gets what he or she wants, and nobody loses what he or she wants.

Method 2—Suppression. Suppression is the *appearance* of submission. Surface harmony is maintained and the conflict is seemingly over, but resentment or fear builds in the parties concerned. The suppressor tends to down play differences, become defensive, and may even become vengeful.

If the issue remains suppressed, morale diminishes, personal interaction decreases, and silence prevails.

Suppression is useful when, for the moment, maintenance of personal relationships is more important than resolving the difficulty; when longer-range goals may be destroyed if surface "diplomacy" is not maintained; or when it is more important for everybody to "be happy" in the immediate situation, which is not relevant to the conflict (e.g., at a party or social gathering).

Suppression is harmful when others are ready and willing to deal with the issue; when the problem is important and nonresolution may be dangerous; when resolution by chance is too risky; or when evasion stops creative conflict or distracts attention from problems which need resolution.

Suppression outcome: A lose/win situation. The person who needs the conflict resolved, loses; the suppressor wins the needed appearance of harmony.

Method 3—Domination. Conflicts can sometimes end when people use power and control to force their position to be accepted. If it is strong enough, the tyrannical use of power always brings conflict to a halt.

Dominators win if they somehow persuade the dominated party that his or her cause is hopeless. There are never any overt conflicts in the relationship between submissive and dominating people. If you have never experienced overt conflict in your relationship to a friend, lover, or parent, then one of you is a dominator, the other is submissive.

Domination is appropriate when the power comes with a regard for the responsibility of the position held; when the position itself requires power; when this method has been previously agreed upon; or when the situation is an emergency, requiring quickly-decided and implemented problem-solving skills.

Domination is inappropriate when the dominated have no way to express their needs or have them met. If people consistently fail to have their needs met, disruption or rebellion may result. Total domination always generates rebellion of some kind . . . eventually.

Domination outcome: A win/lose situation. The dominator forces the other to lose, while he or she wins. However, the relationship between the dominator and dominated always suffers abrasion. For example, when parents always act in a tyrannical way, the parent-child relationship deteriorates.

Method 4—Compromise. Compromise is what grade-school teachers teach as the best solution to conflict. What they don't tell you is that with compromise, everybody loses. Compromise occurs when each party gives up something in order to salvage what may be left. What may be left is always a middle-of-the-road position which may ignore the heart of the matter.

Compromise is appropriate when when both parties have enough leeway to give up part of their position; when there are limited resolution resources on both sides; and when a win/lose situation is undesirable.

Compromise is inappropriate to use when the original position is "loaded" or exaggerated; when the original or resulting position is unrealistic; when the solution is watered-down enough to be ineffective; when commitment to the resolution process is doubted by the parties involved; or when neither party can afford to lose.

Compromise outcome: A lose/lose situation. Both parties lose some of what they originally wanted . . . and possibly all of what they wanted.

Method 5—Creative synthesis. Creative synthesis is the best solution to conflict. Creativity is the process whereby two or more elements are merged, resulting in an entirely different phenomenon or situation (synthesis), yet containing all the original elements in some similar or different form. In conflict resolution, creative synthesis occurs when the abilities, values, and expertise of all parties are validated and respected; and when each party makes its wants, needs, or position clear. With creative synthesis, the emphasis of the conflict is not adversarial, but collaborative. The parties support their own positions while equally supporting each other. When both parties are equally supportive of each other, they pool their collective energies to design strategies for a solution that results in both parties getting what they want. This method of conflict resolution directly challenges the adversarial approach—it asserts that the best solution to any problem completely satisfies both parties concerned, and that each party participates in the resolution process.

Creative synthesis is valuable to use when there is time available to complete the entire process; when both parties know how to support themselves and each other; when they are committed to finding the best solution; or when the parties are well versed in the use of the synergistic process.

Creative synthesis is not useful when conditions of time, ability, or commitment to the problem solution process are absent.

Creative synthesis outcome: A win/win solution. Both parties receive what they want, and perhaps even more than they bargained for or expected.

Exercises and Information

Below is a practical guide for not only solving conflicts, but also resolving them.

Conflict Resolution

Here are eleven practical steps for *resolving* conflict. These steps are only one method of conflict resolution. There are others. Your clients may want to develop another method that works more effectively for them.

Step 1—Describe the *real* issue/conflict. Have both parties write out, as precisely as possible, a description of the conflict from their point of view. Clarity is crucial. Many times people fight on a social level when the real conflict is on a psychological or emotional level. If you can't remember what the conflict was all about within twenty-four hours, it's likely that you fought a battle, but not the war.

> If we justify war [conflict] it is because all peoples always justify the traits of which they find themselves possessed.
> —Ruth Benedict

Step 2—Write how you would like this conflict resolved. Ask your clients to decide what kind of solution they would like to go for in this conflict. They should mentally picture the pros and cons of their imagined outcome. What do they want the result of the conflict to be?

1. No win/no lose (denial)
2. Win/lose (dominating suppressive)
3. Lose/lose (compromise)
4. Win/win (creative synenergy)

Step 3—Decide your own conflict position. There are five basic positions from which to conflict:

1. Engage directly (confrontation)
2. Engage indirectly (manipulation)
3. Hold even (passive resistance/aggression)
4. Postpone (cool off, gather more information)
5. Withdraw (avoidance)

Step 4—Focus on a reduced area or single topic. People often conflict by moving in rapid succession from topic to topic. This method usually occurs when the parties feel defensive, attacked, unsupported, etc. Essential to creative conflict resolution is reducing the scope of the conflict so you can focus on one aspect at a time. Each party usually has both similar and dissimilar areas on which they wish to focus, so it's useful to write all areas down, compare the similar ones, prioritize, and then focus on one at a time.

Step 5—Decide what you want long-range. Ask your clients to think about the kind of relationship they wish to have with the other party after the conflict is over. Have them think about the kind of relationship they want next week, next year, and five years from now. This may also influence their decision in Step 2.

Step 6—Identify forces or pressures. Pinpoint the forces that are acting on your client and the person with whom they are in conflict. What are the needs, feelings, outside influences and wants that they have? What are they for their conflicting partner?

Step 7—List the motives for wanting to win the conflict. What will winning this conflict do for your clients? If they win, what will happen? What will happen to the other party? Is it really in their best interest to win this particular conflict? What will winning do to the relationship? Do they really *want* that outcome?

Step 8—Brainstorm and make agreements. Suggest that your client offer and listen to all possible solutions to the conflict—no matter how impractical, improbable, or impossible they may seem. Then have them make agreements with the other party and *write them down.* They can go over the written agreements and make sure both parties understand them. These agreements define your options at this point in time and are not to be used as ammunition in future conflicts.

Step 9—Make a plan for future action. What is your client going to do? What is the other person going to do? What are they going to do together? Have your client write out a plan of action about how they are going to implement the agreements from Step 8.

Step 10—Check out current status. How has this particular conflict process affected your client's relationship? At this moment, are both parties satisfied? Have them express these feelings in words. If you need to, return to Step 6.

> Force, violence, pressure, or compulsion with a view to conformity, are both uncivilized and undemocratic.
> —Mohandas Gandhi

Step 11—Begin and persist in agreement implementation. Many times, people conflict over long-established habits. These habits take time to replace. Creating new habits requires regular practice and focused effort. Meanwhile, the old ones will keep cropping up. Consistent with your agreement (from steps 8 and 9), begin by making at least one small behavioral change, practice it for a few weeks, and then pick another new behavior to work on as you continue to implement your plan.

Coaching the Conflict Communication Wheel

The best visual representation of the preceding eleven steps is what we call the Conflict Communication Wheel. The purpose of this exercise is to increase the probability of creating a win/win *resolution* to the conflict.

Here is how your clients can generate a Conflict Communication Wheel:

Instructions: When you are alone draw a large circle on a piece of paper. This circle represents your Conflict Communication Wheel's outer edge or rim. Inside this circle, draw a smaller circle to represent the wheel's inner edge or hub. From the edge of the inner circle, divide the wheel into six equal parts or spokes. Label the inside of the hub as 1, and the six newly-created areas divided by the spokes as 2 through 7, respectively.

Remember what you write on this wheel is all you can talk about when conflicting, so don't clutter up the wheel with more than one topic, issue, or conflict. When the other party to the conflict is talking about his or her wheel, be sure to *listen* and not rehearse your reply.

> There never was a time when, in my opinion, some way could not be found to prevent the drawing of the sword.
> —Ulysses S. Grant

- In section 1, the hub or inner circle, write what you think is the *real* issue (step 1 from the previous exercise). Then rate on a scale of 1–10 how important the real issue is to *you* (10 being of critical importance and 1 being almost insignificant). Put the number in the center circle.
- In section 2 of the wheel, write what you believe are the facts of the situation—the who, what, where, when and why—about which you are conflicting (see Step 4). Leave out of this section your own feelings, opinions, or desires.
- In section 3, write your long-range *perception* of the issue. What is your thinking (see Step 5)? Begin each phrase with, "I think . . ."
- In section 4, write your *feelings* about the issue. Begin each phrase with, "I feel . . .," followed by a feeling word (see Step 6).

- In section 5, write out your motives and what outcome you genuinely want (see Step 7). Begin each phrase with, "I want . . ." Make sure you ask for what you really want to have happen.
- In section 6, write out what you are willing to do. Begin each phrase with, "I am willing to . . . ." This becomes a part of the plan for resolving the conflict satisfactorily for both you and your conflicting partner (see Step 9).

When both you and your conflicting partner have completed your own Conflict Communication Wheels on one, single issue, sit down together and share your respective wheels. When you do this; other issues *always* come out. You need to avoid addressing them at this time. When another issue comes out, set aside different time to create a Conflict Communication Wheel on that topic.

Sample Coaching Conversation

Coach: Did you speak to your assistant this week about her poor follow-up on assignments you have given her?

Client: I wanted to, but I realize I have really given her lots to do. She has way too many tasks, so no wonder she is behind.

Coach: Bill, this problem is not going to go away without at least having a conversation with her about your frustrations. This is what we have called a *courageous conversation*. It's just a conversation about what you are feeling and thinking. Ask her to help solve the problem.

Client. When you put it that way, it seems more possible. I know we need to change the situation. I find myself avoiding her and then getting upset about things that aren't done.

Coach: That's why we call it denial. It seems easier to pretend or excuse, but it only gets worse, doesn't it? I want to request that you have that conversation with her this week. We can even rehearse and prepare if you want.

Client: That sounds great. I really must address this. Thanks. Let's practice.

Questions and Inquiries

1. How do you feel about conflict?
2. What is your favorite method for addressing conflict situations?

3. What method of conflict resolution is your weakest?
4. When involved in a conflict, do you conflict creatively or destructively?
5. What method of solving conflict do you want to address during our next coaching session?

Coaching Summary

Communication has had more written about it and spoken about it than any other topic of human interest. In Section 3, Enhacing Communication Skills, we presented six life lessons to add to your coaching practice to help your clients.

The Lessons

The lessons of this section reflect the key skills we believe will assist you and your clients to live more purposefully with high-quality communication, a clear focus, and effective abilities to speak and listen well.

Life Lesson 14

When you know and use the principles of effective communication, you increase the effectiveness of your ability to communicate. This lesson may sound obvious, yet its wisdom lies in the *application* of the lesson. For many people, knowing how to communicate and effectively communicating are two different experiences. Coaching your clients in this and other lessons in this section will allow them to experience the flow and enjoyment of clear communication.

Life Lesson 15

The art of listening is a vital communication skill and is fundamental to all interpersonal relationships. We all know this to be true, but do most of us put this lesson into action? So often the lessons in our book are *reminders* of simple truths—simple, but not easy. If you coach your clients to listen more effectively in all areas of their lives, they will experience profound changes in their relationships, their work, and their self-development.

Life Lesson 16

Successful communication hinges on how well others understand what you are saying. Coaching your clients to increase their awareness of how well they relate their thoughts and feelings is a key coaching skill—a skill that is both modeled and taught. Help your clients recognize how well they express themselves and to what degree coaching would be helpful to them.

Life Lesson 17

Feedback is a way of giving and receiving communication that assists and enhances your relationships. Feedback, or the response we get from our communication, can be through words, actions, or silence. Feedback can tell us how well we communicated. Giving and receiving feedback is how we continually learn to improve what we are expressing, both verbally and nonverbally.

Life Lesson 18

Competition is primitive; cooperation is better; collaboration is best; and a synergistic relationship is superior. This lesson speaks more to the intent of communication than to the process. Collaboration and synergistic communication lead to higher-level relationships. While you can communicate effectively in a competitive framework, expressing a desire of collaboration and synergy is best.

Life Lesson 19

Authentic communication in situations involving conflict is a critical relationship skill for growth and change. Conflict does not imply competition or right/wrong communication. Conflict is actually one of the great human opportunities for authentic communication and for developing purposeful, caring relationships.

Questions for Reflection

1. How would your three closest friend/family members rate your communication skills?
2. What areas of communication do you know you need to improve?
3. In what situations do you default to ineffective communication? What skills from this section of the book would help you improve in these situations?
4. When you speak to someone, are you aware of the feedback you get verbally and nonverbally? Do you seek to rectify any incongruence?
5. Do you communicate best in written word, spoken word, or through actions?

SECTION 4
Living Life with Integrity

Destiny is not a matter of chance, it is a matter of choice; it is not a
thing to be waited for, it is a thing to be achieved.
—William Jennings Bryan

LIFE LESSON 20

Taking responsibility for all of your actions empowers you, strengthens your autonomy, and lets you consciously create your future.

MESSAGES

1. Personal responsibility is different from having responsibilities.
2. The development of your ability to respond authentically to life will dramatically empower you.
3. Your happiness is totally your responsibility. You create your future happiness.

The objectives for Lesson 20 are: 1) To learn that being personally responsible is different from having responsibilities; 2) To develop the ability of your clients to choose authentic responses to life; 3) For your clients to become aware that their future happiness comes *from* them and not *to* them; 4) To help your clients become more complete (whole) persons.

Framework Needed for Coaching Your Clients

When you were young, you responded to environmental stimuli using your inborn reflexes. As you matured, you learned to manage and control your reactions in accordance with what you found to be pleasurable or painful. Reactions that you regularly repeated became unconscious habits.

Many of these habits continue long into adulthood. Reactivity usually becomes the standard way people function.

Consistently reacting to external stimulation essentially makes you a victim of circumstance. Reactivity robs you of choice. When you consistently react to others, you give them the power to determine how you behave. On the other hand, *consciously choosing* how you want to react turns reactions into responses. Taking full responsibility for yourself breaks the dependent, reactive habits of childhood and exercises your freedom to respond to any circumstance the way you choose.

Responsibility allows you to choose *new* responses to old circumstances. It allows you to reprogram your unconscious habits according to your current, *conscious* choices. It brings you the freedom to design and create your current lifestyle and your future.

Many adults believe that responsibilities are the reactions or behaviors expected of them by someone else. For instance, the responsibilities of walking the dog, taking out the trash, or getting good grades in school are behaviors that fulfill the expectations of parents and teachers. Engaging in these responsibilities may or may not meet your own expectations or desires.

The price of greatness is responsibility.
—Winston Churchill

When you were a teenager, you may have heard "Why can't you be more responsible?" or "I can't trust you with the car until you become more responsible." You were probably convinced that being responsible was something at which you were grossly deficient.

Personal responsibility is not exercising good judgment or fulfilling duties. It is something much more important. Your choice of habitual responses forms the foundation of your personal integrity and your lifestyle. Your current mental, emotional, and behavioral habits create your future.

Exercises and Information

Teach your clients that being given responsibility is indeed a gift. If they accept this gift and embrace it as their way of life, they not only develop personal responsibility, they also acknowledge personal accountability and experience total personal freedom. Share with your clients the elements of personal responsibility:

- Their willingness to accept life with all of its challenges, joys, and sorrows
- Their ability to choose from an almost unlimited repertoire of mental, emotional, and behavioral responses
- Never blaming anyone or anything for the outcomes they experience

- Determining for themselves the quality of their own character
- Consciously choosing, setting, and achieving personal goals
- Taking care of their physical, mental, emotional, and spiritual health
- Learning how to *respond* to life, rather than *react* to it
- Living their life in a manner that fosters their personal growth, success, and happiness
- Living as a more complete human being

> My own view of history is that human beings do have genuine freedom to make choices. Our destiny is not predetermined for us; we determine it for ourselves.
> —Arnold Toynbee

Let your clients know that becoming aware of the impact of their chosen habits greatly enhances their personal responsibility. Every action has a result or a consequence. Every response creates an outcome. Their consciously-chosen responses *always* result in consequences. The key to designing their desired future lies in learning about the connection between their present choices and the future consequence of those choices.

Taking responsibility for their present and their future means your clients will take control of the nature and quality of their internal life, and they will determine its pain or pleasure. Only when they've taken this step can they create—or attract into their lives—all the success, abundance, and happiness they desire. Success and happiness come *from* them, not *to* them.

Coaching Exercise

Clients often make other people or circumstances responsible for their own thoughts, feelings, and behavior. Even the language they use reflects avoidance of responsibility:

> "You made me so mad."
> "You make me so happy."
> "If it weren't for _____, I would be happier."

As a coaching exercise, agree with your clients that whenever you hear them speak any of the above phrases, when you hear them blaming others for their particular circumstances, or when they blame childhood experiences for their present condition, you will confront them with their language. After you confront them, teach them more responsible phrases such as:

> "When you say that, I become angry."

"I feel happy when you _____."

"I am responsible for making my own mistakes."

"It is not any one else's fault but my own."

"I am in charge of my feelings, thoughts, and actions."

Sample Coaching Conversation

Client: If it weren't for my boss being so critical, I would be happy with my job.

Coach: Are you saying that your job satisfaction is dependent on your boss?

Client: Yes. He makes my work life simply miserable. I think I'll quit if he doesn't change how he relates to me, and everybody else for that matter.

Coach: It seems to me you are making your boss responsible for, and therefore in control of, your emotional life. Is that right?

Client: I guess so. But that's not right. I want to be in charge of my feelings.

Coach: How would you like to respond to your boss?

Client: I guess I would like to have fun with him, feel more at ease around him, get along with him better.

Coach: What does your boss do that controls how you feel?

Client: Like I said, he is always critical.

Coach: Are you able to choose how you respond to his criticism?

Client: I guess so.

Coach: Let's brainstorm about how many ways you could respond to criticism, then pick one or two to practice with your boss.

> Man is fully responsible for his nature and his choices.
> —Jean-Paul Sartre

Questions and Inquiries

1. How would you like to respond to that person or situation?
2. What influence would you like to have on this person or condition?
3. Can you distinguish between being responsive, being reactive, and having responsibilities?
4. In what area(s) of your life can you assume more personal responsibility?
5. What affect would that have on the outcomes you experience?

6. Do you have the courage to take full personal responsibility for everything you think, feel, and do, without blaming yourself?
7. Can you see how taking personal responsibility results in you becoming the best possible you?

LIFE LESSON 21

Honesty is a much greater achievement than always telling the truth. Honesty means you are authentic in everything you think, say, and do.

MESSAGES

1. When in doubt, tell the truth to yourself and to others.
2. Before you can respond truthfully, you need to be accurately aware of your inner thoughts and feelings.
3. Coaching without truth-telling distracts, distorts, and essentially hinders the process.

The objectives for Lesson 21 are: 1) To learn how truth enhances all relationships; 2) To distinguish between having integrity and being honest; 3) To temper truthfulness with tact; 4) To demonstrate the benefits of honesty.

Framework Needed for Coaching Your Clients

Honesty is much more than always telling the truth. Honesty includes an *awareness* of the truth, being courageous enough to communicate it, and making it a genuine part of your daily personal experience.

Most of us are familiar with lying. We lie when we are afraid of the anticipated consequences of telling the truth. Lying is deliberately changing the facts or deceptively hiding what you know to be true. Honesty is much more than not lying; it is more than simply telling the truth. Honesty is being completely genuine (authentic) in all you think, speak, and do. Being honest with yourself and others is a great skill you have to constantly practice in order to fully develop.

You can be honest in relaying what you saw in an accident and still not be telling the truth. You may not be lying; you may simply be mistaken—you may be honestly inaccurate about what happened. People make honest mistakes all of the time. When you are inaccurate about facts, it's possible you are still being honest but that you simply are not aware of the truth.

In order to be truthfully honest, you must first be conscious of the truth. Being defensive, closed-minded, fearful, or angry always distorts the truth of your experience. When you speak of the truth from any of these perspectives, you are not being honest. To be honest, you need to be sensitive to, open, and aware of your own filters. You must also be curious and confident enough to be receptive to the truth of any situation or relationship.

Being honest about who you really are is probably the most difficult skill to develop. To develop such honesty, you need to know yourself well. When you are accurately self-aware and courageous enough to put yourself out there in all your relationships, you are *authentic*. As a life coach, being authentically yourself within all of your coach/client relationships, models for your clients the way you want *them* to be. Your behavior needs to be the same even when no one is watching or listening. Your actions always need to be consistent.

Some people pride themselves on being totally honest, sometimes brutally honest. In the name of honesty, they volunteer opinions, facts, and judgments in ways that are sometimes painful to others, possibly even destructive. Part of being a mature adult is learning how to temper your truth-telling with sensitivity and tact. Become sensitive to the impact the truth may have on others. Learn tactful ways to share what you believe to be true. Sometimes the better part of honesty is timing. Share your truth at a time when others are ready to hear it, otherwise, you might as well be spitting in the wind.

Finally, honesty involves the realization that your experience is always different than anyone else's. Your view of the world is unique. No one else has your body, your senses, your nervous system, your brain, your history, or your life experience, all of which make up and color your personal truth. Five people can witness the same auto accident and each is likely to provide a slightly different report based on their viewpoint. All will be telling the truth, but their individual truths always differ. Learning about the truth of others, as well as learning about your own, insures you will be as honest and authentic as you possibly can.

> Subtlety may deceive you; integrity never will.
> —Oliver Cromwell

Exercises and Information

People rarely become honest with themselves or others unless they are aware of the personal benefits to be derived from living a life of honesty.

10 Benefits of Being Honest

Present to your clients the following benefits of living honestly

1. Honesty promotes authenticity. Honesty is a reflection of your true thoughts and feelings. If you want people to know who you really are, be honest in your self-expression.

2. Honesty fosters courage. Courage is not the absence of fear. Courage is doing what you know you want or need to do, despite your fear. It takes an immense amount of courage to say what you feel. It is often difficult and takes practice and patience, but the payoffs are enormous.

3. Honesty shows you care. Being honest with yourself and with others shows how much you really care. It also demonstrates self-respect and respect for others. A caring attitude makes people stop and think. Gentle honesty is also very attractive and appealing.

> In dealings between man and man, truth, sincerity, and integrity are of the utmost importance to the felicity of life.
> —Benjamin Franklin

4. Honesty creates a circle of love. Honesty sets an example that invites others to imitate. When others respond with honesty, it can create more interpersonal closeness and authenticity. This often translates into love and can create an ongoing evolution of loving relationships.

5. Honesty shows maturity and self-acceptance. There can often be hurt and pain associated with honesty. A mature person conveys honest expression in a style that minimizes painful impact. When others are hurt, the mature, self-accepting person remains in the relationship to work through any pain experienced by the other person.

6. Honesty fosters a connection. Honesty can bring people closer by creating a safe connection. It forms a context for the relationship within which both parties feel secure enough to be genuine in their interactions. Such a relationship can invite and empower each party to work through some highly personal issues.

7. Honesty feels exhilarating because it is so freeing. Being authentic and saying what you feel and think feels great! By doing so, you break free of the limitations of fear.

8. Honesty eliminates garbage. Hiding true feelings or withholding information creates emotional garbage. This is known as gunnysacking, which requires a lot of self-defeating energy. Being honest from the beginning of any interaction prevents the build-up of emotional garbage and cleans out your emotional gunnysack.

9. Honesty attracts honesty. If honesty becomes an unconscious habit, you will become very attractive to other honest people. A life filled with authentic people is vastly enriched.

10. Honesty can keep you out of trouble. We all know how you can dig yourself deeper into a hole with lies and deceit. So from the start, don't even go there. Keep a clean slate by staying honest, especially when you fear the anticipated consequences.

Exemplifying Honesty to Your Clients

As an authentic life coach, the most powerful way to bring honesty to your coach/client relationships is to be aware of who you are. Become sensitive to your own thoughts, feelings, and behavior. Then, be willing to reveal your authentic self to your clients. Discover and use methods of self-expression that are congruent with who you really (genuinely) are. Become self-accepting and comfortable with accurately communicating and demonstrating your true nature.

Within the helping professions, a long-standing, unwritten rule is that you must avoid bringing your own thoughts and feelings into the helping relationship. But authentic life coaching absolutely requires you to contribute your genuine thoughts and feelings to your coach/client relationships. If you are ignorant of your own thoughts and feelings you will never be able to share them with clients. If you are unaware of the influence your behavior has on others, you will create relationships by chance or out of old habits, neither of which is likely to benefit your clients.

If you are aware of what you think and how you feel, but are afraid to reveal yourself to your clients, you will always be defensive and probably dishonest. When you honestly contribute accurate elements of your personality to your coaching relationships, and you are aware of the positive effect you have on your clients, then you are coaching authentically.

Sample Coaching Conversation

Coach: So, tell me, how did the staff meeting go this week? Were you able to apply some of the coaching and leading strategies we have worked on?

Client: Yes. It felt much better empowering my staff to come up with some of the problem-solving techniques and the tasks to improve our service. But, I am still having problems with Jim.

Coach: Like what. What is he doing?

Client: It's more what he is not doing. He just doesn't offer helpful ideas. He doesn't follow through on suggestions. And he acts bored and distracted in the team meetings.

Coach: And that is probably noticed by the whole team, right?

Client: Oh, indeed. Everyone notices, but no one talks about it publicly.

Coach: This is an example of what is called, the "elephant in the room." Everyone knows it is there, but all pretend it is not. Let's talk about your role in speaking the truth to Jim.

Client: What do you mean, speaking the truth?

Coach: Being honest and authentic as a leader does not mean keeping quiet about the bothersome behavior of a staff member. Have you told Jim how his actions are affecting you and the team?

Client: No, I just put up with it and ignore what I can.

Coach: Do you think it would be helpful to speak to Jim privately about this?

Client: Probably. I have been avoiding it.

Coach: Ok. So the truth I am telling you as your coach is that I want you to handle this and the truth you need to tell Jim is the effect of his behavior. Will you have a courageous conversation with Jim this week?

Client: Yes. It is time.

> The social, friendly, honest man, what'er he be, Tis he fulfills great Nature's plan, and none but he.
> —Robert Burns

Questions and Inquiries

1. Are your actions predictable and congruent with your stated positions?
2. Do you follow through on your promises and avoid making excuses?
3. Is your behavior dependable?
4. Do you respond truthfully (authentically) to constructive criticism?
5. How do you treat confidants?

6. Are you trustworthy?
7. How do you express negative information?
8. Under what circumstances do you lie?
9. Do you exaggerate the positive and diminish the negative?
10. Is your behavior consistent with your stated values, even when no one is watching?
11. Do you take responsibility for your mistakes, omissions, and short-comings?
12. Do you make others' best interests equally important to your own?

LIFE LESSON 22

Anger is a powerful, useful, and natural emotion. Learn how to harness and manage it, and you increase your personal power.

MESSAGES

1. Anger is not a bad emotion.
2. When managed well, anger strengthens your responses.
3. Anger is the usual defense against fear.
4. Depending on how you use it, personal anger can be effectively constructive or powerfully destructive.

The objectives for Lesson 22 are: 1) To clearly distinguish between the emotion/feeling of anger and the expression of it; 2) To learn how to use anger in a creative, effective and constructive manner; 3) To have your clients identify how they habitually express their own personal anger.

Framework Needed for Coaching Your Clients

We usually consider the emotion of anger to be destructive to our psychological and interpersonal health. Most of us grew up associating anger with its expression. When being punished for behaving in destructive ways, we usually did not distinguish between our feelings of anger and the anger-driven behavior for which we were being punished. Over time we began to equate parental disapproval of our *behavior* with the *feeling* of anger, and we began to believe that the natural human emotion of anger was bad, and when we experienced it, *we* became bad.

In childhood, you made many conclusions about anger that were not rational. Many of those conclusions and the behavioral habits based upon them have perhaps resulted in adaptations that may not work well for you as an adult. You may have learned to disguise your anger in anxiety, depression, disappointment, guilt, angelic sweetness, procrastination, passivity, "disasterizing" (always anticipating the worst); ruminating; fear, acts of self-sabotage, and other emotions.

In this way you may often react to the disguise of anger (in yourself or in others) rather than anger itself. Of all the varieties of emotions, anger and fear are probably the most powerful and least understood. To be afraid of anger, or to use it in destructive ways, is very self-defeating. *Anger, however, does need to be controlled, and you can learn how to do that.*

The emotional experience we call anger is nothing more than our bodies providing us with quick, powerful energy. Anger is bodily energy for us to use in order to behave more powerfully. Unfortunately, *how* we behave in anger is often violent, aggressive, or destructive.

While most of us are taught to be nice people, we are rarely taught how to use our anger creatively. Since angry behavior is believed to be not nice, we conclude that anger itself is not nice, and we learn to hold our angry energy inside, deny it, or block its expression. "Nice" people rarely listen to it, learn from it, or practice using it creatively.

Bodily energy is, after all, what allows us to function. All human emotions are the result of changes in bodily energy. Therefore, to determine that one emotion is better or worse than any other is simply foolish. Angry energy allows us to function more powerfully. Anger is meant to empower us, to be *acted upon*. It is not meant to be *acted out*.

We can learn to use anger creatively. In her book, *The Artist's Way*, Julia Cameron writes, "Anger is a map. Anger shows us where we want to go. It lets us see where we've been and lets us know when we haven't liked it. Anger points the direction. We are meant to use anger as fuel to take the actions we need to move where our anger points. With a little thought, we can usually translate the message that our anger is sending us."

Anger becomes entangled in psychological problems when we fear it or when we become angry at feeling angry. Fearing anger makes us defensive. We protect ourselves from what we believe others might think of us if they knew of our anger. We feel ashamed. Out of fear of anger, we diminish our self-assertiveness. We begin to believe something is wrong with us. Fearing our own anger, we never seek to fully express our emotions, thereby restricting ourselves from feeling fully alive. We keep our anger hidden or disguised from others and rob ourselves of relationships which are rich with emotional awareness and sharing.

When we become angry that we experience anger, our anger hardens into hostility. The medical community has established chronic hostility as a risk factor in the development of heart disease. We believe hostility accounts for many more

> The ideal man bears the accidents of life with dignity and grace, making the best of the circumstances.
> —Aristotle

stress-related illnesses than only cardiovascular disease. Hostility leads to abraded relationships and increased stress. In fact, the last few Surgeons General of the United States have agreed that the vast majority of those illnesses for which we seek medical treatment are stress-related.

But anger can also heal us. Cameron writes, "Anger is the firestorm that signals the death of our old life. Anger is the fuel that propels us into our new one. Anger is a tool, not a master. Anger is meant to be tapped into and drawn upon. Used properly, anger is useful."

Anger will always tell us when we have been betrayed by others. It will always tell us when we have betrayed ourselves. It will always tell us that it is time to act in our own best interests. Anger is not the action itself—it is action's invitation.

Exercises and Information

Your clients may not be aware of the circumstances in which they usually feel anger. They may also misunderstand the change in their bodily energy that can trigger anger. Share with your clients some of the most common causes of the anger response.

Situations That Trigger the Normal Anger Response

We usually respond with anger when:

- We feel threatened in some critical way.
- We are very needy and our means of getting our needs met has been threatened or broken.
- Our goal-directed behavior is thwarted.
- We have pent-up rage that is simply seeking an acceptable outlet.
- We are hurt.
- We feel betrayed.
- We don't have *enough* reserves of whatever we perceive to be important to our happiness.
- We simply need to release pain.
- We are anxious or embarrassed.
- We are repeating an emotional pattern that we learned from a parent or other person of significant influence.
- We have used anger before and have believed it to work.

Anger is designed to empower us to address a specific need, to overcome something that is blocking our goal-directed behavior, to stop the hurt, or to protect us from a perceived threat. In all of these conditions, anger is a useful biological mechanism designed to help us survive.

Useful Information about Anger

Below is some useful information about anger that you may want to clarify for your clients. Awareness of these facts can alter long-held conclusions about personal anger, the anger of others, and the expression of anger.

Anger is an inborn, natural, physiological event that provides us with quick energy and power. The physiological changes we label *anger* are not dangerous. They have a negative impact on the body only when they occur when not wanted or needed, or when they are sustained (without expression) over a long period of time.

Anger is a useful motivator that, when expressed in healthy ways, protects and defends us against perceived threats or dangers. It usually occurs under four situations:

- When our intentions or goal-directed actions are blocked (usually called "frustration").
- When we are being hurt in some way (to energize us to get away from or take action against that which is hurting us).
- When our biological needs are not being met and are growing in intensity.
- When we are actually fearful and convert fear energy into anger as a way of lowering our anxiety.

Anger is powerful human energy. Like electricity (another form of powerful energy), it needs to be controlled, but not stopped. Uncontrolled anger is like lightning, it can be highly destructive. Stopped or blocked anger is like a charge in a bell jar— it builds until a destructive explosion occurs. Controlled anger is like electricity moving along wires, it is highly useful.

Healthy expression of anger results in increased self-esteem and genuine peace with yourself and with others. Unhealthy or destructive anger expression usually results in feelings of guilt or shame, sometimes fear. Anger unexpressed increases bodily stress and tension and can lead to depression, even physical illness.

Like all emotional states, anger never lasts forever. It only lasts longer when we continually feed it or fail to express it. Expressing anger reduces the length and intensity of the angry experience. Just as you can reduce the steam pressure in a pressure cooker by either releasing the pressure valve, taking off the lid, or turning down the heat, expressing anger may accomplish all three.

There is a distinction to be made between anger and hostility and hatred. Anger is for the purpose of addressing the four situations above. Hostility may not be energized by anger, but usually serves as a defense against one's own anxiety. Hatred is a strong dislike for someone or something and may or may not involve anger.

When you take full responsibility for yourself, your behavior, choices, and your emotions (including anger), you empower yourself to alter anything you wish about yourself. When you are fully responsible for expressing how you feel, you are more accurately identifying yourself to others. And being clear about what you are feeling at any given moment, clarifies your communication with others thereby enhancing your relationships.

When you acknowledge your anger and use it constructively, make no apology. When you recognize your hostile, anger-filled actions, learn to apologize quickly. Practice taking responsibility for your all your emotions. Learn to forgive yourself (and others) when your emotions are used in harmful or destructive action.

> It is our attitude toward events, not the events themselves, which we can control.
> —Epicetus

The above information will help your clients learn to risk feeling their own anger, express it honestly and openly, and use it to benefit themselves, their relationships with others, and live more emotionally fulfilling lives.

Sample Coaching Conversation

Coach: How did it go with Jim? Did you speak to him?

Client: Yes, but we both ended up raising our voices and being argumentative. I really got angry. He is so difficult for me for some reason.

Coach: And when you get that angry, you feel less powerful than more, right?

Client: Right. I am frustrated and upset.

Coach: A lesson here is that power does not come from force but from controlled expression. Let's think of some ways you can say what you need to say in an uncensored way to release the anger you feel. Then we will plan some practical ways to communicate with Jim. What are some ways you typically release high-level frustration and anger?

Client: I sigh a lot, I mutter a lot, and stomp around the house or office (smiling).

Coach: Do those methods work?

Client: Not really. I guess I need to write down my thoughts—say what I want to say but really shouldn't in public.

Coach: Yes that is one way. What else?

Client: I could say it to you. That would feel good, to just get it out for a few minutes. How about that?

Coach: Yes, I will listen and hold the words for you. Then we can both "dump the trash." How does that sound?

Client: Ok, and then after, I would like to role play with you some ways to speak clearly to Jim so he hears what I want him to hear, without letting myself get extremely angry. I want him to know I am angry, but I don't want to appear rageful.

Coach: Yes, great idea. I am glad you thought of that. Rehearsing an important conversation with someone really helps tone it down, but maintain your honesty and directness in communication.

Questions and Inquiries

1. Are you growing in your emotional life?
2. Are you learning about your anger? Your fear? Your other powerful emotions?
3. Are you risking expressing your anger in healthy and constructive ways?
4. When you authentically express anger, do you experience less stress?
5. Are you distinguishing between passion and anger in the pursuit of your desired outcomes?

LIFE LESSON 23
Being assertive is effective and constructive. Being aggressive is ineffective and destructive.

MESSAGES

1. Self-assertiveness is necessary to get your needs met.
2. Assertiveness is a constructive way to protect yourself.
3. A lack of assertiveness invites people to use or abuse you.
4. Aggression is almost always destructive.

The objectives for Lesson 23 are: 1) To clearly distinguish among assertiveness, non-assertiveness, and aggression; 2) To learn selected assertiveness skills; 3) To learn the connection between being assertive and self-confident.

Framework Needed for Coaching Your Clients

Being able to distinguish among being assertive, non-assertive, and aggressive is extremely important for your integrity. Assertiveness is language and behavior that clarifies you to others and helps to define you, your thoughts, feelings, wants, and needs. It is self-revealing. It is expressive of high self-esteem and self-confidence. It is highly effective in communicating what you want.

Non-assertiveness is remaining hidden. When you don't assert yourself, you are creating an unknown—a void that others fill with their own assumptions about you. They then respond to you as if those assumptions were accurate, which they rarely are. Non-assertiveness may keep you safe from disapproval or rejection, but it also keeps you socially isolated and alone. For anyone to relate to you, they have to know you. If you don't assert who you are in a relationship, the other person never knows you and the relationship either falls apart or fails to develop.

Aggression is always language or behavior that is *against* something or someone. It is rarely *for* you or anything else. We often fool ourselves into thinking that when we are aggressive with someone, it is for a cause or to defend a position. But aggression is *always* aimed against others with the purpose of overcoming them.

Aggression is powerful and usually destructive. It destroys your relationships and your effectiveness. Using aggression, you may win momentary battles, but in the end, you will lose the war. No one likes to relate to an aggressor for very long—it is too painful, intimidating, and fearsome.

Aggression is born out of a mistaken belief that defeating another allows you to win. Usually people resort to aggressive behavior when they feel weak, have low self-esteem, a negative self-image, or believe they are powerless. Resorting to aggression is almost always a defense mechanism against their own fear.

In his book, *When I Say No, I Feel Guilty*, Manuel J. Smith, came up with an Assertive Persons' Bill of Rights*:

1. You have a right to put yourself first sometimes.
2. You have a right to make mistakes.
3. You have a right to your own feelings, beliefs, and opinions.
4. You have a right to change your mind or decide on a different course of action.
5. You have a right to speak up if you feel you've been treated unfairly.
6. You have a right to ask for clarification when you do not understand something.
7. You have a right to ask for help or emotional support.
8. You have a right to feel pain and express pain.
9. You have a right to ignore the advice of others.
10. You have a right to receive formal recognition for your work and achievements.
11. You have a right to say no.
12. You have a right to be left alone when you want to be alone.
13. You have a right not to have to anticipate others' needs. (1985, p.86)

> Justice without force is powerless; force without justice is tyrannical.
> —Blaise Pascal

Exercises and Information

Below are some verbal techniques for helping your clients establish assertiveness. You may want to coach your clients how to use these in daily conversation as well as in conflict situations.

*From When I Say No, I Feel Guilty by Manuel J. Smith, Copyright © 1975 by Manuel J. Smith. Used by permission of Doubleday, a division of Random Rouse, Inc.

Perseverance

The calm repetition of saying what you want. Identify what you want from the person with whom you are speaking and repeat your request over and over again. When you practice this, you learn how to persist without having to rehearse beforehand any supportive arguments, counter arguments, justifications, or angry feelings in order to maintain your position when dealing with others. It always helps if you acknowledge that you heard the person to whom you are speaking *prior to* repeating your request.

Since what you repeat (assert) comes from within you, it is proactive rather than reactive. It is a repeated expression of your own wants, needs, thoughts, and feelings. Once you have practiced this skill until it becomes a part of your unconscious while conversing, you will feel more comfortable ignoring manipulative verbal powerplays, hooks, and attempts to sidetrack the focus of the interaction. You will avoid argumentative baiting and irrelevant logic and stick to your point, remaining focused on your desired outcome. For instance, to the manager of a store say, "I understand your store policy. I realize you want to give me credit for returning this item *and* I want my money back!" Repeat this over and over until you get your money back instead of store credit.

Smoke-Screening

The regular acknowledgment to your partner in an argument that there may be some truth in what he or she says. Acknowledging that the other person may have a point while retaining your own opinion or belief puts a verbal smoke screen between your opinions and the other's argument. Smoke-screening allows you to remain your own judge of what you want to do or say (e.g., "You're probably right in what you are saying. However, I understand it in another way. Will you listen to my understanding?"). Smoke-screening is a verbal assertiveness skill that teaches you to accept manipulative criticism without allowing yourself to *be* manipulated. Once smoke screening becomes a habit, you can receive criticism comfortably without becoming anxious, defensive, or reinforcing people who use manipulative tactics.

Recognizing Information about Others

The simple and often subtle cues demonstrated by your communicating partner that indicate what is important to that person. In almost every conversation, people give verbal clues about what they value. Become sensitive to and learn to recognize

> The only freedom which deserves the name is that of pursuing our own good, in our own way, so long as we do not attempt to deprive others of theirs, or impede their efforts to obtain it.
> —John Stuart Mill

and flag these clues in your awareness. Ask simple questions. Ask for clarification. Ask open-ended questions—questions that cannot be answered with a simple yes or no—like, "Will you tell me more about what your thinking is about that?" If someone is trying to make you do something you really don't want to do, you might say, "Are you really trying to get me to do that right now?" When you develop a genuine curiosity about others, and when you confront them with what they are doing or saying, you become more self-confident about entering into conversation because the focus of your attention is on what the other is saying—not on you or your response. At the same time, you invite conversational partners to talk more easily about themselves.

Expand the Negative

Raising to the level of absurdity the hostile or destructive criticism of another by agreeing with them strongly and sympathetically. This is a difficult assertive skill to master, but once you do, you will learn graceful acceptance of your mistakes and short-comings without having to justify or apologize for them or defend yourself. For example, you might say, "I *know* I'm almost always mistaken about what I do, and [not "but"] this time, I'm still going ahead with what I think anyway." This expansion of the negative allows you to be more comfortable with the negatives of your own behavior without feeling defensive and anxious, or resorting to denial of the truth about your faults or real errors. It also invites your critics to reduce their anger or hostility since you are expressing awareness and acceptance of whatever it is they are criticizing.

Ask for the Negative

Asking for more negative information about yourself. When you feel verbally attacked, you can ask for more negative information about yourself. This effectively invites further criticism which you can use, if it is helpful, or ignore, if it is clearly manipulative. For example, you might say, "Will you tell me more about what you didn't like about what I did (or said)?" This also encourages your critic to be more direct (assertive) in his or her conversation and to use fewer manipulative ploys. This approach often reveals more about your critic than it does about you.

When such negative inquiry becomes a habit, you become more confident about seeking out valuable information as to the effect you have on others or on the situation. Negative inquiry also allows the other person to express his or her genuine feelings. Such expression improves communication.

Honest Self-Revelation

Volunteering information about what you are honestly thinking and feeling at the moment. This verbal habit increases your ability to accept a discussion about both the positive and the negative aspects of your personality, behavior, lifestyle, or intelligence. It also sets an example for your conversational partner, sending the message, "I accept myself and will therefore accept you as well." Nonjudgmental acceptance always enhances social communication and reduces attempts to manipulate by inducing guilt or anxiety.

Offering Workable Alternatives

Offering alternatives or a compromise allows the other person to back down from his or her position without humiliation. If you believe feel that your own self-respect is not in question, offering a couple of alternatives to the issue at hand is a practical strategy. The rule of thumb for this assertive skill is for every "no" you offer two or three "yeses." You can always negotiate or bargain for your goals, unless the alternatives you propose would negatively affect your self-respect or integrity. If the end result reduces your sense of self-worth or self-respect, there can be *no* compromising.

Suggestions for Practicing Assertiveness

- Start by being assertive in small ways. For example, ask your communicating partner to speak more slowly or softly. Build a solid and long-lasting foundation for long-range assertiveness success as a lifestyle.
- Keep in mind that being assertive and asking for what you want doesn't always work. Accept "no"s and rejection as opportunities to find alternatives and return to the first suggestion (above).
- Remember to reward yourself when you have achieved even the smallest goal. You deserve the credit. Ask others to acknowledge your achievement.
- Remember that you have the power to make things happen. You are rarely a victim of circumstance. When you are, you're in charge of how you respond to that circumstance. No one else can determine how you choose your response.

> To be nobody-but-yourself—in a world which is doing its best, night and day, to make you like everybody else—means to fight the hardest battle which any human being can fight, and never stop fighting.
> —e. e. cummings

- Ask for help when you need it. We all need help sometimes. It pays to get the best coaching, teaching, or help. Winners in life always have good coaches.
- Remember that assertiveness is only one mode of expressing yourself. There are many others. Choose your own.
- All lasting and significant change comes slowly. Be patient with yourself. Practice the skill repeatedly and it becomes easier and often automatic.
- Assertiveness is more than role-playing or a technique. It is a lifestyle based on how you see and feel about yourself and how clearly you share yourself with others. Value yourself enough to put yourself out there for others to experience.

Sample Coaching Conversation

Coach: Bill, we have talked much the last few weeks about honest communication and having courageous conversations with important people in your life. How has this changed the way you relate in emotionally-charged situations?

Client: It has improved. I do notice, though, that I dread having those conversations and sometimes put it off.

Coach: And when you put it off, doesn't it build even more and create more anxiety?

Client: Yes, without fail.

Coach: I would like to coach you a bit about the distinction between assertiveness and aggression. Would that be ok with you?

Client: Sure. That sounds helpful.

Coach: Assertiveness is when you express a need you have or a direct communication you need to relate to another, without the intention of causing hurt or discomfort. You express what you need to say and if the other gets hurt or upset by it, that is their reaction, not your desire. You can then continue discussing with them and their hurtful reaction may dissipate. Aggressive communication is what we do when we react by attacking and not responding with our genuine emotions. We actually *do* want to cause hurt or bad feelings for the other. Assertive thought is the act of communicating directly with personal responsibility and an overriding intention to come to a solution.

> In the scale of destinies, brawn will never weigh as much as brain.
> —James Russell Lowell

Client: That is a very helpful distinction. Could you give me some examples?

Coach: Sure. [*Here the coach and the client can create some scenarios to actually practice the skill in this lesson.*]

Questions and Inquiries

1. Over the past two months, can you identify situations where you have been self-assertive? Aggressive?

2. What new assertiveness skills do you want to practice this week?

3. What assertiveness skills might you let your loved ones know you are practicing?

4. How will you improve the way you communicate to others your understanding of what is important to them?

5. On our next call, and in order to practice self-assertiveness, what situations might you want to role-play with me as your life coach?

LIFE LESSON 24

Empathy is the most powerful and effective element in interpersonal relationships.

MESSAGES

1. Empathy is more powerful than sympathy.

2. Empathy enriches your interpersonal relationships.

3. Empathy is a skill you can learn.

4. Empathy can heal and make your life more complete. It enhances your integrity.

5. Coaching empathy is virtually impossible if you have not first developed it within yourself

The objectives for Lesson 24 are: 1) To clearly distinguish among empathy, compassion, support, and sympathy; 2) To teach your clients selected empathetic skills; 3) To help your clients understand the connection between empathy and healthy relationships.

Framework Needed for Coaching Your Clients

Empathy is being consciously aware of, and fully understanding the thoughts, feelings, and needs of another. While empathy is a difficult skill to master, it is invaluable in communication and interpersonal relationships. By developing this skill, you dramatically increase your contribution to any relationship.

When you learn and practice empathy, you make at least two critical discoveries:

1. You are not alone; and
2. All humans are basically the same.

We all seek to survive as best we can. We all want pleasure and attempt to avoid pain. We all desire happiness. We are all motivated by our human needs. We are more similar than different.

Empathy is born of sensitivity to your own experience as well as to the experience of others. When you are sensitive to the affect others have on how you think and feel, your self-awareness dramatically increases. You also become aware of how others think and feel. When you increase your awareness to that extent, you are at a powerful "choice point." You are free to choose how you wish to respond to the immediate relationship based upon conscious awareness and not unconscious reactivity. How you choose to respond at these choice points determines the consequences and results in your life.

Empathy is often confused with sympathy. Sympathy is when you feel exactly the same way someone else feels. When you feel pain inside yourself in response to another's pain—that is sympathy. Feeling sympathy, however, is not always appropriate. Consider what would happen if a surgeon always felt sympathy with his or her patients. In a short time, the doctor would be a physical and emotional wreck!

Empathy is not *agreement* with another. You may or may not agree with the thinking, feelings, and opinions of another person, and you can still be empathetic.

Support is acting in a way that encourages or holds up another person. When you support others, you add your strength to theirs and they become stronger. But being supportive of another's activity is not always very smart. Empathy does *not* always lead to support of another's behavior.

Throughout human history, one general response has proven to be most effective in personal relationships. That response, born of empathy, is compassion. Compassion is most effective when it is the heartfelt response to the information gathered through the experience of empathy. Compassion develops when you have felt safe, valued, understood, and special as the unique person you are.

> All great discoveries are made by men whose feelings run ahead of their thinking.
> —C. H. Parkhurst

But compassion is not complete unless it is directed at yourself as well as toward others with whom you come in contact. Many people find it easier to be compassionate with others, while neglecting or sacrificing themselves. They are self-deprecating, self-critical, and believe everyone else is more important than they are.

On the other hand, there are also those who find it easier to be kind, gentle, and consciously caring about themselves and are constantly unaware of others and how they feel or what they need. At best, they are inconsiderate, at worst . . . selfish.

Treating others as you would like to be treated is considered a golden rule. The more you practice self-compassion, the easier it becomes to show compassion to others. And the more compassionate you are toward others, the more you become compassionate for your own weaknesses as well as your own humanity. Being mean, angry, or violent to someone else reveals how you feel about yourself, and it is certainly neither empathetic nor compassionate.

True empathy allows us to be fully aware of who we are; it also allows us to be fully aware of other people and acknowledge the inner experience of both ourselves and others. Through empathy, we discover our mutual, common humanity. When we discover that, the choice of responding out of compassion becomes much easier.

Exercises and Information

Below are a few coaching exercises that may increase the ability of your clients (and you) to be more empathetic.

- Blindfold yourself for twenty-four hours to strengthen your empathy for the blind.
- Plug your ears for twenty-four hours to learn empathy for the deaf.
- Adopt someone else's body position and imitate their behavior to see how it feels.
- Breathe in the same rhythm as another.
- Impersonate one of your heroes.
- Practice talking to yourself and making faces in the mirror, thereby learning to associate the feelings that go with the speech and facial expressions of others.
- Directly ask others how they are feeling, what they are thinking, and what they want or need at the moment.

Empathetic Response Guidelines

Empathy is the lubricant that smoothes communication and makes it less abrasive. Learning to be empathetically responsive is a skill that can be taught and practiced. Here are some guidelines your clients can practice:

1. Focus your attention on the other person. Become receptive. Maintain eye contact and a responsive posture by remaining fully present in the conversation and psychologically in contact.

2. Make your responses reflect your understanding of the other person's feelings and ideas before responding with your own reactions or thoughts. When you respond without fully understanding another's thoughts and feelings, you risk having your response be inaccurate or not authentically your own. Your conversation is likely to be one of miscommunication.

3. Avoid using clichés or stereotyped phrases. Tailor your language to the other person's level of understanding. Remember that the meaning of your communication is conveyed in the response you receive. If the other does not respond the way you wanted, you must be flexible enough to send your message in another way.

4. Respond frequently. Remember it is okay to interrupt to check out the accuracy of your own understanding of what is being shared. Empathy is being genuinely concerned about the other.

5. Respond to the other person's frame of reference and within it. The influence of events on their frame of reference is more important to communicating with empathy than merely understanding the external facts.

6. Be specific and concrete with your responses. Take your time and allow the other person to pause and formulate his or her responses as specifically as possible. Ask questions when you need clarification.

7. Respond in a voice, tone, intensity, and non-verbal behavior that are equal to the feelings expressed by the other person. The purpose of empathetic communicating is to share meaning through contact.

> It is one of the most beautiful compensations of this life that no man can sincerely try to help another without helping himself.
> —Ralph Waldo Emerson

Coaching Language

Listed below are some initial phrases and sentences, which you and your clients can use to convey empathy:

- "It sounds to me that you're feeling . . ."
- "As I understand it, you felt that . . . Is that right?"
- "To me it's almost like you're saying, `I . . .'"
- "It kind of makes you feel like . . ."
- "The thing you feel most right now is sort of like . . ."
- "What I hear you saying is . . ."

- "I'm not sure I'm with you, but . . ."
- "You feel . . ."
- "I wonder if you're expressing a concern that . . ."
- "It sounds as if you're indicating you . . ."
- "You seem to place a high value on . . ."
- "It appears to you . . ."
- "I read you as . . ."
- "You must have felt . . ."
- "Your message seems to be, 'I . . .'"
- "You communicate (convey) a sense of . . ."
- "So what you seem to be saying (feeling, or thinking) is . . ."
- "I'm picking up that you . . ."
- "If I'm hearing you correctly . . ."
- "So, as you see it . . ."
- "What I guess I'm hearing is that you . . ."
- "I somehow sense that maybe you feel . . ."
- "I really hear you saying that . . ."
- "I wonder if you're saying . . ."
- "As I hear it, you . . ."
- "Your feeling now is that . . ."
- "You appear . . ."
- "I gather that . . ."
- "Listening to you, it seems as if . . ."

> There is only one quality worse than hardness of heart and that is softness of head.
> —Theodore Roosevelt

Sample Coaching Conversation

Client: I really need some coaching today on my relationship with my youngest daughter. We had a conversation that did not go well and that is often the case with her.

Coach: (Modeling empathy) Sure. I hear that you are real frustrated with how that went and you would like to improve the way you and your daughter relate, right?

Client: Exactly. Can we discuss that?

Coach: Of course. That is part of life coaching. Tell me more about what happened and then we can strategize ways to make conversing a better experience for both of you.

Client: She lives in another state and I try to talk with her weekly on the phone. But when I ask about her college classes, or work, or her life at all, she feels I am probing and being critical.

> What we do not understand we do not possess.
> —Goethe

Coach: And that is not the way you want the conversations to go, right?

Client. Right. It is very frustrating.

Coach: Got it. You probably get to the point where you don't even want to call her. Would you like some coaching on ways to attempt to change the way you and your daughter relate?

Client. Yes! Do you have the magic formula?

Coach: Kind of, yes. How well do you believe you exhibit the ability to be empathic with people? Who in your life would feel that you are a good listener, that you really hear them and are able to mirror back to them what they are feeling?

Client: Lots of people—I pride myself on that. My role at work in the human resources department demands that of me, and I believe that my colleagues would agree.

Coach: I don't doubt that. It is often the case that really good professional listeners do not have the same results with family. (chuckles) Do you think you are empathetic in listening to your daughter?

Client: No, not always. I really just want to hear how she's doing, but I do know that my responses sometimes are reactive and I slip into advising her, or making statements that come off as judgmental. I say things like, "you know you really have to start saving money and not using your credit card so much."

Coach: What if we practice a role play? You will play your daughter and I will play you, ok?

Client: Sure.

Coach and client role play with the coach demonstrating empathetic listening, showing the client how to reflect and mirror what his daughter is saying. The coach also models for the client the ability to suspend judgment and just listen to his daughter.

Questions and Inquiries

1. What is your understanding of the distinction between empathy and sympathy?
2. Will you list three or four people for whom you feel empathetic most of the time?
3. With whom do you want to become more empathetic? Why?
4. What can you practice to strengthen you sensitivity and empathy for others?

LIFE LESSON 25
Sharing is the best way to create effective relationships.

MESSAGES

1. Sharing from abundance is different from sharing from need.
2. When you share, you invite the creation of a synergistic relationship.
3. Sharing is not always giving.

The objectives for Lesson 25 are: 1) To distinguish between giving and sharing; 2) To learn the dynamics of self-sacrifice; 3) To learn that sharing who you are is more effective than sharing material things; 4) To help your clients and enhance your coaching practice through sharing.

Framework Needed for Coaching Your Clients

As you were growing up, your parents probably encouraged you to share. Very often sharing meant giving away something that you felt you owned, something that belonged to you. As a dependent, needy child, you were most likely reluctant to give away anything you liked or wanted to keep for yourself.

When claiming and defending your possessions, you were probably told you were being selfish: "Why don't you share that toy with your little sister?" or "Don't be selfish! You have to learn how to share." So sharing became a demand to lose what you claimed as your own.

Nobody likes to lose, especially when we are unskilled at winning for ourselves that which we want or need. As children, we learn that sharing becomes the opposite of receiving; thus, we tend to equate sharing with losing what we have. Sharing becomes the giving away of something we value. Sharing becomes undesirable, even downright noxious. On the other hand, we are told that being selfish is not good. Even as adults, we believe that self-centeredness and selfishness are not virtues.

The result? We rarely practice sharing, unless we use it as a method to get what *we* want. Many of us have learned that if we give something away, we will get it back. "Give and you shall receive" is often quoted, albeit misunderstood. Our culture teaches that if you give enough, you will be happy. So we regularly escalate our giving, especially when we are needy ourselves. We give out of our need *and* belief that giving is what will *get* us what we want.

Actually, giving away what you want returned very rarely works. Giving away something usually communicates that you don't need it yourself. When that happens, sharing becomes just another manipulation for getting others to give to you.

If I give as a method for getting, I become self-sacrificial. Many view self-sacrifice as a selfless act of generosity—and certainly none of us would have grown out of infancy had our parents not been willing to sacrifice what *they* might have needed to address our needs, since we were unable to address them ourselves. However, many adults relate to other adults in a self-sacrificial way.

For example, let's say you and I have eaten our lunch together in the same cafeteria every working day for the past ten years. One Monday, you came to me and said, "Gee, I lost my lunch money yesterday betting on the horse races. So I guess I won't be able to eat lunch with you today." If I was in the habit of self-sacrificial giving, I might say, "That's too bad, Charlie. I'll tell you what, since we have this tradition going, and since you are my best friend, I will give you my lunch money. That way you can eat lunch and I won't." By sacrificing my lunch so my buddy can eat his, I make myself needy by addressing the need of a friend.

The result of self-sacrificial giving is an increase in the obligation of the giver to sacrifice *and* an invitation for the receiver to feel guilty or obligated to give back. Neither of these feelings is particularly healthy.

The healthiest way to give is to share. Instead of giving away all of my lunch money to my friend, I might have given him half of it instead. That way we could both eat, both maintain our tradition, and feel good about the outcome. This is the result of sharing from abundance rather than from need. Sharing is both giving and receiving at the same time. It is not "either or;" it is "both and." Sharing results in win-win outcomes in which both parties benefit. Both parties feel fulfilled. Both engage in giving *and* receiving at the same time. Sharing is not manipulative. It is not self-sacrificial. It is not guilt-provoking. It is not controlling.

In terms of your relationships, the most effective and powerful contribution you can share is yourself. Sharing your authentic self clarifies your half of a relationship. Contributing your gifts to a relationship, while maintaining them as your own, is the positive and beneficial paradox of sharing. When two people share themselves with one another without pretense or deception, we call that intimacy. Sharing your authentic self—who you really are—is the best way to develop intimacy within your relationships. Without *you*, intimacy never occurs.

Sharing is unifying. It is mutually satisfying. It is freeing. Its outcome is synergistic (the sum is greater than its parts). If you want to enhance your interpersonal relationships, learn to fulfill your needs adequately by yourself, or by using a direct request. Only when you are fulfilled can you effectively share. Sharing your abundance is an act of love. It is one of the greatest skills you can learn. It is one pillar in the structure of success attainment. If you fail to share, you fail to succeed in any endeavor.

Sharing "Sharing" with Your Clients

Whenever you have an abundance of anything—time, money, energy, material, knowledge, love, etc.—share it with someone else. As an authentic life coach, you share yourself all the time.

To build your coaching practice, it is wise to share:

- A small gift and letter of appreciation with anyone who refers you to a potential client.
- A congratulatory note for your clients' victories, achievements, and positive creations.
- Your immediate thoughts and feelings about what your clients are focusing on.
- Your relevant life experiences (timed appropriately of course).
- Your thoughts and preparations prior to sessions.
- Any useful ideas you thought about between sessions.
- Anything that will enhance the coach/client relationship.
- Anything that will catalyze your clients' attainment of coaching goals.

Sample Coaching Conversation

Client: I want to follow up on our previous conversations about building my business without causing me to work twenty more hours a week

> You can make more friends in two months by becoming really interested in other people, than you can in two years by trying to get other people interested in you.
> —Dale Carnegie

during tax season. You talked to me about the attraction principle of marketing. Can you coach me today about that?

Coach: You bet! How do you market now? How do new clients come to you?

Client: Fortunately, I have been in business long enough that my clients refer their friends and colleagues to me. But I want to upgrade my clientele to attract those who can afford a higher fee for the experience I bring them, and I want to have accounting staff handle much of the work so that I do not have to do it all.

Coach: Perfect. I assume, like most CPAs, you are less busy in the summer and fall, right?

Client: Yes, that is part of why I want to expand, to get more year-round tax consultation clients, and preparation for the tax filing season.

Coach: So, summer and fall would be a good time for you to find ways to stay in touch with clients and keep them feeling well taken care of by you. Attraction marketing comes from a natural sharing of your skills as well as your authentic self. In other words, you will attract more referrals if you are visible and available, but also if you are seen as someone who is sharing and giving.

Client: I don't understand.

Coach: Find ways to stay in touch with your clients in the "off season" and offer resources, tips, articles. Or, just phone everyone and ask if there are any questions or concerns they have about their tax situation. Then, when you meet with them, share some knowledge or thoughts without charging them, unless it is an official consultation they have asked for. Send them thank-you cards, tax review checklists, and tell them you are expanding your services and would like them to think of some friends who might benefit from seeing you. If you do this authentically, without seeming overly promotional, they will be thankful for your service attitude.

Client: So, you mean giving away some knowledge and resources and keeping them happy with my attention?

Coach: Yes. Sharing yourself willingly is appreciated by clients and they will spread the word about you. Your own clients become your marketing department!

Questions and Inquiries

1. What are some things (talents, skills, abilities, knowledge, material things) of which you have an abundance?

2. What do you give away with no expectation whatsoever of any kind of return?

3. On what occasions do you give in order to manipulate or receive something from another?

4. What will you do to practice "generosity" this week?

LIFE LESSON 26

Stress does not exist outside of you. You are in charge of your stress level and can learn to manage it to your advantage.

MESSAGES

1. You must always cope with stress.
2. Both stressors and stress exist only inside your body/mind.
3. Effectively managing your level of stress is the key to living passionately and healthfully.
4. Coaching your client to more effectively manage stress is a crucial coaching skill.

The objectives for Lesson 26 are: 1) To distinguish between eustress and distress; 2) To learn selected principles of stress-management; 3) To learn practical techniques for coping with unwanted stress in your life.

Framework Needed for Coaching Your Clients

The stress response is a normal, sometimes life-saving, physiological change in your body, designed to energize you to cope with perceived threats. It is often referred to as the flight-or-fight response. This response is a comprehensive physical, mental, and emotional reaction to any internal or external event that we perceive to require immediate action. *Fleeing or fighting* refers to two of the three most common actions used to expend the energy generated by the stress response. The third possible action, which is more akin to our culture, is freezing. Freezing is characterized by a general increase in muscular tension throughout the body, accompanied by muscular rigidity. For example, you are more likely to freeze, as opposed to running or fighting, when a state trooper stops you for speeding.

When the stress response goes off inside you and you use that energy to accomplish what you want, we call it *eustress*. When the stress response remains active for a long period of time or when it goes off—out of old habit—when there is no genuine threat, we call it *distress*. It is estimated that more than 85 percent of the illnesses for which people seek medical treatment are related to distress. Clearly it is to our advantages to learn how to best manage and use stress-response skills.

Identifying those events in your life to which you respond with distress—*stressors*—is important.

You make thousands of internal adjustments and adaptations each day of your life. You usually learn coping mechanisms early, and with time and practice coping with the stressors in your life becomes automatic, an essential skill to smooth functioning and adaptability. Coping mechanisms that are automatic are called unconscious adaptations. You require and use a variety of unconscious adaptations—your continued survival depends on them.

Some coping mechanisms—negative coping mechanisms—come with a high cost. For example, smoking, doing drugs, overeating, or drinking too much alcohol *do* bring immediate relief from stress-related tension or pain. However, any positive effects from these negative coping mechanisms do not last very long and their long-term negative effects can be harmful. When repeated over a long period, they become unconscious habits or addictions.

Exercises and Information

Every person responds differently to the perceived stressors of life. Effective leaders manage their stress levels in specific ways. When you are coaching leaders, the 13 tips below might be very helpful.

> I have had a long, long life full of troubles, but there is one curious fact about them—nine-tenths of them never happened.
> —Andrew Carnegie

How Leaders Manage Their Own Stress

If you clients are leaders of a group, business, corporation, or agency, they are especially prone to high levels of stress. By teaching your clients how an effective leader manages personal stress, you may be able to prevent them from experiencing some kind of physical or mental distress.

Let your clients know that all stress is not bad. Stress only becomes a problem when the stress response goes off when it's not needed, when it stays on longer than what is useful, or when it can't be turned off. You clients can also use stress to motivate and empower them to accomplish tasks, sharpen their thinking, and maintain high levels of energy. The key for them is to learn how to control and manage their stress to maximize performance while avoiding burnout.

Here are thirteen tips your clients can use to manage their stress effectively and creatively:

1. Realize that stress is always an internal physiological response. You are in charge of your stress level, and can learn to manage it to your advantage.

2. View changes and problems as challenges, not as losses or threats. Change is constant. Change is the price we pay for being alive. Search for the opportunities, not the obstacles, inherent in change. Convert the stress of change into the excitement of meeting a new challenge.

3. Have a continuous positive orientation and outlook for yourself and others. Someone once wrote, "The pessimist complains about the wind; the optimist expects it to change; the realist adjusts the sails."

4. Develop flexibility, agility, and tolerance for ambiguity and uncertainty. Ensure flexibility in your approach to stress maintenance by being willing to modify quickly what isn't working.

5. Identify the things you can control and focus your energy and attention on them. Avoid spending time, energy, worry, or thought attending to things over which you have no influence or control.

6. Refuse to get derailed by those who are pessimistic, resistant, or discontent.

7. Take 100 percent responsibility for your stress responses. Failure to take responsibility for your behavior and its consequences decreases your self-confidence and makes you a victim of circumstance (refer to Lesson 20).

8. Refuse to take personally the tensions and conflicts brought about by people around you. Have a community of people who are optimistic, passionate, and oriented around possibility, creativity, and opportunity.

9. Have confidence in your ability to *influence* the events and circumstances around you. You do have an impact, not only with your actions, but also with your thoughts and energy. Success guru, Napoleon Hill wrote, "You have absolute control over but one thing, and that is your thoughts. If you fail to control your own mind, you may be sure you will control nothing else."

10. Take excellent care of yourself physically, mentally, emotionally, and spiritually. Maintaining a balance in all of aspects of your life minimizes your stress and maximizes your health.

11. Frequently debrief with others, giving and receiving feedback that is relevant and important to managing both the risks and possibilities associated with anticipated or desired change.

12. Continually renew and update your knowledge and skills. Never stop learning. Change is continuous and any change, even positive, is stressful. If you are continually learning, you are adequately coping with change.

13. Allow yourself and others the space to experiment with fresh approaches to stress. Encourage the expression of new ideas, solutions, and viewpoints.

> Put your foot upon the neck of the fear of criticism by reaching a decision not to worry about what other people think, do, or say.
> —Napoleon Hill

Negative Coping Mechanisms

Have your clients identify their habitual coping mechanisms for handling stress. Below is a list of *negative* (and often unconscious) coping mechanisms. Following this list is a large selection of *positive* coping methods clients may want to substitute for the negative ones. Invite them to add to the list.

Alcohol. Drinking to change your mood; considering alcohol a "friend" with whom you can relax; drinking to fit in with others.

Tobacco. Smoking to relieve tension or boredom, to fit in with others, or to feel grown-up.

Denial. Pretending nothing is wrong; lying; ignoring any problem or the stressful problem.

Drugs. Abusing coffee, aspirin, street drugs, or prescription medications to relieve or reduce stress.

Overeating. Eating beyond the point of satisfaction; using food to address issues other than hunger, such as boredom, anxiety, discomfort, etc.

Fault-finding. Having a judgmental attitude; complaining; criticizing yourself, others, and the situation to transfer attention away from your own stress.

Illness. Developing a physical problem in order to seek the care of someone else.

Indulging. Staying up late; sleeping in; buying on impulse; wasting time—all to counter the effects of stress.

Passivity. Wishing stress will resolve itself without taking action.

Revenge. Violently acting out your internal feelings of stress.

Stubbornness. Refusing to be wrong or refusing to acknowledge when you make mistakes.

Tantrums. Yelling, moping, pouting, swearing—raging when frustrated.

Withdrawal. Avoiding situations; skipping school or work; keeping your feelings and thoughts to yourself.

Worrying. Fretting over things that aren't important or over which you have no control.

Instructions for your clients: Can you identify your favorite negative coping mechanism(s)? Any of the above may work temporarily for you, but used over a long time, they can destroy your goals, your relationships, your hopes and dreams, your lifestyle, and even your life.

> The reason why worry kills more people than work is that more people worry than work.
> —Robert Frost

Positive Coping Mechanisms

Naturally, there are hundreds of coping methods that are positive in nature and do not exact the heavy toll of negative coping mechanisms. Below are a few positive methods, listed under the categories of mental, physical, spiritual, interpersonal, family, and diversions. If your clients want to manage their stress better, have them pick one or two from each category and practice them until they become automatic.

The list of mental mechanisms includes:

Imagination. Look for humor in your life. Anticipate the future. Daydream, use fantasy or visualize fun, enjoyment, and pleasure. In your mind, create your desired future.

Life planning. Set clear goals for yourself. Plan for the future and design strategies for achieving those goals and plans.

Organization. Take charge of a project. Take charge (responsibility) of your life. Don't let things pile up.

Problem solving. Solve problems by yourself. Seek outside help when you need it. Resolve issues or situations that you habitually tolerate. Tackle problems head-on.

Redefinition. Explore other possible points of view. Look for the positive in every situation. Define the present moment the way it should be. Define a problem as a challenge or opportunity for a new experience or the development of a new skill.

Time management. Practice prioritizing; work smarter, not harder. Delegate your weaknesses to others. Discover and exercise your strengths. Consistently seek more efficient and effective ways to accomplish what you want. Plan time to relax, enjoy yourself, and engage in fun activities.

The list of physical mechanisms includes:

Biofeedback. Learn to listen to the feelings and sensations your body sends you. Come to really know your physical limitations and, if you must exceed them, do so slowly and cautiously.

Exercise. Pursue physical fitness. Fit regular exercise into every day.

Nourishment. Eat only when you're hungry. Stop eating when satisfied. Eat nourishing food for your health. Avoid junk food and all unnecessary drugs (including alcohol, caffeine, and nicotine). Take any vitamin, mineral, or dietary fiber supplements suggested by your physician or nutritionist.

Relaxation. Practice isometric exercises—tensing and relaxing each muscle group in your body. Take a warm bath. Learn the relaxation response and practice it regularly. Listen to soothing music. Design a part of your environment to reflect peacefulness, security, and tranquility. Go into that special place when you want to relax.

Self-care. Energize your work and play. Treat yourself as you would treat a loved child or pet. Strive for self-improvement for the joy of it, and not necessarily to meet some standard or criteria set by others.

Stretching. Take short stretching breaks throughout your day. Learn stretching exercises.

Breathing. Practice breathing exercises, deeply, abdominally, and fully. Learn breath control exercises (panting, holding, timing, etc.).

The list of spiritual mechanisms includes:

Commitment. Involve yourself in a worthy cause. Volunteer some of your time. Invest yourself in a meaningful way. Serve or do someone else a favor. Persist in gaining self-knowledge, growth, goal-attainment, and self-improvement.

Meaning. Find purpose in your life. Create a personal mission statement. Trust the process of life. Generate and nourish hope for your future. Believe in yourself.

> He who has a why to live can bear almost any how.
> —Fredrich Nietzsche

Meditation. Count your blessings. Give thanks. Develop an attitude of gratitude. Share or confess those things about which you feel guilty. Learn mindfulness.

Surrendering. Let go of your problems. Learn to accept the current situation as it is. What exists now . . . *is!* Keep in mind that *everything* changes.

Valuing. Give attention to what you find most valuable. Set priorities and be consistent. Spend your time and energy in ways that meet your values and standards. Use and control your impulses. Develop your own, accurate belief system.

Worship. Share your values, beliefs and feelings with others. Put your faith into action. Celebrate life within a community of caring. Honor your higher power. Recognize the forces operating in the world over which you have no control.

The list of interpersonal mechanisms includes:

Affirmation. Believe in yourself and trust others. Give yourself lots of encouragement and positive, self-affirming statements. Give lots of positive strokes to others as well. Attend to and notice the positive characteristics and qualities you have and the actions you take. Reward yourself.

Assertiveness. Display and state your needs and wants. Learn to ask directly for what you want. Say no with kindness. Be firm when communicating your feelings, thoughts, and opinions (refer to Lesson 23).

Contact. Make new friends. Be a friend to others. Really listen to others and respond from your understanding of their expressed point of view.

Self-expression. Show your feelings. Move your body freely. Exercise and demonstrate your skills and talents. Share your deepest thoughts, feelings, and wishes. Be yourself.

Creating boundaries. Set your own standards and boundaries and let other people know what they are. Accept the boundaries of others. Drop some commitments when you have too many. Under-promise and over-deliver.

Networking. Share desires, projects, and interests with others. Ask for support from family, friends, and acquaintances. Invite others to become involved with you and your activities.

The list of family mechanisms includes:

Balance. Balance the time you spend alone or at work or school with your interactions with family and friends.

Conflict-resolution. Learn conflict-resolving skills that lead to win-win solutions. Intend your conflicts to result in everyone getting what they want. Forgive easily and readily.

Building esteem. Focus on your positive qualities and those of your family members. Acknowledge aloud the things you like or appreciate in your family members.

Flexibility. Be willing to take on new family roles and responsibilities. Become well-versed in many family activities and roles. Remain open to change. Be spontaneous.

Networking. Develop friendships with other families. Make use of the personal and organizational resources available in your community.

Togetherness. Take time to be together, play together, and share time with each other. Build family traditions. Always express heartfelt affection for one another. Limit TV and video games.

The list of diversion mechanisms includes:

Getaways. Spend time alone; daydream; designate a special place where you can be alone; go on a vacation.

Hobbies. Write, paint, remodel, create something, garden, plan and develop projects, engage in sports, learn to play a musical instrument, sing—engage in activities unrelated to your usual ones.

Learning. Take a special class; read; join a club; make learning new things a priority. Never stop acquiring new knowledge.

Music. Play your own instrument. Sing. Dance. Join an orchestra or choral group. Listen to music. Take music lessons.

Playing. Learn new, non-competitive games and play them with friends or family members. Go out with friends; develop a playful attitude; find humor in situations; laugh regularly; go for walks and runs; go dancing.

Working. Engage in meaningful work. Tackle a project unrelated to your usual activity. Keep your mind and body occupied with enjoyable activities.

Sample Coaching Conversation

Client: I am so overwhelmed. There is so much going on with the projects at my company—lots of obligations and then on top of all of that, the computer has been having a temper tantrum.

Coach: (Smiling) Did the computer have the temper tantrum or did you? I know how frustrating technology can be at times. And when that happens on top of the other business stressors, then work can really feel overwhelming and stressful, right?

Client. Right. I could handle a bit of frustration with the computer if I wasn't already overstressed.

Coach: We talked early on in our coaching about how much of the stress in life is chosen by us. Many things that happen to us we do not choose, like car-trouble, plans being changed, weather, etc. but we can choose how we respond to these events. Can you begin to tell me the main stressors that you are experiencing right now, and let's list whether they are from your choices or just circumstantial, ok? I want you to begin to break the stressors down into solvable tasks and take steps to reduce stress and gain a greater sense of control.

Client: That sounds good. Here are some key things that are bugging me: besides the technology frustrations, I have three proposals for conference presentations that have already been accepted and even though the conferences are months away, I know I have to get going on creating the presentation, organizing my thoughts, and working with my marketing consultant on how to leverage those appearances. I am also writing two chapters for new books to be out next year, and the deadline for an article is three months away. Our staff is also redoing our marketing materials, our website, and how our trainings are delivered. We have lots of great ideas, but getting them implemented is the difficulty. That's some of the overwhelm I feel.

Coach: Ok, good. Now take that list and then add to it at home this week, when you can think clearly, perhaps early in the morning. Then, I want you to fax or email me a list of people you could delegate responsibility to, or if you are the one who must complete the task, draw up a timeline to follow to complete it.

Client: Sounds very helpful. I just get bogged down sometimes and feel all the responsibility rests on me.

Coach: Look at the word *responsibility* literally—it means the ability to respond. If you respond to stressors instead of react, you will see more choices of how to handle the event in the moment, rather than let it grow and expand in your mind.

Questions and Inquiries

1. What perceptions do you have that consistently cause your stress level to increase?
2. Do you have a disease or illness directly related to your stress level?
3. What negative coping mechanisms do you regularly use to lower your stress level?
4. What positive coping mechanisms do you use?
5. Can you identify at least five positive methods for coping with stress that you would like to make a permanent and unconscious program in your daily life?

Coaching Summary

The lessons we have offered in Section 4, Living Life with Integrity, are important in that these ingredients to a life filled with integrity are often overlooked or assumed. Just like special ingredients that make or break a gourmet recipe, these lessons are the secret spice that will make your life, and the lives of your clients, extraordinary.

The Lessons

We've highlighted the seven life lessons contained in this section below, along with reminders of how to apply them in your coaching work.

Life Lesson 20

Taking responsibility for all of your actions empowers you, strengthens your autonomy, and lets you consciously create your future. The purpose of coaching is to facilitate in your clients more purposeful and conscious ways of living. While coaching clients on their plans, goals, and intentions, experienced coaches understand that things don't always go according to plan. Most clients need to learn personal responsibility. They need to respond to life in ways that support the results they genuinely desire. Coaching is highly relevant and effective in keeping clients on track when they modify existing habits or make new choices.

Life Lesson 21

Honesty is a much greater achievement than always telling the truth. Being honest means you are authentic in everything you think, say, and do. Being honest is really about being true to yourself through your behavior. Are your clients living authentically? Are they aware of their own "truth" and what is needed to manifest it in their daily lives? Truthful living is authentic living. Authentic life coaching will engage your clients in conversations that help them to become more honest.

Life Lesson 22

Anger is a powerful, useful, and natural emotion. Learn how to harness and manage it, and you increase your personal power. Strong emotions such as anger may be undesirable, but they are not inherently bad. If your clients do not learn to creatively or harmlessly express their anger, it becomes useless and self-defeating. Anger, like the warning light on a car dashboard, serves as a reminder for us to take appropriate action. If clients pay no attention to their anger, or respond inappropriately, their anger will hinder their personal evolution. When your clients recognize and express anger positively, it gives them personal power.

Life Lesson 23

Being assertive is effective and constructive. Being aggressive is ineffective and destructive. This lesson teaches clients the distinction between power and force. Assertiveness is the powerful expression of feelings, desires, or intentions, without intentionally forcing or hurting others. Sometimes assertiveness takes the form of choosing not to say or do anything.

Life Lesson 24

Empathy is the most powerful and effective element in interpersonal relationships. Humans are social creatures; we were meant to be in relationships. Demonstrate to your clients that empathy is an essential element for anyone truly to *be in* any relationship. In order to create an intimate relationship with someone else, empathy is required.

Life Lesson 25

Sharing is the best way to create effective relationships. When we speak of sharing in the coaching paradigm, we are talking about living in and giving freely from a place of abundance rather than a place of lack. Invite your clients to observe how they share, or when they don't. When do they close themselves in and do not share? Authentic life coaching and authentic living require a joyful openness to living and a willingness to share ourselves with others who are important to our lives.

Life Lesson 26

Stress does not exist outside of you. You are in charge of your stress level and can learn to manage it to your advantage. We react stressfully to events in our lives, even positive events. But stressors are like signals—we can make changes to reduce the creation of stress, but most important is our ability to choose how we learn from and respond to stress. Living an authentic, purposeful, fully-engaged life is likely to reduce the accumulation of stress in our lives and head off many stressors that other people assume are part of everyday life. Attitude, action, and accountability are the keys to this life lesson.

Questions for Reflection

1. In what areas of your life are you willing to assume more personal responsibility?
2. What aspects of your life need balancing to optimize your personal integrity (wholeness)?
3. In what ways are you honest and truthful in the contributions to your relationships?
4. Are you completely comfortable with the habitual ways you express your anger?
5. How are you personally assertive in your interpersonal relationships? How could you become more assertive?
6. How can you enhance and strengthen your empathy?
7. What are some of your favorite stress-coping habits? Which to you want to change? Which do you want to develop?

SECTION 5
Achieving Potential

Why should we be in such desperate haste to succeed, and in such desperate
enterprises? If a man does not keep pace with his companions, perhaps
it is because he hears a different drummer.
—Henry David Thoreau

LIFE LESSON 27

Success is a way of thinking, a consciousness. Achieving success is a subjective perception.

M E S S A G E S

1. Success is not a destination, it is a journey.
2. Success is achieving any state with which you are content.
3. The definition of success is highly individualized.
4. Coaching your clients to be successful requires full awareness of *their* definition of success.

The objectives for Lesson 27 are: 1) To clearly distinguish between success as an ongoing journey versus a destination; 2) To learn the *be-do-have* sequence of success; 3) To learn some effective habits that lead to a successful life.

Framework Needed for Coaching Your Clients

Most people define success as either a forthcoming condition at some future point in time, or the achievement of a certain preconceived condition in their lives. The reality is that point or condition is never reached. By the time you arrive at the point you initially labeled as success, you have formed a new perception of where that point or condition is.

We define success as the ongoing expansion and realization of your happiness by the attainment of any states with which you are content. In other words, when you are happy and content with your current state of being, that is success.

We can let circumstances rule us, or we can take charge and rule our lives from within.
—Earl Nightingale

The state with which you are content may not be the same as anyone else's—it all depends on your personal desires and values. Therefore, *success is actually a state of mind*—an individualized positive meaning that one attributes to a specific condition. When clients are content with whatever attained condition they have acquired, an authentic coach considers them to be successful and congratulates them accordingly. Likewise, whenever you are content with your coaching practice, you would define your practice as successful.

In his book, The 7 *Habits of Highly Effective People*, Steven R. Covey reviews a comprehensive search of all the success literature of the past two hundred years. He reports that for the past fifty years or so, something called the Personality Ethic has been very popular. This school of thought is based on the development of skills, techniques, and behaviors—essentially, what *to do* to be a success.

The previous 150 years, however, focused on the Character Ethic—the development of your character. Traits like integrity, humility, simplicity, modesty, and self-discipline were thought to be critical to the creation of success, essentially, who you needed *to be* in order to be successful.

Why the shift? One explanation is that developing personal character takes time, effort, and dedication—not exactly the qualities many people these days are willing to commit to. Right now, everyone seems to be in a hurry, and most people look for shortcuts to results. Therefore, if you believe you can learn a skill or a technique that will more rapidly lead you down the path to success, you may be tempted to take it.

There is a price to pay for taking the route of *doing* prior to *being*. That price is reflected in the hollow question you may ask yourself, "Is this it?" How disappointed would you be if, after reaching the destination that you mapped out and defined as success, you found yourself wondering, "Is this it?"

Perhaps a preferable alternative would be to develop a multifaceted view of success—one that encompasses *being* the best you can be, creating an action plan for what you want in your future, and enjoying all that life has to offer right now.

In his book, *Maximum Achievement*, Brian Tracy writes of six requirements for success*:

1. Peace of mind—freedom from fear, anger, and guilt.
2. Good health and a high level of energy—if we do not have our health or energy, we don't get very much satisfaction from life.

---

*Adapted with the permission of Simon & Schuster Adult Publishing Group from Maximum Achievement: The Proven System of Strategies and Skills That Will Unlock Your Hidden Powers to Succeed by Brian Tracy. Copyright ©1993 by Brian Tracy.

3. Loving relationships—long-term, intimate, mature relationships with other people.

4. Financial freedom—we cannot enjoy life if we're worried about not having enough money.

5. Commitment to worthy goals and ideals—our need for meaning and purpose is the greatest single drive in human nature.

6. A feeling of personal fulfillment or self-actualization—a feeling that we are becoming everything we are capable of becoming.

What is important in Tracy's six-point definition is that all of the requirements have something to do with *who you are*, not with *what you do*.

Once you are the person you want to *be*, and you take actions that support the manifestation of your desired outcomes, only then can your realistically *have* the results you want in life. Lasting success—whatever your definition of success happens to be—always follows this *be-do-have* sequence.

Exercises and Information

Let your clients know that discovering who they are as unique human beings may be the healthiest definition of success in their lives. Since most people remain so focused on events and circumstances outside of themselves, they are often blinded to their own skills and abilities. It is from these internal abilities that all successes arise.

When clients hire you as their life coach, it quickly becomes important that they realize that they are their thoughts, their desires, their actions, their dreams, their habits, and their personality characteristics. Your clients are the best and the worst they choose to be. You need to invite them to shift the sequence of their behavior. For example, one of your clients wants to purchase (*have*) the proper equipment to make his or her business more efficient. The client believes that with the right equipment, he or she will behave (*do*) differently. Then, by changing his or her performance, your client will *be* a better boss. Based on this example, it's clear your client has the sequence of success reversed. Point out to your client that in order to attain lasting success, he or she needs to first ask, "What do I need to modify within me to be a better boss?" and "What changes in my thinking, knowledge, personality, or skills do I need to make?" Once your client becomes aware of the changes required to become a better boss he or she ready to behave differently—and that's all prior to purchasing any equipment.

If clients hire you to coach them toward a more profitable business, the first question you may want to ask is, "Who do you have to become in order to contribute differently to your business so that it generates more income?"

> Your first responsibility is to be the best you can. There's nobody else like you, so why try to be like somebody else?
> —Frank Robinson

Let your clients know that they have the awesome responsiblity *and* the incredible opportunity to create the lives they want. They hold the exclusive power to fill their lives with joy or despair, wealth or poverty, value or insignificance, hatred or love. No one else can create their lives for them. No one else has that power. You and your clients have a whole lifetime to shape your lives to be the best, the happiest, and the most successful.

Sample Coaching Conversation

Coach: So, I read in your client packet and from our first conversation that you want coaching to help your consulting business be more successful, is that right?

Client: Yes. I want to have great clients, to travel to conferences to speak, and have my company make money when I am not there. I want to build a really successful business.

Coach: Tell me how you define success. What would being extremely successful look like for you?

Client: I would have plenty of money, be highly respected by my peers, and be able to take time off to travel to exotic places. To me money gives freedom, and success would imply financial success.

Coach: As a life coach, I do want you to get the success you want, but I'd like to encourage a bigger game. If you became successful in the way you describe, how would you be different? How would a successful life look for you?

Client: The freedom that financial success would give me and my family is the key. I want to be successful in this business so I can live a life with travel, adventure and more time off. Is that possible?

Coach: Many people have done that. Hard work is needed, of course, but working smarter is better than overworking. I like the fact that you see the connection between business success and life success. Who would you have to become to create the success you want?

Client: That is an odd question.

Coach: (Laughing) Hey, that's part of my job . . . to ask odd questions that you don't get asked in other relationships.

Client: Well, I guess I would have to become the successful person I want to be before I achieve the success I want.

Coach: Brilliant insight! I would like to leave you with an inquiry for you to contemplate this week. Don't answer it now, but think about it and write your thoughts about it this week, ok?

> My own view of history is that human beings do have genuine freedom to make choices. Our destiny is not predetermined for us; we determine it for ourselves.
> —Arnold Toynbee

Client: Ok.

Coach: Here is the inquiry: How will you know when you are successful as you describe? What are the descriptors and evidence that will be apparent?

Client: Got it. I will let you know what answers I come up with.

Questions and Inquiries

1. What do you genuinely desire to experience?
2. When you no longer want coaching, how will you be different from when you began?
3. How can you make the greatest difference in your own life?
4. What do you want to create?
5. What is it that you really, really, really, really want?
6. Why do you want it?
7. What is holding you back from getting it?
8. Do you believe you can get it?
9. What motivates you?
10. What do you react to negatively?
11. What do you react to positively?
12. What are your gifts and talents?

> If one advances confidently in the direction of his own dreams and endeavors to lead the life which he has imagined, he will meet with a success unimagined in common hours.
> —Henry David Thoreau

LIFE LESSON 28

Without a vision of your desired future, you allow circumstances to create it for you instead of you creating it yourself.

MESSAGES
1. Keep your dreams in the forefront of your mind.
2. Focusing on your dreams and desires keeps you on track to manifest them in your life.
3. Before you take *any* action, you must first consider the desired outcome.
4. An authentic coach keeps the client's desired outcome apparent at all times.

The objectives for Lesson 28 are: 1) To clearly distinguish between imagining, thinking, envisioning, and reacting; 2) To learn a practical method for generating a powerful, personal vision; 3) To practice creating a personal vision; 4) To understand the value of having a vision of a desired future.

Framework Needed for Coaching Your Clients

Everything that has ever been created by people always begins as an idea, image, or vision in somebody's mind. Successful people keep that idea or vision in the forefront of their minds. Less successful people focus their attention on the immediate actions they perceive to be appropriate or necessary.

Many people move through their lives by simply reacting to the circumstances in which they find themselves, rather than consciously choosing how they want to function.

Unconsciously reacting to events in your life may make living easier and smoother. After all, you don't want to have to consciously think about every little action you take; certainly in emergency situations, you want to be able to react automatically. But keep in mind that by reacting unconsciously you give away your personal power to determine the nature and quality of your lifestyle. Your lifestyle merely becomes a set of habitual behaviors you have learned and unconsciously engage in—behaviors that people or events outside you usually trigger.

To *attain* any consciously chosen outcome in your future, you first need to have a picture in your mind of that outcome. That picture may be very fleeting, but it must be there. Otherwise, you never engage in the behaviors necessary for you to arrive there.

As stated in the previous lesson, to begin creating your desired lifestyle, you must first begin with a vision of how you want to *be*, followed by what you want to *do*, and then what you want the results of your actions to be. The clearer your vision and the more you consciously picture the outcome(s) in your mind, the more likely you are to engage in behaviors that support the creation of that lifestyle.

> Both success and failure are largely the results of habit.
> —Napoleon Hill

Exercises and Information

One of the principles governing how you design and envision your future is: You can't hit a target you cannot see. Ask your clients, "How clearly do you see the desired outcomes for your future way of being? For your future lifestyle? For your relationships to me, as your coach, as well as to others? Are you blindly shooting arrows, hoping to hit a desired target? Are you aware of the targets you want to aim for in your future?"

While generating a clear vision of your desired future is a natural human skill, it also can be learned and strengthened through practice. Here is one exercise for enhancing the ability of your clients to envision their future.

Creating a Vision

Instruct your clients as follows: Begin the visualization process by completely relaxing your body and quieting your mind. Take several deep breaths. Then, incorporating all five of your senses, imagine what you want your life to be like in the future. *See* yourself functioning in a manner consistent with who you want to be. *Hear* yourself speaking as you would if you were already living the lifestyle you want. *Feel* the emotions you would feel if you were happily living the way you desire. Even *taste and smell* how you would like it to be. For example, if you want to live in the mountains, see the house you would be living in; hear the breeze blowing in the pine trees surrounding the house; feel the comfort and warmth of sitting in the living room; smell the fresh scent of pine; taste the food you are eating while looking out the picture window.

Continue to imagine who you want to be in order to have what you desire. What are you like? What skills are you practicing? How are you thinking? What is your attitude toward your lifestyle? Who are you relating to and how are you relating?

Next, vividly imagine *why* you want this lifestyle. Consider appreciating what is required to create this lifestyle, your reasons for wanting it, the happiness or joy related to both the process of creating your vision and the outcomes contained in your envisioned future.

After you have engaged in this visualization process for several minutes, convert what you imagine into a concise *written* description—in the present tense—of what, who, when, where, and especially why you have envisioned this future. Writing a description of your dream transforms your vision into a physical representation, in symbolic form, of your vision. You might even create a collage of pictures or phrases that depict your desired lifestyle. Put this collage in a prominent place where you will see it every day.

Share your vision with trusted people. When you verbalize your vision, you create it once again in words, making it manifest in sound patterns, outside your mind and into the physical world. Language is the second creation of your vision in the external world.

Finally, memorize your written description of your envisioned future. When you can easily recite your written vision from memory, you know you have programmed it into your subconscious. Like the hard drive on a computer, your subconscious mind drives you to make happen that which has been programmed. Without consciously thinking about it, if you *do* know where you want to end up, you will automatically engage in behavior that supports you getting there.

> The essence of success is that it is never necessary to think of a new idea oneself. It is far better to wait until somebody else does it, and then to copy him in every detail, except his mistakes.
> —Aubrey Menen

Sample Coaching Conversation

Following up with the same client as in the previous lesson.

Coach: How was the exercise on the inquiry about success?

Client: It was very interesting. I wrote about how I want my life to be in the future, but I also realized how much success I have in my life right now. What I want in the future is very compelling, however. I don't want it out of desperation or out of having a big ego. I feel compelled to have my picture of success.

Coach: I am so glad you talked about the picture you have of your success. With your permission, I want to coach about creating a compelling vision of your desired future. If you have a clear vision of that future, it is more likely to occur and the steps you take now will move you toward that vision. Of course you can amend it at any time, but it is your future—not mine, not your husband's, not your friends'. It is what you really want.

Client: How do we do this?

Coach: From the work you did last week with the inquiry of success, I would like you to create a descriptive vision of that point in time, when you are that successful person. Speak about it in *first person* as if you are there in that future place and time.

Client: Ok, how do I start?

Coach and client then use the remaining conversation time to create the client's vision. The coach does not speak for the client, but asks questions to evoke the client's response.

> The talent of success is nothing more than doing what you can do well; and doing well whatever you do, without a thought of fame.
> —Henry Wadsworth Longfellow

Questions and Inquiries

1. What do you want your lifestyle to be like in the future?
2. *Why* do you want to create this particular style of living?
3. Who do you have to be in order to create this lifestyle?
4. With whom will you create this?
5. From whom do you need assistance to generate such a lifestyle?
6. For whom will you create this? Yourself? Others? The world? History?
7. How will you and those around you benefit from this lifestyle?
8. When do you want this lifestyle to manifest—A year from now? Ten years? Before you die?
9. How will you feel about yourself once you are living this lifestyle?
10. Upon successfully creating this lifestyle:
    Your physical environment is . . .
    Your emotional environment is . . .
    Your intellectual environment is . . .
    Your social environment is . . .
    Your spiritual environment is . . .

LIFE LESSON 29

Identifying a great number of personal goals and then writing them out is critical to your success in life.

MESSAGES

1. In order to get to where you want to be in the future, you must have clear goals.

2. Goals are different from visions, hopes, wishes, and dreams.

3. Set long-term, short-term, and immediate goals.

4. Always write down your goals.

The objectives for Lesson 29 are: 1) To clearly distinguish between purpose, mission, vision, and goals; 2) To learn how to set your own goals and how to attain them; 3) To clearly identify some of the reasons your clients may be reluctant to set goals; 4) To practice creating a list of life goals.

Framework Needed for Coaching Your Clients

In 1963, Harvard Business School asked one hundred freshmen if they each had a written list of the goals they wanted to attain during their lifetime. Only seven students said they did. Twenty years later, a follow-up survey showed that only 10 percent of those original one hundred had successfully attained what they wanted in life. Remarkably, all seven of the students with written goals were in that 10 percent.

The importance of having personal goals cannot be overemphasized!

Personal goals are different from a personal vision (refer to Lesson 28). They are different from a personal life-purpose or mission statement. Goals are specific attainments that you choose and desire to create, usually relevant to your purpose and/or your personal mission. Your goals are not identical with your purpose, however. Ideally, goals are derived from your vision of what you want your life to be like, but they do not have to be.

Exercises and Information

Let your clients know that their goals can be large or small. They can be relevant to personal development, achievements, personality qualities, or almost any area of life. It is best to have written goals for each day. Every evening, have your clients take five to ten minutes to write down their goals for the next day. Once a week (perhaps Sunday evenings), they should write out their goals for the next week. Once a month, they write out their goals for the next month. Once a year (perhaps January 1st), they write out their goals for the following year. They can take each of these goals from their Life List of Goals (see exercise below).

Your clients may be reluctant to set personal goals, and sometimes the coaching process for goal-setting meets resistance. Clients may resist for a variety of reasons:

> It is impossible to escape the impression that people commonly use false standards of measurement—that they seek power, success and wealth for themselves and admire them in others, and they underestimate what is of true value in life.
> —Sigmund Freud

- They don't believe goals have an important affect on their future.
- They don't take seriously their own power to design their future.
- They believe they are unworthy of happiness or fulfillment.
- They do not take responsibility for the nature and quality of their lives.
- They don't know how to set goals.
- They are afraid of how others might react to their goals and their attainment.
- They fear failing to attain the goals they set.
- They are ashamed of the goals they set in the past that they did not reach.

Identifying some of their reasons for not setting goals is crucial for your resistant clients—and for the coach to be aware of alternative strategies is equally important. For example, if a client is afraid to fail, you might give the client the following message, "It is impossible to succeed without failing. But initial failure at any new endeavor is a valuable lesson to be learned. It is critical to your eventual success."

Writing their goals on paper is a crucial exercise for your clients. As stated in the previous lesson, the process of writing moves the goals outside of your clients' minds for the first time. It translates abstract thoughts or images into physical reality. By memorizing what they've written, your clients can program their goals in their subconscious. They can also revisit and revise their list of goals on a regular basis.

Below is an example of the list of goals rocket pioneer John Goddard made for himself (in Cox, 1998). This can serve as a jumping-off place for you to write your own "Life List of Goals."

My Life List

In 1940, when John Goddard was fifteen years old, he overheard his parents' friend say, "I wish I were John's age again. I would do things differently." Something about that remark seemed to have touched a nerve inside the boy, because he took a blank sheet of paper from his notebook and wrote the words, *My Life List* across the top. He began writing down goals. The list grew to 127 items. When he was seventy five years old, he had accomplished all but fifteen of those original goals.

Here are three examples in each of his categories:

Explore
1. Nile River
2. Amazon River
3. Congo River

Study primitive cultures in
1. The Congo
2. New Guinea
3. Brazil

Climb
1. Mount Everest
2. Mount Aconcagua, Argentina
3. Mount McKinley

Photograph
1. Iguaçu Falls, Brazil

> Are you not ashamed of heaping up the greatest amount of money and honor and reputation, and caring so little about wisdom and truth and the greatest improvement of the soul?
> —Socrates

2. Victoria Falls, Rhodesia
3. Sutherland Falls, New Zealand

Explore underwater
1. Fiji Islands
2. The Bahamas
3. Okefinokee and Everglades

Visit
1. North and South Poles
2. Great Wall of China
3. Panama and Suez Canals

Swim in
1. Lake Victoria
2. Lake Superior
3. Lake Tanganyika

Accomplish
1. Become an Eagle Scout
2. Dive in a submarine
3. Land on and take off from an aircraft carrier

(There were more than forty additional goals in this category!)

> Success seems to be largely a matter of hanging on after others have let go.
> —William Feather

Once your clients have completed their Life List of Goals, their next step is to prioritize them and give them a time frame. They should do this by picking out the goals they want to attain in the next year, the next six months, the next month, the next week, and tomorrow. Then coach them on how to design a *written plan* for the actions they will need to take and/or the preparations they will need to make to attain their earliest scheduled goal(s). Ensure that clients stay focused on their goals for the next year. Have them make a poster-sized collage of pictures and phrases that represent the manifestation of their goals.

As their life coach, you must also make certain that your clients persist in activities that are supportive of their goal attainment. Have your clients revise or add to their goals every January 1st for the upcoming year. When they have attained a listed goal, encourage them to put a check mark beside it or make a whole new list of completed goals and keep it visible. This not only reinforces their desire to reach other goals they have set, but it also demonstrates and exemplifies their success at goal-attainment.

Goal-aware and a goal-oriented people have a much greater chance of fulfilling their desires during their lifetime.

Stepping Stones to Goal Attainment

1. Clearly envision what you want. Imagine your desired future.
2. Intensify your desire. Make the manifestation of your vision a personal, burning desire within.
3. Write down your desired outcomes. Rewrite them regularly.
4. Identify the personal benefits you will derive from your goal attainment.
5. Identify the gap between where you are now and where you want to be when you have attained your goal(s).
6. Develop a strategy that clearly defines a starting point, some progress markers, and how you will be different when you have attained your goal.
7. Make clear choices relevant to your strategy.
8. Write down anticipated time frames for reaching progress markers and deadlines. Work backward from the accomplishment of your goal to the present.
9. Identify anticipated obstacles and hindrances to goal attainment. Plan how you will address them.
10. Gather as much information as you can about how to attain your goals. Talk to others who have accomplished what you want and imitate them.
11. Write a list of all the people you will need to assist you directly or indirectly in attaining what you want. No one ever achieves anything in isolation.
12. Stay focused on your desired outcome and the benefits to be derived from goal attainment.
13. Never quit! Never give up! It's your life. Never stop creating it!

Sample Coaching Conversation

A continuing conversation with the same client in the previous two lessons.

Client: Ok, I have done lots of writing and thinking about my vision of a successful future. Did you read the visioning paragraph I sent you via email?

Coach: Yes I did. Great work. Now we will work today on creating the details of your desired future and begin to create a number of clear and achievable written personal goals.

Client: Great. Let's go.

Coach: A technique I learned from one of my mentors is to write a specific goal on a 3 x 5 note card and then we will fill in the details in a prescribed manner. You can amend this method to what works for you, but do you want to try it?

Client: Sure. Let's do it.

Coach: Ok. I want you to get a pack of one hundred note cards. Then, holding it vertically write a goal in the middle that is part of your vision. One card for each goal, OK? Then in the upper-right corner, write A, B, or C for the relative importance of this goal. If it is critical, it is an A; less critical, but important, it is a B, and so on. Then in the upper-left, make a note of key people or resources to help you meet this goal. On the bottom of the card, still holding it vertically, write the timeline specific to this goal. Do this on each card, for each goal. On the back of the card, you can put the category of the goal, such as wealth, health, fun, finances, etc. Sound doable?

Client: Yes. I got it.

> We can do anything we want to do if we stick to it long enough.
> —Helen Keller

The coach and client continue in the weeks to come to refine these goal cards and to set measurable steps with each goal that lead to the manifestation of the vision and the success the client desires.

Questions and Inquiries

1. What are the five most important values you have for your life?
2. What are the three most important aspirations you have right now?
3. If you knew you only had six months to live, how would you spend your time? What would you like to do between now and then?
4. What have you always wanted to do, but were afraid to attempt?
5. What kind of activities do you enjoy most? Which ones give you the greatest satisfaction?

It is the chiefest
point of
happiness that
a man is willing to
be what he is.
—Desiderius
Erasmus

6. If you had all the money you wanted, how would you spend your time?

7. If you positively knew that you could not fail, what would you attempt?

LIFE LESSON 30
Strategizing is a valuable skill essential to reaching your goals.

MESSAGES

1. There is an important distinction between a plan and a strategy.
2. Strategic planning is the precursor to success.
3. Coach the development of an effective strategy, and your coaching becomes more effective and efficient.

The objectives for Lesson 30 are: 1) To distinguish between purpose, vision, planning, and strategizing; 2) To understand the importance and benefits of strategizing; 3) To learn specific techniques to developing the strategies of your clients.

Framework Needed for Coaching Your Clients

Strategies are the abstract ideas about how you are going to get something accomplished. A strategy:

- Answers the question of how you are going to attain a goal or outcome;
- Defines the nature of the actions needed to create a desired outcome effectively and efficiently;
- Reflects who is going to do the work involved in attaining the results you desire.

A *strategy* differs from a *plan*. A plan is what you generate in order to identify, organize, and schedule the time, energy, and resources you think you need to complete a project. A strategy is *how* you are going to implement the plan. Without strategies, plans tend to lose focus. If you devise a good strategy, often the plan becomes quite obvious.

A strategy is also not the same as a purpose. Your purpose usually defines *why* you are doing what you want to do.—the motivation behind your actions. The best strategy is one that is customized to fit your own personal needs and desires.

A final distinction to be made is that a vision is not a strategy. A vision is an imagined outcome—what you picture in your mind as possible. It is often an image in your mind of how you want your future to be. A strategy specifies *how* you are going to get there.

A clear strategy is how you approach your goal with the highest amount of efficiency and the least amount of wasted energy. When you implement a strategy, you may be only indirectly dealing with a goal. More likely, you are working on the best way to approach a specific outcome. You may think about your relationships to others around you. You may be positioning yourself with respect to your environment, your resources, your plan, and your own approach to creating the results you want. Your strategy defines your *approach* to these areas. Personal success requires at least three elements: the person(s), the goal, and the strategy—referred to as the *who*, the *what*, and the *how*.

Developing a strategy saves you time, effort, energy, and often money. Correct strategies always expand your results. Thomas Leonard, the founder of Coach University, once wrote a paper for his students in which he stated, "Think of Amazon.com. Their original goal was to be the largest seller of books and their *strategy* to achieve that goal was to use the Internet as their storefront. The strategy of using the Internet has proven brilliant. It has expanded their goals so that now Amazon offers music, videos, gifts, software, and who knows what else! Their strategy became even more important than their original goal."

Purposes, visions, missions, goals, objectives, and plans are relatively useless without accompanying strategies. You may actually achieve these things without a strategy, but in the process you will be wasting time and energy, deviating from your chosen path, feeling frustrated by the slowness of your progress, and even prone to getting completely off track.

There are many, effective strategies for virtually any situation in your life. The key is to discover—or develop—the one that best fits your desired outcome. Probably the best method to discover the most effective strategy for your own

> Our plans miscarry because they have no aim. When a man does not know what harbor he is making for, no wind is the right wind.
> —Seneca

success attainment is to find someone who has already accomplished what you want. Go talk to that person or imitate what he or she did.

Exercises and Information

All strategies are never identical. Each must be made relevant to the specific outcomes you desire. Below are some general guidelines for assisting your clients to design personal strategies.

> The significant problems we face today cannot be solved at the same level of think we were at when we created them.
> —Albert Einstein

Ten Tips for Designing Strategies

1. Work with your clients to identify the personal and situational constraints that are involved in their written plan. Can they minimize the limitations created by those constraints?
2. Clients need to determine whether their current ways of functioning or their current strategies actually address the constraints (Tip 1 above) that hinder their ability to create their desired results.
3. Encourage your clients to talk to others about their strategies, especially those who have already accomplished what your clients want to do.
4. Ask your clients to identify people who already possess the skills—ones that your clients don't have—needed to implement their strategy, and invite those people to work with them as a team to implement their strategy.
5. Clients need to identify their own core competencies, as well as those needed to implement their strategies.
6. Encourage your clients to ask others to present strategies or modifications that might enhance their strategies.
7. Ask your clients to consider their strategy from the point of view of an outsider, one who is not involved with its implementation or outcome, to gain a fresh perspective.
8. Clients need to communicate their strategic action plan to those affected by its implementation.
9. Clients should communicate regularly with everyone involved in the implementation of the strategy. Ensure that your clients make strategic course corrections based on feedback from all involved.

10. Clients need to recognize and reward all participants who helped in their strategic implementation.

Sample Coaching Conversation

Coach: Today, I read in your coaching session prep form that you wanted some coaching on specific steps and strategies to get to your goals for your life and business. That's great, because our coaching is about developing multiple strategies, or multiple action plans (maps). What are some of the strategies you have thought about to achieve your various goals?

Client: One is that every morning I look at my vision statement and then look at the goals for each area. That seems to help me stay focused and motivated maintain action.

Coach: That's great. Let's take one of the goals and look at multiple strategies for it, ok?

Client: How about the book? I really want to get that done in twelve months.

Coach: And what strategies do you already think will work?

Client: Well, there are nine chapters plus the introduction and references, so I thought a chapter a month is a good goal. Then I thought of taking each chapter and breaking it down into sections.

Coach: Good ideas. Now, when will you do this specifically? What discipline strategy would be helpful?

Client: I know my energy and mind are best in the early morning when it's quiet and private. So I want to do my writing in the morning, about two hours a day. I can even do that on Saturdays without interrupting the entire weekend.

Coach: Great awareness. That is very good. Any other strategies that could be added to help you complete this book.

Client: No. What else?

Coach: I offer this for your consideration. How about if you send your chapters as you complete them to some friends or colleagues who are willing to review them as you progress. They will help you know how it is read, what is unclear, or what is missing for them as a reader.

Client: That's good. I know a couple who would be thrilled to see me complete this book.

Coach and client continue to work on creating several strategies for each goal. The more possible strategies the better. Then the client can choose from several. If only one strategy is created, the chance of failure and frustration is greater.

Questions and Inquiries

1. What is the most creative and efficient way to make _____ happen?
2. What is the smartest or most clever way to create _____?
3. What is a better way to accomplish what I want, other than how it has been accomplished before?
4. What might be an unconventional way to accomplish a similar outcome?
5. What is *my way* for doing what would create my success at _____?
6. What would happen if we reversed the process, turned it around or upside down, did it backwards, or looked at it from the reverse angle like a mirror image?

> Nothing is more terrible than activity without insight.
> —Thomas Carlyle

LIFE LESSON 31
The attitude you adopt determines whether you are successful in creating a lifestyle you enjoy.

MESSAGES

1. Your attitude is the position you adopt relevant to any situation.
2. Choose your attitudes wisely.
3. Your attitude is the context into which all your life experiences fall.
4. Coach with a positive attitude toward life and toward developing one in your clients.

The objectives for Lesson 31 are: 1) To understand the four possible life positions; 2) To learn the benefits derived from maintaining a positive mental attitude (PMA); 3) To learn how to develop your own positive mental attitude.

Framework Needed for Coaching Your Clients

In aeronautics, *attitude* is defined as the position of an aircraft relative to a given point of reference, usually ground level. In psychology, *attitude* is a manner of acting, feeling, or thinking that demonstrates one's own disposition, opinion, or emotional state. In coaching, an attitude combines both of these definitions. For coaches, an attitude is the mental and emotional position one adopts relative to a given reference point, person, or situation that reflects how the client thinks, feels, or acts.

If you adopt a positive attitude toward life, you are more likely to create positive outcomes. Likewise, if you adopt a negative attitude, you are more likely to generate negative results.

There is a well-known aphorism: "Success attracts success while failure attracts more failure." Certainly, when you strive for success with a PMA, you are better able to attain it, and being paralyzed by failure attracts further failure.

When you put your mind to work with a PMA and a general belief in the positive outcome you desire, you are guided toward creating whatever your definition of success might be. Conversely, if you fill your mind with negative thoughts and fears, you stop anticipating what the outcome *might* be and inadvertently attract the very outcome you wanted to avoid.

Exercises and Information

Transactional Analysis (TA) is a theoretical system of psychotherapy and applied communication created by the late Eric Berne. TA postulates that people adopt only four "life positions" vis-à-vis others. These four life positions or attitudes clients can adopt with respect to themselves in relation to other people. The four positions are: "I am okay, and you are too; I'm okay, and you are not okay; I'm not okay, and you are okay; I'm not okay and neither are you." During any given time period, people might move from one position to another. Usually, clients have their favorite life position and when they are functioning from it, they will likely behave in predictable ways.

As a life coach, you may want to familiarize yourself with the information charted below. When clients display the behavior outlined below in any of the four quadrants, their attitude or life position they have adopted will become apparent.

> A positive mental attitude (PMA) is the single most important principle of the science of success!
> —Napoleon Hill

LIFE-POSITION CHART

Life Position #1—I'm of value, you are too (+ +)

Common Interpersonal Dynamic	Let's get on with . . . our relationship, our lives.
Usual Personal Action	Become your best. Act in your best interests first, then the best interest of others. Succeed. Become a "winner."
Common Phrases	Thank you. I appreciate what you do. I like you. Let's get on with it.
Usual Outcomes	Joy, excitement, fulfillment, gratification, enthusiasm for being alive.
Use of Time	Use time well; spend time in contact with others; make time for what's important to you.
Extreme Position	Live. Grow. Create what you want. Implacable optimism.

Life Position #2—I'm of value, you are not valuable (+ −).

Common Interpersonal Dynamic	Get rid of . . . you, the problem.
Usual Personal Action	Crusader. Fight against. Destroy. Throw away.
Common Phrases	If it weren't for . . . (you, the situation, others). Go away. Leave me alone. I wish you'd change. I want them out of my life.
Usual Outcomes	Lose relationship. Anger. Fury. Frustration. Aggression against.
Use of Time	"Kill" time.
Extreme Position	Rage and violence against. Homicide.

Life Position #3—I'm not of value, and you are (− +).

Common Interpersonal Dynamic	Get away from . . . you, or the situation.
Usual Personal Action	Lose. Run away from. Escape. Fail.
Common Phrases	I don't know. You know better than I do. I don't care. I don't want anything from . . ."
Usual Outcomes	Embarrassment, shame, disgust, emptiness, depression, boredom.
Use of Time	Pass time. Wait for time to pass.
Extreme Position	Self-deprecation. Violence against self. Suicide.

Life Position #4—I'm not of value, and neither are you (− −).

Common Interpersonal Dynamic	Get nowhere with . . . you.
Usual Personal Action	Needy. Poor. Indigent. Dependent. Helpless.
Common Phrases	Why bother? Who cares? I can't and you can't either. We're helpless. We are victims.
Usual Outcomes	Humiliation, passivity, disorientation, feeling alienated and alone, nothing is accomplished,
Use of Time	Mark time (maintain the status quo). Waste time.
Extreme Position	Emotional withdrawal. Insanity. Denial of reality.

> It is our attitude toward events, not the events themselves, which we can control.
> —Epicetus

When your clients adopt attitudes of "okay-ness" about themselves, they are exhibiting PMAs and self-concepts about who they are. When they interact with others who have PMAs, they are most likely to create relationships that enhance not only their lives, but the lives of those with whom they interact.

If your clients adopt positive attitudes about themselves, but they view *others* negatively, they tend to believe they would be better off without others.

When your clients adopt negative attitudes about themselves, they become their own worst critics. They treat themselves shabbily and invite others to treat them in the same way. If, at the same time, they view others positively, they will try to distance themselves from them. If, however, your clients see others in the same negative way they see themselves, any personal relationships they might develop will be based on mutual negativity and will justify their resistance to getting anywhere in life.

No one succeeds at anything in life without relationships! The nature and quality of your relationships determine the nature and quality of your life. The only life position or attitude you can adopt that ensures positive relationships is, "I'm of value and you are too!"—and that is a PMA about yourself *and* everyone else.

> Nothing is life is to be feared. It is only to be understood.
> —Marie Curie

Benefits of a Positive Mental Attitude

When your clients take charge of their mental and emotional lives and develop and maintain a PMA, they generate many positive rewards for themselves. In Napoleon Hill's classic book, *Think and Grow Rich*, he lists ten rewards that your clients can reasonably expect to gain if they maintain a PMA:

1. A success consciousness, which attracts only the circumstances that make for success.
2. Sound health, both physical and mental.
3. Financial independence.
4. A labor of love in which to express yourself.
5. Peace of mind.
6. Applied faith, which makes fear impossible.
7. Enduring friendships.
8. Longevity and a well-balanced life.
9. Immunity from self-limitation.
10. The wisdom to understand yourself and others.

The penalties of a negative mental attitude can include:

- Mental and physical ailments.
- Self-limitations that trap you in mediocrity.
- Fear and all its destructive consequences.
- Hatred of the means by which you support yourself.
- Many enemies and few friends.
- Worry.
- Victimization by negative influences you encounter.
- Subjection to the will of others.

What choices will you make? What choices will you encourage your clients to make? Your clients can fill their minds with negative thinking, or they can develop and maintain a positive mental attitude. If they choose the latter, how might they go about it?

Developing Your Clients' PMAs

How can you catalyze a PMA in your clients? Of course, the choice is always up to your clients—they hold the power to develop a PMA or not. When a client does want to develop a PMA and asks you for coaching, what can you do? Below are some time-tested ways to develop a PMA. Given the unique personal histories of your clients, you may want to customize the following principles to each client as you see fit:

- Discover what your clients really want most in life, and, as a team, relentlessly pursue it.
- Have your clients help others attain goals that are similar to their own.
- Ask your clients to identify who they feel is the most successful person in the entire world and emulate him or her in every way.
- Mutually determine what kind of resources your clients needs to attain success.
- Have your clients think big—but they need to keep in mind that greed, more than anything else, has destroyed the most ambitious people.
- After your clients learn what they can from their errors, tell them to forget all the mistakes and failures of the past by focusing attention on their current situation and their desired future.
- Make certain your clients write a plan of action, then, implement the plan.
- Your clients need to fill their minds with positive affirmations about themselves, others, and their future.
- Help your clients to make a daily habit of saying or doing something that makes someone else feel better or more important.
- Your clients need to realize they always have a choice about how to respond to any situation. They should always choose to respond positively.
- Encourage your clients to contact and speak with anyone they know they have unjustly offended or hurt, and then offer sincere apologies and ask for forgiveness.

- Encourage your clients to replace bad habits with new, alternative ones that work better for them.
- Make certain your clients remain focused on their desired outcome.
- Your clients need to avoid toxic relationships—and substances—and close their minds to anyone who wants to exert a negative/destructive influence on them or those they love.
- Your clients should avoid self-pity, which is the classic destroyer of self-reliance and self-confidence. Your clients need to believe that they are the only people upon whom they can (and should) depend at all times.
- Make certain your clients realize they can never control or change others. They can only control and change themselves.
- Help your clients understand that personal power does not come from possession of money or material things alone.
- Encourage your clients to live in a style that best fits their physical, emotional, and spiritual needs.
- Help your clients develop an attitude of gratitude. They should keep a gratitude journal and make a minimum of five entries a day. This will attune their minds to attract the situations and outcomes they desire.
- Your clients need keep their bodies fit; their minds will follow suit.
- Your clients should learn to like people just as they are. They need to keep an open mind to all subjects and toward all people, no matter what their appearance, color, creed, or lifestyle.
- Your clients need to abstain from negative conversations, especially gossip or tearing down others.
- Make certain your clients know and fully accept that love is the finest medication for human bodies, minds, and souls. Love changes the entire chemistry of the body and our mental attitudes. It also extends the space we occupy in the hearts of others.
- Help clients *believe in their own ability to be free* and to exercise free choice.

The development and maintenance of a positive mental attitude is important for you and your clientele. Indeed, a PMA is crucial to all personal achievement and success. More than any other personal quality, the nurturing of a PMA empowers you to create a genuinely successful lifestyle and a genuinely successful *you*!

Sample Coaching Conversation

Coach: I want to do a *coaching checkup*. How is it going overall with your desired outcomes in your business and your personal life? You seem a bit overwhelmed these last few weeks.

Client: I am. My business seems to have slowed; there have been personnel difficulties, website challenges, and other frustrations. It just is not as fun as it was in the beginning.

Coach: So, how is all this frustration affecting you mindset or attitude.

Client: My attitude right now is one of fear, frustration, and mild anxiousness.

Coach: This is not a common pattern for you. In the time I have known you, you almost always put a positive spin on everything. What has worked for you in the past when chaos erupts?

Client: Well, I always tackle the things I can change and roll with the ones I can't. But right now, it seems more stressful than usual. However, your question makes me think that it is only a matter of perceived overwhelm and I can tackle the tasks at hand, one at a time, and start to *clear the clutter*, so to speak.

Coach: Right. And you don't have to do it all yourself. Remember delegation? You have people who can help you. And the other thing I want you to know is the *position or attitude* you take greatly affects your behaviors and your emotional reactions. How could you shift your thinking to take a different position than you currently have?

Client: Good point! I know when I have an *attitude of gratitude* for what is going well and a more positive outlook on how I want things to be, then positive change seems to occur.

Coach: That is one of the simple truths of life that we all need to be reminded of from time to time.

Client: Thanks. I will consciously shift my position and attitude about all this and start doing what I can, and getting help from others when I need it.

> To be without some of the things you want is an indispensable part of happiness.
> —Bertrand Russell

Questions and Inquiries

1. On a daily basis, how much time do you spend in each of the four life positions?
2. What is your favorite life position?
3. How does your life position affect your relationships?

4. What kinds of self-talk will enhance your positive mental attitude?

5. What attitude(s) to you want to modify or replace as a result of our coaching?

LIFE LESSON 32
Your level of commitment is absolutely critical to your long-term success and achievement.

MESSAGES

1. When you are truly committed, your creation of outcomes is self-supported.

2. Genuine commitment is the necessary ingredient for accomplishing anything in life.

3. Authentic life coaching requires that you be committed to the realization of *your clients'* desired outcomes.

The objectives for Lesson 32 are: 1) To clearly distinguish between commitment and involvement; 2) To learn how to increase the level of commitment of your clients; 3) To learn and use methods for maintaining a high commitment level.

Framework Needed for Coaching Your Clients

Success is usually determined by how committed you are to the attainment of your desired objectives. Until you are committed, you maintain a "go half-way" mentality. You may become involved in your success—you may even strongly wish for your desired outcomes—but unless you are *committed* to your success, you will likely give up when confronted with the first obstacle or setback.

Your subconscious mind is extremely powerful in generating energy for your use. Your subconscious mind is the source for all the enthusiasm and excitement you feel when you begin to move progressively toward accomplishing your goals. In his book, *Maximum Achievement*, Brian Tracy writes that "to generate this motivation, your superconscious mind requires *clear, specific goals to which you are completely committed*" before it can release ideas and energy for goal attainment.

Not only does a high level of commitment call for your mind to produce personal motivational energy, it also powerfully attracts others to contribute to your endeavor.

Fear is the primary reason for a lack of commitment: fear of failure; fear of succeeding; fear of your own incompetence; fear of losing your identity; fear of rejection; fear of personal abandonment. Regardless of the nature of the fear, when you lack commitment to any goal, the goal is weakened and the motivational energy to continue the pursuit of success is lessened. This general weakening predisposes you to lose your goal-attainment altogether. If you want to increase your level of commitment, eliminate any and all fear pertaining to the successful achievement of your desired outcomes. The best way to minimize your fear is to stay focused on the clear goal you want to attain.

> The three great essentials to achieve anything worthwhile are first, hard work; second, commitment or stick-to-itiveness; third, common sense.
> —Thomas Edison

Exercises and Information

All your clients need to be committed not only to the coaching process, they also need to commit themselves to the attainment of their coaching goals.

Increasing the Commitment Level of Your Clients

The motivation and energy of your clients toward goal-attainment increases when their desired outcomes serve a personally felt need. For example, when we need food, we are motivated to seek out and eat food. Our *need* is hunger. When the need is strong, the motivation is strong, and the level of commitment is raised. So, if your clients really *need* what they desire to have, they will more likely commit themselves to its attainment (as well as to your coaching).

When your clients don't really need something, they will not focus their energy or time on reaching their desired goal. No matter how much your clients say they want a specific outcome from coaching, if they don't perceive a real need for the outcome, they will be less committed to its attainment and less committed to coaching for its realization.

When clients increase their perceived needs to the point at which their successful achievement becomes a burning desire, and they believe attaining that achievement is critical to their well-being, they will become highly committed to do whatever it takes to be successful.

The journey to success begins with the desire your clients show for it. Share with your clients some of the suggestions below for increasing their desire *and* their level of commitment:

- Write down and regularly review your goals.
- Regularly remind yourself of the outcomes you desire.
- Regularly review the benefits of attaining those desired outcomes.
- Surround yourself with pictures depicting your successful attainment of the results you want.
- Believe in yourself and in your ability to be successful.
- Write out time frames for marking your progress.
- Reward yourself for reaching the milestones that mark your progress.
- Identify possible obstacles and design strategies to overcome them.
- Learn from other people how you can most efficiently reach your goals.
- Devise a plan.
- Create several alternative strategies for implementing the plan.
- Take actions that support the creation of your desired outcome(s).
- Persist.
- Persist.
- Never quit.
- Persist.

If your clients commit themselves to these activities, their success is essentially guaranteed!

Tips for Fostering Commitment from Others

Share with your clients some of the following tips they can use to strengthen the commitment levels of people around them. Have them keep in mind that fear may motivate people to perform, but commitment is enhanced only in an atmosphere of fearlessness.

To invite others to commit themselves, you need to:

> Our greatest weakness lies in giving up. The most certain way to succeed is to always try just one more time.
> —Thomas Edison

- Always express confidence and optimism about yourself, your vision, your work, and your group or organization.
- Develop a team of capable, competent people. Acknowledge them regularly.
- Draw out and use the talents and abilities that others have.
- Involve other people in any decisions that directly or indirectly affect them. Communicate to them the influence they had on any final decision.

- Invite feedback from others. Value and appreciate it; don't interrupt when they are giving it.

- Express gratitude for others taking the risk of giving you constructive criticism.

- Reward new ideas about how to accomplish tasks.

- Invite others to risk making mistakes, and trust their process of doing so.

- Both publicly and privately express your trust and confidence in other people.

- Exhibit a non-hostile, positive sense of humor, especially in sensitive or stressful situations.

- Set realistic standards for yourself and others. Encourage others to live up to them. (See Lesson 5.)

- Share with others your own values and convictions, even when they are not popular.

> Genius is perseverance in disguise.
> —Mike Newlin

Sample Coaching Conversation

Coach: So, how is the book writing going? Any progress?

Client: Not much. I have piles of information and resources and some notes of the outline and chapters, but every time I sit down to write, I get distracted by other commitments.

Coach: Let's talk a bit about that word, commitment. I am sure you have lots of things you are committed to, and I bet you have many duties you also feel obligated to, right?

Client: That's true. Some are obligations, some are projects I have committed to.

Coach: How much do you want to write this book? How excited would you be on the day the manuscript is complete and sent to the publisher?

Client: Very excited. I am so thrilled that I got the publishing contract and I have a year to complete it, but I just am not showing much commitment to begin writing.

Coach: In my experience, when people decide to be really committed to something, it is like they turn up the volume. It becomes compelling, not just interesting, or not even exciting. It becomes a compelling reason to commit. Can you commit to that level for this book?

Client: Yes I can. That really helps. If I keep the end goal in mind and then break down the doable steps of completing it, I can feel committed. And I also see that I can have other commitments, but I need to block out my writing time. I am freshest in the early morning, so that is when that commitment will be met.

Coach: Great insight. And it does sound now like you have distinguished between being obligated to write the book and being committed to completing the book, right?

Client: Right. Thanks.

Questions and Inquiries

1. In a range from one to ten, how committed are you to coaching?
2. What can we do as a team to enhance your commitment to attaining your coaching goals?
3. What fears do you have that are diminishing your commitment to your goal-attainment?
4. If you were to persist in doing what you are doing now, what might you reasonably expect the outcome to be?
5. If you don't want that expected outcome, what might you commit to change today?

What makes the difference between a Nation that is truly great and one that is merely rich and powerful? It is the simple things that make the difference. Honesty, knowing right from wrong, openness, self-respect, and the courage of conviction.
—David L. Boren

LIFE LESSON 33
A life that is balanced both internally and externally is crucial to creating a satisfying life.

MESSAGES

1. Your body is genetically programmed to maintain physiological balance.

2. An imbalanced life is the context for physical, mental, emotional, social and spiritual difficulties.

3. Maintaining a balanced life is an ongoing dynamic.

4. Authentic life coaches support their clients' efforts to balance their lives.

The objectives for Lesson 33 are: 1) To understand what having a balanced life really means; 2) To learn the principles of creating balance and harmony in your life; 3) To practice creating balance within your clients' own lives; 4) To learn some coaching techniques to catalyze your clients' life balance.

Framework Needed for Coaching Your Clients

Almost all the people we coach seek balance in their lives. Successful CEOs want to balance their personal life with their work. Professionals want to balance their leisure time with their professional commitments. Employees want to balance their family life with their job responsibilities. These are all situations that are *external* to your body. They are complicated by the influence of others and are outside your personal control. Knowing how to balance your *internal* state is crucial. Internal balance results in maximum wellness, energy, and vitality.

When one or more of your basic needs goes unfulfilled, you become unbalanced. When you are out of balance, you become *dis*stressed. If a basic need that's out of balance becomes large enough, something in your life will break down or stop functioning normally.

Is your life balanced? Personal balance is not something you attain once and for all. There are actually two kinds of balance: static and dynamic. Static balance is when all energy is motionless. Dynamic balance is like a gyroscope—energy moves and changes all the time, but the gyroscope remains balanced. Dynamic balance is a state of internal calm and contentment despite the external chaos going on outside you.

Dynamic balance can also be like standing on a teeter-totter with one foot on each side of the center fulcrum. If you put more weight on your left foot, the right end of the teeter-totter goes up and its angle to the ground increases. Maintaining balance in your life is a dynamic, ever-changing process. Designing and living a balanced life is often very simple—but it is never easy. Develop the habits described below and your success at creating a balanced life is almost certain.

> Those who do not find time to exercise will have to find time for illness.
> —Earl of Derby

Exercises and Information

Here are some principles and coaching techniques designed to help your clients create balance in their lives.

Eliminate Distractions

Many material possessions, demanding people, and stressful circumstances all distract your clients from achieving dynamic balance in their lives. Ask your clients to divest themselves of as many of these distractions as possible. Gaining or regaining balance in life requires your clients to become relentless in eliminating influences that push or pull them off center. Don't let making more money or having more material possessions be the central focus of your clients' lives. People who have done this in the past are notoriously unbalanced and are usually very unhappy.

Prioritize Values

The ability of your clients to maintain the order of their priorities, whatever they may be, is crucial to living a balanced life. A balanced order of priorities might be 1) self-care and self-responsibility; 2) your spousal relationship; 3) your parent-child relationships (if you have children); 4) your friendships; and 5) your work or job. Unfortunately, many clients have these healthy priorities reversed, valuing their jobs foremost and their friendships next. These clients tend to spend little time with their children and even less time alone with their spouse. They rarely, if ever, take responsibility for their own self-care. They become needy and expect someone else—usually a spouse—to take care of them as their parents did. By the time they achieve their job goals, they have become so out of balance with the rest of their lives, they often become ill, divorce, or burn out.

Be Fully Present in the Moment

This means clients are not preoccupied with the past or future. You need to train your mind and body to remain focused on whatever is happening now. Have clients view what's happening now, even if it is routine, as if they were experiencing it for the first time. For example, teach clients to greet a friend as if they hadn't seen him or her for a long time, even if they spent time with this friend only yesterday.

When clients focus their attention on what's happening now, they acknowledge all that exists in the moment, without evaluating it in any way. This takes practice, but the emotional balance is worth it.

Learn and Practice Self-Centering Skills

Meditation, relaxation, stress-reduction, active listening, thought control, and monitoring of energy drains and sources are all self-centering skills. After you engage in an activity, do you feel energized? Do you feel more alive? If yes, then write that activity on a list titled Energy Resources. For activities that make you feel drained, depressed, or less enthusiastic than before, write them on another list under the heading Energy Drains. Once both lists have several entries, you may begin to see how you could choose to balance your activities.

Below is an exercise designed to help you identify energy drains in your life and replace them with energy resources.

> We are what we repeatedly do. Excellence then, is not an act, but a habit.
> —Aristotle

Energy Drains And Resources. Take all the time necessary to identify and think about the following areas of your life. Replace the energy drains with those things that are energy resources for you. Begin balancing your energy, and you begin balancing your *life*.*

Identifying and eliminating energy drains
    Relationships

        _____ There are people in my life who continuously drain my energy.
        _____ I have unreturned phone calls, emails, or letters that need to be handled.

---

* The following worksheet is adapted from Take Time for Your Life by Cheryl Richardson copyright © 1998 by Cheryl Richardson. Used by permission of Broadway Books, a division of Random House, Inc.

_____ I lack quality friendships in my life.

_____ I feel a void in my life created by the lack of a romantic partner.

_____ There is a relationship I need to end.

_____ There is a phone call(s) I dread making, and it causes me stress.

_____ I miss being a part of a loving and supportive community.

Environment

_____ My car is in need of cleaning and/or repair.

_____ I'd like to live in a different geographic location.

_____ I have appliances that need repair or upgrading.

_____ My home is not decorated in a way that nurtures me.

_____ My home is cluttered and disorganized.

Body, Mind, and Spirit

_____ I eat food that is not good for me.

_____ It's been too long since I've been to the dentist or had a medical check-up.

_____ I do not get the sleep that I need to feel fully rested.

_____ I'd like to exercise regularly but never seem to find the time.

_____ I have a health concern for which I've avoided getting help.

_____ There are books that I'd love to read but never seem to find the time for.

_____ I lack a spiritual side to my life.

Work

_____ My work is stressful and leaves me exhausted at the end of the day.

_____ My office is disorganized and I have trouble finding what I need.

_____ I'm avoiding a confrontation or conflict at work.

_____ I tolerate bad behavior from a boss or coworker.

_____ I am not computer literate and it gets in the way of my productivity.

_____ I know I need to delegate specific tasks but am unable to let go of control.

_____ With email, voicemail and snail mail, I'm overloaded.

Money

_____ I pay my bills late.

_____ I spend more than I earn.

_____ I don't have a plan for my financial future.

_____ My credit rating is not what I'd like it to be.

_____ I do not have a regular savings plan.

_____ I do not have adequate insurance coverage.

_____ I have debt that needs to be paid off.

Energy resources

Relationships

_____ I enjoy the company of special friends.

_____ I share my life with a soulmate.

_____ I have a family (blood or chosen) that loves and supports me.

_____ I spend time having fun with people who make me laugh.

_____ I am part of a loving and supportive community.

Environment

_____ I have a special soul-nurturing place in my home just for me.

_____ I listen to my favorite music regularly.

_____ I've let go of all the stuff I no longer need.

_____ I keep fresh flowers in my home and office.

_____ My home is neat, clean, and well organized.

Body, Mind, and Spirit

_____ I exercise regularly.

_____ I have eliminated caffeine from my diet.

_____ I have a way to relax that eliminates stress and keeps me feeling centered.

_____ I eat healthy and nutritious foods.

_____ Each day I read something inspirational to keep my attitude positive.

_____ I set aside regular time for solitude and silence.

Work

_____ My commute is stress free.
_____ I have a mentor who guides and encourages me.
_____ I always take lunch breaks.
_____ I have colleagues who inspire and respect me.
_____ I take mental health days when I need them.
_____ I enjoy my work.
_____ I feel energized at the end of most work days.

Money

_____ I am fully insured and protected.
_____ I save money consistently.
_____ My taxes are paid and up-to-date.
_____ I've made smart investments that earn me top dollar.
_____ I enjoy being generous and easily share my wealth.
_____ I pay my credit cards in full each month.

Act with Conscious Awareness and Deliberation

To act deliberately means you base your actions on full awareness of the consequences resulting from them. You are *not* reacting solely to external stimulation. Acting deliberately is a matter of conscious choice. Acting with conscious awareness is to be proactive.

Keep in mind that *all* actions (even non-action) have consequences. Sometimes these consequences are negative and not wanted; sometimes they are desired and positive. But they are never absent. The trick to balancing your life is to learn which choices and actions result in the consequences you really want.

Live in Personal Integrity

Integrity means wholeness or completeness and is the result of integrating all aspects of your life—your mental, emotional, physical, relational, spiritual, and social aspects. Living a life of integrity implies harmony. When you have integrity, you behave in ways that are true and honest to who you really are. Expand your self-concept and, your life experience becomes enriched.

Know You Always Have Choices

Your past does not determine your future. Regardless of your present situation, you can always choose how you want to respond. Your thoughts, feelings, and behavior are under your control. Become consciously aware of your personal power to choose.

Avoid Making Judgments

Objective judgment is an oxymoron—your judgments are always subjective because they are your own. More often than not, a judgmental attitude is an unconscious attempt to protect yourself or promote yourself at someone else's expense. Lose your judgmental attitude toward yourself as well as others and you lighten your emotional attachment to outcomes beyond your control . . . it is a great balancing dynamic.

> Happiness is inward, and not outward; and so it does not depend on what we have, but on what we are.
> —Henry Van Dyke

Sample Coaching Conversation

This conversation occurs early in the coaching relationship after an initial session about the client's goals.

Coach: Part of my role as your life coach is to expand our conversation beyond work, achievement, or performance goals. You have some great ones, but I also want to talk about life goals and life balance. Is that ok with you?

Client: Absolutely. I want to have more balance in my life. I would like some coaching in that area, definitely.

Coach: Tell me about your life balance now. When do you experience it? Or have you ever?

Client: Every so often I take a day to refocus all my priorities. I block out my calendar so I can make it to my son's soccer game. My wife and I will schedule a get-away weekend. I will play golf and tennis by rearranging some appointments at the law firm. But then everything goes back to normal and I have to juggle time again to get in balance.

Coach: First of all, juggling things for temporary balance is not having a balanced life. I get an image of you on a tightrope juggling balls, you almost fall, regain your balance, and then complete the traverse.

Client: Yes! That is what it feels like.

Coach: I believe that having a balanced life is an ongoing, dynamic intention we hold, and we may make small course corrections when we are out of balance. But, it is not as drastic or temporary as in the tightrope metaphor. Does that sound right to you?

Client: Yes, I agree with your statements. I would like balance of work, family, and leisure time so they all have a place in my life. How do I do that with all the commitments and duties at work?

Coach: You actually came up with some great strategies earlier. You mentioned time-blocking. Do you feel you control your calendar or does it control you?

Client: It pretty much controls me. My secretary schedules some appointments in the time that is open.

Coach: Ok, here is a secret. If you block out time before other appointments are scheduled then you control your timeslots. I know, of course, that *urgencies* come up, but you are more likely to do what you want if it is on your calendar.

Client: I can do that. In other words, I pre-block timeslots for me, or family, or fun, and all it needs to say on the calendar is that it is booked.

Coach: Right. Now here is a request: You and I have talked earlier about incorporating your values in balanced living, and you stated values of family, fun, golf, reading, etc. What I want you to do is look at your calendar over the last sixty days and write down categories of how your time was spent. Our values may be stated one way, but how we devote our time can say something quite different. Will you do that? I think it will be quite enlightening.

Client: Yes, I will. I will make chart and approximate the number of hours alloted to each category.

Questions and Inquiries

1. What areas of your lifestyle are in need of more balance?
2. What activities do you need to stop in order create more balance in your life?

3. What actions do you need to take (start) in order to create a more balanced lifestyle?

4. What do you need to do to maintain bodily balance? Eat differently? Move differently? Rest more? Take care of yourself first?

LIFE LESSON 34
Living in the present moment is important.

MESSAGES

1. In the present moment, everything can be perfect.
2. All we directly experience is the immediate moment.
3. Being fully-present in the moment is a key to successful living. Neither the past nor the future actually exists. Living in the present moment is all we ever do and is all we ever experience.

The objectives for Lesson 34 are: 1) To help your clients understand what living in the present moment really means; 2) To realize that you can begin to make life changes in the present moment; 3) To help clients develop a plan to appreciate and use in the present; 4) To help your clients view themselves "as they are".

Framework Needed for Coaching Your Clients

Physicists tell us that the concept of time is precisely that—a concept. What we call time is not a *thing* that actually exists. The passage of time is a mental construct, not an actual experience. If time does not exist, except in our minds, then the past and the future do not exist either. Only the present experience exists, and that is always changing, always different.

We usually think of time as linear, with the past on one end of the time line, the present in the middle, and the future at the other end. If we live in the past, we are not likely to respond accurately to our current situation. Similarly, if we always focus on the future, we tend to ignore what is happening right now, and inappropriately respond to present conditions as if the anticipated future events were already taking place.

If we look more critically at our life experiences we realize that we never experience anything other than in the present moment. Sure, we can remember a past, but remembering is a present-time activity. We can anticipate and even plan for a future, but anticipating and planning are also present-time activities. Our direct experience *always* occurs in the present. All personal experience is caught in the eternal now.

Psychologists tell us that functioning as if the past is what we experience now is one source of psychological depression. However, if your memories of the past are enjoyable, living in the past can be more pleasant than living in the moment. Psychology also tells us that anticipating a future and responding as if it were happening now is a source of much anxiety. Depending on the quality of our memories, thinking about the past can precipitate sadness and depression or joy and satisfaction. Depending on what we anticipate for a future, we can become anxious or eager, panicked or enthusiastic. So it is in everyone's best interest to live in the present moment to create enjoyable memories as well as a desired future.

Buddhism tell us that clinging to the present is the source of all suffering. Trying to hang on to the ever-changing moment is indeed a very difficult, if not an impossible task. Like jumping onto a moving freight car, hanging on to the moving moment can also be dangerous.

Present-moment living means that you focus your attention on what is actually happening *right now*. It means expanding your momentary awareness to include what is happening outside of your body, inside your mind, and within your body all at the same time. It means deliberately responding to your current perceptions without cluttering them up with past memories or future anticipations. Realize that only in this eternal moment, the possibility for life improvement and perfection exists.

You may be wondering, "What about the benefits derived from past experience? What about the advantages of planning and working to create a desired future? Are we really doomed to repeat the past if we do not learn from it?"

Certainly, everything you've learned is based upon accumulated experiences that are now memories. Planning for and anticipating future events affect the creation of new experiences and are positive skills and viewpoints to be encouraged, strengthened, and used. They are necessary places to visit occasionally, but *you don't want to live there!* Living in the past or future is to live in memory or fantasy. It deprives you of awareness of your current situation and the ability to respond accordingly.

> The best thing about the future is that it comes only one day at a time.
> —Abraham Lincoln

Exercises and Information

To assist clients in experiencing the power of present-moment awareness, consider the following techniques and adapt them as desired.

1. Ask your clients to have a morning ritual of self-centering. This can include a morning meditation, prayer, inspirational reading, journaling, or visually focusing on nature and being still.
2. Take any of the quieting techniques above and use them as a stress-buster during the day. We often recommend that clients view this as a pause button on their CD player, or like a wake-up call. For just five minutes or so, take some time to become present-centered.
3. Practice mindful awareness. This is an exercise we often give our clients. For any routine activity (e.g., morning shower, grocery shopping, driving, or walking) notice the details of the sights, sounds, smells, and sensations. Slow your brain down and notice the colors, smells, physical feel, emotions, and beauty of everyday experiences.

Sample Coaching Conversation

Client: Wow . . . what a week! I accomplished a lot and learned of potentially new projects and opportunities.

Coach: Sounds very good. I read about all you accomplished in your coaching prep form. I want to hear about the exciting opportunities.

Client: I was asked to speak at two conventions in the next few months and now have to get moving on creating my Powerpoint presentation and the keynote address that goes with the title. I also was asked to be one of six authors in an edited update of a book on leadership. And, I have some ideas to expand my speaking and training business, improve the website, evolve some collaborative business relationships, and other little things.

Coach: Great. All of these things seem to fall in line with the vision and purpose we have worked out before. But here is a coaching question: How are all these projects for the future affecting you in the present? Are you living in the future of all those possibilities and probabilities? Or are you letting the anticipation and excitement, and maybe the anxiety of all these things, influence your daily life?

> The happiness of life is made up of minute fractions—the little, soon forgotten charities of a kiss or smile, a kind look, a heartfelt compliment, and the countless infinitesimals of pleasurable and genial feeling.
> —Samuel Taylor Coleridge

Client: Nice reminder. Of course it is influencing my daily life. I even sleep poorly because I know all the work I have to do and I tend to procrastinate.

Coach: Life coaching is often like a wake-up call you get in a hotel room. I am here to remind you to live a great life now, not in the future. Your future projects are all fabulous, but if you live in that future, you don't enjoy the now. Can you see how you can do both?

Client: I like that metaphor of a wake-up call. I could set an alarm on my computer to remind me to meditate for a few minutes, to go for a morning walk, and or to take a midday break. I have done that in the past and it helps. So, what you are saying is use the present as grounding for all that I want for the future. After all, the future is only predictable, not guaranteed.

Coach: I could not have said it better myself. Now, will you set up your reminder system today?

Client: Yes.

Coach: One last request. Go back over your coaching goals about life balance, time with family, etc. For those that require a focus on the present, put them on a note card and tape them to your computer screen. That is another way to be reminded to live on purpose.

Client: Great idea. I will do that today too.

> Life is what happens to us while we are making other plans.
> —Thomas LaMance

Questions and Inquiries

1. What aspects of your daily life are based on present experiences?
2. What old habits do you want to replace with new, present-moment ones?
3. What experiences *come in handy* in your daily life?
4. What do you worry about, as if the future were already happening?
5. Is what's happening right now pleasant, painful, or neutral?
6. Are you enjoying being in the moment?
7. What can you think about, focus on, or do right now to make your eternal now more enjoyable?

LIFE LESSON 35
You are always a leader for someone, especially for yourself. Lead your own chosen life.

MESSAGES

1. Leadership skills can be effective or ineffective.
2. Leadership skills can be learned.
3. As a life coach, you are always a leader to your clients.
4. An authentic coach leads by example.

The objectives for Lesson 35 are: 1) To help your clients understand what being a leader really means; 2) To identify the most effective leadership skills; 3) To develop your client's own leadership style.

Framework Needed for Coaching Your Clients

During the past two decades, there has been a plethora of books and articles written about the nature of effective leadership and how leaders develop. Further research in the last ten years has clearly demonstrated that all of us can learn the skills used by effective leaders.

Each of your clients can develop the qualities of leadership required to be effective in any situation. Indeed, everyone is a leader to someone at some time in their lives: older siblings are leaders of younger ones; older students are leaders of their younger classmates; parents are the leaders of their children; bosses are leaders of their employees; employees can be leaders of their colleagues.

At some point in your life, you will be looked to lead, whether you like it or not. It doesn't matter if you are a sibling or a senior VP in a high-tech firm, a military general or a parent. To be successful in any endeavor, you will have to use at least some qualities of leadership.

Even if you weren't prepared early in life to be a leader, you can still learn skills and techniques to help you take the helm of an organization, or your life.

> The higher we are placed, the more humbly we should walk.
> —Cicero

Leading by Leading

When asked about his style of leadership, General Charles DeGaulle once said, "I find out where the majority of Frenchmen are heading and run out in front of them." Clearly, that is one model of effective leadership.

A second model for leadership is patterned after wolves. The leader of a wolf pack usually runs in the middle of the pack—faster runners ahead, slower runners behind. The leader *pushes* those in front to go in a specific direction and to move at a certain pace, and *pulls* those behind to encourage them to keep the pace and follow. This style of leadership works well for many effective leaders. Regardless of the personal leadership style that fits you and your specific situation, certain time-honored personal characteristics of leaders exist that have proven very effective.

Exercises and Information

Below is information about the characterisitcs, myths, styles, and definitions of leadership.

Ten Characteristics of Effective Leaders

Here are some of the qualities you may want to catalyze in clients who aspire to enhance their leadership skills.

1. Leaders have a keen sense of who they are. They know themselves, their strengths and weaknesses, their values and their value, and the uniqueness of their own perceptual reality.

2. They are genuine in their self-expression. They don't put on false fronts simply to win the approval of others. They truly are what they show to others. They are aware of and develop their inner life.

3. They maintain an openness to change. They are receptive to new ideas, new ways of doing things. They listen without prejudice. They are flexible and prepared to consider a fresh approach.

4. They take total responsibility for themselves, for the nature and results of their behavior, and sometimes for the actions of others.

5. They fully understand the importance of character in all their contributions and creations. They are committed to being guided by the positive qualities of character.

6. They balance their personal contributions with the contributions of others. They understand the value of synergy in all their relationships. They respect and value the contributions of others.

7. They are care-frontational. They express themselves authentically and fully integrate their self-expression with compassionate caring for the people with whom they relate.

8. They teach/coach more through *being* than through *doing*. The quality of their silence communicates more than long speeches.

9. They place the immediate moment into the context of the future. They focus on the big picture, the long-term effects, and their desired outcomes, while they are fully present in the moment.

10. They create value within all their relationships. Service to others is their creed. They know that the more they assist others to get what they want, the more likely they will be fulfilled.

Myths and Realities of Leadership

Why aren't there more leaders? Why are people so reluctant to assume the leadership role? One possibility is they are fearful or ignorant of what contemporary effective leadership truly means. Discuss with your clients their notions about leadership. Then, share with them some of these myths and current realities about leadership today:

Myth 1. Leaders are a small band of special people endowed with the ability to understand the mysteries of leadership.

Reality: Leadership can be learned and everyone plays a leadership role at some time in life. Effective leadership is everyone's business.

Myth 2. Through personal power and control, leaders maintain a tight ship so that their followers toe the line and their organizations run like clockwork.

Reality: Contemporary leaders delegate personal power and good decision-making authority to others. They challenge the process of how things have always been done. They shake up the status quo with new ideas, new methods, and sometimes a totally new vision and purpose for the process of attaining desired outcomes.

Myth 3. Today's leaders are renegades who destroy tried-and-true ways of conducting business by attracting rebellious followers and engaging in courageous actions.

Reality: Leaders are not defiant for defiance sake. They challenge the existing reality out of a deep faith that others can adapt, grow, learn, and realize their unique human potential.

Myth 4. Visionary leaders seem to have some psychic powers that allows them to know what is going to happen.

Reality: Having a vision of the desired outcome is important for leaders, but everybody can dream and learn ways to make their dreams a reality. The vision of leaders may not come from original thought. They might adopt it from others or learn what best expresses the values of the culture.

> Leadership is the ability to get other people to do what they don't want to do and like it.
> —Harry S. Truman

Myth 5. The more you control others by incentive, power, manipulation, coercion, or intimidation, the better followers will perform.

Reality: Genuine leaders know that the more they control, the less likely they will be trusted and the less likely others will excel. They serve and support others.

Myth 6. It is lonely at the top because leaders must remain cool and aloof from those they lead. Only a select few know about the strategic plan the leader has in mind.

Reality: Leaders' actions are far more important than a strategic plan or their words, no matter how practical, inspirational, or enthusiastically expressed, and being aloof is not a prerequisite. Credibility and consistency of action are the most critical determinants of whether a leader is followed over time.

Myth 7. Leadership is a position, and the position is superior to any other.

Reality: Leadership is a process of relating that involves the use of personal and interpersonal skills and abilities whether applied from a position of leadership or not.

Whether your clients are parents, teachers, bosses, friends, executives, colleagues, or role models, they can all be leaders. Your clients should hone their leadership skills according to the *realities* of today's world.

Leadership Styles

If any of your clients aspire to be effective leaders, or if they are already in a leadership position, they will want to develop the top 10 characteristics of leaders listed below.

1. Charisma. Charismatic leaders instill faith, respect, and trust; they have a gift for seeing what others need to know and need to think about; and they are enthusiastic and convey a strong sense of mission.

2. Courage. Courageous leaders are willing to express, support, and stand up for their ideas, even if they are not popular. They do not give into others' opinions in order to avoid conflict or confrontation. They will do what is right even if it causes personal hardship.

3. Intellectual stimulation. Good leaders provoke thought in their followers, stimulating them to think, solve problems, and create *for themselves*. As a result, followers believe their thinking and input are important, enhancing their ability to contribute to the organization.

4. Individual consideration. The best leaders treat each individual as unique. They coach, advise, teach, and assist people who need it. They are open and really listen to (consider) their followers.

5. A clear vision. Effective leaders have already pictured in their minds a detailed image of the outcomes they want to create for their followers. They have the ability to communicate their vision to their followers and to instill enthusiasm or support for that vision within them.

6. Judgment. Great leaders use good judgment. By using rational thinking, logic, analysis, comparisons, and anticipatory scenarios, they arrive at sound conclusions, make wise decisions, and create alternative courses of action. They are realistic and use their experience and knowledge to bring a personal perspective to decisions.

7. Respect for others. The best leaders honor the individual values, talents, and skills of their followers. They never belittle or humiliate. They never discount the ideas of others, even when they disagree. They value everyone's contribution to the overall effectiveness of the group or organization.

8. Dependability. Good leaders keep their promises, follow through on their commitments and take full responsibility for their own actions. They always acknowledge their mistakes and seek to correct their actions in the future. Followers can count on them to be consistent in their behavior. They work effectively by themselves and as a member of a team.

9. Flexibility. Great leaders are able to cope with and effectively function in everchanging situations. They handle multiple issues, one at a time. They change how they think, feel, and behave as the situation warrants it. They are open to change and accept it when it happens.

10. Integrity. This is the most important quality a leader can have. They act in accordance with generally accepted moral and ethical standards. They do not abuse their position of leadership. They are truthful in all they think, say, and do and all elements of the leader are integrated.

> Leaders are the custodians of a nation's ideals, of the beliefs it cherishes, of its permanent hopes, of the faith which makes a nation out of a mere aggregation of individuals.
> —Walter Lippmann

Definitions of Leadership

Share with your clients the following definitions of *leadership* and *leadership style*.

Leadership is the personal ability to motivate others to do willingly what they have the ability to do but might not spontaneously do on their own. It consists of receiving a positive response from others and utilizing that response to bring about a desired action.

Leadership style is the usual manner in which an individual displays leadership qualities. It implies that an individual has a special effect on others that commands respect, admiration, or affection and causes them to follow.

Help your clients identify their own leadership style among the four styles presented below. Thereafter, they can more easily identify the leadership styles of other people influencing their lives.

FOUR MAJOR TYPES OF LEADERSHIP STYLES

The Negative Leader	Behaves in ways that invite others to dislike, fear, avoid, undermine him or her if they feel they can get away with it, or passively get even.
The Positive Leader	Inspires admiration, respect, support, and cooperation.
The Objective Leader	Relies on the reality of the situation, uses objective information to govern his or her actions, and is not afraid to make decisions and implement them based on his or her understanding of facts.
The Subjective Leader	Relies on opinions or projected wishes, tends to use bias and prejudice in his or her actions, and vacillates out of fear of making wrong decisions.

Your coaching clients need to know that regardless of their personal leadership styles, effective leaders recognize that leadership depends on at least three factors:

- The leader's personal characteristics
- The wants, needs, thoughts, and values of others
- The reality of the current situation

Effective leaders know that if they fail to take into account any one of these three factors, their leadership becomes ineffective or useless, if not downright dangerous.

If your clients want to develop their independent style of leadership, they need to:

- Become aware of the abilities of their subordinates
- Learn their own job or role
- Guide others toward realistic goals
- Affect change
- Take responsibility for decisions and actions of the group they lead
- Engage in self-development

Whether leaders influence by personal example, persuasion, or empathetic feedback, they win others over by demonstrating a willingness to act among followers, rather than forcing compliance. Therefore, the relationships leaders develop with others is crucial.

Become the leader of your own life! Take charge of your success, your happiness, and your lifestyle. After all, you are the CEO of your own life.

As an authentic life coach, you should realize that effective leading means catalyzing the success of others. This defines your role in the coach/client relationship. How well you lead your clients, and how well you catalyze their success, determines your effectiveness as a coach.

> A leader is best when people barely know that he exists.
> —Witter Bynner

Leadership: Getting Out of the Way

Leadership can be best defined as the communication ability to relate to others in such a manner that they willingly do, and do well, what needs to be done.

Leaders take part in and continually practice their language skills, known as *the conversations of leadership*. For your clients to learn the language of leadership, they must first know the culture of the group they are in. They must then be able to articulate a vision within that culture. Leaders need to be well informed about what is happening within their culture and how that culture relates to the rest of the world. They need to be aware of innovations, emerging trends, regulations, and the competition.

Making sense of the culture and how it fits in the world requires more than facts. Leaders need to understand how things interrelate and how those relationships impact the lives of their followers. Leaders do this by creating an *integrated vision* of the whole field relevant to their desired outcomes or results. They then have to be able to speak of that vision in a way that elicits enthusiastic support from followers who then want to promote and support the manifestation of that vision. Of all the abilities of leaders, learning to read the world and produce a powerfully attractive vision of the future is the most critical to success attainment.

Once your followers have the same vision as you, the leader, then a common mission needs to be discussed, created and agreed upon. For a sports team, the mission might be to win the championship. For a business endeavor, the mission might be to capture 10 percent of the market share. For a service organization, the mission might be to deliver the best service for the benefit of the customer. Your mission might be to become successful in designing and creating a lifestyle of happiness and love. Regardless of the nature of a mission, it remains an important declaration of how leaders intend to position themselves in the culture and the outcome they are committed to achieving.

Leaders communicate with people to form alliances with them. An alliance is created when two parties—people or organizations—mutually agree to support each other while retaining their own autonomy for individual action. The basis for an effective alliance is trust. Leaders learn how to engender trust by being consistent and dependable, truthful and caring, respectful and compassionate. Without trust, alliances are weakened or dissolved.

There is no such thing as individual leadership. Leadership is always a social relationship between people. To have an effective organization, leaders must assign and delegate authority. They expand their base of followers by catalyzing responsibility and authority within their followership. In a chemical reaction, a catalyst causes two or more elements to combine *without changing itself and without participating in the results*. Catalytic leaders stay out of the way of their followers. This creates a team of followers, and the leader becomes their coach. Well-coached teamwork is essential for anyone interested in playing in a big game. Catalytic leadership will also continue the process of producing new leaders.

Leadership is sorely needed in every aspect of our lives today. Catalytic leadership generates followers, team-players and new leaders. It is the soil from which grows new followers, new teams, new leaders, and new life.

Sample Coaching Conversation

Client is a vice president of marketing at a Fortune 100 company who wanted coaching to improve her leadership and people skills.

> **Client:** I want to talk today about the results of my assessment. Generally, I got good marks as far as the results of our team were concerned, but there were common comments about me being *aloof* and *micromanaging*.
>
> **Coach:** Tell me more. What did they mean by those words?
>
> **Client:** When we debriefed, some of them said that that was the first time in a long time that I asked what any of them thought about the team or about my leadership. Although they were a bit mistrusting, they were appreciative that I was listening. But, they said, I often appeared as a problem solver and did not let them do their jobs in their own creative ways.

Coach: So you would like to be a better leader and maybe more of a coach-like manager?

Client: Yes. I know that I sometimes lead by *command and control* and I would like my leadership to be more *empowering and participatory*.

Coach: That is a very good start. That awareness already shows good leadership. Now the way to continue to evolve your leadership position and be trusted by your team is by example and actions, not just words. Are you ready to shift the way you lead your team?

Client: Say more about what you mean by leading by example.

Coach: Sure. Have you known people in your life that you considered leaders for you or mentors for you and yet they were not *officially* in that role? These would be people you looked up to, emulated, admired, and were inspired by more for *who* they were and *how* they were, than for what job they held.

Client: Oh yes, I can think of several. I would like to be that kind of leader.

Coach: You, as defined your job responsibilities, are a leader. But you also want to develop a staff of leaders. Everyone is a leader to someone. I would like to request that you lead more by encouragement and trust of what you have assigned or delegated and then check in to see how you can support them, not take over the work, ok?

Client: I get it. Trust them more and *coach* them to do the best job they are responsible for. Model leadership by my style and my actions. I like that. I will try that more this week and report back to you. Is it a good idea to let my staff know of my intention?

Coach: Sure. That show's great leading by example. I think they will be inspired by your authenticity.

Questions and Inquiries

1. In what areas of your life do you want to take the lead?
2. What is your favorite leadership style?
3. What leadership skills do you want to develop?
4. How does your being—your personality—affect your leadership style?

LIFE LESSON 36
To become an effective leader, you must first become a good follower and teammate.

MESSAGES

1. To lead effectively and authentically, you must know how to follow and how to be skilled at being a team member.
2. Your skills at "followership" predicts your leadership style
3. Dancing comfortably between leading and following is the hallmark of a competent leader.

The objectives for Lesson 36 are: 1) To explain to your clients the concept of followership; 2) To learn how to be an effective member of a team; 3) To understand the concept of leading by stepping out of the way.

Framework Needed for Coaching Your Clients

Very few people aspire to be a great follower. The notion of following usually has negative connotations. The word *followership* is not even found in the English dictionary. Learning to be a follower as a necessary skill in training for leadership is often completely ignored. We don't generally take pride in our abilities to follow. But the ability to actively choose to follow is the basis for our democratic society: We follow the laws, we follow our leaders, we follow one another in lines, we follow the Constitution (usually); we follow our parents and teachers. Without followers, there can be no leaders because the function of a leader is usually defined by the responsive activities of his or her followers.

More often than not we build personal relationships in which someone leads and someone follows. You've heard the expression, "There are too many cooks in the kitchen." When too many people try to lead and there are too few followers, personal and organizational relationships break down. In order to create success, we must follow.

By focusing on followership first, we develop an understanding of the followers' needs and generate a group of skillful followers. They, in turn, enable leaders to lead, thereby reducing the responsibility for success that is usually carried by leaders alone. When leadership is shared, followers become a team, and from the team new leaders emerge.

Exercises and Information

Orient your clients to the notion of effective followership by inviting them to play with some of the exercises below.

Effective "Followership" Skills

Your clients need to realize that developing their following skills allows them to more quickly become team players. Becoming members of a team will move them more efficiently toward becoming successful at any endeavor that requires more than one person to achieve. Below are some skills your clients can develop in order to become great followers.

Invite your clients to increase their conscious awareness. Followers need to be aware of themselves, others, and the reality of the situation.

Self-awareness implies not only knowledge of your own personality, it also means you are aware of how your personality affects people around you and the situation you are in at the moment.

Sensitivity to others (who they are, what they need, how they think, and what they do) is critical, not only to being a good leader, as stated in the previous lesson, but to being an effective follower. If the running back on a football team is not aware of who the others players are, how they think about the play, and what they do, then that running back can not follow the rest of the team and move the ball toward the goal.

Being aware of the reality of the situation means that you understand the dynamics that are operating in any given environment. Without an awareness of your environment or culture, you will no doubt be ineffective in anything you attempt within that context.

Ensure that your clients learn about the vision of their leader. Integrate their visions of how they want to be into the vision of whomever they are fol-

> My grandfather told me that there are two kinds of people; those who do the work and those who take the credit. He told me to try to be in the first group; there was much less competition there.
> —Indira Gandhi

lowing. If they don't know about the vision of their boss or leader, your clients need to ask him or her to articulate it for them. If they are not aware of the vision the leader has for the organization, they become a wandering generality within it, and may contribute to its success only by chance.

Clients need to contribute their own ideas and thoughts about how best to attain the goals of the group/leader. Their beliefs, ideas, and thoughts may be a positive contribution to the overall effectiveness of goal-attainment.

Your clients need to learn the rules of the game so they can follow accurately. Most organizations function like a game with certain rules to follow and rewards for those who follow them. Those who don't are punished.

> To lead people,
> walk behind them.
> —Lao-Tzu

Help your clients increase their level of self-esteem. Encourage your clients to view themselves as valuable, positive influences on the leadership, as well as on the rest of the followership.

Great followers become an asset to their leader. The last people to be cast aside are those deemed most valuable to the leader/organization. Great followers learn how to address and solve problems that the leader confronts. They learn how to relieve the leader of stress and how to support him or her in effectively pursuing the leader's purpose and mission. When your clients are a great asset to their leader, they will succeed.

Teach clients to go the extra mile. Great followers know that doing a little bit extra—doing more than asked, making a positive contribution, and doing it enthusiastically—will turn them into valuable resources for the leader and the rest of the team. It also prepares the follower to become a good leader.

Benefits of Being a Team Member

In today's business world, you will never succeed if you behave as a Lone Ranger. The pace of business—indeed the pace of life—is so rapid, and the rate of change so fast, that no person *alone* can effectively succeed. We need to be a team. And we need to know how to be team players.

The most common characteristic of good team players is their willingness to subordinate personal desires and goals to those of the group or team while respecting their special roles within the matrix of the team. Like a link in a chain, each role is important, but it comprises only one part the whole chain. The strength of the chain is totally defined by the strength each individual link.

The overall health and effectiveness of any team is dependent on the health and effectiveness of its members. For a team to achieve its desired outcomes, each member must do his or her job and do it well.

Your clients must be aware of the benefits of being a part of a team. These benefits vary according to the composition of the team. However, there are some positive benefits to be derived from being a member of *any* team. Here are a few to share with your clients:

> The most important single ingredient in the formula of success is knowing how to get along with people.
> —Theodore Roosevelt

Companionship and camaraderie. Almost every veteran of military service knows of the great friendships and camaraderie formed in a platoon. When you are a participating member of a team, you are not alone. Someone else's strengths complement your weaknesses, and vice versa. You share laughter, common purposes, tears, common values, and you have a sense of truly belonging to something larger than yourself.

The responsibility for success and the burden of failure are shared. When a team succeeds, everyone gets credit. When it fails, everyone shares the burden.

You are made stronger. Single sticks are easy to break, but bundle that single stick with a number of similar ones and you cannot break it.

You learn. Gaining different perspectives from teammates enriches your own point of view, allows you to make better decisions, and increases your knowledge base.

You can count on your teammates' support and assistance. When all members of a team are aware of their interdependence, everyone supports each other. Such dependability leads to a realistic sense of security. Safety exists in numbers.

Sample Coaching Conversation

Continued conversation with the same client as in the previous lesson.

> **Coach:** So what did you learn this week about your leadership?
> **Client:** I really had some great experiences with the staff. And I found that I did less. I almost felt guilty because I did not step in with solu-

tions or ideas unless they asked. I told them I assumed they could do their jobs and even offer creative ideas for the department's strategies without being asked. They really liked my new, *coach-like leadership*.

Coach: That's really great. What you are learning here about leadership is that it is not always about doing, often it is about empowering. You, even as a designated leader, sometimes have to *get out of the way*. There are times you need to be a *follower*. I call that *leading from behind*.

Client: That is what I experienced. My son and I had a talk last week about wolves and what he learned in school. He informed me that the alpha wolf in a pack leads the pack from the middle. As the lead wolf, he makes sure the ones in front keep pace and that the ones in the rear stay with the pack. That is really what we are talking about isn't it?

Coach: What do you think?

Client: Although I do not want to think of my team as a pack of wolves, I do like the analogy of leadership.

Coach: Great. And wolves get an undeserved bad rap. They are great examples of family, team, leadership, and survival.

Questions and Inquiries

1. In what areas of your life do you want to follow?
2. In what areas do you want to function as a team member?
3. What would you like to learn from following?
4. On what kind of teams do you aspire to participate?

Coaching Summary

How to achieve success has been a ubiquitous topic of trainers, speakers, preachers, books, tapes, seminars, products, and philosophers. Use Section 5, Achieving Potential, with your coaching clients to help them maximize their personally defined vision of success.

The Lessons

Use these ten lessons as experiments, as starting-points of coaching conversations, or as possibilities for your clients to achieve outcomes *they* would define as successful.

Life Lesson 27

Success is a way of thinking, a consciousness. Achieving success is a subjective perception. As life coaches, we believe that this lesson seems obvious. We also know what's obvious for us is not always obvious to our clients. When you propose this lesson and related exercises to your clients, ask them if they find the approach relevant, effective, and useful *for them*. If not, go to the next one. Success for your clients must be defined by them—not you.

Life Lesson 28

Without a vision of your desired future, you allow circumstances to create it for you instead of you creating it yourself. This lesson for us is one of the hallmarks of authentic life coaching. It has been said that, if you don't know where you are going, how will you know when you get there? We believe authentic living is living on purpose. A purposeful life must have a vision of an intended future. Planning your personal vision is a systematic creation. Having a life coach as a partner can help immensely.

Life Lesson 29

Identifying a great number of personal goals and then writing them out is critical to your success in life. The almost magical value of *writing* goals and detailed plans is one of the little-known secrets to creating the life your clients desire. The more detailed the written plan, the more intentional focus is required of your clients. When written details lead to focus, strategies, and flexibility, clients more easily adapt to changing circumstances. After all, a plan is merely a blueprint. Modifying a blueprint is much easier than modifying an existing structure. When envisioned and strategic details are clearly written at the beginning of any creation, modifications are more easily accomplished.

Life Lesson 30

Strategizing is a valuable skill essential to reaching your goals. Strategy comes after planning. You can't have an effective strategy without a clear direction and an outcome in mind. Work with your clients to co-create multiple strategies for achieving their goals, desires, and intentions for their future. Multiple strategies allow for flexibility and the identification of relevant alternatives. If you only create one strategy, the chances for disappointment are greatly increased.

Life Lesson 31

The attitude you adopt determines whether you are successful creating a lifestyle you enjoy. Take a stand for your life. Successful living is determined by envisioning, planning, implementing, and commiting. Dreaming and wishing do not create success. Pair this lesson with discovering your life's purpose and you will be extraordinary beyond your wildest dreams.

Life Lesson 32

Your level of commitment is absolutely critical to your long-term success and achievement. Success never comes without action. Your role as coach is to be the catalyst, motivator, and accountability partner for your clients and their performance. The most successful people in the world did not achieve greatness by individual effort. In some manner, coaching and mentoring were available to them. Now that the profession of life coaching has emerged and evolved, people who want a coaching approach to designing and creating their life can obtain it.

Life Lesson 33

A life that is balanced both internally and externally is crucial to creating a satisfying life. In order to have a balanced lifestyle, you must pay attention to all aspects of your life. This does not mean that each area of your life needs the same amount of attention. Total life coaching addresses the whole person and the creation of an inner life and outer lifestyle that are optimally balanced.

Life Lesson 34

Living in the present moment is important. This lesson is a wise statement for all ages. We all know it's true, but we live in defiance of its simple truth. Live in the *now* more often. Be aware of your past and learn from it. Plan and design your future, but live *today*.

Life Lesson 35

You are always a leader for someone, especially yourself. Lead your own chosen life. Effective leading is being purposeful and committed. While you are wise to seek guidance and leadership from others and obtain great coaching, you ultimately lead your own life. Take responsibility for your choices. Be joyful and choose your own personal path. You can always take another route, or adjust to the unexpected. All leaders make course corrections frequently.

Life Lesson 36

To become an effective leader, you must first become a good follower and teammate. Great leaders know when to follow. Sometimes we describe authentic life coaching as leading from behind. A coach is a resource and a guide, but may not know the exact path of the client. You are only aiding your clients as they chart their own courses. Followership is a key to great coaching, it is also a skill your clients can apply to their personal and business lives.

Questions for Reflection

1. How will you know when you are successful?
2. Can you name three people (living or dead) you view as successful? Why do you think they were successful?

3. If you do not define yourself by your job or role functions, what would success be for you?

4. What would a balanced life be for you? How would your life change if it was more balanced?

5. Within your current lifestyle, where are you a leader? Where are you a follower?

6. What methods do you use to become centered or present-oriented? Which could be used more often? Which could be added to your unconscious habits?

SECTION 6
Learning Cognitive Skills

True enjoyment in life comes from the activity of the mind.
—Albert Einstein

LIFE LESSON 37

Your thinking habits are the most powerful tools you have for creating anything you genuinely desire.

MESSAGES

1. If you want to change your lifestyle, begin by modifying your thinking.
2. What you think defines who you are.
3. You can learn how to modify your thinking habits.
4. Clear thinking is a prerequisite to great coaching.

The objectives for Lesson 37 are: 1) To help your clients identify the types of thinking skills; 2) To learn how to become a clearer thinker; 3) To learn how to maintain an open mind; 4) To understand the power of your thoughts; 5) To acquaint yourself with other aspects of your mental life.

Framework Needed for Coaching Your Clients

We often take for granted our ability to think. To do so is perilous to functioning as a human being as well as to enjoying a lifestyle of your own creation.

The Power of Thought

If you realized how powerful your thoughts are, you would never again think a negative thought. Your thinking not only programs your subconscious mind, it modifies your biochemistry. You are what you think, regardless of whether or not you are aware of your thinking. Indeed, you become in the future what you think in the present!

As a man thinketh
in his heart,
so he is.
—Proverbs 23:7

Thoughts are non-material events, energy impulses. Thinking energy is consciousness, intelligent consciousness. As far as we know, human beings are more intensely conscious—possess more thinking energy—than any other creature on earth.

Our powerful thinking ability, however, is like a double-edged sword—one edge can lead to extreme unhappiness and misery, the other can create an experience of ecstatic joy. Consistent habitual thoughts manifest themselves in bodily changes. Positron emission tomography (PET), a scientific technology for monitoring biochemicals in the central nervous system, has clearly demonstrated that negative thoughts actually create stress chemicals in the body. If you regularly think fearful thoughts, you become a fearful person. You may defend yourself by running or hiding from your own perceived threats. If you focus on angry, vengeful, or resentful thoughts, you become hostile, aggressive, and often depressed. When you think and feel negative thoughts, you negatively affect all of your relationships.

Your thoughts about *yourself* are the most influential kinds of thoughts. Who you are and how you value yourself determine your attitude. Your attitude determines how you treat yourself. How you treat yourself informs others how they should treat you. When you think negatively about yourself, you treat yourself poorly, inviting others to treat you likewise.

The most accurate and beneficial way to think of your genuine self is in terms of energy. Start thinking about yourself as an informational field of energy rather than a solid, physical body. Your body is mostly water—liquid, not solid. On a cellular level, your physical body consists of a huge number of energy stores, of mitochondria and an even larger number of cells. Trillions of messenger molecules inform each cell precisely how to function. At an even deeper level, you are pure energy. Not dead energy, but fully alert, alive, intelligent energy. Your energy is intelligent enough to create and organize some seven trillion actions within your body every second. Now that's intelligent power!

What is conscious and unconscious thought? On a fundamental level, it is nonmaterial energy containing information that creates and manages all bodily functions. When your thoughts are negative, you create negativity. When your thinking is positive, you generate positivity. You always have the choice about *what* you think, *when* you think, and even *whether or not* you think. You are always choosing the *meaning* you give to those biochemical events in your brain and throughout your body. Most of these choices, however, are unconscious. They are programmed into your subconscious functioning by the information in your DNA and by your repetitive and reinforced thinking.

When you *consciously choose* to reprogram your thinking, you influence and control your life from the inside out. When you stop your thinking—as in meditation—you erase the static between self-generated information and information contained in the thoughts of others. When you stop your conscious thought, you open your mind to other informational energy. You can become consciously aware of what Carl Jung called the "collective unconscious." You don't have to be a mystic to experience informational intelligence greater than your own. Contemporary physicists have shown that we are, on a fundamental level, a field of energy within an energy field of infinite possibilities.

The nature and quality of your habitual thinking patterns creates and determines the nature and quality of your life. Change your thinking habits and you change your life. If you are unhappy with who you are, or with your situation, begin changing it by first changing your thinking habits.

> Every good thought you think is contributing its share to the ultimate result of your life.
> —Grenville Kleiser

Exercises and Information

Norman Vincent Peale once said, "Change your thoughts and you change your world." If any of your clients want to do either, below are some helpful suggestions.

Changing Your Thinking

If you sense your clients are thinking negative thoughts, encourage them to replace these thoughts immediately. Let your clients know that *doing* the right things, *having* the right things, or *saying* the right things is never sufficient. They must also *think* the right things. Only then can they create lives that are balanced and in harmony with what they genuinely desire.

There are several ways for your clients to start changing their thinking. Here are a few suggestions.

Create an overall vision of your desired future. Write down a comprehensive description of that vision. Write their vision in the present tense as if it was already manifest. Memorize the description (memorization signals that the information has been programmed into the subconscious mind). Refer to this description regularly. Revise it often.

Make a written list of at least 200 goals—some small victories, some huge dreams—you would like to reach during your lifetime. Think thoughts that support the manifestation of your desired vision. Update the list regularly. Write "victory" beside each one you attain or accomplish.

Consciously practice filling your mind with affirmations and images of yourself functioning within your desired lifestyle. Write down these affirmations. Record and listen to them regularly. Collect pictures representing your desired outcomes. Put self-esteem affirmations on the mirror. Regularly paint, draw, sculpt, or otherwise make visual your goals.

You might suggest to your clients that they help *others* realize their dreams as well. They are more likely to create what they desire if they help enough other people get what they want. (Incidentally, this principle is one of the wonderful aspects of authentic life coaching.) When your clients focus on the positive nature and quality of their thinking, they powerfully increase the probability that they will generate a real abundance of happiness for themselves.

Detecting the Closed Mind

The human mind is a fantastic source of creative energy. Our mental activity is the driving force behind our evolution.

> There is nothing either good or bad, but thinking makes it so.
> —William Shakespeare

Let your clients know that new ideas have changed the face of the earth. New concepts have altered how we live. Creative thinking has benefited each of us in countless ways. So why is it that so many of your clients keep their minds closed to receiving new information?

The primary source of a closed mind is *fear*. Many clients close their minds and remain in their comfort zones rather than risk the usual cognitive disruption created by new and different ways of thinking. Keeping an open mind is a perceived and feared risk. As revitalizing as a receptive mind might be, clients often prefer to defend the familiar, the comfortable, and the regular routine by not letting any new thoughts or information leak into their awareness.

Whenever we filter out new information, we think only those thoughts with which we are familiar. We often remain controlled and driven only by our unconscious thought patterns, which we incorporated when we were children. When we disrupt our unconscious programming, we feel unsafe and anxious. Clients who feel unsafe, insecure, or anxious are most likely to be closed-minded. It's their favorite defense mechanism.

It's tragic that our natural curiosity as children is deadened (if not killed) in the name of protecting ourselves from change. Yet authentic life coaching provides a safe relationship out of which natural curiosity and new thinking can emerge. Remind closed-minded clients that shutting their minds to the receipt of new information only maintains their old ways of thinking and being. Keeping out novel, and perhaps beneficial information virtually guarantees a dull and boring life.

Close-minded clients may invent excuses and rationalizations to make their closed mind seem normal or rational. Sometimes they will spend more time and energy thinking up excuses for keeping their mind closed than they would use if they simply tried out the new idea or action.

When you hear a client say one of the following common statements, you can be fairly certain you are coaching someone with a closed mind.

> Thinking is the hardest work there is—which is probably the reason so few engage in it.
> —Henry Ford

"But we've always done it this way!" "If it ain't broke, don't fix it." If it has been good enough up until now, that in and of itself is a good reason for not ever considering another approach, another possibility, or another way of thinking about an issue. The issue and the mind are closed.

"I just know we'd be unsuccessful if we tried it your way." This is a common manifestation of a closed-mind—in this instance, a fear of possible loss. Somehow we tend to believe that doing something differently requires the loss of an old habit. Ask yourself, however, "Did I lose my ability to walk when I learned how to ride a bike?" or "When I learned to drive a car, did I force myself to forget how to ride a bicycle?"

"It's too much trouble to change." Learning new ideas, new skills, or new habits requires effort, focused concentration, and practice. It certainly requires a lot less effort to close our minds than to engage in new ways of thinking and functioning. In the name of laziness or safety, the closed-minded person always avoids trouble at the price of paralysis and stagnation.

"Don't rock the boat" or **"don't make waves."** These phrases reflect our fear of loss of control. We spend most of our childhoods learning to control something. We practiced controlling our environment, others, or ourselves. If we were punished when we lost control as children, maintaining control became much more important to us as adults than learning anything new.

"It can't be done, it's impossible." When confronted with this kind of statement, you know your client feels helpless, powerless, and has a closed mind. He or she feels more powerful engaging in familiar thinking than in attempting something new at which he or she might be awkward or fail. Defending this perceived helplessness by closing the mind helps your client maintain the illusion of safety.

The Exercise of Map-Making

Thoughts are merely electrochemical events in our brains. When clients change the electrical firing patterns of the nerve cells within their brains, their whole reality—or mental map—changes. Alter the biochemistry of a tiny area of the mid-brain and the emotional responses to *everything* are altered!

What to say to your clients about mental maps. The world inside your mind is like a map. It is an electrochemical representation of what has stimulated your brain. The map is not the actual terrain, only a symbolic image or conceptualization of what is out there in reality. This map may or may not be accurate about how it represents the outside world. However, you rely on this map, this representation in your mind, to learn how to survive and function in the world.

If the map in your mind is inaccurate, false, outmoded, or just plain garbled, then your behavior will be confused, inappropriate, difficult, problem-generating, and perhaps even crazy. You would be like the driver of a car trying to follow a map of Chicago while driving in Los Angeles.

One major problem with map-making in our heads is that we are born only with those maps in place that resulted from genetic programming. A more difficult problem is that the external situation is constantly changing, making our maps obsolete, useless, and sometimes even dangerous.

The biggest aspect to keep in mind about map-making is that maps require constant revision. It doesn't seem fair that most of our life-long habits were developed by the age of five. After all, what right does a little five-year-old have to determine how I, as an adult, will behave or function? What right does he or she have to determine my behavior right down to the language I speak, how I relate to others, my thinking and emotional habits, and the basic nature of the map I now use to help me navigate my world?

Consider coaching sessions as essentially exposure to new experiences and the practicing of new skills—especially new thinking skills. Such exposure and practice are the best methods of map-making and revision. In order to fully enjoy being alive, we must learn new ways of functioning and new skills. We must revise old habits that have become painful or inappropriate and heal our wounds. We must expose ourselves to new experiences and situations, and practice new ways of thinking and problem solving—new ways of evaluating the information we are constantly taking in. We need to keep accurate old maps that are working well, but we must update and build new versions of the maps in our minds (refer to Lesson 2).

Stinkin' Thinkin'

Your clients may already know that their reality is caused by their thinking. What they might not know is that they respond not to events occurring outside of them, but rather to their *perception* of those events and their *evaluation* of those perceptions.

If your clients become anxious when thinking about giving a speech to an audience, you may want to ask, "What's so dangerous about giving a talk in public? Your *thinking* and your *evaluation* of public speaking send the signals to your body to gear up for a threat." Thus, your clients' thoughts are what generate the anxiety (stress) response.

When examining your clients' negative ways of thinking, a number of undesirable patterns crop up repeatedly. Whatever the origin, all are simply bad habits developed over the years. Fortunately, because they have been learned, they can also be replaced. First, however, the dynamics of these negative thinking patterns must be recognized and understood.

Your clients are usually unaware of their negative thinking habits. Before they can replace any thinking habit with another, they need to become aware of the habit they wish to replace. Here are a few common—often unconscious—negative thinking habits. Share them with your clients when they engage in these thinking patterns so they might become consciously aware of them and practice chosen alternatives.

> My life has been filled with terrible misfortunes—most of which never happened.
> —Mark Twain

Making assumptions. This is a pattern of making assumptions and then responding to them as if they were true or happening immediately. Most worrying is an anxious response to an assumed event. Replace assumption-making with responding only to facts or objective events. Always seek accurate information concerning events about which you worry.

Self-criticism. Many people engage in an internal monologue of self-criticism or put-downs, which always lowers their self-esteem. Replace criticism with realistic self-praise and affirmation.

Perfectionism. This is the belief that you and your actions must always be perfect in order to be acceptable. Perfectionist thinking always breeds bodily tension, fear, and hyperactivity. It also leads to attempts to control everything. Replace perfectionist demands with "adequacy."

> You have absolute control over but one thing, and that is your thoughts. If you fail to control your own mind, you may be sure you will control nothing else.
> —Napoleon Hill

Cynical monologue. These thoughts diminish the joy you have in a given moment, create distrust in your relationships, and lower self-esteem. Replace cynicism with creative alternative values—ones that you feel good about.

Mind reading. This is the tendency to assume you know what others are thinking or feeling, and act as if those assumptions were true. It also occurs when you assume you know why others act the way they do without first checking it out. For example, "He never smiles at me, so I know he doesn't like me or will reject me" is a common type of mind reading.

Fallacies of control. When you think that you are controlled by external forces such as fate, happenstance, chance, or circumstances, you commit one of the fallacies of control. You commit another fallacy of control when you believe you are responsible for or in control of the pain or happiness of everyone around you.

Power to change another. This is a belief that you have the ability or power to change how another person behaves. Common to difficult relationships, this belief is a fallacy. Believing that if you talk long enough, yell loud enough, or get even often enough the other person will change is an example of distorted thinking.

Later reward fallacy. This means that you think all your pain, suffering, giving, self-sacrifice, or self-denial will eventually pay off in some way. The statement, "After all I've done for you, just look at the thanks I get" illustrates this type of thinking.

Disasterizing. Sometimes called *catastrophizing*, this is when you magnify the significance of unpleasant events and behave as if they were bound to happen or were happening now. For example, you make a mistake at work or have a bad day and you think, "This is the end of my job. I'll never be able to succeed. I'm a stupid failure."

Filtering your thinking. Filtering is when you focus on a negative detail in a certain situation and dwell on it exclusively, thereby perceiving the whole situation to be negative. Sometimes you filter all positive feedback through a negative self-image and color everything negatively. Discounting a compliment is an example of this.

Disqualifying a positive action or event. Attributing to luck any positive occurrence or successful behavior. For example, when you achieve a coaching goal, you think, "Well that was a lucky fluke. I'm sure I could never do that again."

Thinking you are better or worse than anyone else. Comparative thinking is a mistake because everyone is different. Everyone has unique personal qualities.

Thinking in "shoulds." You make heavy, often unwanted demands on yourself or others, based on your own perfectionist standards. Change the *shoulds* to *coulds* and you can live up to your notion of perfection. Thinking in *coulds* rather than *shoulds* brings to your thinking the power of conscious choice.

Polarized thinking. Sometimes called black and white thinking, an example would be when you make a mistake or fall short of personal standards you think, "I guess I'm a complete failure."

Over generalizing. You believe that a single negative event guarantees a continuous pattern of unpleasant happenings. Making assumptions that the future will always be like this is an example of over generalization. The words, *always* and *never* characterize this kind of thinking.

Personalization. You take on the responsibility and guilt for events you never caused. For example, a child receives a poor grade and the parent personalizes the poor grade by thinking that there must be something he or she did wrong.

Emotional reasoning. This is when you feel a certain way and then decide that things really are that way. You feel unloved, so you decide you are unlovable. You feel rejected, so you think there is something wrong with you.

Remind your clients that their negative thinking styles reinforce harmful perceptions of themselves, of others, and of the reality of the situation. They have practiced these habits for many years and replacement of these habits requires awareness, persistence, and a desire to feel better about the experience of being alive. Suggest to your clients that they change their "stinkin' thinkin'" habits not by trying to get rid of them, but by practicing new, more accurate thinking habits until they become as automatic as the old, mistaken ones. When your clients think accurately, they lower their stress and raise their level of self-esteem.

> Your success and happiness lie in you. External conditions are the accidents of life, its outer trappings. The great enduring realities are love of service. Resolve to keep happy, and your joy shall form an invisible host against difficulty.
> —Helen Keller

Seven Ways to Manage Your Mental Life

Below are seven suggestions you can offer your clients to aid them in more effectively managing their cognitive life.

1. Visualization. This consists of four essential elements: frequency (how often you engage in imagery about your desired outcome or creation); vividness (the sensory-rich clarity of your image); intensity (how much emotional energy is evoked when visualizing); and duration (how long you engage in imagining your desired creation).

> We never understand a thing so well, and make it our own, as when we have discovered it for ourselves.
> —René Descartes

2. Affirmations. These are verbal statements that are positive, present tense (as if you are describing a currently existing condition), and personal (relevant to you and not a comment on anyone or anything else).

3. Verbalization. This is when you speak aloud to yourself or to others, a description of your desired outcome, the process of how you are creating it, and the reasons why you want that new creation to be made manifest. Ask someone else to inquire about your progress and become accountable to him or her.

4. Acting the part. This is when you behave as if you have already attained the outcome you desire. Walk, talk, and act exactly as if you were already the person you desire to be within that new condition or creation.

5. Feeding your mind. Identify someone who has already successfully created what you want to create and imitate what that person did. The more you read, listen, watch, and learn about any subject, the more confident and capable you feel in that area, and the more you identify with and reprogram your subconscious with the identified content.

6. Associating with positive people. Form a mastermind group of two to five people who are of like mind and with whom interacting strengthens you and empowers you to attain your desired creation.

7. Teach others what you are learning. Teaching another is one of the best ways to learn anything for yourself. You become what you teach. You teach what you are.

The principles involved in developing mental mastery are repetition and practice. Combined into one overriding principle, repetitive practice is the most powerful conscious activity we have for programming our subconscious with new habits.

Edit Your Memories

A large part of conscious and unconscious thinking is remembering. Your clients' memories may fill up a lot of their thinking time. However, it may be wise for clients to edit their memory bank.

If a client has an auto accident, the instant of the accident becomes a memory. The only place the accident remains, or recurs, is in that memory. Indeed, every instant in the present moment, immediately becomes a memory.

Thankfully, a great deal of what we experience becomes a permanent part of our memory banks. If it were not so, we would not learn as much or as rapidly as we do. Our ability to remember is one of the finest, natural skills we have. It only becomes a problem when our memory banks are filled with negative contents.

Your clients' emotions, thoughts, anticipations, judgments, desires, problem-solving skills, intentions, creativity, and values evolve not so much from their immediate experiences as they do in response to their remembrances of past experiences. When they respond from a collection of negative memories, they color their present internal state with negativity, depression, and darkness—their present-day experiences become depressive, unhappy, and miserable.

Perhaps we all need to revise and update our thinking and memory content. As an authentic life coach, you know you can always fill your memory bank with pleasant, delightful memories. You can always anticipate the best, positive future events for yourself and your clients.

Since the quality of your present-moment experience and your bodily reactions to it depend on the content of your mental life, why not fill your mind with the best thinking, most positive memories, and the greatest anticipations you can conjure? If we were to do that with the actual positive events—the accidents of life that are delightful—or the exciting anticipations of our future, we would certainly create a context for every moment to be lived fully and enjoyed thoroughly. Teach you clients this way of thinking. They might like it—and you might become a better, more effective life coach!

> The only people who never fail at anything are those who don't try anything.
> —Earl Nightingale

Sample Coaching Conversation

Client is a mortgage broker who just started with a new firm. He has been in sales before, but mostly car sales at a dealer with many repeat customers.

Coach: How was your progress this week? Any successes in getting new clients?

Client: Some, but this is not as easy as it was being the sales leader at the Mercedes dealer. There is more competition in this business.

Coach: Maybe, but there are a lot more people buying and refinancing homes than are buying new cars. So do you think you can get some of that business?

Client: I believe I can most of the time, but there are times, like when I lose a customer, or a closing is canceled, that I feel frustrated and start thinking negatively.

Coach: I imagine that when you first started in the car sales business you had some similar experiences.

Client: Yes, that is true. I do believe I can be very successful in the mortgage business and I like the excitement of it. There really is a huge supply of customers. I just need to see that our company can make it easy and financially sound for them. It is really a no-brainer for those with good credit.

Coach: I already hear your thinking changing. Remember earlier when we talked about the importance of positive attitude? This is the next step. From a positive outlook comes positive or possibility thinking; thoughts affect beliefs and beliefs determine behaviors. Moreover, to many great thinkers words, are seen as a form of energy—what you think creates your experiences.

Client: Boy, that really strikes a chord. . . Now I believe I can shift into positive thinking whenever I hear those negative voices in my head.

Coach: As a fieldwork assignment, I'd like you to list at least 10 affirmations that support your desired changes. Are you willing to do that?

Client: Ok. I will do that.

Questions and Inquiries

1. What are some ways you can change your negative thinking patterns?

2. Can you identify with any of the previously described thinking styles? If so, which ones?

3. With what new thoughts and thinking habits are you willing to fill your mental life?

4. What memories do you wish to keep? Which ones do you wish to repress?

LIFE LESSON 38
Everyone has the ability to develop creative thinking skills.

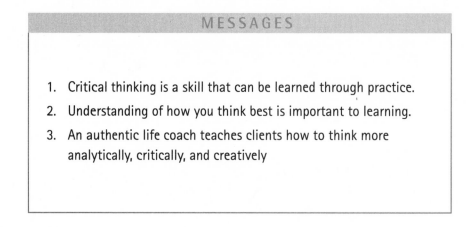

MESSAGES

1. Critical thinking is a skill that can be learned through practice.
2. Understanding of how you think best is important to learning.
3. An authentic life coach teaches clients how to think more analytically, critically, and creatively

The objectives for Lesson 38 are: 1) To distinguish between analytical and creative thinking; 2) To learn how to strengthen clients' thinking skills; 3) To learn how to think creatively; 4) To deepen your understanding of your clients' thinking abilities.

Framework Needed for Coaching Your Clients

As he mentioned in earlier lessons, if we do not allow for variation in our behaving and thinking habits, our actions and thoughts become stagnant and result in the same old outcomes.

Everything around you that is manmade began as an idea in somebody's mind. As complex as it may seem, human culture all started with someone thinking differently from how they were taught to think. The evolution of civilization requires the generation of new ideas, new concepts, and new thinking habits.

Analytical Thinking

As human beings we have the ability to reason. For thousands of years this ability has been studied and discussed; Plato and Aristotle wrote volumes on logic, rational thought, and reasoning. They saw value in thinking logically and rationally. To comprehend and understand our world, analytical thinking is crucial.

Almost all analytical thinking is based on the principle of cause and effect. If you want to understand any event, you need to identify its cause or causes. For example, medical science operates on the model of finding the causes of symptoms, treating those causes, and helping the symptoms to disappear. A diagnosis is an attempt to identify the symptoms of a specific problem and think back to the cause(s) in a linear fashion. The assumption is that when the cause is identified and modified, the symptoms can also be changed.

The diagram below shows the conventional analytical thinking pattern—moving in a linear fashion from recognizing a problem to finding a solution. We have been taught that when confronted with a problem, we should analytically select a possible solution based on our experience, education, and work. At least until after we have experimented by trial and error with the possible solutions we have chosen, we exclude all other possibilities from our thinking. Then, we work within a clearly defined direction toward the usual solution. In short, we analyze the problem to identify the causes and we select a solution from our mental storehouse. We try the solution to see if it works to solve the problem. If it doesn't, we either give up or try another possible solution.

$$\text{problem} \rightarrow \rightarrow \rightarrow \rightarrow \rightarrow \text{solution}$$

As you can see, analytical thinking, as beneficial as it is in some areas, remains narrow, exclusive, and linear. The pattern of analytical thinking allows our minds to simplify and effectively cope with a complex world. We can function automatically and routinely because we have successfully repeated this analytical thinking pattern until it becomes unconscious.

Analytical thinking works well, except when it doesn't. Unconscious, linear, analytical thinking habits make it difficult to come up with new ideas, creative solutions, and ways to expand your own thinking habits—especially when confronted with new or unusual information. You and your clients need to think in new ways whenever you are in a new situation. That is where creative thinking proves most valuable.

> The fundamental fact about the Greek was that he had to use his mind. The ancient priests had said, "Thus far and no farther. We set the limits of thought." The Greeks said, "All things are to be examined and called into question. There are no limits set on thought.
> —Edith Hamilton

Creative Thinking

When you think creatively, you deviate from your past thinking habits. You think outside the box. You break out of your established (usually unconscious) thinking habits, ignore conventional wisdom, and generate new ideas, new solutions, and new thinking patterns.

Creative thinking styles include:

- Making novel combinations—combining things in new ways.
- Thinking in metaphors and analogies—imagining other perceptual paradigms, looking at other world views.
- Making unique connections—connecting the previously unconnected.
- Thinking in opposites and reversals—viewing things from another angle.
- Actively looking for the exception—the accidental—and discovering what you are not looking for.

Please note that these creative thinking styles do not produce the creative experience. They only form the thinking context in which creativity is enhanced. These styles liberate your creativity by disrupting your conventional thinking patterns (usually the analytical one) and stimulating new thinking habits by allowing you to consider unlikely informational relationships.

Exercises and Information

Below are selected principles and exercises to achieve clear and creative thinking habits. Share them with your clients on an individualized basis.

Generating Ideas

Brainstorming is probably the most familiar way for your clients to generate ideas to solving problems. Your clients can brainstorm alone or with others. Effective brainstorming involves five basic principles: (1) generate as many ideas as possible; (2) avoid making judgments; (3) write down ideas as they occur; (4) elaborate on every idea; and (5) allow the subconscious to work on focused ideas.

> Remember happiness doesn't depend upon who you are or what you have; it depends solely upon what you think.
> —Dale Carnegie

1. Generate as many ideas as possible. Have your clients engage in possibility thinking. If you brainstorm with your clients, begin by mutually looking for as many ideas as you can. Know that *quantity breeds quality*—if only because of the laws of probability. The more times you swing a bat at a baseball, the probability increases that you will hit it! If you never risk missing, you'll never swing!

> Great minds discuss ideas; Average minds discuss events; Small minds discuss people.
> —Eleanor Roosevelt

2. Avoid making judgments. Once you've generated the maximum number of ideas, avoid making judgments about any of the ideas. Nothing kills creative thinking faster than evaluative judgments. *Don't* ask silently or aloud, "Why won't this work?" If you must question yourself, ask "How can this be done?" Rather than concentrating on generating a large quantity of ideas, clients have usually learned the habit of immediately judging them. Creative thinking is more difficult, if not impossible, when you prematurely reject ideas.

3. Write down ideas as they occur. One of the best ways to defer judgment is to write down all ideas as they occur, which creates them symbolically in the external world. By immediately writing their ideas down, clients freeze them in time and grant them enough importance to externally manifest them for the first time.

The human brain keeps track of no more than nine bits of information at any given moment. So, writing down ideas not only translates them from a mental abstraction into a concrete reality, it also allows clients to keep a record of them. Listing ideas helps clients to remember them, speeds up their thinking, keeps them focused, permanently captures the ideas for later reference, and invites your clients to focus on alternatives or elaborations.

4. Elaborate on every idea. Suggest to your clients that they carry a pocket-sized spiral notebook with them at all times and write down possible solutions to problems immediately as they occur. After they have written down all their ideas during a given timeframe, ask that they review them and elaborate on their ideas. Elaborating on their written ideas improves them.

In his book, *Cracking Creativity*, Michael Michalko gives credit to Bob Eberle for ordering these seven principles into the useful mnemonic device, *SCAMPER*.

> **S** = **S**ubstitute? Can I substitute something for the idea?
> **C** = **C**ombine? Can I combine it with some other idea?

A = **A**dapt? Can I adapt the idea to the general subject I am considering?

M = **M**agnify? **M**odify? Can I enlarge the idea? How can I change it or add to it?

P = **P**ut the idea to some other use? Are there new ways to use this idea?

E = **E**liminate? What can I delete from this idea. What is not necessary? Can I simplify it?

R = **R**earrange? **R**everse? What other arrangement might be better? What is the opposite? How else can they be viewed?

Offer clients the following example of Thomas Edison: Contrary to popular belief, Edison did not *invent* the electric light bulb. What he did was elaborate on the idea of the light bulb to perfect it as a readily available consumer item. He also experimented with over ten thousand light sources to find one that would give off light without burning up. In the process, he invented an entire practical system for electric lighting including conduits, dynamos, and a means for dividing the current to illuminate many light bulbs at once.

5. Allow the subconscious to work on focused ideas. Once your clients have elaborated on their ideas, it is time for them to allow their subconscious to work on the ideas. Since subconscious programming is what drives most behavior, if your clients want to implement new ideas, have them begin by programming these new ideas into their subconscious minds. They can most effectively accomplish this by focused attention, practice, and repetition. Have them memorize their ideas so that they can recite them rapidly, aloud, and without pause. When they can recite their ideas from memory you know they have programmed them into their subconscious. Their unconscious will then work on the idea twenty-four hours a day.

Most great ideas do not arrive suddenly, popping up from the unconscious mind. Only after focusing her attention, practicing experiments, and repeating actions did Madam Curie, in a dream, generate the configuration of the benzene ring. For that discovery, she won the Nobel Prize for Science. Thomas Edison sometimes slept on a table in his laboratory so he could begin working the moment he awoke and not forget anything his subconscious delivered while he was unconscious.

Creative thinking requires a concerted effort to generate ideas and strengthen the thinking habits presented in this section.

Sample Coaching Conversation

Client: Boy, what a week I've had. We've got lots of things to talk about today.

Coach: Tell me where you want to start.

Client: Well, I am fresh out of ideas about how to build my practice. I'm not getting the clients I used to get, my income is diminishing, and I anxious about my financial future.

Coach: Let's brainstorm a little about what you might do to revitalize your business.

Client: Sounds great.

Coach: I'd like to make a distinction between analytical thinking and creative thinking, because I think it would add clarity to our brainstorming. First of all, let's think analytically about the current state of your business and how it got there. What you have learned about what works and what doesn't work? What trends you are observing? And how you have built your practice up to now? After that, let's think creatively about what you want to do in the near future and engage in possibility thinking on how you would like it to be and what changes would support the creation of a stronger practice.

Client: So you are distinguishing between thinking analytically about what's happening now and the causes of it, and thinking creatively about my future and what needs to be done to increase my income stream.

Coach: You got it. So here is my request of you and a fieldwork assignment for our next call. Take a piece of paper and draw a line down the center of it. Title the page as *Thoughts About My Business*. Label the left column *Analysis of my current situation and how it came to be*; label the right column *New ideas and strategies for growing my business*. Then, bring the lists to our next session. Is that okay with you?

Client: That sounds like a neat idea. I'll do it and maybe next week we can brainstorm together about both lists.

Coach: Sounds good to me. And on our next call, we will continue the conversation about new and creative adjustments to your overall business plan.

Questions and Inquiries

1. How are you willing to work at developing your creative thinking habits?
2. What new thinking habit are you willing to practice for the next three weeks.
3. Do you understand the difference between analytical and creative thinking? What is the distinction? Write it down.

LIFE LESSON 39
Paradoxical thinking is crucial to the full understanding of your world.

MESSAGES

1. Paradoxical thinking is essential to being receptive to new information.

2. Understanding the paradoxes of knowledge expands your awareness of personal reality.

3. To be able to think paradoxically is a valuable thinking skill.

4. Coaching your clients' thinking skills presumes a personal awareness of paradoxical thinking.

The objectives for Lesson 39 are: 1) To learn what paradoxical thinking is; 2) To become aware of the value and significance of paradoxical thinking; 3) To effectively manage the apparent paradoxes within your clients' personal reality; 4) To learn some developmental techniques to enhance your paradoxical thinking skills.

Framework Needed for Coaching Your Clients

If you are an effective coach, you will always present statements to your clients that are inconsistent with their common experience. Your clients may find what you say to be unbelievable or absurd at first, and yet true in fact. If your clients are going to understand, incorporate, and use what you share that is contradictory, unbelievable, and inconsistent with their current experience, they must enhance their cognitive skill of *paradoxical thinking*.

Most clients hire a life coach because how they currently think and behave no longer works well for them—or they feel ignorant of what they need to learn or do differently to get where they want to be in life. Your clients need to be able to

Whenever you find yourself on the side of the majority, it is time to pause and reflect.
—Mark Twain

cognitively process, incorporate, and use information that they currently don't understand, don't believe, or find inconsistent with their current experience. In short, they have to think paradoxically.

The strongest form of paradoxical thinking is to be able to hold in your mind the truth of two apparently mutually exclusive ideas. Instead of thinking that *either* this or that is true, the paradoxical thinker thinks *both* this and that can be true.

Clients who think paradoxically are more likely to expand their awareness of the nature of their reality.

The circular Yin Yang symbol is a well known Chinese image—a visual representation of paradoxical thinking. Contained in the black color (yin) is a small element of white (yang), and within the white color (yang) is a small element of black (yin). Both black and white are identical in shape and size, and both are contained within a whole circle.

An example of this ancient dynamic is an element of spring that shows itself at the peak of winter; as one extreme fades, its opposite emerges. Nothing in life is either black or white, rather a variable shade of grey.

Thinking that ideas are mutually exclusive is indicative of a compartmentalized or closed mind. Albert Einstein himself proposed that physical matter and energy are essentially the same. He determined that life is not divided into matter and energy, but matter and energy are merely different forms of the same elemental (essential) phenomenon. Where *you* might have difficulty believing that light is *either* waves *or* particles, physicists who think paradoxically have no trouble with the idea that light is *both* particles *and* waves.

You are a physical being, a psychological being, and a spiritual being, and perhaps other beings all rolled into a whole human being—and you are *both unique* and paradoxically *the same* as other human beings.

Exercises and Information

When your clients want to strengthen their thinking habits, the exercises below are very useful.

Exercise in Paradoxical Thinking

Invite your clients to brainstorm and make a list of all possible actions that initially seem to be mutually exclusive (e.g., experiencing sadness and happiness at the same time, noticing the human body to be solid, liquid, and an energy field simultaneously). Go over the list and ask your client to acknowledge each action from a perspective of *both/and* rather than an *either/or* viewpoint. Point out that seemingly mutually exclusive viewpoints can be equally accurate.

The goal of the above exercise is to practice evaluating all actions and their anticipated consequences from a paradoxical viewpoint.

During each contact with your clients, when you hear them engaging in black-or-white thinking, gently invite them to consider their thoughts from an all-inclusive viewpoint.

Sample Coaching Conversation

Client: I really need some coaching today on problems I'm having with members of my team at work. As you know, as a team leader I have been assigned a project to develop a more effective software program with my team. Some of my team members think the whole thing is unnecessary and a waste of time.

Coach: Well, it sounds to me like you could use some new thinking about your resistant team members. Why do you think those team members' resistance is so strong.

Client: I don't know. They're either for or against it. At least, that's how they're coming across to me.

Coach: What if the those team members are actually afraid of change and very comfortable with the status quo?

Client: I've never thought about it like that.

Coach: Well, in this case you may want to expand you notion of resistance to include both fear and comfort and possibly feelings of inadequacy. If you thought about the problem in this way, it would expand your options about how to address their resistance and increase the likelihood of arriving at a win-win solution.

> What we do not understand we do not possess.
> —Goethe

Client: That's a new way to think about it for me. I can see the value of considering how their resistance can actually be helpful to working on completing our assignment.

Coach: Let me suggest that you use this type of paradoxical thinking whenever you catch yourself looking at problems in a black-or-white manner.

Questions and Inquiries

1. What are some other ways to view your coaching goals, attainments, and chosen actions toward creating what you want?

> Thought makes the whole dignity of man; therefore endeavor to think well, that is the only morality.
> —Blaise Pascal

2. Have you considered all the possible ways of interpreting the actions of others?
3. Do you always understand and consider the point of view of the person with whom you are interacting?
4. When in doubt about your own interpretation of thoughts, feelings, and events, do you seek out different interpretations from many others? Even when you are certain, do you ask for confirmation as well as invite other points of view to be shared?
5. How else might you interpret any event in your life, especially traumatic events?

LIFE LESSON 40
Identifying your learning style, coupled with reinforcement, facilitates all learning.

MESSAGES

1. Without positive or negative reinforcement, learning does not take place.
2. Your personal attention is the most powerful reinforcement for learning.
3. Efficient learning depends upon your learning style.
4. Effective coaches identify and reinforce their clients' learning styles and personal changes.

The objectives for Lesson 40 are: 1) To understand the distinction between positive and negative reinforcement; 2) To become selective in what you reinforce with your attention; 3) To become familiar with your personal learning style; 4) If desired, to change your learning habits by practicing new ones.

Framework Needed for Coaching Your Clients

When any human response is attended to, that response is reinforced and the probability of it recurring is increased. In other words, what we attend to becomes stronger in our lives—even if the attention given is negative, such as punishment or pain. Amazingly, the reinforcement power of negative attention is about five times stronger than that of positive attention. For example, if you say, "I really like you," to a client every day for five days, and then on the sixth day you say in anger, "I really hate you," the client is more likely to remember the latter and be emotionally attached to it longer.

Education is that which remains when one has forgotten everything he learned in school.
—Albert Einstein

As an authentic life coach, your selective attention to the changes, attainments, progress, and accomplishments of your clients needs to be consistent. *Never* make your clients wrong! Remain constantly constructive by giving regular positive reinforcement to their new behaviors, changes, and attainments. The most common forms of positive reinforcement include recognition, acknowledgement, praise, reward, offering congratulations and even greeting cards or small gifts. You become the champion and greatest fan of your clients and their aspirations.

One of the most useful models of human learning has been the systems model. A systems approach breaks down the process of learning into elements, categorizes them, and then systematizes them into identifiable components that can be more easily addressed by the life coach in the coach/client relationship.

There are four basic phases to human learning:

1. The input phase: information gathered through the five senses.
2. The elaborative phase: incorporating the sensory information in a cognitive context or mind set.
3. The processing phase: the attribution of personal meaning to the perception (information and mindset).
4. The output phase: the verbal and/or nonverbal expression of an idea or thought.

Each phase determines what is learned, how learning happens, and how learning is expressed. Each phase must be adequately operative before efficient learning occurs.

Categories of stimuli that affect each phase of learning contain elements your clients use in unique combinations. These combinations are referred to as learning styles. Your clients' learning styles consist of their favorite combinations of elements within each of the four phases of learning.

You become a more effective life coach by identifying client learning styles and providing positive reinforcement to your clients when they practice new behavioral habits, skills, and thinking patterns. Like representational systems, learning styles are said to be visual, auditory and tactile/kinesthetic.

Learning Style Stimuli

The unique personal combination of these stimuli elements and how you use them to learn anything comprises your learning style.

1. Environmental—sound, light, temperature, design, distractions.
2. Emotional—motivational level, anger/anxiety, persistence, responsibility, confidence.
3. Sociological—friends, co-workers, self, team, authority, rules, or laws.
4. Physical—perceptual processing, intake, output, time limits, mobility, bodily function, practice.
5. Psychological—thinking that is analytical, creative, intuitive, systematic, or rational; focus, cerebral preference, a tendancy to be impulsive or reflective.

Exercises and Information

Transactional analysis defines a unit of attention as a *stroke*. We all need such strokes to remain healthy and to evolve. There are three categories of strokes: positive, negative, and none. People learn to invite negative strokes when they believe positive strokes are unavailable, because negative attention is experienced as better than no attention at all. Negative strokes are more powerful, last longer, and usually have more energy than positive strokes. Likewise, people invite positive strokes either by direct requests or engaging in socially expected or culturally approved behavior. People avoid strokes by isolation, lack of purposeful engagement in a task or social situation.

> Common sense is instinct. Enough of it is genius.
> —George Bernard Shaw

Completing Your Stroking Profile

All interactions between people are for the purpose of getting or giving strokes, or for maintaining a stroke economy. Your clients can make use of the table below to map out their characteristic stroking patterns and think about and perhaps change their stroking patterns within themselves and their relationships.

Instructions: Place a checkmark on the line that most accurately reflects how often you give, take, or ask for (directly or indirectly) either positive or negative strokes.

STROKING PROFILE

		Give	Take	Ask For
Always	10			
	9			
Very Frequent	8			
	7			
Frequent	6			
	5			
Often	4			
	3			
Seldom	2			
	1			
Never	0			

Positive Strokes

		Give	Take	Ask For
Never	0			
	1			
Seldom	2			
	3			
Often	4			
	5			
Frequent	6			
	7			
Very Frequent	8			
	9			
Always	10			

Negative Strokes

Using the chart above, a client can evaluate his or her own stroking habits. Ask your clients to note how often they accept, reject, seek, offer, or ask for strokes. Eventually, your clients will create a social network wherein they consistently give and receive attention sufficient to fulfill their need for strokes.

Assessing Learning Styles

When you and your clients are aware of their learning styles, coaching becomes more effective, stroking patterns more powerful, and the attainment of coaching goals becomes quicker.

Here is an assessment tool to help your clients discover their favorite learning style. If your clients agree with the statement, put an "X" over the bullet beside it. If they disagree or don't know, leave the bullet empty.

List A

- People say you have terrible handwriting.
- You don't like silent filmstrips, pantomimes, or charades.
- You would rather perform or listen to music than view art.
- You sometimes leave out words when writing, or sometimes you get words or letters backwards.
- You can spell aloud better than when you have to write something down.
- You remember things that you talked about in the coaching conversation much better than things you have read.
- You dislike copying materials from books or bulletin boards.
- You like jokes or verbal riddles better than cartoons or crossword puzzles.
- You like games with lots of action better than board or card games.
- You understand material better when you read aloud.
- It seems like you are the last one to notice something new in your environment.
- You find reading a map difficult.
- You usually struggle to keep neat notes or records.
- You like to use your finger or a ruler as a guide when reading.
- You hum frequently or whistle to yourself when you are working.
- You hate to read from the computer, especially when the background is busy.
- Sometimes when you read you mix up words that look similar.

> All the education and all the knowledge in the world can't help the poor soul who has no common sense.
> —Benjamin Franklin

List B

- It seems like you always have to ask somebody to repeat what he or she just said.
- Sometimes you find yourself staring out the window when you are really trying to pay attention to something.
- Often you know what you want to say, but you just can't think of the words. Sometimes you are accused of talking with your hands.

- You may have trouble understanding a person who is talking to you when you are unable to watch the person's face while he or she is speaking.
- You would rather receive directions via demonstration rather than in spoken form.
- When you watch TV or listen to the radio, someone is always asking you to turn it down.
- Spoken words that sound similar (bell-bill, pin-pen) give you trouble. Sometimes you can't tell them apart.
- You have trouble remembering things unless you write them down.
- You like artwork better than music.
- You have to go over most of the alphabet in order to remember something like whether "M" comes before "N."
- You tend to answer questions with "yes" or "no" rather than with complete sentences.
- Often you forget to give verbally received messages (such as telephone messages) to people unless you write them down.
- You are always drawing little pictures on the edges of your papers, or doodling on scratch paper.

Now tally the checked bullets for both List A and List B, keeping the totals separate. Consider clients with more bullets checked for List A auditory learners; if the number of checked bullets for List B is higher, they are visual learners. If the number of checked bullets on both lists is high, they probably learn best by touching and doing and are kinesthetic learners.

Sample Coaching Conversation

> Knowledge is the antidote to fear
> —Ralph Waldo Emerson

Coach: You mentioned in your email to me yesterday that you are having some frustrations with a couple of your staff. Tell me more about it and let me know how you want to be coached in regard to that.

Client: This is really one of the main goals of my coaching. I get busy during tax season and need to have staff stay on top of their responsibilities and follow through on what I tell them to do. I had to reprimand two of my staff this week for not completing files as I asked, and our new receptionist did not give me messages that should have been directed as urgent. I have a big client that is very upset that I did not return his call.

Coach: So, you would like coaching on how to have these sorts of things not happen and for things to run as smoothly as possible, even during the hectic months of tax season, right?

Client: Right. If we could do that, then I would be thrilled. I need employees who do as they are instructed and can be counted on.

Coach: let's coach a bit about your style as "boss" or manager. How do you think your employees view you? If I interviewed them, how would they describe your role.

Client: Oh, I am sure they see me as the boss. And when things aren't going right, I get a bit edgy and demanding. I really don't want to be that way, but I can't have sloppy work that affects my work and reputation.

Coach: Got it. Would you like to be more of a coach-like manager than a boss? You still are the leader and owner of the business, but what if you could coach your employees to be more like you need them to be, and encourage and teach them along the way.

Client: That sounds good, but is that possible?

Coach: There is a truth in life that what people pay attention to is what shows up more, even if it is not desirable behavior. We humans are creatures of habit and we sometimes do things that are not what we want, but negative thinking causes us to be out of sync. Have you ever heaed of *The One Minute Manager*?

Client: No, I haven't.

Coach: The main them is "catch people doing something right." What the authors Blanchard and Johnson are saying in that statement is the fact—and we all do it—that we usually pay more attention to what people do wrong than what they do right. How often do you authentically praise or comment to your staff on things they did well?

Client: Not very often. I assume they know when they do well. And when I criticize them, it is only to get them to do better.

Coach: I know. That is our default human response. Would you be willing to experiment this week, after reading *The One Minute Manger*? Blanchard even teaches how to still ask for performance change or improvement, but only after noticing what staff does well. Your staff will really respond differently to you if you begin to recognize and comment on what they are doing right. Are you willing to try this?

Client: Sure. I will get the book tonight. Sounds helpful.

> It is not enough to acquire wisdom, it is necessary to employ it.
> —Cicero

Coach: Great. So experiment with reinforcing good working habits and behaviors this week and we can coach more next week about making this new habit for you a standard operating procedure.

Questions and Inquiries

1. Under what circumstances do you withhold positive attention (strokes)? Why?
2. Will you monitor yourself for the next few weeks to determine the ratio between the amount of time you spend attending to problems and difficulties vs. attending to solutions and positive events?
3. What are five personal qualities you want to strengthen in yourself by focusing your attention on them?
4. How can you modify your habits of attention (stroking patterns) to insure you are reinforcing behaviors that support your attainment of desired outcomes.

Coaching Summary

How we learn what we learn is unique to the human experience. As Section 6, Learning Cognitive Skills, shows our thinking capabilities are highly evolved, yet often underutilized and minimized in our everyday experience.

The Lessons

The four lessons in this section are designed to help you and your clients become more purposeful and powerful in the application of your thinking skills.

Life Lesson 37

Your thinking habits are the most powerful tools you have for creating anything you genuinely desire. The techniques and exercises in this lesson are designed to help you use thought more powerfully to create your desired future. Examining our thinking habits can be enlightening because, like all habits, they become routine and need reexamination. Keep thinking habits that work, modify those that don't.

Life Lesson 38

Everyone has the ability to develop creative thinking skills. Analytical thinking is another kind of thinking. After applying systems thinking, our brains can analyze data and review available choices. But this analysis need not be done alone. Today, life coaches are available to assist clients in co-creative analysis.

Life Lesson 39

Paradoxical thinking is crucial to the full understanding of your world. In Western culture we have a proclivity to think in terms of black or white, either/or. Paradoxical thinking allows us—in fact *forces* us—to think in terms of both/and by permitting separate realities to coexist. Philosophers and writers throughout history have emphasized the importance of embracing paradoxical thinking. Experiencing paradoxes is often what shakes up our current belief systems and allows us to see things in new ways.

Life Lesson 40

Identifying your learning style, coupled with reinforcement, facilitates all learning. It has been said that what we resist, persists or what we pay attention to is created. These simple principles are often forgotten. Your clients want to create desirable change in their lives and, like most humans, they also have some challenges in their life or business that need changing. The lesson here is to teach your clients to give attention to what they want and utilize the coaching relationship to reinforce the creation of new behaviors, habits, and skills.

Questions and Statements for Reflection

1. Can you describe three times when a shift in your thinking has been instrumental to a desired outcome?
2. When in your life has systems thinking been of value? Cite examples from your life and write them down.
3. Recall a time or situation in your life when analytical thinking was crucial to a successful outcome. What type(s) of thinking were utilized prior to the analysis?
4. Have you ever experienced the positive aspect of paradoxical thinking? What is a most recent example?

SECTION 7
Creating High-Quality Relationships

We can't all be heroes because someone has to sit
on the curb and clap as they go by.
—Will Rogers

LIFE LESSON 41
Succeeding at any endeavor is dependent on the nature and quality of your relationships.

MESSAGES

1. Specific principles exist to create high-quality relationships.
2. You can follow a known process for developing the relationships you want.
3. Fifty percent of the quality of your relationships depends on the nature of what you contribute to it and the people involved.
4. Coaching interpersonal relationship skills is a fundamental aspect of life coaching.

The objectives for Lesson 41 are: 1) To understand the basic principles of beneficial interpersonal relationships; 2) To develop life-enriching friendships; 3) To learn exactly how we go about creating the kinds of relationships we genuinely desire.

Framework Needed for Coaching Your Clients

Successfully creating a desired life is completely dependent on the nature and quality of inter-personal relationships. No one even survives without some kind of inter-personal relationship(s). As an authentic life coach, you need to be a genuine expert in creating high-quality relationships and in catalyzing the same in your clients.

Creating Rich Relationships

Developing a desired lifestyle is impossible if you don't relate to others. We are social creatures. We cannot exist completely on our own.

> In separateness lies the world's greatest misery.
> —Gautama Buddha

Most of us are not highly skilled at creating enriching relationships. Many of us take pride in our sense of independence and believe ourselves to be separate from others. Sometimes we feel we don't even belong in our own families—especially if we grew up in frightening, hostile, or troubled families. We seek emotional safety by mentally dividing the human species into two different categories: *me* and *everybody else*. Mentally and behaviorally, we isolate ourselves from others. We fear and fail to recognize that we are of one species . . . human.

When we habitually isolate ourselves from others, our relationships become psychologically bankrupt, empty of any kind of emotional richness. Such relationships die, and their deaths seem to prove to the loner that he or she is indeed different, separate, and alone.

How can we enrich our relationships? First, we need to recognize, whether we like it or not, that we are all interdependent. While we are all individuals, we still depend on each other for food, shelter, transportation, clothing, and overall life fulfillment. Each of us is woven into a delicate fabric of interdependence.

Secondly, we need to distinguish between friends and acquaintances. Acquaintances are any people we might know. Friends are people in whose company we feel completely accepted. We enjoy interacting with them and trust them completely. Without any fear, we comfortably share our personal thoughts, ideas, opinions, and especially our feelings.

Reinventing Friendship

In the so-called battle between the sexes, one of the first casualties is non-erotic friendship. Friendship between men and women has been so sexualized that someone once defined the Platonic friendship as that brief interval between the introduction and the first kiss.

In our culture, deep friendship simply doesn't receive the hype of the sexual relationship. Psychologists have stated for years that friendship is the third most important relationship in our lives. The relationship between life partners is primary. The parent-child relationship comes second, followed by that durable bond of respect, affection, and mutual enjoyment—the genuine, non-sexualized friendship.

For hundreds of years, friendships between men were taken as the standard of all human relationships. Male friends were like brothers. The brotherhood of men was the desired goal of civilization and the resolution to war. Today, many men are often afraid of close, deep friendships with other men because they don't want to be viewed as homosexual. They may also be afraid of friendships with women, because if they befriend another woman, they fear the loss of their mate or partner. Because we have sexualized intimate relationships, friendships have

Life Lesson 41   333

lost much of their value and influential power. Non-sexualized male/female friendships remain minimal, and with such losses, our need for friends remains unmet.

Almost every male-female encounter is so romanticized or sexualized that the encounters are seen as a "hunt-and-surrender" interaction rather than as a potential for partnership, team-building, collaboration, or cooperation. The time has come to make the bonds of deep friendship society's highest and holiest calling.

Let's desexualize friendship and reclaim our birthright as human beings to develop and nurture our innate need and capability to share our hearts and minds in intimate relationships with *both* men and women. Let's remove sex or competition that hinders or blocks us from forming friendships. Let's make the bonds of affection and the expression of love not only okay, but a desired goal between people regardless of gender.

Exercises and Information

After your clients acknowledge the notion of interconnectedness, you need to make them aware of what Stephen Covey calls "emotional deposits" made into relationships. In essence, we need to balance our relationship accounts by not withdrawing more than we deposit.

Make your clients aware of the five types of emotional deposits below and their counterparts, as described by Covey*:

1. *Kindness vs. unkindness.* Every act of kindness nourishes a relationship. Every unkind act poisons it.
2. *Keeping vs. breaking promises.* Trust is based upon promises kept. Relationships break when trust is violated through broken promises.
3. *Honoring vs. violating expectations.* Healthy relationships are based upon mutual expectations. We need to respect the expectations we have of ourselves and honor the expectations others have of us. When we violate the expectations of others, the relationship weakens.
4. *Loyalty vs. duplicity.* Loyalty is exemplified when we speak well of others when they are not present. Duplicity (being two-faced) is when we speak well of others when they are present, and negatively about them when they are absent. Friendships thrive with loyalty; they die with duplicity.
5. *Regret vs. Pride.* Recognize that we all make mistakes. When you or someone else makes a mistake, apologizing sincerely and forgiving

* From Stephen Covey, 7 Habits of Highly Effective People. Originally published by Simon & Schuster. Copyright ©1989 by Stephen Covey.

> The way to make a true friend is to be one. Friendship implies loyalty, esteem, cordiality, sympathy, affection, readiness to aid, to help. The real friend is he or she who can share all our sorrows and double all our joys. Radiate friendship and it will return seven-fold.
>
> —B. C. Forbes

completely is a huge emotional deposit. If we are so insecure and prideful that we never apologize, we make an equally huge emotional withdrawal from the relationship. (1989, pp: 190–197)

Your clients need to develop the habit of making emotional deposits in all of their relationships. Doing so will make them rich with emotional health, abundance, and delight.

General Principles of Successful Human Relations

Familiarize your clients with the following general principles of interpersonal relationships:

1. People differ, so treat them differently.
2. You get more from others by helping them feel important than you do by making them feel afraid. Building their self-esteem raises your own.
3. Actions result more often out of old habit or emotion than they do from logic or new information.
4. You have to like people (including yourself) to get along with people.

The Coach/Client Relationship Skills

The life coach/client relationship is a very special one. As a life coach, you need to exemplify and teach your clients about the following:

Attend. What we attend to becomes energized and grows. Attending to your clients means staying present with them when conversing. Your attentiveness demonstrates their worth by giving them your undivided concentration. Likewise, when you give a task your full attention, you reveal its worth. If you coach your clients in face-to-face sessions, always maintain eye contact. Stay relaxed and open.

Listen. Actively listen to understand what your clients are saying, feeling, thinking, and wanting you to know. Listen to what is *not* being spoken. Do not interrupt or silently rehearse your reply.

Empathize. Get into the perceptual worlds of your clients. Experience their feelings. Seek full understanding of their positions and viewpoints.

Communicate understanding. Respond with your understanding of what your clients are communicating. Check it for accuracy *before* you express your own thoughts or feelings.

Respect. Behave toward your clients as if each is valuable, precious, one of a kind. They are!

Accept. Acknowledge *who* your clients are now and distinguish between who they are and what they do. Acceptance is not necessarily condoning. Never try to force change upon your clients.

Assert without being aggressive. Never suffer in silence. Let your clients know your precise thoughts and feelings.

Self-reveal. Be open and receptive. Express your thoughts, feelings, wants, needs, dreams, and hopes freely and spontaneously. Share your strengths and weaknesses. Without judgment, let your clients know what is really going on.

Speak directly. Don't use defensive smoke screens like sarcasm, teasing, long-winded lectures, withdrawing, or sulking. Talk to your clients directly even if doing so means conflict. Ask directly for anything you want, using the words, "Will you. . .?"

Focus on now. When conversation bogs down, talk about what is going on between you and your client *here and now*. Don't bring up the past. Express what you like and don't like about what is happening now, in the moment.

> If I accept you as you are, I will make you worse; however, if I treat you as though you are what you are capable of becoming, I help you become that.
> —Goethe

The Process of Creating Any Relationship You Want

If your clients are interested in enhancing interpersonal relationships they currently have or want to develop, familiarize them with the following step-by-step exercise. This process can be used with spouses, children, supervisors, employees, parents—anyone with whom you want an effective and beneficial relationship.

Follow these steps and you will make rapid progress down the path of creating a relationship you desire—the realization of a personal, high-quality relationship!

Step 1. Relax your body and mind. Take ten deep breaths. Take 15–30 minutes to imagine the kind of relationship you would like to have with someone in particular. Picture in your mind how you will be, how you will connect, how you will communicate, how you will feel.

Step 2. Write a detailed description of the nature and quality of your desired relationship. Write it in the present tense. For example, "We enjoy daily walks together." *Only after you've written it down*, share your vision with the other person. Directly ask your relationship partner to engage in steps 1 and 2.

Step 3. Begin to integrate, in writing, the two individual relationship descriptions into a single write-up. Leave nothing out of either person's vision. Avoid falling into a discussion of the relationship you already have. Stick to describing what you *want it to be like* between the two of you.

Step 4. Commit the common vision to your memory, word for word. You might try reading it out loud twice a day, rewriting it daily, or reviewing it several times a day. Only if you can recite from memory the description of your common vision will you know you have programmed it into your subconscious mind.

Step 5. Recite aloud your intention to create your common vision. At least twice a day, make eye contact with your partner as you say, "It is my intention to create with you a relationship characterized by . . ." and then recite the description of your common vision. Speak only when you make direct eye contact. If you break eye contact, stop speaking.

Step 6. Brainstorm together the *ABCDs* (Actions, Behaviors, Choices, and Decisions) you can make to support the manifestation of your common vision. Without judgment, write down as fast as you can your ABCD list. Go for quantity rather than quality.

Step 7. From your ABCD list choose a *single* activity to practice daily for three weeks. It takes three weeks for any new habit to become automatic and therefore unconscious. When you practice daily that single, important activity, it will be an automatic habit by the end of those three weeks. Then select a second habit you wish to engage in and practice that one for the next three weeks. There are seventeen sets of three-week periods in a year. If you commit to your subconscious mind seventeen new habits that you know will support the creation of your desired relationship, in a year's time you will have transformed the relationship.

> As we close ourselves inward, we create a sphere of safety that becomes smaller and smaller until it has room enough only for ourselves, removed from anything or anyone who could ever love us, from anyone who would touch, caress, or heal us.
> —Wayne Mullerg

Step 8. Tell at least one other trusted person—a friend, coach, teacher, or confidant—of the habits you are practicing. Have them ask about your progress and hold you accountable to them.

Step 9. Evaluate the nature of your current relationship with your partner. Become aware of any resistance you have to owning the negative contributions you make to the relationship. Resistance is always fear-based. If you don't become aware of the things you want to change, you will never discover better alternatives.

Step 10. Make a conscious choice to develop a key habit that is a positive alternative to any negative one discovered in Step 9. You cannot unlearn old habits; you can only replace them with new ones.

Step 11. Let yourself experience all of the emotions generated by the discrepancy or gap between what exists now and your desired, envisioned relationship. Avoid engaging in past patterns of reaction. Stay focused on the relationship you are creating.

Step 12. Tolerate the chaos, difficulty, and awkwardness of engaging in new habits. New creations always evolve from a disruption of the status quo. Keep the common vision you have with your relationship partner in the forefront of your mind. Remember that all new activities are difficult before they become easy through practice, and chaos is the context from which creations arise. Only in the chaos and confusion of newly plowed ground is the earth in the proper state to receive the seeds of new plants. Mistakes lead to creations.

Step 13. Persist in practicing the ABCDs that support the creation of the common, desired, and envisioned relationship. Practice your key habit everyday for twenty-one days.

Step 14. Without judgment or criticism, acknowledge yourself as the source of the new relationship, as well as the choices and energy involved. Take 100 percent responsibility for creating your common vision.

Step 15. Reinforce and strengthen all habits, ABCDs, and new experiences with positive attention. The simplest form of positive attention is expressing appreciation to your relationship partner such as "Thank you for . . ." Keep an "Appreciation Journal" and make five entries daily.

Step 16. Regularly acknowledge you and your relationship partner as a team as you move toward the fully manifested creation of your desired relationship.

Sample Coaching Conversation

> **Client:** This past weekend my wife and I got into a big argument. She is an executive VP in a large company and spends 60 to 80 hours a week either at work or traveling. We hardly spend any time together at all.
>
> **Coach:** I understand your relationship is not what you would like it to be. So, how would you like it to be between you and your wife?
>
> **Client:** I don't know. I just resent the amount of time she is away. It's like she's married to her job.
>
> **Coach:** Rather than focusing on the nature of your unsatisfactory relationship as it is today, are you willing to focus on the kind of relationship you would like to have with her in the future?
>
> **Client:** Yeah, that sounds good. How do I begin that?
>
> **Coach:** First of all, I want you to write down a detailed description of the nature and quality of the relationship you really want. Do this without talking to her about it, so it is not influenced by what she does or doesn't want. Next week, we will strategize about how you can contribute to the creation of that ideal relationship. Okay.
>
> **Client:** Sounds good. I guess I never really thought about what kind of relationship I would really want to have. I'll have that description by our next coaching call.

From this point on, the coach will guide the client through the 16 steps above.

Questions and Inquiries

1. What is the quality of each of your current relationships? Your primary one?
2. What do you contribute to the relationship as it is now?
3. Do you like who you are and what you bring to any relationship?
4. What are the most positive characteristics you bring to your relationships?
5. What are your best talents and skills you use within the relationship?
6. What *new* interpersonal skills and habits do you want to develop?

LIFE LESSON 42

Accurately assessing the nature and quality of a current relationship is crucial to changing it.

MESSAGES

1. Most people create their adult relationships by using old habits of social interaction.

2. Identifying your current social skills helps you to discover alternative methods of interaction that work better for you as an adult.

3. If you are unaware of where you are in a relationship, it is virtually impossible to create changes within it.

The objectives for Lesson 42 are: 1) To understand the ABCs of WAR (*Wrecking A Relationship*); 2) To learn how to be non-sexually, yet intimately connected; 3) To assess your clients' current relationships; 4) To discover your clients' level of satisfaction with a given relationship; 5) To understand the evolution of relationships.

Framework Needed for Coaching Your Clients

The first interpersonal relationship we ever have is that between us as children and the adults around us. Many of the social skills learned within that first child-adult relationship are maintained throughout our lives. It is crucial to living happily as an adult, that we revise our childhood relationships and learn how to relate to others as adults.

Understanding Mature Interpersonal Relationships

We are social creatures, yet most of us grow up completely ignorant of the nature of mature interpersonal relationships. As adults, we often remain untaught and unskilled in how to create happy and satisfying personal relationships, even though our happiness is powerfully affected by the nature and quality of our relationships with others.

Relationships grow, change, and mature. Interpersonal relationships begin at birth. Early childhood is characterized by dependence, in which the child completely depends on parents for survival and care.

Dependent relationships grow into codependent relationships. Codependent relationships form when two dependent individuals lean on each other for care, need fulfillment, and quality of lifestyle, rather than standing on their own two feet.

Co-dependence evolves into independence during adolescence. How skilled the parents have been at encouraging independence within their children determines the nature of this transition. Most of us are aware of how psychologically difficult the shift can be from co-dependence to individual autonomy. Independent adults are self-caring and self-supportive. They create their own lifestyles.

Healthy, independent adults form interdependent relationships with mates, peers, coworkers, friends, and colleagues. Teamwork, cooperation, and collaboration characterize interdependent relationships.

Moving out of sequence through these phases of relationship growth is virtually impossible. You cannot create an interdependent relationship if you have never gone through an independent stage of development. Likewise, when childhood co-dependence is unsatisfactory, the evolution to independence proves difficult at best, impossible at worst. After all, we don't expect a plant to flower before it has matured—and it rarely blossoms if it has been stunted in its early growth. Nor does it grow to its full potential when crushed as a sprout.

There is another phase of interpersonal relationships which is rarely noticed or acknowledged. This kind of relationship is the most mature of human interpersonal relations and evolves only after we have successfully completed the first four phases: dependence, codependence, independence, and interdependence. We call this additional, fifth, phase an inter-developmental relationship and sometimes refer to it as *synergistic*.

The following is a description of an inter-developmental relationship enjoyed by two individuals who have matured *through* the interdependent phase of relationship growth:

> Both individuals are independent and get their needs met by themselves or in other relationships. They realize that the outcomes of relating are greater than either could create alone. Both parties share a common vision that gives pur-

Fate makes our relatives, choice makes our friends. —Jacques Delille

pose and direction to their relationship. They trust themselves, each other, and the relationship. They know that the sum of their energy (synergy) is greater than their individual efforts. They synergize when interacting with one another. Neither party is dependent on the other for anything. They take a side-by-side position, facing the future with individual confidence and assurance that what they create as independent grown-ups is more important than their individual goals. They view problems and challenges as mutual opportunities to grow with no need to change the other or modify the other's agenda. They usually enjoy the relationship and have fun within their interaction. As individuals, they have resolved personal issues of pettiness, conflict, ego, self-promotion, striving, power, etc.

If we learn and practice the skills necessary to form inter-developmental relationships, we blossom into psychologically mature people. When we practice inter-developmental relationship skills, we manifest our greatest human potential and are more likely to create lifestyles of delight, satisfaction, and happiness.

Exercises and Information

It is much more difficult to create high-quality relationships without being aware of the quality of the relationships you currently have. Therefore, it becomes very important to realistically assess your current relationships and clarify their characteristics at the moment.

Assessing Your Relationship

Teach your clients that relationships are formed to satisfy personal needs. We all have physical, mental, and emotional needs. Some personal needs are genetic, some are learned, some reflect our values, and some are based on our beliefs. If those needs go unsatisfied, the relationship dissolves or becomes conflicted.

Our primary relationship is any relationship that satisfies the greatest number of our needs. Realistically, no single relationship can fill all of our needs because needs change and relationships change. Relationships grow or deteriorate according to how well our personal needs are addressed by them.

Coach/client relationships catalyze the identification and fulfillment of the needs that clients bring to the relationship. When assessing relationships, it is important for coaches to remain judgment-free. Your coaching intent is simply to identify what *is* and not to evaluate it as either good or bad.

What follows are a few relationship assessment scales that your clients can use to focus on areas of any relationship they may want to change. In the process they are also likely to discover how satisfied they are with important areas of their relationships.

Relationship satisfaction. How satisfied are you and your partner in this relationship with the following aspects of your relationship? (Adapt the areas to fit the relationship being assessed.)

RELATION SATISFACTION SCALE										
Communication	1	2	3	4	5	6	7	8	9	10
Cooperation/Helpfulness	1	2	3	4	5	6	7	8	9	10
Conflict Management	1	2	3	4	5	6	7	8	9	10
Emotional Intimacy	1	2	3	4	5	6	7	8	9	10
Finances	1	2	3	4	5	6	7	8	9	10
Parenting	1	2	3	4	5	6	7	8	9	10
Respect	1	2	3	4	5	6	7	8	9	10
Sexual Intimacy	1	2	3	4	5	6	7	8	9	10
Spirituality	1	2	3	4	5	6	7	8	9	10
Mutual Support	1	2	3	4	5	6	7	8	9	10
Synergy	1	2	3	4	5	6	7	8	9	10
Time Together	1	2	3	4	5	6	7	8	9	10
Overall Quality of the Relationship	1	2	3	4	5	6	7	8	9	10
Scale	*1*	*2*	*3*	*4*	*5*	*6*	*7*	*8*	*9*	*10*
		Not satisfied at all			*Somewhat satisfied*			*Very satisfied*		

Private assessment of a current primary relationship. This is a private assessment tool designed to capture your perceptions, beliefs, and opinions regarding a specific relationship. This assessment is for your own private use and will not be shared with your relationship partner. It is essential that your answers honestly reflect what is true for you *at this time*. Some of these areas may not apply to your relationship. Respond only to those areas you want to develop within your current relationship.

Love is: _____

_____

_____

yes__ no__ I love my partner.

yes__ no__ I believe my partner loves me.

yes__ no__ I respect my partner.

yes__ no__ I believe my partner respects me.

yes__ no__ I appreciate who my partner is—his or her talents, characteristics, etc.

yes__ no__ I believe my partner appreciates me.

yes__ no__ I support my partner.

yes__ no__ I believe my partner supports me.

yes__ no__ I accept my partner for who he or she is now.

yes__ no__ I believe my partner accepts me.

yes__ no__ I acknowledge my partner regularly and often.

yes__ no__ I believe my partner acknowledges me.

yes__ no__ I affirm my partner every chance I have.

yes__ no__ I believe my partner affirms me.

yes__ no__ I know my partner better than anyone else does.

yes__ no__ I believe my partner knows me.

yes__ no__ I am committed to creating a quality relationship with my partner.

yes__ no__ I believe my partner is committed to creating a quality relationship with me.

yes__ no__ I am committed to creating a synergistic relationship with my partner.

yes__ no__ I believe my partner is committed to creating a synergistic relationship with me.

yes__ no__ I will personally evolve in order to contribute anything necessary to create the relationship we want.

yes__ no__ I believe my partner will evolve in order to contribute anything necessary to create the relationship we want.

yes__ no__ I look forward to being with my partner after being separated for any length of time.

> You can make more friends in two months by becoming really interested in other people, than you can in two years by trying to get other people interested in you.
> —Dale Carnegie

Write the one main reason why you do or do not look forward to being with your partner.

_____

_____

_____

List at least five more reasons why being together or working together is pleasant or unpleasant.

1. _____
2. _____
3. _____
4. _____
5. _____

    yes__ no__ I have treated my partner with care during the last month.

List five instances:

1. _____
2. _____
3. _____
4. _____
5. _____

    yes__ no__ My partner has treated me with care during the last month.

List five instances:

1. _____
2. _____
3. _____
4. _____
5. _____

    yes__ no__ I have behaved uncaringly (intentionally or unintentionally) toward my partner in the last month.

List five instances:

1. _____
2. _____
3. _____
4. _____
5. _____

    yes__ no__ My partner has behaved uncaringly toward me in the last month.

List five instances:

1. _____
2. _____
3. _____
4. _____
5. _____

yes__ no__ I have accused, nagged, or criticized my partner in order to change the following five things, and he or she has not done so.

1. _____
2. _____
3. _____
4. _____
5. _____

yes__ no__ My partner has accused, nagged, or criticized me in order to change the following five things, and I have not done so because I could not or did not wish to change them.

1. _____
2. _____
3. _____
4. _____
5. _____

Circle the items above you could have changed or corrected if you *really* wanted to do so.

yes__ no__ My relationship with my partner has a positive influence on my job/work performance. How?

_____
_____
_____
_____

yes__ no__ I believe that, up to this point, I have been making a greater effort than my partner to make our relationship successful.

Describe.

_____

_____

_____

_____

yes__ no__ My life is more interesting and more fulfilling because of our relationship.

Describe.

_____

_____

_____

_____

yes__ no__ I have seriously considered the possibility of dissolving this relationship. If yes, how many times in the last six months? ___

yes__ no__ I know of others with a better relationship than ours. If yes, why is their relationship better?

_____

_____

_____

_____

yes__ no__ In the beginning, I believed our relationship would be a success.

If yes, list five elements you believed would contribute to this success.

1. _____
2. _____
3. _____
4. _____
5. _____

yes__ no__ Knowing what I do now about our relationship, I would choose the same partner if I had to do it all over again.

yes__ no__ If I could get out of this relationship without any inconvenience, without any major cost, bitterness, or hardship on our colleagues, friends, and/or children, I would choose to do so.

yes__ no__ I was happier in the beginning of our relationship than I am now.

If yes, give at least three reasons why.

1. _____
2. _____
3. _____

yes__ no__ There are negative things I learned about my partner after we were committed to each other.

List five.

1. _____
2. _____
3. _____
4. _____
5. _____

yes__ no__ I am satisfied with our sexual relationship.

Describe at least five things with which you are or are not satisfied. Why or why not?

1. _____
2. _____
3. _____
4. _____
5. _____

yes__ no__ I am satisfied with our financial situation.

Why or why not?

_____

_____

_____

List ten disadvantages or unsatisfying aspects for you in this relationship.

1. _____
2. _____
3. _____
4. _____
5. _____
6. _____
7. _____
8. _____
9. _____
10. _____

List at least five reasons why your relationship is advantageous or satisfying for you.

1. _____
2. _____
3. _____
4. _____
5. _____

What is the one major area in your relationship that needs improvement?

_____

_____

_____

yes__   no__   I like my partner.

What do like most about your partner?

_____

_____

_____

_____

yes__ no__   I believe my partner likes me.

What do you think your partner likes most about you?

_____

_____

_____

_____

The ABCs of WAR (*wrecking a relationship*). If you want to *destroy a relationship* by waging a relationship war, here is your weaponry! Put a check mark in the box next to the weapon(s) you use.

❑ *Accusing*	❑ *No Affection*
❑ *Blaming*	❑ *Obstinacy*
❑ *Criticizing/Complaining*	❑ *Pessimism*
❑ *Defensiveness*	❑ *Quarreling*
❑ *Emasculating*	❑ *Rejection*
❑ *Fifty-Fifty Attitude*	❑ *Self-Pity*
❑ *Gender Inequity*	❑ *Triangulating*
❑ *Hostility*	❑ *Undermining*
❑ *Indifference*	❑ *Vindictiveness*
❑ *Jealousy*	❑ *Workaholism*
❑ *Keeping Score*	❑ *X-Raying (Mindreading)*
❑ *Lack of Self-Love*	❑ *Yelling*
❑ *Manipulation*	❑ *Zoning Out*

The ABCs of creating a high quality relationship. If you want to *create a high quality relationship*, here are the tools! Put a check mark in the box beside the tool(s) you use or would like to develop.

❑ *Activities Together*	❑ *Behaviors that Benefit*
❑ *Consideration*	❑ *Decisions Made Jointly*
❑ *Energy for the Relationship*	❑ *Examine your Relationship*
❑ *Forgiveness*	❑ *Giving to one Another*
❑ *Habits that Affirm*	❑ *Imagination*
❑ *Joy*	❑ *Kindness*

- ❑ *Love*
- ❑ *Negotiation*
- ❑ *Prioritizing*
- ❑ *Respect*
- ❑ *Trust*
- ❑ *Visions Shared*
- ❑ *Yearn to Build a Quality Relationship*
- ❑ *Meditation*
- ❑ *Open-mindedness*
- ❑ *Quiet Time*
- ❑ *Solitude*
- ❑ *Uplifting Each Other*
- ❑ *Working Together*
- ❑ Zeal about Your Relationship

Coaching Language

Invite your clients to make the following phrases an unconscious part of their working vocabularies.

- ■ "It is my intention to create with you a relationship characterized by ___."
- ■ "The kind of relationship I want with you is one of ___."
- ■ "In order to create the relationship we both want, I am willing to ___."
- ■ "Please tell me what kind of relationship you want with me."
- ■ "How would you like it to be between us?"
- ■ "What can we do together to create the quality of relationship we both want?"
- ■ "What can I contribute to our relationship that will improve it?"

> Friendships, like marriages, are dependent on avoiding the unforgivable.
> —John D. MacDonald

Sample Coaching Conversation

A long-term coaching client wants to have a few conversations about improving her marriage. Sometimes coaches can refer this "case" to a specifically trained relationship coach. This sample conversation is for clients who are not experiencing severe conflict and do not need marriage therapy, but for those who want their relationship to be the best it can be.

> **Coach:** You wrote that you wanted to focus on improving your marriage relationship. What is it you want to improve?
>
> **Client:** I'm not really clear. I really love my husband and there are no serious problems. I just want our relationship to be outstanding. We

seem to often be distant and distracted by our jobs, our children, and other things. I guess that is natural, but I want it to be different.

Coach: Super. Just like the business coaching we have been doing, if you are clear about what you want and then purposefully focus on the desired outcomes, it is more likely to happen. Relationships are no different.

Client: How do I begin?

Coach: In our earlier coaching, we had conversations and even completed some assessments of the current state of your business. Let's do the same with your marriage. Are you willing to honestly complete some questionnaires about the current state of your marriage? These would only be for you for now. If your husband seems interested we could do it together or I could refer you for a few sessions with a relationship coach.

Client: Yes, that sounds good. We have actually talked about this and he is very open and feels the same. We love each other dearly and we want our relationship not to be mediocre.

Coach: Ok. What I want to do is schedule a session with both of you and if your husband shows the same enthusiasm, there will be some assignments and some assessments I will give you both to create the vision of how you want the relationship to be and what you want to currently improve upon. This would include communication, fun, sex, everything. Is that ok with you? You don't have to share intimate details with me. You would just have to share the results and answers with each other. Our coaching would be about hearing and understanding and then mutually creating the relationship you want.

Client: That sounds perfect. Let's start with the assessment forms and dialogues and then continue with coaching for the changes needed.

Questions and Inquiries

1. Of all your relationships, which one would you like most to improve?
2. What kind of relationship (if any) do you want with this person?
3. What kinds of contributions can you make to the relationship that will improve it?

4. Will you contribute differently to the relationship even if the other person does not?

5. Will you keep a "gratitude journal" for each relationship you would like to change?

6. If you want to terminate a relationship, how will you do that while maintaining your personal integrity and caring?

LIFE LESSON 43

The nature and quality of all human relationships are determined by the nature and quality of the character of those involved.

MESSAGES

1. All successful relationships in life evolve from the character of those people involved in the creative process.

2. Positive character traits create positive interpersonal relationships.

3. Negative personal character traits create negative interpersonal relationships.

4. Positive character traits can be taught and developed.

5. Effective life coaching occurs when both the coach and client put character development first.

The objectives for Lesson 43 are: 1) To identify and develop the character traits that create personal happiness and fulfillment; 2) To learn the process of character development.

Framework Needed for Coaching Your Clients

Good character is the inner motivation to do what is right according to the highest standards of human behavior, in every situation, whatever the cost. We all have the opportunity to develop our character by working on personal qualities that conform to our value system and generate the greatest amount of personal happiness and fulfillment.

The quality of all human relationships consists of the contributions given to them by the people in those relationships. Since we are social creatures what we bring to our interpersonal relationships always reflects who we are and the quality of our character. The quality of our character consists of our personal mix of character traits. When our character is full of positive traits, we experience pleasure, fulfillment, and happiness in our relationships. When it is made up of negative traits, we may experience empty relationships.

We acquire character traits through a number of influences. A genetic component to individual character qualities is likely—a propensity to develop character in particular ways. Parents are probably most influential in exemplifying character traits for children to imitate, practice, and incorporate. The effect that role models, friends, and peers have on us also contributes to the development of character. Finally, life events, particularly the challenging ones, influence the development of our personal character.

In any relationship or endeavor, the quality of the character of the people involved can facilitate or hinder the attainment of success of that relationship. Fortunately, the character traits of very successful people throughout history have been well chronicled. Such human qualities can be taught, learned through practice, and coached.

> I have a dream that my four children will one day live in a nation where they will not be judged by the color of their skin but by the content of their character.
> —Martin Luther King, Jr.

Exercises and Information

Invite your clients to identify any of the following positive character traits that are important to them to find in others. They can then identify traits that they would like to incorporate into their character. Ask them to make the perceptual/behavioral shifts necessary to seek out and develop the desired character trait. When developed within individuals, these traits lead to the creation of high quality relationships and great success.

CHARACTER IN A HIGH QUALITY RELATIONSHIP

ALERTNESS vs. Carelessness	Being fully awake and aware of what is going on around me and within me.
ASSERTIVENESS vs. Aggression	Clearly expressing my genuine thoughts, feelings, opinions and desires to be self-revealing.
ATTENTION vs. Ignoring	Strengthening the behavior of others by focusing on it and/or highlighting it. Seeing with receptive eyes a world of ceaseless wonders.
AUTHENTICITY vs. False fronts or ulterior (hidden) motives	Responding from genuine self-awareness and letting my true thoughts and emotions be known.
BEING PRESENT vs. Distracted	Living in the present moment. Not obsessing about the past or worrying about the future.
BOLDNESS vs. Fearfulness	The willingness to assert what I have to say or do, knowing that it is in the best interests of all concerned.
COMPASSION vs. Indifference	Empathic awareness and caring for the suffering of others.
CONTENTMENT vs. Envy	Being satisfied with who I am and what I have in the present moment.

CREATIVITY vs. Repetition	Addressing each task or activity as if it were new and seeking new ways of being in relationships.
DECISIVENESS vs. Paralyzing hesitancy	The ability to acknowledge important factors in any given situation, and take direct action based upon perceived accurate information.
DEFERENCE vs. Rudeness	Choosing to limit my actions so as not to deliberately offend the values or tastes of those around me.
DELIBERATENESS vs. Rashness	Taking into account the possible consequences of my actions; my own wants and needs; the desires and needs of others; and the reality of the situation prior to taking action.
DEPENDABILITY vs. Incongruity	Making my actions congruent with what I have said, and actually doing whatever I agreed to do, even when it requires unexpected sacrifice.
DETERMINATION vs. Faintheartedness	Taking purposeful action and persisting in attaining the right goals at the right time, regardless of any resistant opposition.
DILIGENCE vs. Slothfulness	Persistently using my time and energy to accomplish the tasks assigned to me or those I have agreed to do.
ENDURANCE vs. Discouragement	The inward strength and stamina to withstand resistance and continue to do the best I can.
ENTHUSIASM vs. Apathy	Being passionate and joyful in all the actions I take.
FAITH vs. Denial	Recognizing and accepting that there are other dimensions to life than what is experienced through our five senses.
FLEXIBILITY vs. Rigidity	Willingness to modify actions, change plans, and alter my thinking according to the direction of those in authority OR based upon new information and feedback.
FORGIVENESS vs. Rejection	Letting go of any resentment about the hurts that I may have done or others may have caused. Releasing myself from vengeance and self-deprecation.
GENEROSITY vs. Stinginess	Giving from the abundance of my material and personal resources to those in greater need of them.
GENTLENESS vs. Abrasiveness	Being considerate and expressing personal concern for others' well-being.
GIVING vs. Selfishness	Sharing from abundance and consideration of the needs of others.
GRACE vs. Rigid Stubbornness	Gentle acceptance of what is and smoothly flowing in my responses to others.
GRATITUDE vs. Criticism	Communicating to others (by actions and words) what I appreciate about them and the beneficial impact they make on my life.
HONOR vs. Disrespect	Acknowledging the value and benefits others have on my life, regardless of who they are as human beings.
HOPE vs. Discouragement	Anticipating that all results will work out the best for all concerned.

> I care not what others think of what I do, but I care very much about what I think of what I do: That is character!
> —Theodore Roosevelt

Character cannot be developed in ease and quiet. Only through experience of trial and suffering can the soul be strengthened, ambition inspired, and success achieved.
—Helen Keller

HOSPITALITY vs. Isolation	Welcoming other people and ideas with open consideration of them and a desire to address them authentically, without fear or malice.
HUMILITY vs. Pride	Acknowledging that all achievement is a result of cooperation, collaboration, teamwork and what others bring to my life.
IMAGINATION vs. Mindlessness	Creating in my mind new images, new ideas, and new consequences to my actions.
INITIATIVE vs. Reactivity	Recognizing and doing what needs to be done before I am asked to do it.
JOYFULNESS vs. Self-pity	Maintaining a positive attitude, even when involved in negative circumstances. Celebrating being alive.
JUSTICE vs. Corruption	Taking personal responsibility to support and advocate what is fair, true and in the best interests of all concerned.
KINDNESS vs. Discourteousness	Allowing my caring concern to be expressed in little actions, brief words of encouragement and expressions of courtesy and respect.
LOVE vs. Indifference	Being continuously appreciative and caring for others and putting their best interests on an equal bearing with my own.
LOYALTY vs. Unfaithfulness	Expressing my genuine, positive thoughts and feelings about someone whether or not they are present, and whether or not they will find out.
NURTURING vs. Neglect	Engaging in those task necessary for positive growth.
OPENNESS vs. Defensiveness	Practicing receptiveness and empathy toward others, toward my environment and toward the universe.
ORDERLINESS vs. Confusion	Eliminating clutter in my mind and in my environment, and arranging both to become more effective and efficient.
PATIENCE vs. Irritability	Acknowledging a difficult situation and withholding an action or directive to remove it immediately.
PEACEFULNESS vs. Turmoil	Remaining serene within (internally) even when my external environment is chaotic.
PERSUASIVENESS vs. Argumentative	Expressing personal "truths" without debasing or disrespecting the viewpoints of others.
PLAYFULNESS vs. Inhibited	Expressing child-like spontaneity while engaging in pleasurable (fun) activities with delightful laughter.
PUNCTUALITY vs. Tardiness	Demonstrating the value of another's time by doing what needs to be done and doing it in a timely fashion.
RECEPTIVE vs. Closed-minded	Taking in information without prejudice even when I disagree.
RESOURCEFULLNESS vs. Wastefulness	Using in a practical manner anything that others have over looked or discarded.
RESPONSIBILITY vs. Helplessness	Being able to respond from within and doing so in accordance with my own and others' expectations of me.
REVERENCE vs. Disregard	Maintaining a sense of awe about the preciousness of life, of being alive and of all that life has to offer.

SECURITY vs. Anxiety	Confidence in my ability to creatively cope with anything life has to offer.
SELF-CONTROL vs. Self-indulgence	Making decisions, choices, and taking actions that are congruent with the highest values and standards of human behavior.
SENSITIVITY vs. Callousness	Being acutely aware of the genuine emotions, needs, and attitudes of my own and those of others around me.
SILENCE vs. Noisiness	Quieting the body, mind and internal chatter so as to allow for revitalization of my spirit.
SINCERITY vs. Hypocrisy	Making my actions consistent with my values and a desire to be transparent in my motives.
THOROUGHNESS vs. Incompleteness	Finishing the tasks I begin as fully as I can.
THRIFTINESS vs. Extravagance	Spending only what will accomplish the task before me...and nothing more.
TOLERANCE vs. Prejudice	Becoming aware of the diversity of individual character development and valuing who they are as human beings, even when I don't condone their actions.
TRUTHFULNESS vs. Deceit	Never hiding or distorting my reporting of facts, regardless of the anticipated outcome.
VIGILANCE vs. Carelessness	Communicating the worth of others by focusing my attention on them and their wants and needs.
VIRTUE vs. Vice	Behaving ethically and morally in all the actions I take even when to do so puts me in jeopardy.
WISDOM vs. Stupidity	Responding to all situations in life from the best knowledge and awareness I have.
WONDER vs. Discounting	Cultivating a profound and vibrant curiosity about all events and surprises in my life.
ZEAL vs. Dispassionate	With passion and high energy, cherishing each moment, each event, each contact in my life.

Coaching to Create Good Character

As an authentic life coach, your task is to catalyze the development of good character in your clients. Begin by having a dialogue with your clients about what personal qualities they define as traits of good character. Make use of the list of positive character traits provided (above). Define and make a list of the aspects of good character your clients want to develop, strengthen, or practice.

Provide an example of some person who displays (or has displayed) the traits listed. Have your clients pick one trait to practice for three weeks. At the beginning of each coaching contact, ask your clients to report on instances in which they engaged in behavior that reflected their chosen character trait. Reinforce the practice of that trait by offering your congratulations, acknowledgement, appreciation, or praise. After three weeks of practice, ask your clients to select and

If there is
righteousness in
the heart,
there will be beauty
in character.
If there is beauty in
character,
there will be
harmony in the
home.
If there is harmony
in the home,
there will be order
in the nation;
If there is order in
the nation,
there will be peace
in the world.
—Chinese proverb

practice their next desired character trait, and so on. By the end of a single year, your clients will have incorporated seventeen chosen qualities of good character. Such integration will definitely enhance their character . . . and their destiny.

Sample Coaching Conversation

Coach: Did you get a chance to review the list of positive character traits I sent you?

Client: Yes. What a great list of traits to aspire to.

Coach: At your request, this will be a focus of our next several coaching conversations. Did you notice any traits that you would like to improve in your own life?

Client: I think I could improve on several. One I picked immediately is *flexibility* instead of *resistance*. Under duress, I tend to get rigid and resistant to change. Yet what I admire in a couple of associates is their flexibility. Afterall, things don't always go according to plan.

Coach: That's true. So, if that is the trait you would like to upgrade in your life, here's a request for you. I would like you to look for opportunities to practice flexibility in the next three weeks. That is how long it takes to form a new habit or incorporate a new trait. You will have lots of opportunities. In addition, I would like you to read that word several times each morning to turn it into an operating system in the back of your mind. Can you do that?

Client: Sure. That sounds doable and fun, actually.

Coach: Well see, you are showing flexibility already! Over the course of the next few months, you can practice a new trait every 3 weeks and by the end of twelve months, you will have improved or adapted seventeen admirable and desirable character traits.

Client: Great. Let's do it.

> The measure of a man's real character is what he would do if he knew he would never be found out.
> —Thomas Macaulay

Questions and Inquiries

1. Why is the development of your character important to you?
2. What are some of the benefits of developing specific character qualities?
3. What character qualities do you want to develop in yourself?
4. How will you invite others to develop desirable character qualities?

LIFE LESSON 44

Creating genuine relationships is critical to building a successful life.

MESSAGES

1. Intimacy is not necessarily sexual in nature.

2. Genuine relationships are created when two or more people express who they really are, what they truly think and feel, and what they want or need.

3. Ideally, the purpose of all human interaction is to create genuine relationships.

4. Effective life coaching is based upon genuine relationships.

The objectives for Lesson 44 are: 1) To understand what intimacy is and is not; 2) To learn the skills required to build a genuine relationship; 3) To learn how to be non-sexually, yet intimately connected; 4) To distinguish between your persona and your true self.

Framework Needed for Coaching Your Clients

We are always in relationships with others. If we do not connect with others, we may survive as a biological entity, but we are something less than human. To become fully human, we require intimate connections with other people. It has been said that "Even a hermit needs a crowd to escape from"—we are relationship beings at our best, and at our worst.

Carl Jung first made the distinction between persona and genuine self. The persona is composed of aspects of our personality that we show the world. Like the facade of a building, it is the outer self. The persona allows us to cope with the world outside us. It also protects us against intrusion from the outside world. It is the defensive structure of our personalities.

The genuine self is our true character—what lies behind the public facade. It is the personal, inner reality of our personality. Often referred to as the real self, it is the inner self. Both the persona and genuine self are necessary to who you really are. They define your true character.

Emotional Intimacy vs. Physical Intimacy vs. Sexual Intimacy

Emotional intimacy between two people revolves around the basic concept of accepting each other "as is." Intimacy is being able to share your thoughts, feelings, and opinions about something you have experienced, something you believe in, or something you dream about. You share without fear of judgment, criticism, or physical or emotional abandonment. Intimacy is freedom to share the real you with someone; freedom to feel happy, joyful, tired, sad, or angry—knowing that you will not be rejected or ridiculed.

Emotional intimacy is not how much we do for our partner, it is how we *are* with our partner. It is an attitude that is receptive and inviting, and not threatened by challenge, change, and growth.

An authentic life coach invites clients to form emotionally intimate relationships, beginning with the coach/client relationship.

In coaching, emotional intimacy involves a decision to trust and share *and* a decision to be the recipient of the other person's trusting and sharing. Intimacy is born of your inner character and is expressive of both your persona and your real self. In truly intimate relationships, each party is totally vulnerable and open with the other.

Emotional intimacy means validating and accepting each other's feelings rather than justifying negative behavior that may have resulted from those feelings. During coaching, when your clients tell you they are hurt by something you say or do, you need to acknowledge this hurt rather than defend what you said or did. The perception held by your clients is the only thing that matters.

Intimacy means being interested in or caring about anything and everything that is important to your client, no matter how trivial it seems or personally challenging it is to you. By allowing yourself to become vulnerable, both in your sharing *and* in your listening, you and your client grow as individuals and in intimacy.

Many people mistakenly equate physical intimacy with sexual intimacy. Physical intimacy is our need for nurturing, for physical affection—hugs, kisses, touches, holding hands, physical strokes etc. Sexual intimacy can and usually does include physical intimacy, but physical intimacy does not have to include sexual intimacy.

> I have often thought that the best way to define a man's character would be to seek out the particular mental or moral attitude in which, when it came upon him, he felt himself deeply and intensively active and alive. At such moments, there is a voice inside which speaks and says, "This is the real me."
> —William James

Using sex to fulfill our need for physical nurturing and using physical nurturing to fulfill our need for sex *does not work*. We can never have enough physical nurturing to satisfy our need for sex, and we can never have enough sex to satisfy our need for physical nurturing. They are two separate and distinct needs, each of which must be fulfilled separately in order to have an intimately satisfying primary relationship.

Of course, authentic life coaching prohibits any form of sexual contact with clients.

Exercises and Information

Intimacy is the crucible in which all effective, positive relationships are formed.

> The deepest principle in human nature is the craving to be appreciated, the desire to be important.
> —Andrew Carnegie

Basics Concepts of Intimacy

Here are some basic concepts to keep in mind when coaching your clients to build more genuine, intimate relationships.

Risk. Both you and your clients *risk* revealing yourselves as you really are, without letting the possibility of judgment or opinion (approval/disapproval) deter or alter that revelation.

View. Invite your clients to *view* any statements about them as an expression of another person, and not necessarily an accurate description. This means that all statements from others more often than not, reflect the character (likes and dislikes, feelings, wants, limitations, etc.) and perceptual world of the speaker.

Learn. Help your clients *learn* to see "different-ness" and disagreement as opportunities for growth and new understanding, rather than put-downs or criticism.

Commit. *Commit* yourself to work through whatever emerges within the coach/client relationship, until all the feelings are out in the open, all information is shared, and mutual satisfaction is achieved. Ask your clients to participate in this process with genuineness.

Accept. *Accept* that your clients cannot change their feelings by acts of will. Rather, each of you must be in charge of establishing your own boundaries so you do not get into resentment-collecting.

Clarify. Both you and your clients need to *be clear* about stating your boundaries, expectations, and wants. You also need to view the boundaries as limitations and needs rather than ultimatums or attempts to control the relationship.

Understand. Make certain that your client develops a clear, *internal understanding* of the fact that *neither of you intends to hurt or use the other.*
Tell your clients that you intend to give your all, but *only* to the extent it is congruent with what your clients desire from coaching.

> Until you have become really in actual fact a brother of everyone, brotherhood will not come to pass. Only by brotherhood will liberty be saved.
> —Feodor Dostoevski

Important Elements to Creating Genuine, Intimate Relationships

Share with your clients the following list of personal qualities and techniques which, when shared with someone else, characterize a genuine, intimate relationship. Have your clients customize the list to best suit their personalities.

- Cooperation
- Compassion
- Creativity
- Compatibility
- Consideration
- Consistency
- Communication
- Dependability
- Sensitivity
- Self-care
- Humor
- Playfulness
- Romance
- Self-dependency
- Self-love
- Mutual Respect
- Non-self-sacrificial Giving
- Understanding of Self and Partner
- Self-awareness

Tips for Developing Non-sexual Intimacy

1. Practice listening to your intuitive, genuine inner voice for what you truly think and feel, as opposed to what others want you to think and feel.
2. Avoid assuming others are like you, or projecting your own image onto anyone else.
3. Don't allow others to create *you* by conforming to their expectations, criticisms, accusations, or value systems.
4. Avoid trying to change others. It is a colossal waste of your time and is impossible.

5. Practice sharing your genuine thoughts, feelings, joys, successes, strengths and weaknesses, fears, concerns, wants and needs, hopes and dreams, and whatever expresses your true self.

Sample Coaching Conversation

Coach: Tell me how you have progressed with the two to three friendships you were attempting to be more authentic with. Eric, Peter, and Kevin, is that right?

Client: I had a very real conversation with Eric and Peter. It was actually very enlightening. They felt, as I did, that they wanted a few male relationships that were closer and more authentic, so we agreed to spend our time together differently and to talk about real stuff in our lives, and not have just superficial or impersonal conversations.

Coach: Great. I believe that what you are really trying to create is personal intimacy. We often confuse intimacy with sexuality and they are really two separate things. Have you ever had a female relationship in your life that was intimate, but not sexual?

Client: Oh, sure. I have considered a couple of women really good friends and that is all they are. But I could talk to them about anything and it was not anything sexual, it was very intimate and trusting.

Coach: Exactly. Many men report that same experience. What you are attempting to do with your male friends is to create non-sexual intimacy too. To have both male and female relationships that are high quality and authentic is really a big part of living a fulfilling life, do you agree?

Client: Yes. I'd like to improve that area of my relationships. If I develop this new level of intimacy with two or three men, then that would do it.

Coach: It sounds like you are well on your way. We will revisit this over the next few weeks, OK?

Client: Sure, I would appreciate that.

Questions and Inquiries

1. Do you understand the distinction between intimacy and sex?
2. Are you afraid to be open, honest, and expressive of who you are?

3. In the next three weeks, which one of the important elements to creating genuine, intimate relationships do you want to practice and develop within your coaching relationship?

4. Do you trust yourself? Others? The world?

5. Do you hide behind a persona out of fear of being rejected, criticized, hurt, or abandoned?

LIFE LESSON 45

Friendships are a special kind of interpersonal relationship that you must consciously create.

The objectives for Lesson 45 are: 1) To understand the basic reasons for forming friendships; 2) To learn how to become a good friend; 3) To learn the value of service in friendship.

Framework Needed for Coaching Your Clients

Lasting friendships rarely develop without conscious awareness, deliberate choices, nurturing effort and a desire to be a friend.

Lessons in Friendship

True friendship is a soul-level, awesome connection. By being in awe we are energized, uplifted, and filled with new ideas. Feeling a sense of understanding and of being understood, we are validated and encouraged; we *know* we are not alone. Our friends inspire us to grow. What we admire in them motivates us to rise higher. They become the mirror in which we see our better selves. We are spiritually invigorated by the wisdom and beauty we see in our friends.

Despite the importance of friends, we are rarely taught the *skills* of friendship. We grow up never knowing our own abilities for contributing to friendship, and often waste irretrievable hours, even days or years, relating to people who are toxic to us, who demand our time and energy for no good purpose. We harm ourselves psychologically, emotionally, and spiritually when we have not developed strong friendly relationships with others.

Exercises and Information

You clients cannot change anyone else in order to build a better friendship; they can only change themselves and modify what they bring to the friendship. You may want to teach your clients the following nine lessons so they might create, maintain, and evolve true and lasting friendships.

> I will destroy my enemies by converting them to friends.
> —Maimonides

1. *Give your friends more than they expect.* Give, not for their sake or the sake of the friendship, rather, give for the joy you create by giving.
2. *Be quick to accept and forgive the hurts that are always involved in friendship.* You can't realistically expect to dance closely and never step on one another's toes. When you apologize and ask for forgiveness, look your friends directly in the eye. Don't let little conflicts injure a great friendship.
3. *Consciously choose your friends.* Co-dependent friendships are unconsciously chosen. Intentionally choose your friends on a soul-level.
4. *Always tell the truth to your friends.* Tell the truth about yourself, them, and your friendship. Ralph Waldo Emerson once described being permitted to speak the truth as one essential criterion for friendship.
5. *Acknowledge who your friends are now.* Accept that your friends may grow, change, and evolve. Sometimes your own growth as well as your friend's growth will result in the dissolution of the friendship. Realize that such transitions are natural and rejoice in them. Be patient with emerging friendships.
6. *Risk loving deeply.* All great friendships involve great risks. Even if you are afraid, risk being loving in your friendships.
7. *Spend time alone.* This will increase your self-awareness and the likelihood that you will take full responsibility for your own thoughts, feelings, and actions regarding your friendship and your life.

8. *Honor your friendship with gentle respect.* Trying to force a friendship is like tearing open a flower bud to make it bloom faster. Forcing the evolution of friendships destroys them.

Learn and practice these nine lessons in friendship and within your lifetime you may evolve more than just five true friendships. You will certainly become a true friend yourself.

Friendship Dynamics

Your clients form different types of friendships with different people. Identify with them the type of friendships they want to form and clarify with them the type of friendships they already have. Help them to modify their friendships if they so desire.

Below are some common types of friendships and their characteristics, to share with your clients.

Dependent-dependent (co-dependent) relationship. In this relationship each person involved looks to the other to address their own wants and needs, and does not trust their own ability to be happy alone.

> A friend is a person before whom I may think aloud.
> —Ralph Waldo Emerson

- *Why they bond:* Each partner has a mutual need for support. They lean on each other for fulfillment of the needs they can't fill themselves.
- *Undermining forces:* Any move by either partner to become independent.
- *Conflicts:* Withholding reassurance, support, or love.
- *Why the friendship dissolves:* One partner finally outgrows the other or becomes self-dependent.
- *What each needs from the other:* Reassurance, because they have not grown up with the notion of being autonomous.
- *Direction for growth:* To see each other as independent and develop self-support skills and confidence. Give permission and encourage the other to see themselves as grown-ups.

Dependent-controlling relationship. This relationship is one wherein one person manipulates or tries to control the other as a means of getting the other to address their desires and needs.

- *Why they bond:* Each partner has a mutual weakness that is accepted by the dependent and denied by the controlling person.
- *Undermining forces:* Anything that adds to the dependent person's strength; anything that diminishes the controlling person's power or perceived control.
- *Conflicts:* The dependent person becomes a bigger burden or decides to grow up; the controlling person withholds material and emotional support.
- *Why the friendship dissolves:* The dependent person develops self-esteem, the mutual activities are completed, and the controlling person can leave without feeling guilty.
- *What each needs from the other:* The dependent person needs room to grow; the controlling person needs to grant more freedom and be less threatened by letting go of control.
- *Direction for growth:* To grant themselves and each other the right to *personhood*.

Dependent-competitive relationship. This relationship is one wherein one person depends on the other who competes in order to "win" his/her own need fulfillment, dominate the other, or destroy the other's ability to function independent of the relationship.

- *Why they bond:* There is a need for love and admiration (adoration) on the part of the competitive person and a need for support and security on the part of the dependent.
- *Undermining forces:* The competitive friend's need to be the center of attention causes the dependent partner to cling to them; the dependent partner's anxiety overwhelms the other.
- *Conflicts:* The dependent friend tends to be an emotional burden (needy and demanding, sometimes passively); the competitive partner is unable to give the dependent partner security and emotional support.
- *Why the friendship dissolves:* There is too much insecurity for the dependent person to manage; the competitive person becomes over-burdened or bored and wants to move on.
- *What each needs from the other:* The dependent person needs to risk more and be a more active friend by becoming more of an independent person; the competitive partner needs to temper his or her self-preoccupation.

- *Direction for growth:* To reach an acceptance of each other's needs in an atmosphere of honesty in which the competitive person can admit his or her dependency on the partner's stability, and the dependent person can admit manipulating the other by acting helpless.

> Be a friend to yourself, and others will.
> —Scottish Proverb

Controlling-controlling relationship. This relationship is one wherein each person attempts to manipulate and control the other (as opposed to themselves) in order to change the behavior of the other.

- *Why they bond:* Each has similar ambitions, goals, and intellectual style; each sees the other as complimentary to his or her own goals in life.
- *Undermining forces:* Dissimilar opinions about how to achieve goals and any change that alters the balance of power.
- *Conflicts:* Money, control, permission, or autonomy.
- *Why the friendship dissolves:* One or the other can't stand being controlled or the ensuing state of low self-esteem that manipulation creates.
- *What each needs from the other:* Greater freedom and autonomy.
- *Direction for growth:* for each to accept his or her own imperfections and allow the other person space to be imperfect.

Controlling-competitive relationship. This relationship is one wherein each person attempts to control the other by competitive withholding what the other wants or needs from them.

- *Why they bond:* Each feels incomplete without the other.
- *Undermining forces:* Changes in the relationship that devalue love as a powerful influence.
- *Conflicts:* Each withholds whatever the other wants.
- *Why the friendship dissolves:* Relationship fatigue due to a continuous conflict over who is right, best, or more important.
- *What each needs from the other:* A greater understanding of and a willingness to satisfy mutual needs.
- *Direction for growth:* To learn to go it alone and still be together.

Competitive-competitive relationship. This relationship is one wherein each person is self-absorbed and competitively compares themselves to the other in order to feel "better than" the other.

- *Why they bond:* Each believes they have found the kind of person they have always wanted as a friend.
- *Undermining forces:* Too much success creates an imbalance in the equality they once shared.
- *Conflicts:* Withholding attention and time due to intense preoccupation with self and career.
- *Why the friendship dissolves:* Insecurity becomes so great that the support and appreciation received falls short, so each seeks another person to fill his or her needs.
- *What each needs from the other:* Applause, mutual respect, tolerance of moodiness during periods of self-doubt, and patience.
- *Direction for growth:* For each to trust his or her own self and the other's friendship, and to forgive hurtful comments and actions made under stress.

Service to Friends

Twenty-five years ago, John Greenleaf, a former director of management research at AT&T wrote a book titled *Servant Leadership*. In it he identified and described the term servant leaders as those who get more excited about making others more successful than themselves. The servant leader lives by the purposeful motto, "I'm here to care for people and help them become successful." In a true friendship, you are there to help your friends become more successful and satisfied in life.

> It is one of the most beautiful compensations of this life that no man can sincerely try to help another without helping himself.
> —Ralph Waldo Emerson

With the rise of technology, the depersonalization of activity in the workplace, and the general busyness of our lifestyles, people are interacting less and less in the spirit of service. Friendships suffer.

Service to others is one of the most natural and healthy skills in which we can engage. If parents were not able to serve the needs of their children, the human species would extinguish itself in one generation. If teachers were unable to serve the learning needs of their students, human knowledge would never be transferred to the next generation.

There are thousands of service agencies and clubs throughout the world. One of them, Rotary International, has a motto, "Service above self." The point of the motto is to learn to love people and use things, not vice versa. This success principle of service is what is most frequently violated in interpersonal relationships. You cannot continually violate this principle and expect to remain friends with anyone.

Service is distinct from fixing. When you fix something, the implication is that something is broken. A value judgment usually separates the "fixer" from what or who needs fixing. When you fix something or someone there exists an inequality between you and the friend you desire to fix. Such inequality creates an imbalance in the friendship, and breeds confusing expectations. Friendships need to be served not to be repaired, but to enrich them. This was Mother Teresa's basic message: "We serve life not because it is broken but because it is holy."

> There is no higher religion than human service. To work for the common good is the greatest creed.
> —Albert Schweitzer

Authentic service in your clients' friendships can be the antidote for many psychological and social ills. It's a primary way to reach your personal potential as a unique human being—a special friend. Service bonds people in friendship and leads to success and personal evolution.

There is much misunderstanding about the definition of service. What is it? Some people confuse helping others with serving them. Very often helping friends may be debilitating to those we help. When people can do for themselves, or when they need the practice to strengthen their own skills, then helping by doing for them, tends to weaken them . . . not help them. There always exists an inequality between the helper and the one being helped. Helping often implies indebtedness or obligation to reciprocate. It often invites those being helped to feel guilty about their own need for it. "Please Mother, I'd rather do it myself," characterizes the rebellious cry needed to strengthen autonomy and avoid being "helped" into dependency.

Sample Coaching Conversation

Client is a manager at a manufacturing company and was just transferred to a new city three months earlier.

> **Coach:** Good morning, Larry. How are things going? I am especially curious, now that you have been there three months, how are you connecting in your new location?
>
> **Client:** I like the job and I like this location, but my wife and I really miss our old friends. Me especially. She seems to stay in touch by phoning and emailing them, and even planned a trip to visit them. But I feel like I am in a whole new place.
>
> **Coach:** You are, but I hear you. Friends are so important and you lived in San Diego a long time. Would it help to reconnect with a few friends from back there?

Client: That might help, but I also want to make new friends here. I think we will be here for several years. We like it and my job is great, so this is not a short-term stay.

Coach: Okay. Let's start with a few key friends you already have. Can you list three to five people with whom you would like to revive your friendship?

Client: Sure, I can think of two women and two men. I have always had women as good friends. They are easier to talk to. But my two male friends are special guys that I did a lot of stuff with. I miss that.

Coach: How would you like to stay in touch? How often? What do you think they want?

Client: I am not sure. I don't know what they want? So, you are probably going to ask me to ask them, right? (chuckles)

Coach: Good idea (laughs). Will you do that?

Client: Yes, I can. I guess I will call each one, be honest about missing our relationship, and see if they have any desire to write, call, or stay in touch like I do. I know them well. They would like to do something. And with the guys, I want to plan a fishing trip or something. We did that in San Diego and we can do that still, even though I live here.

Coach: Great. Next session we can brainstorm techniques for cultivating friendships and connecting with people in your new locale.

Questions and Inquiries

1. What kinds of friendships do you have now? How would you characterize them?
2. Why have you bonded with each of your friends?
3. Whom do you want as a friend who is not one already?
4. In what ways can you be of service to the friends you have?

LIFE LESSON 46

The highest-quality interpersonal relationships are based on love.

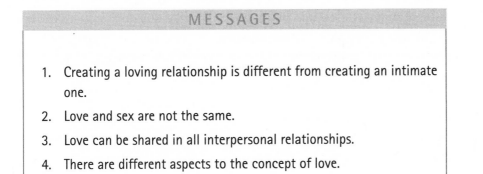

MESSAGES

1. Creating a loving relationship is different from creating an intimate one.
2. Love and sex are not the same.
3. Love can be shared in all interpersonal relationships.
4. There are different aspects to the concept of love.

The objectives for Lesson 46 are: 1) To understand what love is in a primary relationship; 2) To learn the difference between the expression of love and human sexuality; 3) To learn to take full responsibility for your sexuality; 4) To become aware of behavior and language that kills and reinforces a loving relationship.

Framework Needed for Coaching Your Clients

The word *love* has so many definitions and has been used in so many contexts that it has almost become meaningless to your clients. Each of them usually has his/her own definition of love. Often these definitions were formed in childhood and may no longer be relevant or applicable to adult relationships.

Myths of Love

Creating a loving relationship is often difficult and unpredictable. Only within the past eighty years has love been the primary reason for people to marry. Prior to that, many people were married for political, economic, and legal reasons. Par-

> To love is to admire with the heart; to admire is to love with the mind.
> —Theophile Gautier

ents often arranged the marriages of their children. Love had very little to do with it.

Even in contemporary culture, marriage for love seems under attack. That attack is waged by couples who attempt to do too much. The effort required to be full-time parents, full-time employees, full-time business owners, full-time spouses, full-time homemakers, and full-time lovers is simply overwhelming. The attempt to manage all the demands of everyday life may prove fatal to loving relationships and to the marital relationship itself.

Additionally, people usually believe several myths about loving relationships. When these myths are crusted by the realities of daily living, couples experience disappointment, betrayal, and they often exit the relationship in search of another that more adequately fulfills their mistaken beliefs about love and relationships. Below are some of those myths.

Myth 1. How you feel about your partner and how your partner feels about you are the two best predictors of a successful relationship.

Response: No feeling or emotion lasts very long. How you feel about someone else is usually based upon an idealized image or upon a need you want the other to fulfill. Whether your image is of an ideal boss, friend, spouse, or parent, no one usually lives up to that image. In any case, it is no one's job to fulfill your needs but your own. A better predictor of how happy your relationship will be is how well you arrange for your own needs to be met. The happiest of relationships are formed when both parties have accurate and authentic knowledge of each other and when each party takes full responsibility for his or her own needs and for the needs of the relationship. Ask directly for whatever you want or need from your relationship partner.

Myth 2. The better you and your partner know each other, the better you will communicate. If you really know someone, you will be able to communicate even without words. After all, if you really love someone, you will know what he or she wants. If they fail to meet your unspoken needs, that means they don't love you.

Response: The reality is that your ability to communicate is entirely independent of whether or not you either know or love someone. Being in love never enables you to read your partner's mind or heart, let alone know when your partner is hungry, needy, angry, sad, or feeling sexy. Communication means a willingness to tell your partner about your genuine inner experience. Make no assumptions that your partner will know otherwise.

Myth 3. If my spouse comes from a loving family, he or she will be loving to me, and we will have a loving relationship.

Response: Not true! Closeness and love in someone's family of origin is based upon a parent-child relationship. Adult-adult relationships require different ways of relating, different expressions of love, and different styles of caring.

Myth 4. It is better to live together before marrying to discover if you can make a solid relationship.

Response: The divorce rate is *not* lower for couples who have lived together prior to marriage. Marriage vows seem to alter the psychological makeup of a relationship, making leaving the relationship more difficult. Public acknowledgement of a couples' mutual commitment to a relationship often strengthens their resolve to make a go of it.

Myth 5. Love and sex are the same.

Response: As stated before, you can never get enough sexual contact to fulfill your need for love, and you can never get enough love to satisfy your need for sex. They are two different needs. A parent may love her children, but never have sexual feelings toward them. A boss may love his or her employees, and never engage in sexual conduct with them. A friend may love another person of either gender, and never express that love sexually.

> Respect is what we owe; love, what we give.
> —Phillip James Bailey

Your clients need to demythologize their concepts of love in light of their current adult-adult relationships. Couples need realistic information about the nature of love, the nature of a happy committed partnership, and new skills to help them build a mutual, need-fulfilling, and happy relationship.

Exercises and Information

During their childhood, most of your clients were never taught the nature and aspects of love. In the business world, the word *love* is almost never heard—let alone discussed. In platonic relationships, conversing about your love for the other is often taboo.

Secrets of Love

Your clients may need to acquaint themselves with the following "secrets" about love and being a lover.

Secret 1. *The power of thought.* Love begins with our thoughts. We become what we think. Loving thoughts create loving experiences and loving relationships. Affirmations can change our beliefs and thoughts about ourselves and of others. If we want to love someone, we need to consider their needs and desires.

Secret 2. *The power of respect.* You cannot love anyone or anything unless you first respect them. The first person you need to respect is yourself. To begin to gain self-respect ask yourself, "What do I respect about myself?" To begin to respect others—even those you may dislike—ask yourself, "What do I respect about them?"

Secret 3. *The power of giving.* If you want to receive love, all you have to do is give it. The more love you give, the more you will receive. To love is to give of yourself authentically, freely, and unconditionally. Practice random acts of kindness. The secret formula of a happy, lifelong relationship is to always focus on what you can give instead of what you can take.

Secret 4. *The power of friendship.* To find true love you must first find a true friend. Love does not consist of gazing into each other's eyes, but rather looking outward together in the same direction. To love someone completely you must love them for who they are, not what they look like. Friendship is the soil through which love's seeds grow. If you want to bring love into a relationship, you must first bring friendship.

> The great secret of successful marriage is to treat all disasters as incidents and none of the incidents as disasters.
> —Harold Nicholson

Secret 5. *The power of touch.* Touch, which breaks down barriers and bonds relationships is one of the most powerful expressions of love. Touch changes our physical and emotional states and makes us more receptive to love.

Secret 6. *The power of letting go.* If you love something, let it be free. Even in a loving relationship, people need their space. If we want to learn to love, we must first learn to forgive and let go of past hurts and grievances. Love means letting go of our fears, prejudices, egos, and conditions.

Secret 7. *The power of communication.* To love someone is to communicate with them. Let the people you love know that you love and appreciate them. Never be afraid to say, "I love you." Never let an opportunity pass to praise and acknowledge someone. Always leave someone you love with a loving word.

Secret 8. *The power of commitment.* If you want to have love in abundance, you must be committed to it. Commitment is the true test of love. If you want to have loving relationships, you must be committed to loving relationships. When you are committed to someone or something, quitting is never an option. Commitment distinguishes a fragile relationship from a strong, loving one.

Secret 9. *The power of passion.* Passion ignites love and keeps it alive. Lasting passion does not come through physical attraction alone. It comes from deep commitment, enthusiasm, interest, and excitement. The essence of love and happiness is the same, all we need to do is to live each day with passion.

Secret 10. *The power of trust.* You cannot love someone completely unless you trust that person completely. Act as if your relationship with the person you love will never end. Trust is essential to all loving relationships. Trust yourself, trust others, and trust the world. It is the foundation of love.

Healing a Relationship with the Language of Love

As an authentic life coach, you may want to share with your clients the following list of affirmations. Suggest to your clients that they should agree with, regularly state, and habitually behave according to these affirmations. Can you imagine the healing change in a primary relationship if each person viewed himself or herself and their relationship from a perceptual paradigm colored and shaped by these affirmations?

- "I want to know and give attention to your needs."
- "Your emotional needs are more important than my desires."
- "I want to stop blaming."
- "I want you to feel loved, valued, understood, and listened to in our relationship."
- "I want you to feel confident that you are my best friend, the top person in my life."
- "I want to generate positive energy in our relationship."
- "I want to quit feeding the negative when we disagree."
- "Help me not to offend your spirit."
- "I want to listen to your feelings and honor them."
- "I want to help you raise your self-esteem all the time."

- "I want to be a forgiving, trusting partner to you always."
- "I want my daily behavior to be loving behavior toward you."
- "If I behave unlovingly, please alert me so that we can talk about it."
- "I want to make our relationship and home joyous, loving, and enthusiastic."
- "I accept responsibility for creating a climate of positive values in our home and relationship. Please help me."
- "I want to learn how to process anger creatively. I give you permission to be angry and I promise not to attack you when I'm angry."
- "I need your help with my anger. Help me to express my anger in a way that does not hurt you."
- "I want to do more learning and less protecting of myself."
- "My intent is to learn and truly understand rather than to defend and protect my ego."
- "I want to explore the thoughts behind our negative emotions so that we can correct them, understand each other better, and live together without threat."
- "I want to build comfort and harmony into our relationship more and more."
- "I want to explore how you are affected by my behavior so we can both gain more freedom and more intimacy."
- "I want to be able to share your pain and have you receive my warmth and caring in return."
- "I want to learn to say I'm sorry when I have offended your spirit."
- "I want you to know that I'm grateful for you and I want us to enjoy an increasingly fulfilling and loving relationship together."

Sample Coaching Conversation

> Perhaps love is the process of my leading you gently back to yourself.
> —Antoine De Saint-Exupery

The following excerpt is from a relationship coaching session with the husband and wife. The husband was a coaching client for several months but requested relationship coaching to make what he called "a good marriage great."

Coach: Thanks for both of you being willing to take a more purposeful look at your relationship and how to make it even better than it is now. What is it you hope to accomplish from our coaching together?

Bill: Like I discussed with you a few weeks back, part of my life coaching has been to balance work and family and that discussion led to some desire to be more loving as a husband and to have our relationship be more prominent in my goals. We have a very good marriage and we have no major problems, but we want it to be the best it can be.

Shannon: That's right. I was so thrilled to hear Bill wants to work on this together. To me family and our relationship is the most important goal. Everything we do is so we can be loving and mutually supportive to each other.

Coach: Great. This is the power of relationship coaching. You don't need marriage therapy and yet you want your relationship to be the best it can be. What have you discussed with each other that would be evidence of a more satisfying marriage?

Shannon: I want more time together as a couple and more loving. I don't mean more sex or even better sex. That would be nice, but it is really okay now. What I mean is more intimacy, more time, and more romance. And Bill agreed that would be his desire too.

Bill: That's right. We just need some coaching on how to make that happen.

Coach: You have been married twenty-seven years. And while sex is a part of loving, it is not the only expression of loving. I will let you guys talk about the desire for improving sex if you want, but I really want to focus on the improvement of expressing and feeling love.

Bill and Shannon together: Yes. That is what we want.

Coach: If three months from now, your relationship was more like you want it to be, what would be different? Bill, how about you answer that first?

Bill: We would be spending more time together. Time with each other, not just in the same room watching TV or reading. I know we both want more focused time together, but sometimes it seems like we force it.

Shannon: We both know early in a relationship you want to be with each other all the time, both for romance and sex, but also because you want to be with the other person. As we got comfortable, we seem like most couples to have settled in and it does not happen as naturally.

Coach: Exactly. That is true of many of our habitual patterns. So what would make this time together more *on purpose* while still feeling natural?

Shannon: You know, we do great on vacations or short getaways. Getting away from our routine always spices up our love life, but we also communicate more.

> Often the difference between a successful marriage and a mediocre one consists of leaving about three or four things a day unsaid.
> —Harlan Miller

Coach: So how could you have more of those getaways or time together. I know you can't take unlimited vacations, but what could you do?

Bill: When our kids were still at home, we used to trade baby-sitting with other couples and do getaway weekends. Now that our kids our out of the home, we could do that even more easily.

Shannon: That's true. That would be fun, say once every two months. We can afford it if we book the time.

Coach: Good idea. The lesson here is to *come from love* and give love a place to seed and sprout. It is obvious you two love each other, but you want it expressed more and not always by making love, but by giving love. Is that right?

Both: Yes.

Coach: I have a request for this week. If you agree, I would like you each to practice being loving by doing something loving with your partner. Bill, I want you to do something for Shannon on the even numbered days, and Shannon, I want you to do something for Bill on the odd numbered days. Sometime during the day, express love in a way you would like. It could be anything—a card, a massage, a surprise gift— but make it an example of what you really feel when you think of being loving. See your partner as the object of that love and practice showing it *on purpose*. And I also would like you two to schedule out three getaway weekends, OK? Can you do both of these requests?

Bill: Sure. Sounds great.

Shannon: You bet.

Questions and Inquiries

1. What are some of the differences for you between love and sex?
2. How do you express your sexuality in your primary relationship?
3. How do you express your love in relationships?
4. What are the distinctions between a loving and an intimate relationship?
5. How do you want to increase your capacity for love?
6. How do you want to increase your capacity for intimacy?

LIFE LESSON 47

Romance and taking responsibility for your sexual life enriches the primary relationship of couples.

MESSAGES

1. Romance is not necessary in a relationship, but it certainly enriches it.
2. Romance can be learned and maintained in a loving relationship.
3. To learn how to take sexual responsibility for your life.
4. Coaching the development of romance is an important skill for an authentic life coach.

The objectives for Lesson 47 are: 1) To learn the relationship benefits of romance; 2) To help your clients understand the difference between love, romance, and their sexual life; 3) To create and maintain a romantic primary relationship; 4) To learn the currency of romantic exchange; 5) To understand the elements of romance with a primary partner.

Framework Needed for Coaching Your Clients

When coaching a couple seeking to create a mutually desired relationship, you will often hear, "Can you coach us on how to bring more romance into our relationship?" Every couple, at some point, experiences what it's like to have romance in their lives. Many decide to marry based upon their romantic feelings for one another. They believe their romance will last that long—but unfortunately, it usually doesn't. When romance wanes, couples may seek coaching to re-energize it.

Most of us yearn for more romance in our lives and we try to make our primary relationships more romantic. Often with the aid of soap operas, novels, magazine stories, and movies, our desire for romance dramatically increases.

> Love is ever the
> beginning of
> Knowledge, as fire
> is of light.
> —Thomas Carlyle

With a generous amount of romance in our lives we tend to feel more alive, see beauty everywhere, feel full of creative energy, and our experience of being alive becomes more enjoyable and colorful.

But a long-term, mutually satisfying relationship cannot be solidly built on romance alone, because romance tends to fade over time. Since romance is composed of one part *fantasy*, one part emotion, and one part *non-rational enjoyable actions*, the realities of life tend to overshadow the romance we felt earlier within our committed, primary relationships. No one can continuously sustain a romantic high over the long term. You may even be afraid that if you allow romance to flourish, you will only be hurt or disappointed when romance dwindles or disappears altogether.

The good news is that you can have it both ways: a romantic relationship that is also practical and a realistic and responsible relationship that is also filled with romance.

The Art of Romance

Dinner by candlelight, romantic music floating dreamily in the background, dancing the night away in your lover's arms, aware only of each other and the intensity of the passionate love you share. Ah, romance! Maybe . . .

According to John Gottman (2000), America's leading marriage researcher at the University of Washington in Seattle, lasting romance means partners connect in small ways—often and everyday! According to Gottman, the magic ratio is 5 to 1: five positive interactions for every one negative interaction. Five deposits in the relationship bank account for every one withdrawal. Candlelight dinners and dancing may sound romantic, but don't count on them to make up the difference if your everyday account of positive interactions is consistently overdrawn!

Interestingly, the word *romance*—with its modern day connotation of unordinary, adventurous, idealized, or imaginative acts—has Latin roots as the language spoken by the common people during the last centuries of the Roman Empire. The word *romans* referred to the everyday languages of the people, now collectively known as the *romance languages* of French, Spanish, Italian, etc. Tales of chivalric love were often told in *romans*—the common language—which led to the use of the word *romance* to denote a *love story*.

In modern times our notion of *romance* or a *love story* is rooted in how we communicate and relate to each other in the common, ordinary events of life. What counts is the everyday language: hugs, smiles, kisses, holding hands, putting your arm around your partner, massaging his or her shoulders, touching the face, *really* listening, cuddling, an unexpected phone call just to say hello, eye contact, gentle touches, gentle words—repeated often and everyday!

To be attentive to performing little acts with no ulterior motive other than to simply to express your love, that's the secret—the art of romance!

Exercises and Information

Let your clients know that real-life romance cannot be calculated or produced by a certain formula. It cannot be forced. But each of us can choose to crowd romance out of our lives or to contribute to a primary relationship climate in which romance is allowed to flourish.

Methods to Create a Romantic Relationship

If your clients want coaching on how to increase the level of felt romance within their relationship, the following suggestions may prove beneficial.

Focus on partner. Develop an ability to focus only on those aspects of your partner in which you take great delight. If he or she has a great sense of humor, attend to it with a "thank you." If your partner is a terrific cook, thank him or her for making such great meals. Romance blossoms when you attend to and highlight the joyous, delightful parts of your partner's mind, body, and spirit. Attending to such aspects will make your partner more significant in your relationship and your life.

> The best portion of a good man's life is his little, nameless, unremembered acts of kindness and love.
> —William Wordsworth

Focus on self. Develop this same selective attention to yourself as well. Regularly generate a romantic image of yourself by thinking of yourself as loved by someone very special—your partner! After all, of all the people your partner could have chosen to love—you're the one. Loving and paying attention to yourself brings you a greater awareness of loving and paying attention to others.

Live with romance. Imagine that it is possible to live with romance. Romance does not develop in response to demands, complaints, criticism, tears, emotional withdrawal, tantrums, or threats. You cannot bargain for it. You cannot buy it. As a gentle and fragile force, romance cannot overpower negativity without some kind of window of opportunity. Such a window is your imagination. Imagine the romantic and you help create the climate necessary for romance to grow.

Ask. Learn what turns your partner on to romance. What may be romantic for you may be a turn-off for your partner. Ask your partner directly what he or she experiences as romantic; then tell your partner what you consider to be romantic.

Often the small, unspoken gestures count the most. Your attitude is crucial. If you feel obligated to buy your partner a gift, that sense of obligation very quickly smothers any spark of romance. Become curious and receptive to your own romantic tendencies and share them with your partner.

Schedule unhurried time. Make space in your mind as well as your schedule for relaxed, unhurried, uninterrupted attention to one another and to your relationship. Schedule that time and declare it sacred. Define it as your time together and alone with no pressure from outside forces such as children or job worries.

Imagination. Become more aware of your own non-rational, free, creative, and imaginative side. We all have it. Read poetry to each other, listen to music together, prepare favorite and special meals, plan new adventures, seek out delightful experiences together. Draw out the beauty and excitement you want to experience in each other and the world you share.

Keep a Journal. A "romance" journal is a wonderful place for your clients to record all the romantic happenings in their lives. Those ideas and events on which we focus our thoughts and to which we attend become stronger and more dominant in our lives. If your clients want more romance in their lives, have them write about it, think about it, act on it, and record it.

Invite clients to describe in their journals the most romantic times they have experienced. Have them list at least ten things they consider to be romantic. They need to be specific: what, how, when, and where. When the opportunity arises, have your clients share this information with their partners.

Now, have your clients list ten gestures their primary partners consider to be romantic. If your clients don't know, teach them how to ask their partner directly for this information. Have clients converse with their partner about romance and record what they learn in their journal for future reference.

Taking Responsibility for Your Sexual Life

Make the distinction with your clients between romance and sexual expression. Clearly, not all sexual activity is romantic, and not all romance is sexual.

After clients have been in monogamous relationships for a few years, what happens to their sexual interest and desire? Does it increase in intensity and pleasure? Does it fade into some kind of mechanical routine? Does it deepen and become more passionate? Where does the energy go that was once so ecstatic at the beginning of a sexual relationship?

Teach your clients that one of the primary causes of fading sexual passion is the development of a sense of responsibility for the emotions of another, including sexual pleasure. We often grow up believing we are responsible for the feelings of others. Phrases such as "You make me so angry," "You make me so mad," and "My happiness depends on you," when heard by a small child, generate the belief that he or she is responsible for, and can alter, the emotional lives of others. This childhood belief is often carried into adulthood when we feel responsible for, among other feelings, the sexual pleasure of a partner.

> Sexual pleasure, wisely used and not abused, may prove the stimulus and liberator of our finest and most exalted activities.
> —Havelock Ellis

Phrases such as "You turn me on," "Your lack of sexual interest turns me off," and "I don't want to pursue my own sexual fulfillment because I am afraid you will reject me," invite clients to feel dependent on others for their own sexual happiness. It discounts their own power and responsibility for meeting their needs and modifying their own feelings, including those about sex. In our coaching practice, we have found that there is a direct correlation between the amount of caring *for* the emotions of others and the decline of sexual desire, if nothing else than from personal neglect.

When clients feel responsible for the feelings of others, they often adjust their own behavior to try and change the way their partners feel. Not a good idea! The reality is that *no one* has the power or ability to change how another feels. What someone feels is that person's own experience and is totally dependent on his or her own perceptions, thoughts, beliefs, and attitudes. Your clients have no control over anyone else's experience and to *assume* that responsibility is an error.

One sure way for a client to lose passion for life—including sexual passion—is to inaccurately assume responsibility for the happiness or pleasure of a sexual partner, or anyone else for that matter. To do so allows that person's own sexual happiness to become neglected, his or her sense of power to diminish, and self-esteem to erode. When that happens, sexual interest and desire fades.

What can you advise your clients to do?

Practical Prescription for Deepening Sexual Desire and Fulfillment

When your clients take the responsibility to follow the six basic directions below, their enjoyment of a powerful and fulfilling sex life increases dramatically.

Take responsibility for your own pleasure and satisfaction. Touch another only if it feels good to do so. Make contact with your partner only if you enjoy the contact. Take the initiative if you want sex. Become responsive to your own feelings and desires.

> Lord give me
> chastity—but not yet.
> —Saint Augustine

Have sex when you *both* desire it. To make love when neither you or your partner feel loving or desirous of sexual pleasure diminishes the enjoyment of engaging in sexual behavior for both of you.

Share absolutely everything. Share your experience of the moment. Be there in the moment. If your experience is pleasurable, share it. If your experience is thought-wandering, share it. If you are not fully involved in the moment, stop your sexual activity.

Laugh. Have fun. Enjoy your sexual feelings. Sex is not only meant to be a source of human reproduction, it is a source of emotional satisfaction as well. Maintain an attitude of playfulness. Keep your sexual life uncluttered with any feelings other than enjoyment.

Stop if you want to. Stopping is not rejection. Stopping is not bad or a commentary on your sexual adequacy; it is a choice. It may be the most responsible choice you make at any given moment. After all, sexual fulfillment is a result of being responsible for your sexual feelings and making responsible choices about how you use your own sexual energy.

Give your partner permission to use your body for pleasure, and vice versa. Freedom comes with responsibility. When you give your partner blanket permission to use your body for his or her own pleasure, it frees you to pay more attention to how you are using your partner's body for your own pleasure.

A Coaching Exercise on Sexual Exploration

One exercise you might want to share with your clients to help them learn to take sexual responsibility with their partners is called "Sensory Exploration."

Instructions: Without clothes on, explore every square inch of your partner's body with each of your five senses: sight, sound, taste, touch, and smell. Take your time. Without judgment—"good," "bad," "pretty," "ugly," etc.—describe your own sensations. For example, what does your partner's shoulder blade look like? How does it sound when you tap it? What does it taste like? Is it warm or cool? Moist? Hard? Soft? Close your eyes and feel its shape. Does it have an odor? Is it smooth or rough? After you fully know your partner's shoulder blade and have shared that information, move on to another part of the body—and be sure to share what you discover.

Sample Coaching Conversation

Continuation of relationship coaching with Shannon and Bill from previous lesson.

Coach: I am anxious to hear about the last two weeks. How did it go with creating more space and time for your relationship?

Bill: Really great. We did some simple things together, had a great getaway weekend and the odd/even day of being loving was really a good experience.

Shannon: I agree. And I think we broke the rules. I think there were a few days we both did loving things for each other.

Coach: Hmm. Sounds like a good rule to break. In fact, in today's coaching conversation, I wanted to coach and teach a bit about increasing romance in your relationship. Does that sound like something you would like?

Shannon: Sure.

Bill: I would like to learn to be more romantic and I know Shannon would like me to as well.

Coach: Okay. The experience you had the last couple of weeks is a beginning. You spent quality time together and some of it probably was romantic. But, we often think romance entails big events like candlelight dinners, vacations, an evening with dim lights and wine. Those are all great, but romance is actually enhanced by everyday noticing and commenting on the uniqueness of your partner. We need five positive comments to offset any negative encounter. Now I know you want to increase the feeling of love and togetherness you experience, even when you are apart, right?

Bill: Yes, that is what I want from coaching. We have a really good relationship now, we just wanted to make it even better.

Shannon: Yes. The best it can be for both of us.

Coach: Romance is couples connecting in small ways everyday and wanting the best for your partner and helping them reveal and cherish their uniqueness. If that happened more in your relationship, do you think that would feel more romantic?

Bill and Shannon: Sure.

Coach: Great. I may be teaching more than coaching here today, but I want you each to begin to notice and comment in a loving way on the *little things* you love and adore or are grateful for in your partner. Would you do that this week?

Bill and Shannon: Yes.

Coach: Okay, so here is my request. I would like you to experiment with noticing the little things in each other this week. Notice them and comment with phrases like, "You know honey, I want you to know how much I appreciate you making our house feel so comfortable." Or, "I love the way you laugh and smile when you are talking about funny things you share about work." I am sure you can discover lots of opportunities to say loving statements throughout the day. Are you willing to do this?

Bill: Sure, sounds fun.

Shannon: Yes, I like this already. In fact, I want to tell Bill right now that I really, really appreciate him for suggesting the coaching. I feel more romantic already.

Bill: Okay coach. This is good.

Coach: Have fun being loving and romantic with each other this week. This might become a great new habit.

Questions and Inquiries

1. How do you define love?
2. What changes do you want to make in how your express your sexuality?
3. What actions do you consider to be "romantic?"
4. What actions does your partner consider to be "romantic?"
5. Are you willing to learn to speak the language of love?

LIFE LESSON 48
Resolving conflict in relationships requires a balance of power.

MESSAGES

1. There are many types of power-based relationships.
2. Creating a balance of power in your relationships requires time, practice, effort and care.
3. No one interacts very long without conflict.
4. Resolving conflict in a close relationship is a complicated skill all of us can learn.

The objectives for Lesson 48 are: 1) To help your clients understand what a power-balance is in a relationship; 2) To learn some power-balancing skills and to have the courage to implement them; 3) To learn the rules for constructive fighting in a close relationship.

Framework Needed for Coaching Your Clients

Almost all conflicts within any relationship are a result of an imbalance of personal power. A very important life-coaching skill is being able to coach clients regarding the re-balancing of power in their relationships.

The Power of Teamwork

The healthiest and most powerful relationship is the one in which the individuals involved view themselves and their partners as a unit, a team. Like a couple's tennis match, each partner can play their own game, but they need to integrate their play into a synergistic relationship in order to form a successful match.

Synergy in a relationship is when, a couple—a balanced team—is more than the sum of the contributions made by each of the participants. For example, a family is much more than the total contributions made by its members.

Basic synergistic relationships are created when two or more people collaborate and cooperate to create a relationship they genuinely desire. The participants are unified as a single team while at the same time maintaining their individuality. If all the members of a football team acted on their own with no adjustments made for the team endeavor, winning would be impossible.

If you only pursue your own interests, your primary relationship will wilt from neglect. On the other hand, if you lose your personal identity to the relationship, your relationship will most likely die as well. The trick that leads to success is to balance the time and energy you spend working on your own growth and development with the time and energy you expend participating fully in your primary relationship.

> Courage is the first of the human qualities because it is the quality which guarantees all others.
> —Winston Churchill

Maintaining such a balance is a never-ending effort. The energy to balance comes from the tension between the two positions. Lose that tension, and you lose the desire and energy to maintain your balanced relationship.

When you have a balanced, synergistic relationship, you have more power than you would otherwise—power that can be used to accomplish common goals, more easily create commonly desired outcomes, and help you grow more rapidly.

Exercises and Information

We don't often like to admit that we keep score in our interpersonal relationships, but we all do. This lesson will help your clients look at how people create balances of power and how they can move toward establishing mutually affirming, respectful, and perhaps even loving relationships.

Creating a Power-Balance in Relationships

In order to successfully create power-balanced relationships, clients have to buy into three basic assumptions about themselves and their partner:

1. Everybody has intrinsic worth that is a birthright, not a product of status. We all have the same worth.
2. Each of us is different; respect for and preservation of differences is vital.
3. Differences *cannot* be used to rank someone's worth, since we all have equal worth.

Share the following points with your clients on how to create healthy, balanced, and powerful relationships.

1. **What clients must do for themselves:**
   - Take care of themselves first
   - Create and maintain healthy and realistic self-concepts
     Take responsibility for creating and expressing their feelings in constructive ways
   - Take responsibility for their choices. Support themselves psychologically and economically
   - Take responsibility for creating and maintaining their health at optimal levels

2. **What your clients can expect their partners to do:**
   - Provide support and encouragement as they grow and change; challenge behaviors that are destructive
   - Stand with them in times of trouble and be one source of comfort; work with them to assess and divide tasks
   - Work with them to develop skills for resolving conflict, including seeking professional coaching, teaching, or assistance
   - First make choices that are good for them and then for the benefit of their partner
   - Negotiate agreements, keep those agreements, and if they choose to break an agreement, notify their partner first
   - Cherish the relationship and make choices that nurture it
   - Respect their religious beliefs and practices
   - Give up any idea of changing them

3. **What your clients can expect to do for their partner:**
   - Exactly the same as they want and expect to receive

4. **Issues partners need to clearly understand:**
   - Money: salary, budgets, financial goals, knowledge of expenditures, etc.
   - Sex: team policies, rules of engagement, etc.
   - Time: overtime, compensatory time, time off, leisure time, etc.
   - Children: discipline, division of labor, etc.
   - Other relationships: fraternization policies, outside influences and activities, what is off-limits or against the rules, etc.
   - "Job" description: the extras, contributing ideas, limits of responsibilities, etc.

5. **Recognizing and appreciating diversity:**
    - Get to know the cultural background and traditional activities of your partner
    - Understand your partner's perceptual paradigms
    - Acknowledge gender differences between women and men
    - Acknowledge individual preferences, desires, and aspirations

6. **Barriers to creating healthy, power-balanced, mutual and loving relationships:**
    - Wanting things to be different without doing anything differently
    - Failure to ask, "How am I contributing to this situation?"
    - Reluctance by partners to say how they feel
    - Reluctance by partners to ask for what they want
    - Choosing to feel powerless or helpless
    - A need to be right that is stronger than the value (importance) of the relationship
    - Jealousy, envy
    - Holding on to resentments, grudges, and the past
    - A blaming mentality
    - A punishing mentality
    - Areas of life kept secret or hidden and an unwillingness to talk about them
    - Reluctance to seek coaching or professional help
    - Continuing to engage in behavior that is self-destructive

Basic Rules for Constructive Fighting In Relationships

Fighting can be either destructive or constructive. Destructive fighting can be mutually damaging and can lead participants further apart and destroy the entire structure of a relationship. Constructive fighting allows partners to grow into a new togetherness. It can increase the love each partner has for the other and can provide the foundation for a healthy, happy, synergistic, and growing relationship. Constructive fighting in any close relationship is a skill, an art—and it can be learned.

Below are a few simple ground rules to learn and practice so that, even in the heat of battle, a fight can be highly rewarding and constructive. And, if not that good, at least the fight is more likely to result in a win-win solution to any given conflict.

Rule 1. Recognize that the purpose of a conflict is to define yourself in relation to the other. It should not serve as an attempt to manipulate or control the behavior of your partner.

Rule 2. State your complaint as precisely and as accurately as possible. Immediately after you clearly state your complaint, follow up with one or two suggestions as to how the complaint might be reasonably solved.

Rule 3. Ask for and give information regarding major points raised in the conflict. Make sure you understand the precise complaint. Make sure your partner understands the real complaint, and make sure the complaint is real.

Rule 4. Stick to one topic until a satisfactory resolution is achieved. Don't jump from complaint to complaint just to voice backlogged resentment.

Rule 5. Confine yourself to statements of your own feelings and understanding. Don't deny or make statements about your partner's feelings or understanding. This is dirty fighting. Your partner's understanding is as real to him or her as your understanding is to you.

Rule 6. Don't make assumptions about how your partner will react and then respond as if those assumptions were real. Run "checks" to be assured of how your partner really would respond. Do this by asking for information or feedback from your partner.

Rule 7. Don't muddy the waters by making counter complaints or demands of your own. This is the counterpart to Rule 5.

Rule 8. Understand that the best defense is a good offense. If your partner begins to attack you, it is probably because he or she feels cornered. Avoid making broad, sweeping judgments regarding the personality of your partner. It merely means you feel you are losing. Give each other room to compromise without losing face.

Rule 9. Stay with the feeling and attitudes you are experiencing at a given moment and communicate them. Remember Rule 1. To raise feelings you had in the past is, at best, meaningless, for they are gone and cannot be changed. Forgiveness does not mean trying to prove one or the other right or wrong regarding some past event; it is a willingness to change and move forward.

> Almost all married people fight, although many are ashamed to admit it. Actually a marriage in which no quarreling at all takes place may well be one that is dead or dying from emotional undernourishment. If you care, you probably fight.
> —Flora Davis

Rule 10. Take time to listen to your partner. Don't rehearse in your mind what you are going to say while your partner is talking. Really listen—there's time! Then listen to your own feelings and responses to be sure they are real and immediate. Listen to what and how you speak so that *what you say* is the same as *how you say* it. Don't try to shout each other down.

Rule 11. Always avoid sarcasm. There is no better way than sarcasm to close communication lines.

Rule 12. Remember that there are never any losers in a constructive fight. If you win at the expense of your partner's loss, then the conflict was destructive and you have both lost. If you resolve the complaint you both win, for you have communicated well and have probably grown closer as a result.

Practice these rules first on "small" areas of conflict. You will feel silly at first. Everyone feels awkward and frustrated when first learning a new skill. With practice, you can become comfortable using these rules—they will become automatic and you will no longer have to concentrate on them so intently during the conflict. When this happens, conflicts with your partner will become the means through which your relationship can grow on a solid foundation. Constructive fighting is an art that all couples can master. Enjoy learning it.

Healthy Conflict Resolution in Power-Balanced Relationships

Methods for solving conflict in a relationship can be positive and constructive, or they can be negative and destructive, depending on the nature of the conflict-solving behavior.

Unhealthy ways to handle conflict. Here are some methods for managing conflict that result in diminishing the health of the relationship.

> It is better to create than to be learned; creating is the true essence of life.
> —Reinhold Niebuhr

- Avoid it
- Turn conflict into a power play or a contest of wills
- Gunnysack small issues
- Choose to be a victim
- Become a blamer
- Become a judge
- Become a punisher
- Prove that your partner is wrong

- Attempt to create power over your partner
- Assume righteous indignation and demand an apology
- Triangulate the relationship by involving a third party

Types of conflict. There are many kinds of relationship conflicts. Here are but a few.

- Prevalence of preference—who will get their way?
- Unspoken expectations
- Minor grievances/little resentments
- Hidden agendas
- Broken agreement or major breech of trust
- Betrayal

Conflict resolution skills. Some of the best tips for resolving relationship conflicts are:

- Say how you feel
- Take responsibility for your feelings
- Clarify the issues
- Ask for what you want
- Listen without interrupting or rehearsing a reply
- Repeat in your own words what your partner has said
- State what your partner wants
- Negotiate
- Apologize
- Make restitution

Pre-conflict guidelines. Before you engage in any conflict, it is wise to follow some of the guidelines presented below.

1. Determine that both parties in a conflict are committed to talk through resentments as soon as they recognize them.
2. Establish that both parties are willing to develop and practice conflict resolution skills.
3. Schedule conflict resolution sessions at suitable times (not when the conflict issue has erupted with high emotionality). Address spontaneous conflicts later if either partner prefers.

4. Recognize and acknowledge conflict-laden situations and subjects. Don't ignore them.
5. Understand that you needn't be completely clear about negative feelings to begin conflict resolution.
6. Establish that both parties are willing to relinquish destructive goals such as proving they are right, retaliation, revenge.
7. Approach the conflict resolution session with curiosity.
8. Recognize that your expectations don't create obligations, unless these have been established previously through negotiation.

Conflict resolution guidelines. When he or she is already engaged in conflicting, your client may want to follow these guidelines:

> We have the power to make this the best generation of mankind in the history of the world—or to make it the last.
> —John F. Kennedy

1. Sit so that eye contact is easy.
2. Listen to each other without interrupting.
3. Repeat what your partner said to ensure you heard it accurately: "You feel ___ and what you want is ___."
4. Omit the words *always* and *never*. Don't use the word *why*. These all sound like accusations or requests for justification.
5. Ask for what you want and if it's something your partner is willing to give.
6. Speak with care.
7. Be ready to go for the win-win solution.
8. Don't agree to a compromise that you don't really accept merely to stop the conflict.
9. When you're done, reaffirm your appreciation of each other and lighten up the situation by doing something fun.

Skills clients can use to create balance. After conflicting, it is very important for people to re-balance the personal power each has in the relationship.

- Let go of old behaviors.
- Give up the idea of changing your partner and get to work on changing yourself.
- Set limits for yourself.
- Create new personal behaviors.
- Refuse to change back into old ways of protection and defense.
- Create new methods of support for new behaviors.

Sample Coaching Conversation

Coach: I see that one of the areas you wanted coaching on today is the conflict you are having with your spouse. Tell me more about it.

Client: The issue is that he makes promises and takes on tasks but his follow-through is poor. It has gotten to the point that both me and the children complain and even laugh about it. They take bets on what excuse he will come up with on each occasion. He is predictably irresponsible and unreliable.

Coach: And you too are frustrated. How have you communicated to him? What feedback have you given him?

Client: I have had numerous conversations about it with him. There are times I just want to demand he change or else. Yet, there are many valuable contributions he makes to the family.

Coach: It sounds like all of you gossip and complain behind his back, is that right?

Client: Definitely. It is becoming a bad situation.

Coach: I would like you to think of the family as a collection of individuals all with unique strengths and weaknesses. Would you say that this situation between you two leading to an imbalance of power and strength in the marriage?

Client: Absolutely. We need to do something as it is becoming cancerous.

Coach: First of all, I would invite you to go back and use the relationship assessments that you've completed and have a conversation with him on how his tendency to over promise and under-deliver is negatively impacting the entire family and your marriage particularly. Then you can ask him what he can do to be more aware of how that is affecting his relationship to you and the kids. Then suggest to him some alternative ways he could behave that would resolve this issue for you.

Client: I will do that this week. Great idea. Thanks!

Questions and Inquiries

1. What rules for constructive fighting do you want to learn and practice?
2. What is your favorite method for conflicting?
3. What new conflict management skills do you want to learn?

4. In your daily life, with whom do you usually conflict? Are your conflicts constructive? What changes will you make to insure they are constructive?

LIFE LESSON 49

You can consciously create the kind of relationship you want with family members.

MESSAGES

1. A family is a dynamic network of interpersonal relationships.
2. If you are a parent, you are the family leader.
3. Effectively parenting teenagers is a highly developed skill.
4. Communication between family members is crucial to the health of the family unit.
5. Coaching healthy family relationships also affects all interpersonal relationships outside the immediate family.

The objectives for Lesson 49 are: 1) To understand the phases of evolution that nuclear family relationships go through; 2) To learn how to become a leader within your family; 3) To learn some parenting principles; 4) To learn family communication skills.

Framework Needed for Coaching Your Clients

One of the most common goals coaching clients have is to create a balance between their professional and personal lives. They know that if things are bad at work, their home lives are negatively affected, and that if their family lives are bad, the value of their work outside the home is diminished.

Everywhere in the United States, couples are breaking up their primary relationships and altering their family dynamics in the process. Moreover, for their own economic survival, a majority of families have both parents working outside the home. Traditional family patterns are no longer sustainable in our contemporary society. Dissolution of the family sometimes seems the only answer, even the most desirable one.

Make yourself as happy as possible and try to make those happy whose lives come in touch with yours. But to attempt to right the wrongs and ease the sufferings of the world in general is a waste of effort.
—James Weldon Johnson

One theory as to why today's families seem unable to make it is that people are applying old-fashioned family patterns to their own family situations. Couples are trying to fit themselves and their children into the same mold in which their primary families functioned. Such an approach may have worked for past generations, but it's obviously not working now.

Exercises and Information

If your clients want to develop balance between their roles and functions outside the home and their roles as family members, they need to develop *new patterns* of family relationships. Clients who are parents are the primary teachers of their children. As parents they need to understand and exemplify to their children ways to survive the contemporary stress and pressure they may be experiencing.

Share with your clients the following descriptions of the developmental phases most families go through. These may be new patterns for your clients that will help them to understand and clarify their family circumstances.

Phase 1

This might be called the Idealistic Bubble Phase. Most young couples see themselves in idealistic terms. If they don't perceive themselves idealistically, they most certainly idealize their partner—"He/she is everything I ever wanted in a man/woman." They also build an idealized view of what their lives together will be like—"Being married to him/her will be so wonderful" or "We'll be *so* happy all our lives together!" This phase might last three to six years.

Phase 2

This could be referred to as the Disappointing, Bubble-Bursting Phase. When we come to really know another person, any idealized image we may have held usually comes crashing down. The realities of daily work and family demands become apparent. Disappointment sets in—"He/she just isn't the same person I married" or "I never knew he/she was like that before I married him/her." Thus, the romantic, bubble-like phase of relationship bursts. Typical responses to this disappointment include anger, criticism, sadness, frustration, shock, blame, and usually powerful attempts to reinstate the original image we had of ourselves or our partner. While we might want our role in the marriage to change, we often expect our partner to keep on filling the original role in which we cast them. Couples often look to their children to maintain their original fantasies about how the family was going to be. Sometimes couples attempt to make their children into "cement babies"—looking to them to bond their family together. When families become centered around children rather than around the marital relationship, the whole family structure is in trouble. Invariably children grow up and, the family dynamic changes forever. The bubble-bursting phase usually lasts anywhere from one to ten years.

Phase 3

This is the Look-At-Who-I-Am-Phase. This phase arrives when couples begin to see themselves and their children as they really are, and not the ideals they thought they were. After feeling perhaps disappointed in the roles they have played as workers, spouses, and parents, couples begin to discover they are no longer those things—they are real gown-ups in an adult world. They begin to differentiate between who they are as individuals and the roles they fill: spouse, parent, worker, employee, professional, etc. They discover their personal identities and begin to display them outside their former idealized roles. This self-discovery phase might last five to seven years.

Phase 4

This is the Realistically Reaching-Out Phase. It begins after each partner comes to know themselves and their family members extremely well. Each starts to build new connections with other members of the family. Couples and parents who made it through the first three phases and who are still relating well to one another now begin to reach out with their genuine—not idealized and not role-determined—personalities. Each partner is determined to be him or herself in the relationship. Each wants to be accepted, even loved, for who they really are. To gain such love, partners must reconnect to each other and their children. The primary dynamic of this phase is getting to know and understand each family member and to recognize that family member for who he or she *really is*. This phase may last anywhere from three to five years or a lifetime.

Phase 5

This can be called the Self-Dependent, Reconnected Phase. Each family member in this phase is free of childlike dependencies and idealized expectations of themselves. They enjoy their realistic self-awareness and trust themselves to fulfill their wants and needs. They freely choose to be in contact with other family

> Who of us is mature enough for offspring before the offspring themselves arrive? The value of marriage is not that adults produce children but that children produce adults.
> —Peter De Vries

members, not out of a dependent need, but from delight derived from such contact. This phase can last a lifetime.

If we teach our clients that a normal family evolves through these phases and that these phases make up the usual pattern of development, they might understand more about the dynamic they are involved in and how they can better balance their family life with their work life. A good understanding of the phases of marriage and family development is the foundation upon which each couple and their children can build strategies for happily passing through each one, together.

Parenting

Without a doubt, your clients' parents failed them. All parents fail. No parent is ever adequate to provide their children with enough love, caring, support, wisdom, etc. to completely meet their needs. Parents naturally fall short—there is *no way* to be a perfect parent.

Parenting is the toughest job in the world. It's also the most important. It is more important than any job outside the family. Your clients can teach their children almost all the skills they'll need to survive in the world, but they usually don't teach effective parenting! How could they? All they have to draw upon is the trunk full of parenting experiences they filled when they were children. When your clients have children, they haul out the trunk from their psychological attics, dust it off, open it up, and behave exactly the way their parents behaved toward them. "When I was a kid, I swore I'd never treat my children the way I was treated," says a young mother who then proceeds to behave precisely the way her mother did. Or, in their rebellion, your clients determine to do just the opposite of what their parents did. The results? Their children become just like them.

Since all the parenting we get is inadequate to a certain degree, as grownups we have at least two vital tasks. First, we need to supplement the good parenting we got from our parents with other sources of positive mothering and fathering skills from other models. Second, we need to forgive our parents for their unavoidable inadequacies *not for their sake, but for our own!*

To forgive our parents means to let go of the resentment, guilt, fear, feelings of inadequacy, or angry rebelliousness that resulted from their natural failures. Forgiving them frees us to supplement our family time together and learn new ways of behaving and parenting. It allows us to become the parents *we* want to be. It permits us to get the parenting we never had, to learn the parenting skills we were never taught, to more fully become our own grown-up selves. Once clients are free to be their grown-up selves *and* to be parents, they automatically set the example for their children.

> The reason parents no longer lead their children in the right direction is because the parents aren't going that way themselves.
> —Frank McKinney Hubbard

Parenting is life's toughest job, but we can learn to do it better, however imperfect that still may be, by freeing ourselves from our own childhoods, and finding and developing present-day relationships that fill our psychological gaps to make us more completely ourselves—unique human beings who happen to love, care for, and support those other small human beings we call our children.

> The most important single ingredient in the formula of success is knowing how to get along with people.
> —Theodore Roosevelt

Top Twelve Ways to Effectively Parent Teenagers

Surviving the teenage years of their offspring can be as difficult for your clients as going through adolescence all over again. Today's life for a teenager is entirely different from when your clients were that age. But some of the underlying principles and values to parent a teenager have remained the same. Below are some very important principles designed to help your clients creatively survive their children's teenage years.

Trust your teenage children implicitly and watch them like a hawk. You need to be two-sided about this one. Your child needs and deserves your trust, but at the same time still needs your protection and guidance. A key to understanding your teenager (and their self-concept) is knowing who his or her friends are. When chauffeuring your teenager and his or her friends, *listen* to their conversations. Make a point of getting to know the parents of your child's friends. Allow your son or daughter to bring friends home. In fact, encourage the use of your house as a meeting place. Remember, you can't watch like a hawk unless you can see your child!

Lead by example, walk your talk. Teenagers are very sensitive to hypocrisy in adults. Make sure that your actions are consistent with your own values. They are watching you to see how well your values are functioning. For example, if you preach honesty and then cheat on your income taxes, you send a mixed message to your child. If you want to raise your teenager to become an honest adult, be one yourself. You need to be clear about what you value. Your actions will communicate louder than your admonishments and punishments.

Pick and choose your battles. Is blue hair, a bald head, or a pierced eyebrow really so terrible? Remember long, unwashed hair, bellbottoms, and love beads? Your kids need room to experiment with who they are just as you did when you were a teenager. For behavior that is dangerous, inconsiderate, vindictive, or intolerant, draw your battle lines and stand your ground. Maintain confidence in yourself and your values, regardless of how much they seem to be attacked by your teenager. However uncomfortable it is for you, testing your integrity and dependability is one of the normal tasks of adolescents. Don't fire your big guns over small issues.

Be a wall. Make and maintain as few family rules as practical. However, when your teenager has broken a family rule, be swift and consistent in implementing the understood consequences, or allow the natural consequences of their chosen actions to occur. If there is one message all teenagers need to get, it is that there are always consequences to their actions and they have the power to choose their actions, therefore the power to choose the consequences.

Develop your sense of humor. Don't take yourself, or your job as a parent, too seriously. Look for and learn to see the absurdities of daily life. Laugh a lot. Develop your sense of humor . . . you will need it. Laughter is a great stress reliever and laughing together is a gentle way to strengthen your relationship with your teenager. Periodically let go of your role as parent. Often you can afford to be fun around teenagers.

> A lot of parents pack up their troubles and send them off to a summer camp.
> —Raymond Duncan

Learn from your children. Your children are becoming young adults. They are eager to be heard even if they do not tell you much about themselves. One way to connect with your children is to pay attention to what they are passionate about. Whatever it is, become a student—their student. Without trying to change or control them, ask them about the political demonstration they are participating in, the music they enjoy listening to or playing, the skills they have learned while skate boarding. Attend their plays, sporting events, and recitals. You may not initially understand their passions, but you can become a student and learn to appreciate their skills and interests. You may even find that you have something in common! Become your teenager's greatest fan. Don't play their games. Only coach them if asked. Stay in the bleachers. Cheer them on. Stay off their playing field.

Honor their individuality. Avoid comparisons. Comparing your teenager to one of their older or younger siblings, to the way you were when you were their age, or to a friend or neighbor's child implies that your teenager is in some way the same as other individuals. Remember, they are one-of-a-kind. Celebrate and value their uniqueness.

Loving them unconditionally doesn't mean that you always have to like their behavior. Just as you must distinguish between who your teenager is and their behavior, you must also make the distinction between loving versus liking. Your son or daughter may at times behave in a way that makes him or her pretty unlikable. If your teenager knows you love who he or she is *unconditionally*, you can let your teenager know what you dislike about a certain behavior without damaging the relationship. In fact, teenagers have a reputation for trying to behave unacceptably from time to time. Teens need to know that they are loved *and* that a specific behavior is unacceptable. Be consistent, fair, and swift in implementing the known consequences for unacceptable behavior.

Don't ask to be included, but if you are invited, say yes. Your teenage child is beginning the process of separating from you. You need to begin the process of letting go. Teenagers need to exclude their parents from much of their lives if they are to eventually leave home as autonomous adults. The hallmark of good parenting is how well your offspring are able to happily function without you. They need to exclude you in order to successfully separate from you. However, if they extend an invitation to you to do something together, say yes. There is no greater gift they can give you than the gift of themselves.

Plan for your obsolescence. Your years of active parenting are coming to a close. Your teenager is putting you out of a job. It is a bittersweet transition. To succeed as a parent your children must ultimately leave you to create their own lives. What future will you create for yourself when the nest is empty? Plan for and create your own lifestyle without them. Your ability to let go and to look forward to the next phase of your life will help your teenager separate from you and take the next step toward his or her own independence and into young adulthood. One of the last great gifts you can offer your teenager is the example of how to live a fulfilled and happy life of your own.

Actively listen. Listening to teenagers is like hugging a child; it validates them, makes them feel valued and loved, and affirms their importance to you. Listen, not with the intention to reply, to change their minds, to control them, or to change their behavior, but with the intention to understand. Become genuinely curious and interested in what is going on inside your teenager's mind, what he or she is feeling and thinking. Listen to update your knowledge. Your teenager is rapidly changing; listen for those changes.

With pride and acknowledgment, acknowledge that your job as parent is now transformed. Take pride in your accomplishments as a parent. Acknowledge your teenagers as the fine, developing adults they are. Then gradually abdi-

Instant availability without continuous presence is probably the best role a mother can play.
—Lotte Bailyn

cate your role as their parent and primarily responsible for their welfare. They need to practice being their own best parent. They will imitate you, if you have been their best parent. They do not need to be controlled by you. They need your love and support, and the permission to become adults in their own right. But they won't unless you transform your job as their parent.

Becoming a Family Leader

Whether or not we like it, children look to parents for leadership. Leading our children is an awesome responsibility. Without leadership, children have no direction. Without direction, they have nowhere to go, nothing to learn, nothing to teach, and no skills to master. Without leadership, families drift, flounder, or dissolve.

As we stated in an earlier lesson, one of the most critical skills of any leader is the ability to listen genuinely. Listening is not just hearing. It's not simply comprehending. Rather, it combines hearing and understanding with a purpose. Skilled listening allows us to reproduce, point for point, someone else's point of view (see Lesson 15.)

Carol McCall, founder of The World Institute for Life Planning Group, writes, "Who are the leaders you go to for advice, coaching, feedback? Not to the practical ones who tell you exactly what to do, how to do it, when to do it. You go to the leaders who listen, brainstorm without censorship, and who are the least bossy. It's because by discussing your problems and circumstance with them, you then know what to do about it yourself" (2000, p. 89).

McCall has coined the term *empowered listening* to describe listening with a gentle curiosity, a genuine interest and an empathy for another's experiences. Empowered listening requires silence and timing and very little speaking. It encourages the speaker to be original, creative, autonomous in their thinking, and courageous in their behavior. According to McCall, "Empowered listening is a skill that requires the listener to give up the right to interpret/make up what's being said and remain present to what's being spoken. The speaker is heard outside the boundaries of our personal judgments, opinions, and evaluations."

Leading your children by engaging in such listening validates them, affirms their own thinking and feeling, increases their sense of self-worth, diminishes their hesitancy to express themselves, and challenges and empowers them to develop their true potential. Empowering listening nurtures and catalyzes a healthy, loving parent/child relationship. It is the essence of effective parental leadership.

Family Communication

Language is the most common way we psychologically connect with others. There is one major difference between communication within your family and communication with the world at large—the emotional health of your family members is at stake! Families get into difficulty when members are prevented from expressing certain feelings, needs, thoughts, ideas, awareness, or opinions.

Just as effective communication in general involves many skills, healthy communication among family members requires basic rules. There are two categories of communication rules that families can consciously or unconsciously develop: positive and negative.

Examples of negative rules governing family communications might include: "Don't show your emotions"; "Don't ask for hugs, attention, or reassurance"; "Don't talk about dad's drinking or mom's affair," "Don't point out hostility at the dinner table"; "Don't ask for help, express anger, show you've been hurt, talk about sex, notice mistakes and problems, disagree with family members, show affection, or point out any kind of dysfunction!" The list of communication prohibitions, or negative rules, could be extremely long.

Negative communication rules are created and continually reinforced in families by fear of rejection or disapproval, a fear sometimes strengthened by violence. As we stated in the beginning of this book, unspoken messages have a way of becoming lessons which need to be learned. Lessons ignored grow into problems. Problems not addressed become crises. Continued family crises become chaos, leading to the dissolution of family relationships. It is always better if we allow for communication and listen to messages between family members before this cycle has a chance to begin.

Negative family communication rules. There are certain kinds of communication that will spiral the communication process in a negative direction. Here are but a few.

1. *Denial.* A parent asks a child (or spouse), "What's the matter?" The response, "Nothing," denies current thoughts and feelings.
2. *Incongruent messages.* When *what* is said is belied by *how* it is said, you are sending an incongruent message. When you say one thing but mean another, you are communicating incongruently.
3. *Mind-reading.* You are guilty of mind-reading when you make assumptions about another's thoughts, feelings, and anticipated

behavior, and then respond as if they were true. Usually we voice these assumptions in the form of accusations or criticisms.

4. *Trying to prove you're right.* When you try to manipulate (change) someone else's viewpoint or repeat yourself using different phrasing, you are trying to prove your position right and the other's wrong.

5. *Deletion* involves leaving parts of a message out or being very indirect. Instead of saying, "I'd like to go to a movie," you say, "It's a lousy night for TV isn't it?"

Positive family communication rules. Likewise, there are types of communication that will enhance the communication process in a positive direction. Here are a few of them.

1. *Give absolute freedom* (permission) for all family members to verbalize (not act out) what they feel, see, want, think, and sense. Instead of asking, "What's the matter?", ask "Will you share with me what is going on with you now?

2. *Ask directly for what you desire, want, or need.* In English, there is only one way to ask directly for anything. Use the words, "Will you . . . ?"

3. *Listen to yourself.* Hearing yourself helps uncover your own communication errors and disorders. Monitor your tone of voice, pitch, the speed of your speech, body language, and affect on others.

4. *Ask for clarification and elaboration.* Avoid criticism, generalizations, and accusations.

5. *Take your time.* Make sure what you communicate reflects completely what you mean.

6. *Tell the truth.* Speak the truth gently and temper it with tact. The more a family shares the truth, the stronger a unit they will become.

Sample Coaching Conversation

Coach: How is it going with your goal to establish more work family balance?

Client: Not so good this week. My youngest son is driving me nuts. I just cannot seem to gain the improvement I want in our relationship. He's 17 and just won't communicate with me. Our attempts often end in silence or anger. Things were fine in his younger years. My husband and I discuss this and he says it is just a phase but I am tired of this phase.

> When I was a boy of fourteen, my father was so ignorant I could hardly stand to have the old man around. But when I got to be twenty-one, I was astonished at how much he had learned in seven years.
> —Mark Twain

Coach: How would you really like things to be different?

Client: I want my son and I to be able to talk, to listen to each other, and to avoid this cloud of fog over the conversation. We seem to have created some tension that prevents any attempt at a fresh-start to communication.

Coach: Do you think this is something that requires different professional help, such as a family therapist or counselor?

Client: Oh no. My husband and I took parenting classes at our church. Everything was fine until he turned sixteen.

Coach: You know, language is the most common way we connect with those we love. If you were your son, what do you think he is hearing from you?

Client: That's a good question. I wish he could answer that because I really want to know. I want to communicate and to show that I want to spend special time with him, not to smother or intrude upon his life, but to have some regular communication about more joyful things. What is he excited about, or frustrated about? And does he even know what I am up to? I just do not want this wall between us.

Coach: You obviously love your son and want things to be better. What other ways could you communicate to him in depth about what you want? Let's brainstorm a bit.

Client: I could send him an email. He is always on the computer (laughs).

Coach: Don't laugh, that might be good. What else?

Client: I could write him a letter or card.

Coach: You could send him a video of you talking, or a CD recording.

Client: You know, those sound funny but they might work. I could do something totally out of the ordinary to get his attention and for him to see my real desire to just love him.

Coach: Great. Any of those you want to try? You need to find a way to communicate differently than you have been.

Client: This may sound risky, but I want to write down some key thoughts and then use our video camera to tape me and tell him it is a special message for him. Then I hope we can open communication in the future. I like this idea. I can show my humor, say all I want to say, and invite him to write or make a video back to me.

Coach: Wonderful. I will also offer, if you think it is helpful, a name of someone who specializes in relationship and family coaching. In four sessions he can make a space for dialogue and empowered listening.

It is not family therapy, but family coaching. If you get interested, let me know. Good luck! We will talk again next week.

Questions and Inquiries

1. Are you open and receptive to what your family is learning, teaching you, enjoying, and how they are changing?
2. Do you exemplify the qualities and character you want your children to learn by imitating you?
3. Is yours a child-centered family or a marriage-centered one?
4. Are you prepared for the changes in your parent-child relationships as the children become adults?
5. Are you proactive in all your family interactions?

LIFE LESSON 50

Appreciating differences and valuing diversity enriches your relationships and your life, and broadens your humanity.

The objectives for Lesson 50 are: 1) To deepen appreciation for human differences; 2) To value individual diversity as essential for relationship evolution and cultural enrichment; 3) To learn ways to identify and incorporate differences to create synergistic outcomes and relationships.

Framework Needed for Coaching Your Clients

With the mapping of the human genome complete, we now know that genetically speaking, human beings are 99.97 percent the same. Genetically, human differences are miniscule compared to human similarities. Yet on the social and cultural level, we are very different. If we were not, human evolution would stop and our interpersonal relationships would be boring at best and constricted at worst. Shared individual differences are essential for expanding our "humanness." Without diverse individuals in relationships, human life would be little more than biological and cultural stagnation.

Any culture, whether it's familial, organizational, societal, or national, consists of webs of people, bound to one another through trust, mutual need, and compatible aspirations. Culture is based on shared individual differences in knowledge, experience, skills, history, talents, and dreams. Culture develops and grows when membership in it benefits *everyone* who lives or works within it; it inevitably dissolves when those involved cease to benefit. Culture crumbles when even a few powerful members no longer value human differences or appreciate diversity.

As a life coach, you need to value and appreciate the differences in your clients. We have often said that as life coaches, we learn more from our clients than we ever do from books or even our formal education. Imagine how boring coaching would be if all your clients were the same. Imagine how predictable your life would be if all your friends and colleagues were exactly like you. Imagine how restricted your knowledge would be, if everyone else knew only what you knew. Now imagine how rich your life experience would become if you were influenced by the unique personalities of many people from divergent backgrounds. Imagine how satisfying your coaching practice might be if your clients called you from different countries, spoke different languages, and shared with you all of their unique differences. We believe that it is important for coaches to highly value the differences in their clients. It is equally important to coach clients to value individual differences in others as well.

> The oppression of any people for opinion's sake has rarely had any other effect than to fix those opinions deeper, and render them more important.
> —Hosea Ballou

Exercises and Information

Share this diversity checklist with clients who want to enrich their lives by learning about others and integrating their uniqueness into their own lives.

Diversity Checklist

Here is a checklist for assessing how well you have integrated human diversity into your life.

- I have an attitude of genuine curiosity about how others differ from me.
- I have assessed my relationships with family, friends, and colleagues. I am aware of how each affects my personal and professional success.
- Without fear or anxiety, I interact with people who are different from me.
- I regularly ask for feedback from others on what hinders my growth and the development of the qualities and skills I want.
- I make a point to meet with acquaintances from other cultures and ethnic backgrounds.

- I encourage my friends and acquaintances to share their different opinions, thoughts, feelings, and judgments.

- I ask for assistance or counsel from people whom I know hold mind-sets different from my own.

- I establish a good relationship with at least one or two key members of the varied cultures to which I belong, such as family, clubs, organizations, social networks, workplace, special interest groups.

- I identify relationships outside my own perceptual paradigms that expand my awareness and aid in the achievement of my goals and desires.

- I guard against focusing too much on my tasks and details and not enough on the people involved.

- I seek out people who can give me useful information, unique perspectives, and offer support or critiques.

- I participate in cultural traditions and events different from those with which I grew up.

- I stay in touch with people in my past who have added value to my life.

- I invite others to share their unique ideas, even if they have little relevance to my life.

- I champion diversity efforts in my workplace, in my social network, and within the organizations to which I belong.

- I view every person as a source of new knowledge. I can learn something from everyone I meet.

> Prejudice is the reason of fools.
> —Voltaire

Sample Coaching Conversation

Coach: What do you want to focus on today?

Client: Remember when we talked about meeting new friends here? I am trying to do that, but so far no one special is emerging. I am meeting lots of people and I like them, but don't feel compelled to make them my new friend, if you know what I mean.

Coach: I do know what you mean. That will come in time. In the meantime, who are you associating and working with?

Client: Actually, in this job there is a lot of cultural diversity. There are employees from Asia, Europe, and a generally more diverse community than what I experienced in my previous job.

Coach: That is great. What a great opportunity to learn about different cultures and viewpoints.

> It's amazing how much can be accomplished if no one cares who gets the credit.
> —Blanton Collier

> Resolve to be tender with the young, compassionate with the aging, sympathetic with the striving and tolerant of the weak because sometime in your life, you will have been all of these.
>
> —George Washington Carver

Client: I do agree, but I am a bit uncomfortable knowing what to do to open relationships with those from Singapore, Africa, Hong Kong, and even Europe. I am just at a loss.

Coach: No problem. Learning comes from being curious and genuinely wanting to know about the other person and their experiences. You can even use your discomfort to start a conversation by saying something like, "How has it been for you to move here from Singapore?" People love to talk about themselves and remember, they may feel more out of their comfort zone than you do. Reach out and just be curious.

Client: That sounds very doable. Thanks for the tip. I really like learning about different cultures and I hope someday I get a chance to work overseas for a period of time. I will be more direct in asking those from different cultures about their experience and see where that leads.

Coach: Great. I will wait to hear how that goes. Have fun! You will gain a new richness of experience from this opportunity.

Questions and Inquiries

1. What person who I don't really know will I contact within this next week? Why?
2. What ethnic cultural activity (such as Hanukah, Swedish Dance of Lights, Kwanza, Cinco de Mayo) will I engage in within the next month?
3. Where might I travel to learn first-hand about another culture?
4. What are the culturally unique qualities, strengths, and skills of the individuals with whom I work?

Coaching Summary

Section 7, Creating High-Quality Relationships, has focused on ways to create healthy human relationships. Humans are relationship beings, and yet nurturing interpersonal relationships seems to be one of the greatest challenges we face. Unhealthy relationship skills are a root cause of divorce, hatred, abuse, and loneliness.

The Lessons

In the ten lessons of this section, we offered tips and techniques to address these challenges. If your clients have established as coaching goals the creation of healthy relationships, they will benefit from practicing the skills described here.

Life Lesson 41

Succeeding at any endeavor is dependent on the nature and quality of your relationships. Becoming fully human depends on the nature and quality of your interpersonal relationships. You can be very independent and self-reliant, and at the same time be in relationships that reflect collaboration, creativity, self expression, and the expression of love.

Life Lesson 42

Accurately assessing the nature and quality of a current relationship is crucial to changing it. Your relationships mirror many of the life lessons in this book. Are you learning these lessons? If you want to modify the quality of your interpersonal relationships, are you accurately assessing their current nature?

Life Lesson 43

The nature and quality of all human relationships are determined by the nature and quality of the character of those involved. Your character is reflected in all of your actions and relationships. Love, integrity, honesty, and compassion are but a few of the key components of successful relationships discussed in this lesson. Interpersonal relationships are two-way streets. The character of the people with whom you relate also determines the quality and health of those relationships. You have the ability to modify your own character and select relationships with people whose character traits are important to you. You have no power to change the character of another person. That's always up to him or her.

Life Lesson 44

Creating genuine relationships is critical to building a successful life. In this lesson, we amplify the essential connection between the nature of relationships and the creation of a successful life. In business as well as personal growth, the most successful people have created mutually helpful and rewarding relationships. Without such relationships, the experience of being alive is often empty and lonely.

Life Lesson 45

Friendships are a special kind of interpersonal relationship that you must consciously create. Almost everyone desires to have friendships outside our families. We believe that much of the loneliness and angst in our modern society is from wanting our friendships to be different, but not consciously creating the kind of friendships we desire. Learning this life lesson enhances your ability to build and maintain close friendships throughout your lifetime.

Life Lesson 46

The highest-quality interpersonal relationships are based on love. Teachings from all major religions and collected wisdom have consistently advocated this obvious but often neglected truth. Learn and practice this life lesson and you will have great success in all your endeavors.

Life Lesson 47

Romance and taking responsibility for your sexual life enriches the primary relationship of couples. Romance is consistently and frequently acknowledging and expressing the love you feel in ways both you and your partner understand as romantic. Romance is recognizing the uniqueness of the person you love and not keeping that recognition a secret.

Life Lesson 48

Resolving conflict in relationships requires a balance of power. A power differential is the cause of most breakdowns in relationships. People in the most successful relationships recognize and learn that shifts and compromises in personal power are required to create maximally healthy relationships. Power is not the same as force, it is the expression of a person's gifts, knowledge, passion, and desires. A balance of power includes valuing each individual's unique power, but not becoming coercive, manipulative, or controlling.

Life Lesson 49

You can consciously create the kind of relationship you want with your family members. Becoming fully conscious and behaviorally purposeful within the family is the goal of this lesson. Take an inventory of the family relationships you have now and envision and create those relationships in accordance with how you would like them to be. Engage in possibility thinking and make use of intentional creating. Design a family life that conforms to your highest and best aspirations.

Life Lesson 50

Appreciating differences and valuing diversity enriches your relationships and your life, and broadens your humanity. Remind your clients that diversity is enriching and allows them to weave a human tapestry of interpersonal relationships that has many different colors, fabrics, and textures.

Questions for Reflection

1. What relationships in your life are being neglected? How could you nurture them?
2. Can you identify three relationships in your life that are high quality? What makes them so?
3. What relationships would you like in your life that you don't have now?
4. If you were in a relationship with yourself, how would you feel about you?
5. How do people in your life know they are special to you? How do you express love?
6. Is conflict something that builds a wall in relationships, or is it something you handle with care?

SECTION 8
Understanding the Past to Create a Desired Future

> Memory is the cabinet of imagination, the treasury of reason, the registry of conscience, and the council chamber of thought.
> —Saint Basil

LIFE LESSON 51

Your personal history is a valuable resource for creating your desired future.

> ### MESSAGES
>
> 1. Who you are today is a result of all the experiences contained in your personal history.
>
> 2. If you are content with who you are, you would change nothing about your past.
>
> 3. You have the ability to erase (forget) or modify your memories, thereby affecting the present.
>
> 4. Use awareness of your history to create your desired future.
>
> 5. Maintain a mental and emotional orientation to your current state and your desired future outcomes.

The objectives for Lesson 51 are: 1) To become aware of and accept your personal history and all its experiences; 2) To learn ways to modify your memories, thereby influencing how you experience your current reality; 3) To use your personal history as a base from which to create your desired future.

Framework Needed for Coaching Your Clients

Like it or not, all of the experiences you had in the past have resulted in who you are today. Some of your experiences may have been painful, even tragic; some may have been highly pleasurable. Regardless of the nature or quality of these experiences, they are all contained in your memory. Some behavioral scientists believe that *every* informational message sent through your senses are recorded somewhere in your memory. Everything you've felt, thought, learned, read—everything—lives on in your mind.

Both conscious and subconscious memories affect and influence who you are and how you function today. Memories are like physical scars, some of them remain as clear as they were when you first had the experience. Some memories can be modified by the intensity of the initial experience, by your perceptual abil-

They may forget what you said, but they will never forget how you made them feel.
—Carl W. Buechner

ities and habits, and by further experiences subsequent to the initial one. Although some scars (memories) heal differently from the original tissue and remain visible for the rest of your life, regardless of how you have healed or not healed from your experiences, the memories contained in your unique personal history continue to influence how you experience your current reality.

When consciously creating your future, you need to be selective and discriminating about which memories you choose to learn from and which ones you will forget. You can choose to use memories or new experiences to support the creation of your desired future. You don't have to remain a victim of your past unless your experiences prove useful to creating what you want now and what you want in the future.

Authentic life coaching always remains focused on the client's present and future, unless remembering the past is useful to enhance the client's current reality or increase the probability that he or she will create the future of his or her envisioned dreams. If however, a client's experiences negatively clutter present-day functioning, or if they hinder creation of a client's desired future, then the client may benefit from psychotherapy to modify or heal from those historical events. Then they may coached on how to modify and move beyond them. Coaches could still work with the client if he/she is capable of maintaining focus on the present & future.

Exercises and Information

Few people aspire to become isolated in their current condition or situation. Your clients probably hired you to help them discover a direction for their lives based upon their desired destination. Focusing on the past in an attempt to heal from it is the model for therapy, not for authentic life coaching. But understanding your clients' pasts may prove useful in order to identify the talents, strengths, and abilities they can use to consciously create their desired future. It may also prevent them from working at careers or relationships that they fall into rather than determining for themselves what they really want by way of a lifestyle.

Powerful and influential people are aware of how their past has influenced— if not determined—their current way of living. They are aware of who they are, where they came from, what drives them now, and what values and principles guide their current choices, thinking, and actions. They shape their own lives and their future by using their past as a guide and a fundamental foundation upon which to build their current reality and their anticipated future.

Coaching Tips

Below are some coaching tips to make the best use of your clients' personal histories as aids to assist them in generating fulfilling present lifestyles and to move ever closer to their genuinely desired future.

Invite your clients to do the following:

- Periodically ask them to clarify their personal priorities, values, and guiding principles. As change inevitably occurs, these aspects of their lives may also become different from what they were in their past.
- Ask them to realign their priorities, values, and habits with how they are currently spending their time and energy.
- Request that they make regular adjustments in their life course based upon their own sensitivity and awareness, as well as feedback from others.
- Ask them to identify the skills and abilities they have developed in the past that will be most helpful (or necessary) for attaining success in the future. They may want to ask others for their ideas on how they can learn or develop relevant new skills.
- Preferably daily and definitely weekly, request that they reflect on what they learn from each day. Suggest that they carry a pocket-sized notebook to jot down new learning.
- Invite your clients to advise others on the creation of their desired future, life planning, or career development. One of the most effective methods for permanent learning is to teach others what they are learning.

> Wish not so much to live long as to live well.
> —Benjamin Franklin

Sample Coaching Conversation

This sample conversation is with a client who has exhibited some *mindset* and *attitude* difficulties toward the past due to beliefs about himself that started in childhood. He is a successful entrepreneur, but every so often these attitudes and beliefs based on past experiences draw him backwards.

Coach: Thanks for the update via email this week on your progress to create new habits of self-care and a project focus. I was glad to see the steps you had made. How would you like to use our coaching today?

Client: Where I am really stuck is in the negativity that crops up when I feel overwhelmed. I hear my *inner critic* say, "You don't know what you are doing. What do you know about running a business?"

Coach: I hear you. If I were a therapist we might explore whose voices those are, when that belief began, and I might hear your story of how long that has been a challenge for you. But, as a coach, I try to help you learn from the past and not focus on it. In other words, we all have a past, and the key to life design with coaching is to learn from the past while creating your future. So, would you like to work on ways to make your mindset and inner dialogues more positive and purposeful?

Client: You bet, that is indeed what I want. I have been to hours and hours of therapy and I understand when all this began and where it comes from, but I want to have it not hold me back.

Coach: Great. That is exactly why I took you on as a client. You are motivated to unhook from your past and to design and create your desired future. This may sound trite, but it is true. Our past is important, but it is past. We must learn from it and use what we learn to make the changes we want in our life now. When we begin to be more on purpose with our life, we are more at choice. In other words, I want you to learn new ways to act based on practicing new beliefs and new attitudes. Behaviors and beliefs are changeable, but they require practice, just as any new skill does, understand?

Client: Yes! That is exactly what I want.

Coach: So, how about this. If your life story thus far was someone else's story, what are the lessons and how would you write a sequel with a positive outcome? In other words, since you are the author of your life now, can you begin to conceptualize and then practice new belief systems and behaviors? Would you be willing to co-create fieldwork and experiments with me to try on new behaviors and habits?

Client: Yes. Let's do it.

Coach: I would request that you make a list of five negative statements you often hear in your head about yourself. Then write the opposing or positive belief on the other side of the paper. Next, I would like you to look at these five positive beliefs every morning and every evening this week and report back to me your experience with new behaviors and actions that might have occurred during the week as a result of these positive beliefs, OK?

Client: Yes I will, that sounds exciting. I am ready to go.
Coach: Great. Please email me your progress this week.

Questions and Inquiries

1. What skills learned in childhood do you still use in your daily life?
2. What habits learned in childhood are no longer serving your best interests? With what do you want to replace them?
3. What kinds of abilities are required to create your envisioned future?
4. What aspects of your memory do you want to modify or erase?
5. What memories do you want to keep alive? How will you maintain or strengthen them?
6. With what memories will you enrich your present life?

LIFE LESSON 52

You can choose to leave a personal legacy that makes a positive difference.

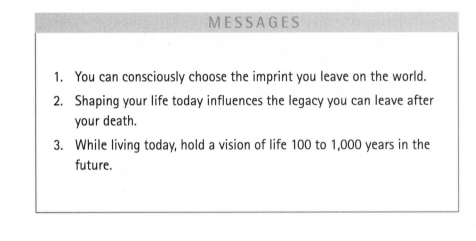

MESSAGES

1. You can consciously choose the imprint you leave on the world.
2. Shaping your life today influences the legacy you can leave after your death.
3. While living today, hold a vision of life 100 to 1,000 years in the future.

The objectives for Lesson 52 are: 1) To become aware of the affect your life has on the future; 2) To be able to shape your current lifestyle with a personal legacy in mind; 3) To become content with the memories you leave others after you die.

Framework Needed for Coaching Your Clients

We usually think of a personal legacy as the bestowal of money, property, or material goods to our descendents. Usually this type of legacy is described in a legal document such as a will or bequest. This is one kind of legacy.

A second kind of legacy is the affect your life has on the future of those who are remain alive after you die. Make no mistake, the nature and quality of your life does live on, if nowhere else than in the memories of your descendents. Like ripples from a stone tossed into a still lake, the influence of your life spreads far beyond the immediate present.

Authentic life coaching takes into account the future impact of a client's life while creating that life in the present. How many of your clients would change how they live if they considered the impact their current choices *will* have on those people (not only their own descendents) who live long after they die? For example, would parents continue to argue and fight in the presence of their children if they realized that every argument changes who their children are now and who they will become in the future? Would you continue to live as you are, if you knew you were creating the memories your descendents will have of you? Are we considering our grand-children's grandchildren as we make decisions and choices today? If not, *why* not?

Let your clients know that they *can* and *do* make a difference. If they want to have a significant, lasting impact on those around them, on their families, in their careers, or on their communities, they would be wise to invest themselves in learning to lead the best life and become the best person they can be. They need to realize that the nature and quality of the way they lead their lives has a ripple effect on everyone who comes in contact with them—that effect is the legacy they leave after their death.

> Men make history and not the other way round. In periods where there is no leadership, society stands still. Progress occurs when courageous, skillful leaders seize the opportunity to change things for the better.
> —Harry S. Truman

Exercises and Information

In order to clarify their legacy, it is often useful for clients to create a "timeline" that extends from the immediate present into the far distant future. Below is an example of such a timeline.

Creating a Legacy Timeline

Invite your clients to create a personal legacy timeline (example below). Place their legacy goals on each of the lines for the time periods specified. They might choose to represent their various goals and aspirations with different colors. They can even draw diagrams or pictures that remind them of their envisioned, desired outcomes. Keep in mind that their legacy timeline does not have to be linear. Experiment by making it circular, a spiral, or a wave.

Today _____ **1 week from now** →

e.g., Create a positive and enjoyable memory for my grandchild

1 week from now _____ **1 month from now** →

e.g., To write down my genealogy and family tree as detailed as I know

> You must be the change you wish to see in the world.
> —Mahatma Mohandas Gandhi

1 month from now   **1 year from now**

→

e.g., To increase my estate by at least 10 percent

1 year from now   **5 years from now**

→

e.g., Complete the college trust funds for my grandchildren.

5 years from now   **10 years from now**

→

e.g., Complete writing my autobiography or memories for my family and any others who are interested

10 years from now   **50 years from now**

→

e.g., Establish an ongoing business that is vibrant and continues to have a positive impact in the culture

50 years from now   **100 years from now**

→

e.g., My influence continues on how people live in their business and personal lives

100 years from now   **500 years from now**

→

e.g., I will be remembered for several generations for the contributions I made and the way I lived my life

One of the benefits of completing this exercise is that it allows your clients to set goals in the context of their present life and beyond. You can repeat this exercise with your clients as often as you wish. View the legacy timeline as a living document, one that will evolve, change, and grow.

Envisioning a Legacy

Share with your clients the following method for generating a vision of the legacy they want to leave.

Begin by getting comfortable. Breathe deeply and relax your body. Become aware of everything that supports you, physically, emotionally, mentally, and spiritually—the chair, the floor, the earth; the conditions and people that give you emotional nurturing; your favorite ideas and thoughts; your values and beliefs; your world view. Imagine these are your roots; they are what anchor you to yourself, to others, to your environment, and to the world.

Now review your personal history. Ask yourself, "Where did I come from? Who were my ancestors? How did they live? What hopes and dreams for the future did they have? What influenced my great-grandparents, my grandparents, my parents, and my siblings?"

In your imagination, leap beyond your lifetime, beyond your death. Ask yourself, "What kind of a world do I want for my children? My grandchildren? My great-grandchildren? My grandchildren's grandchildren? What direction do I want us to go in? What kind of lifestyle do I wish for them to have?"

Think about what you would like to leave your great-grandchildren? What do you want future generations to have? What memories of you would you like them to hold? What stories about you do you want them to hear? How do you want to be remembered one hundred years from now? A thousand years from now?

While holding that envisioned future firmly in your mind, in all its clarity and richness, ask yourself, "What part of this dream do I want to come true during my lifetime? What foundation can I lay today, upon which my dream for the future will be created?"

> The greatest use of life is to spend it for something that will outlast it.
> —William James

This foundation might be immediate, local, and personal, or it might be national or global. Think about how this dream can fit into your life now. What actions, behavior, choices, and decisions can you make today that are supportive of creating the future you have envisioned? These will be your legacy. These can be your contributions to the history of humanity and the world.

Begin to bring your awareness back to the present moment. Put your envisioned future into writing. Write yourself a letter that describes what you want your legacy to be. Once a year, perhaps on your birthday, review it. Share your desired legacy with friends who will be a part of creating your envisioned future.

Sample Coaching Conversation

Many coaching clients older than fifty have already had a successful life, but they want coaching to live more purposefully, more authentically, and to keep creating new ways to succeed, both personally and professionally. We often refer to their coaching conversations as *legacy coaching* and the following represents a snippet of such coaching.

Coach: So, we have been coaching for many months now about structuring your business, creating more life balance, and focusing on the creation of new strategic alliances with your consulting business. When you began coaching, I suggested that eventually we would talk about your future and your legacy. This week you wrote that you were ready.

Client: I am. I went back over my original forms and exercises about life purpose and this week it seemed that it was time to have that conversation. Everything is going well in work and my home life. I have really appreciated the coaching and the changes I have made in my life. But, now I want to change our focus for a time to the legacy of my life.

Coach: Wonderful. This is a key part of total life coaching and to me, one of the most exciting conversations. I believe that by looking at the legacy you want to leave you will design a future that will profoundly affect how you live in the present.

Client: Great. How do we do that?

Coach: There are many ways. Let me suggest that we start with two conversations and related fieldwork assignments. One is for you to write your own obituary. Have you ever done that?

Client: I remember doing that in a psychology class, but I was only twenty-three. That was ages ago.

Coach: Ok, so one assignment for this week is for you to write an obituary for yourself. What would you like it to say? What would be included? Will you do that?

Client: Yes, I will. What is the other assignment?

Coach: The other we can actually do right now. I want you to imagine that you are in the future fifty years after your death, and you are meeting with a wise being that is able to have you glimpse things that have happened since your death—kind of like the movie *It's a Wonderful Life*. You are able to see all the connections to the life you led with others and to lives you touched. Tell me all that you see as you look at a visual history of the legacy you left.

> He who bends himself a Joy doth the winged life destroy. But he who kisses the Joy as it flies lives in eternity's sunrise.
> —William Blake

The client begins to relate in detail with prompting from the coach what has occurred since his or her life ended, all the people who carried on his or her legacy in some way. This type of coaching conversation can go on for many sessions, but is quite enlightening for a client who wants to leave a lasting legacy. We urge you to consider this final lesson for clients ready for the *legacy conversation*.

Questions and Inquiries

1. What do you want your future to look or feel like after you are gone?
2. What actions can you take today to increase the probability that your desired future will indeed be made manifest?
3. How do you want your descendents to live?
4. How do you want planet Earth to be in a thousand years? A million years?
5. While considering your great, great grandchildren's memories of you, what do you want them to be?

> The only thing necessary for the triumph of evil is for good men to do nothing.
> —Edmund Burke

Coaching Summary

In Section 8, Understanding the Past to Create a Desired Future, we offered two lessons key to assisting clients to appreciate the value of their history, and to consciously choose the legacy they wish to leave. It is important to use these lessons when your clients want to move beyond just living a good life to designing a future for which they want to be remembered.

The Lessons

In this section we discussed the importance of learning from your unique personal history as a means of designing a desired future. We also considered the value of thinking about, and planning for, the legacy you want to leave after your death.

Life Lesson 51

Your personal history is a valuable resource for creating your desired future. Most people allow their history to control their present. We believe your clients' past is a positive resource rather than a liability. Coaching your clients to create a compelling future is preferable to allowing them to continue being victims of their past.

Life Lesson 52

You can choose to leave a personal legacy that makes a difference. The power of this lesson becomes evident when clients have attained many of their original coaching goals and are living what they deem to be a successful life. This is the time to expand the coaching conversation to focus on their personal and professional legacy. This shifts the emphasis of life coaching from problem solving and goal attainment to creating a future that continues to impact others after the clients' death.

Questions for Reflection

1. What elements of your personal history are valuable in creating your desired future?

2. What memories of your past are currently hindering your life? What are you doing to modify or move beyond them?

3. For what contributions to your life and work do you wish to be remembered?

4. What are you doing now to impact future generations in a lasting way?

Afterword

In the introduction, we stated that the primary purpose of this book is to enhance your professional practice, satisfy your curiosity, and empower you to change your life.

We have selected 52 life-taught lessons that our experience tells us coaching clients are most often desirous of learning. Which lessons do you need to learn? Which ones have you already mastered? Which can you focus on with your clients?

We believe that the most effective life coaching comes from authentic people whose lives reflect who they really are as human beings, and who contribute to the development of the very best of human potential in all their professional relationships. Does your authenticity catalyze the attainment of your client's desired outcomes?

In order to build a career as a life coach, you need to have a sustainable coaching business. After reading this book, are you better equipped personally and professionally to create a thriving business?

As life coaches ourselves, we wish for you to evolve fully into the life coach you desire to be. More than that, we want you to continue to learn those life lessons that will assist you in creating the lifestyle of your dreams and your clients' dreams. We hope this book has helped you to do precisely that, and will continue to be a resource for that noble desire.

References

Berne, E. (1996). *Games people play: The basic handbook of transactional analysis.* (New York: Ballantine.)

Blanchard, K., & Johnson, S. (1982). *The one minute manager.* New York, NY: William Morrow.

Cameron, J. (1992). *The artist's way: A spiritual path to higher creativity.* Los Angeles: Tarcher/Putnam.

Campbell, J., & Moyers, B. (1988). *The power of myth.* New York: Doubleday.

Cashman, K. (2000). *Leadership from the inside out.* Provo, UT: Executive Excellence Publishing.

de Chardin, P. T. (1971). *Christianity and evolution.* New York: Harcourt Brace & Jovanovich.

de Chardin, P. T. (1976). *The phenomenon of man.* New York: Perennial.

Chopra, D. (1993). *Creating affluence: Wealth consciousness in the field of all possibilities.* New York: Amber-Allen.

Chopra, D. (2000). *How to know God: The soul's journey into the mystery of mysteries.* New York: Harmony Books.

Covey, S. (1989). *The 7 habits of highly effective people.* New York: Simon & Schuster.

Cox, D. (1998). *There are no limits: Breaking the barriers in personal high performance.* Franklin Lakes, NJ: Career Press.

Frankl, V. E. (2000). *Man's search for meaning*, Fourth Edition. La Placentia, CA: Beacon Press.

Greenleaf, R. K. (2002). *Servant leadership*. New York: Paulist Press.

Guillaumont, A. (1976). *The gospel according to Thomas*. Boston: Brill Academic Publishers.

Hill, N. (1937). *Think and grow rich*. Meridian, CT. Ralston Society Publishers.

Kelsey, M. T. (1976). *The other side of silence: A guide to Christian meditation*. New York: Paulist Press.

Kun, T. S. (1962). *The structure of scientific revolutions*. Chicago: University of Chicago Press.

Leonard, T. (1994). *Spiritual path*. Coach University, Teleclass Workbook.

———. (1998). *The portable coach*. New York: Scribner.

LeShan, L. (2003). *The medium, the mystic, and the physicist*. New York: Allworth Press.

LeShan, L., & Morgenau, H. (1982). *Einstein's space and Van Gogh's sky*. New York: Macmillan.

Maslow, A. (1962). *Toward a psychology of being*. Princeton, NJ: Van Nostrand.

McCall, C. (2000). *Listen! There is a world waiting to be heard*. New York: Vantage.

Michalko, M. (1998). *Cracking creativity*. Berkeley, CA: Ten Speed Press.

Nadler, G., & Hibino, S. (1998). *Breakthrough thinking: The seven principles of creative problem solving*, (Revised 2nd Edition.) Rocklin, CA: Prima Publishing.

Remen, N. (1997). *Kitchen table wisdom: Stories that heal*. East Rutherford, NJ: Putman.

Richardson, C. (1998). *Take time for your life*. New York: Broadway Books.

Sayama, M. (1982). *Samadhi: Self-development in Zen, swordsmanship, and psychotherapy*. Albany: State University of New York Press.

Smith, M. J. (1985). *When i say no, i feel guilty*. New York: Bantam Books.

Tracy, B. (1993). *Maximum achievement*. New York: Simon & Schuster.

Index

taking responsibility for your sexual
life, 384–385
sharing
vs. giving, 206
negative connotations of, 205–206
yourself, in relationships, 207
silence
as communication buster, 126
singing
as spiritual practice, 85
Smith, M. J., 193
smoke-screening
as assertiveness technique, 194
speaking skills
as communication-sending skill,
150
raising your practice standards, 51
spirituality/spiritual development
acceptance, 93–94
aspects of spiritual life you need to
catalyze, 98
common elements of spiritual
development, 96
common spiritual practices, 85–86
communication and, 92
eastern philosophy clients and, 105
embracing death, 95
energetic expression of emotions,
94
Generation X client, 105
human contact and, 95
meditation and, 91–92
mystic/metaphysical client and, 103
paradigm shifts and, 102–103
paths to learn about spirit, 83
personal benefits from, 84
principles of, 84–85
qualities/characteristics of spiritual
person, 86–87

realize and appreciate your spiritual
nature, 81–89
religious client and, 103
removing dualism, 92–93
setting boundaries of, 59
spiritual signposts, 90–91
spiritual stress coping mechanisms,
216–217
tips for coaching development of,
86, 97–98
what it is not, 81–82
you and your clients are already on
spiritual path, 101–108
spiritual path
metaphor of, 101
you and your clients are already on
spiritual path, 101–108
standards
catalyzing high personal/profes-
sional standards, 47–52
evaluating, 46
responsibility for personal standards, 45–53
static balance, 262
strategic thinking
high personal/professional standards, 50
strategy
benefits of, 244
defined, 243
vs. plan, 244
vs. purpose, 244
tips for designing, 245–246
vs. vision, 244
stress
eustress vs. distress, 211
natural stress response, 210–211
negative coping mechanisms for,
213–214